# ADULTS WITH LEARNING DISABILITIES

*Clinical Studies*

# ADULTS WITH LEARNING DISABILITIES

## *Clinical Studies*

*Edited by*

**Doris J. Johnson, Ph.D.**
*Professor and Head*
*Program in Learning Disabilities*
*Department of Communication*
*Sciences and Disorders*
*Northwestern University*
*Evanston, Illinois*

**Jane W. Blalock, Ph.D.**
*Director of Professional Services*
*Atlanta Speech School*
*Atlanta, Georgia*

G&S

**Grune & Stratton, Inc.**
Harcourt Brace Jovanovich, Publishers
Orlando New York San Diego London
San Francisco Tokyo Sydney Toronto

*Grune & Stratton, Inc.*
Orlando, Florida 32887

Distributed in the United Kingdom by
*Grune & Stratton, Ltd.*
24/28 Oval Road, London NW 1

Library of Congress Catalog Number 86-27141
International Standard Book Number 0-8089-1795-1
Printed in the United States of America
86 87 88 89 10 9 8 7 6 5 4 3 2 1

# Contents


Preface vii

Contributors ix

1. Introduction and Definition of the Problem 1
   *Doris J. Johnson*

2. Principles of Assessment and Diagnosis 9
   *Doris J. Johnson*

3. Primary Concerns and Group Characteristics 31
   *Jane W. Blalock and Doris J. Johnson*

4. Intellectual Levels and Patterns 47
   *Jane W. Blalock*

5. Abstract Reasoning and Problem Solving 67
   *C. Addison Stone*

6. Auditory Language Disorders 81
   *Jane W. Blalock*

7. Auditory Processing by Learning Disabled Young Adults 107
   *Lois L. Elliott and Lu Anne Busse*

8. Problems of Conceptualization and Language: Evidence from Definitions 131
   *Bonnie E. Litowitz*

9. Reading Disabilities 145
   *Doris J. Johnson*

10. Disorders of Written Language 173
    *Doris J. Johnson*

11. Problems in Mathematics 205
    *Jane W. Blalock*

12. Nonverbal Disorders and Related Learning Disabilities 219
    *Doris J. Johnson*

13. An Experiment in Group Therapy with Learning Disabled Adults 233
    *Louise Rosenblum*

14. Issues and Concerns in LD College Programming 239
    *Susan A. Vogel*

15. Summary of Problems and Needs 277
*Doris J. Johnson and*
*Jane W. Blalock*

Appendices 297

Author Index 317

Subject Index 324

# PREFACE

The purpose of this volume is to highlight the multiple long-term needs of adults with learning disabilities. Our concern for this group arose out of long term follow-up studies of children with language disorders as well as many self-referrals from adults who requested testing and remediation.

These studies and observations indicated that learning disabilities are not totally alleviated with Special Education and the problems are not simply academic handicaps. They interfere with many aspects of schooling, social life, independence and occupations.

Hundreds of adults have been tested in our Center and each has added to our understanding of learning disabilities. While similar tests and tasks were used with all of the adults, their individual problems and levels of ability prevented the use of identical test batteries. Some authors in the volume saw only a small sub-set of the total population but their findings are significant for future research and for an understanding of certain cognitive and linguistic problems of the group.

The volume is intended as a textbook for courses in learning disabilities and as a resource to Psychologists, Special educators, Vocational Rehabilitation workers, Social Workers, and other professionals who may see this population.

We wish to express our thanks to many people who have worked with us during the past several years. First, we acknowledge the contributions of our colleagues who have contributed chapters in this book. Having interdisciplinary studies enhances our understanding of this unique population. The methodology used by psychologists, audiologists, linguists, and social workers is important for future research in the field.

We are indebted to the graduate students who spent many evenings with us in the testing/tutorial program. Their clinical skills, observations, and sensitivity to the needs of the adults were deeply appreciated. Those who assisted with data analysis also lightened our load.

Several secretaries contributed to the multiple drafts and final manuscripts. In particular we acknowledge the help from Lou Detlefsen, Mary Ellen Shamory, Mary Rooney, and Betsy Mitten. Betsy deserves extra thanks for the fine art work in all of the figures.

Roy Wood, Dean of the School of Speech, has been very supportive of the entire program in Learning Disabilities for many years. He has been responsive to our ends in the research, teaching, and clinical programs and we appreciate his support.

Finally, we are grateful to the many adults with learning disabilities from whom we have learned so much. We have been inspired by their tenacity and hope the future holds greater promise for them.

# Contributors

**Jane W. Blalock, Ph.D.**
*Director of Professional Services*
*Atlanta Speech School*
*Atlanta, Georgia*

**Lu Anne Busse, Ph.D.**
*Graduate Research Assistant, Audiology*
*Northwestern University*
*Evanston, Illinois*

**Lois L. Elliott, Ph.D.**
*Professor of Audiology and Otolaryngology*
*Northwestern University*
*Evanston, Illinois*

**Doris J. Johnson, Ph.D.**
*Professor and Head*
*Program in Learning Disabilities*
*Department of Communication Sciences and Disorders*
*Northwestern University*
*Evanston, Illinois*

**Bonnie E. Litowitz, Ph.D.**
*Adjunct Associate Professor*
*Linguistics and Learning Disabilities*
*Northwestern University*
*Evanston, Illinois*

**Louise A. Rosenblum, M.S.W.**
*Social Worker*
*Mental Health Services*
*Northwestern University*
*Evanston, Illinois*

**C. Addison Stone, Ph.D.**
*Associate Professor*
*Program in Learning Disabilities*
*Department of Communication Sciences and Disorders*
*Northwestern University*
*Evanston, Illinois*

**Susan A. Vogel, Ph.D.**
*Adjunct Professor*
*Department of Special Education*
*Northeastern University*
*Chicago, Illinois*

# ADULTS WITH LEARNING DISABILITIES

*Clinical Studies*

# 1

# Introduction and Definition of the Problem

DORIS J. JOHNSON

The letter in Figure 1-1 is a plea written by a 30-year-old man who has average mental ability but cannot read beyond a first grade level. He has held the same job as a foreman in a factory for over five years and is well-respected by his coworkers. He is very conscientious about trying to learn and remember new signs in the factory, particularly those concerned with danger. He is married and has children who are beginning to read. As he observes the pleasure his children gain from books, and as he looks toward the future, he wants to try once more to learn to read so that he can "go on with his learning." He is fully aware of the knowledge that can be obtained from print.

Yet, his problems are not limited to reading and writing. He has numerous auditory disorders. For example, he is unable to say the days of the week, the months of the year, or the alphabet in order. He cannot rhyme nor segment words into phonemes, and he has problems with word retrieval and syntax.

In contrast, he has fine mechanical skills and good visual-spatial abilities. He has always been motivated to learn, but he dropped out of school at the age of 16 because the repeated failure was so painful.

Case studies of children and adults such as these have been reported in the literature for decades. Many insightful physicians, educators, and psychologists noted that certain children did not speak, read, write, or calculate normally even though they had at least average intelligence (Ewing, 1930; Hinshelwood, 1900; Morgan, 1896; Nettleship, 1901; Orton, 1928; Thomas, 1905; Wallin, 1921). Many had superior mental ability. Thompson (1969), for example, describes the learning problems of Edison, Auguste Rodin, General George Patton, and Woodrow Wilson. According to Simpson (1979), even famous authors such as Gustave Flaubert, W. B. Yeats, and Agatha Christie had difficulty learning to

ADULTS WITH LEARNING DISABILITIES
ISBN 0-8089-1795-1

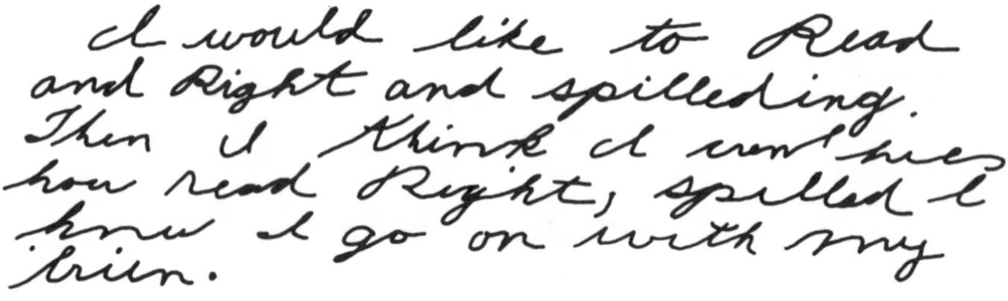


**Figure 1-1.** Writing of a 30-year-old man.

read and write. Similarly, Patten (1978) describes Einstein's unusual problems in learning to speak and calculate.

Prior to the recognition of specific learning disabilities, many of these people were misplaced with the deaf, the mentally ill, or retarded. Others remained in the regular classroom with little or no assistance. Gradually, however, their unique needs were recognized and differential diagnosis was emphasized (Ewing, 1930; Gesell & Amatruda, 1948; Myklebust, 1954; Orton, 1937). In addition, educators who saw the need for special instruction developed remedial programs (Fernald, 1943; Gillingham & Stillman, 1956; McGinnis, 1963; Myklebust, 1952; Strauss & Lehtinen, 1947).

Although there was gradual awareness of learning disabilities, it was not until the late 1960s that comprehensive assessment and special education were provided in public schools. Several factors fostered the growth of such programs including legislation, parental pressure, teacher preparation, and the development of professional organizations. Growth of the field also was enhanced by the use of more general terminology.

Before the late 1960s, terms such as minimal brain dysfunction (M.B.D.), brain injury, neurological impairment, perceptual handicap, dyslexia, or aphasia were used. Since these labels designated only subgroups within the total population, it was necessary to select a term that was broad enough to encompass the broad spectrum of symptoms exhibited by this heterogeneous group (Kirk, 1963; Myklebust, 1963).

## LEARNING DISABILITIES DEFINITION

Although terminology and emphases vary somewhat, most definitions have three major components. The first, often known as the exclusion clause, is intended to differentiate specific learning disabilities from other types of learning problems. That is, the definitions state that learning disabilities are not due primarily to sensory impairments, mental retardation, physical handicaps, emotional disturbance, cultural disadvantage, or lack of instruction (Federal Register, 1977; National Advisory Committee on Handicapped Children, 1968;

National Joint Committee for Learning Disabilities, 1981; see Appendix). This does not mean, however, that a child can have only one handicap. On the contrary, many have multiple problems. The major objective is to highlight the needs of children and adults who have specific deficits even though they have integrities and opportunities for learning.

A second component of the definition states that individuals with learning disabilities have a *discrepancy* between their mental ability and performance in one or more areas, such as listening, speaking, reading, writing, mathematics, and/or various areas of nonverbal behavior such as spatial orientation. A few definitions, however, have not included statements regarding nonverbal problems. This omission is of concern since these disorders can be very debilitating both socially and vocationally (Johnson & Myklebust, 1967; Kronick, 1978; Myklebust, 1975). Throughout this volume we will emphasize that learning disabilities are not simply academic handicaps. Although problems of oral language, reading, and other forms of verbal behavior cannot be minimized, it is clear that adequate participation in society requires many nonverbal skills.

The implementation of the discrepancy clause has been of concern in recent years since many school systems and agencies have been required to quantify the underachievement in order to obtain special services. While some have made provisions only for students with *severe* discrepancies, it is our impression that every handicapping condition, including learning disabilities, may be mild, moderate, or severe. Many of the adults evaluated in our Center have a history of mild chronic problems that interfered with their vocational or educational mobility.

The third component of most definitions indicates that the disabilities are a result of some factor *intrinsic* to the individual (Hammill, Leigh, McNutt, & Larsen, 1981; National Joint Committee definition, 1981). Earlier definitions state that the problems are due to a disturbance in some basic psychological process such as perception, memory, or conceptualization (National Advisory Committee on Handicapped Children, 1968). The shift in emphasis from the word "processing" is a result of several factors, including problems of defining and measuring specific processes, theoretical differences in the field, and, perhaps, to occasional misuse or misinterpretation of the concept. For example, certain reading disabled students who were found to have deficits in perception or memory were given extensive training on tasks such as discrmination of nonverbal figures or repetition of digits rather than on the primary area of underachievement (e.g., reading or spelling). Similarly, children with language disorders at times were taught to discriminate environmental sounds when they needed work on verbal learning. When they made less progress than expected, there was a tendency, at times, to deemphasize processing. In our program we emphasize the need for direct work on the primary areas of underachievement in conjunction with disturbances in processing. For example, we do not expect a student to learn to spell without direct instruction, but we think the instructional procedures should vary with the nature of the error pattern.

Students who spell phonetically, but cannot learn words that must be memorized visually, need different forms of instruction from those who omit sounds or syllables.

While there are differences of opinion regarding the definition and theories of learning disabilities, the body of knowledge in the field continues to grow here and abroad. The problems are not unique to a single culture nor socioeconomic level. Although the identification of such individuals often begins in countries or communities where there is ample stimulation and instruction, it is evident that learning disabilities occur throughout the world (Duane & Leong, 1985; Rawson, 1972; Strong, 1972; Tarnopol, 1977).

## LONG TERM NEEDS

Most programs for learning disabilities began at the elementary or preschool level with the hope that early identification and remediation would alleviate the problems. Several follow-up investigations, however, indicate this was not always the case. While many children made substantial gains, they also had residual disorders (Behrens, 1963; Cooper & Griffith, 1978; Critchley, 1973; Horn, O'Donnell & Vitulano, 1983; Johnson, 1980; Kline & Kline, 1975; Kronick, 1978; Rawson, 1968). In some respects, this outcome could be expected since the environment demands more of an individual with age, particularly in higher levels of symbolic behavior and conceptual thinking.

When it became evident that services were needed beyond the elementary years, special education was mandated for secondary schools and various types of programs were developed (Alley & Deshler, 1979; Ansara, 1972; Mann, Goodman, & Wiederholt, 1978; Wiig & Semel, 1976; Zigmond, 1978). In addition, a special institute was funded by the Office of Education at the University of Kansas to study the nature and needs of learning disabled adolescents (Meyen & Deshler, 1978).

More recently, programs have been developed for students at the college level (Cordoni, 1979; Chapter 14). The young adults themselves have been very active in trying to obtain services from higher education, mental health facilities, and vocational rehabilitation agencies (Brown, 1980). It is gratifying to see the increased assistance from these agencies as well as from business and industry. Nevertheless, a greater awareness of persistent learning disorders is needed to help these people actualize their potential (Bender, 1956, 1975; Blalock, 1981; Bryant, 1978; Cruickshank, Morse, & Johns, 1980; Rogan & Hartman, 1976; Silver, 1984; Silver & Hagin, 1964).

Because of the ways in which exceptional learners are assimilated into society and because of the heterogeneous nature of the population, it is difficult to know what percentage of the group has special needs. Kronick (1979) states that some individuals narrowed the gap that separated them from their intact peers and are viewed by others as "normal," whereas in other instances the gap has widened. She says this latter group is perceived as incompetent and frequently in crisis. Some may be among the delinquent population or in correctional institutions (Berman, 1977; Jacobson, 1974; Keilitz, Zaremba, & Broder, 1979; Mulligan, 1972; Pasternack & Lyon, 1982). Others may be unemployed or among the mentally ill; still others are undoubtedly in the mainstream of society, having progressed or adjusted to their limitations. Some, however, are still trying to cope with their problems and are actively seeking various types of help. For the most part, it is the latter group who requested services in the Learning Disabilities Center at Northwestern University. While we recognize this may be a rather select sample, particularly because many adults referred themselves, it is our feeling that a description of their collective problems may be useful in planning for the educational, vocational, and psychosocial needs of other learning disabled individuals.

## REFERENCES

Alley, G., & Deshler, D. *Teaching the learning disabled adolescent: Strategies and methods*. Denver: Love Publishing, 1979.

Ansara, A. Language therapy to salvage the college potential of dyslexic adolescents. *Bulletin of the Orton Society*, 1972, *22*, 123–139.

Behrens, T. *A study of psychological and electroencephalographic changes in children with learning disorders*. Unpublished doctoral dissertation, Northwestern University, 1963.

Bender, L. Research studies from Bellevue Hospital on specific reading disabilities. *Bulletin of the Orton Society*, 1956, *7*, 1–3.

Bender, L. A fifty-year review of experiences with dyslexia. *Bulletin of the Orton Society*, 1975, *24*, 5–23.

Berman, A. Neurological dysfunction in juvenile delinquents: Implications for early intervention. *Child Care Quarterly*, 1977, *1*(4), 264–271.

Blalock, J. Persistent problems and concerns of young adults with learning disabilities. In W. Cruickshank & A. Silver (Eds.), *Bridges to tomorrow: Vol. 2, The best of ACLD*. Syracuse, NY: Syracuse University Press, 1981.

Brown, D. Steps to independence for people with learning disabilities. Washington, DC: *Closer Look*, 1980.

Bryant, T. The effect of student failure on the quality of life and community mental health. *Bulletin of the Orton Society*, 1978, *28*, 8–14.

Cooper, J., & Griffith, P. Treatment and prognosis. In M. Wyke (Ed.), *Developmental dysphasia*. New York: Academic Press, 1978.

Cordoni, B. Assisting dyslexic college students: An experimental program designed at a university. *Bulletin of the Orton Society*, 1979, *29*, 263–268.

Critchley, M. Some problems of the ex-dyslexic. *Bulletin of the Orton Society*, 1973, *23*, 7–14.

Cruickshank, W., Morse, W., & Johns, J. *Learning disabilities—The struggle from adolescence toward adulthood*. Syracuse, NY: Syracuse University Press, 1980.

Duane, D. & Leong, C. (Eds.) *Understanding learning disabilities: International and multidisciplinary views*. New York: Plenum Press, 1985.

Ewing, A. *Aphasia in childhood*. London: Oxford University Press, 1930.

Fernald, G. *Remedial techniques in basic school subjects*. New York: McGraw-Hill, 1943.

Gesell, A., & Amatruda, C. *Developmental diagnosis*. New York: Paul B. Hoeber, 1948.

Gillingham, A., & Stillman, G. *Remedial training for children with specific disability in reading, spelling and penmanship*. Cambridge, MA: Educators Publishing Service, 1956.

Hammill, D., Leigh, J., McNutt, G., & Larsen, S. A new definition of learning disabilities. *Learning Disability Quarterly*, 1981, *4* (4), 336–342.

Hinshelwood, J. A case of dyslexia: A peculiar form of word-blindness. *Lancet*, 1900, *2*, 1451–1454.

Horn, W., O'Donnell, J., & Vitulano, L. Long-term follow-up studies of learning-disabled persons. *Journal of Learning Disabilities*, 1983, *14*, 542–553.

Jacobson, F. Learning disabilities and juvenile delinquency: A demonstrated relationship. In R. Weber (Ed.), *Handbook of learning disabilities: A Prognosis for the child, the adolescent, the adult*. Englewood Cliffs, NJ: Prentice-Hall, 1974.

Johnson, D. Persistent auditory disorders in young dyslexic adults. *Bulletin of the Orton Society*, 1980, *30*, 268–276.

Johnson, D. & Myklebust, H. *Learning disabilities: Educational principles and practices*. New York: Grune & Stratton, 1967.

Kline, C., & Kline, C. Severe reading disabilities: The family's dilemmas. *Bulletin of the Orton Society*, 1973, *23*, 146–159.

Kline, C., & Kline, C. Follow-up study of 216 children. *Bulletin of the Orton Society*, 1975, *25*, 127–144.

Keilitz, I., Zaremba, B., & Broder, P. *The link between learning disabilities and juvenile delinquency: Some issues and answers*. Englewood Cliffs, NJ: Prentice-Hall, 1974.

Kirk, S. *Behavioral diagnosis and remediation of learning disabilities*. Proceedings, Conference on Exploration into the Problems of the Perceptually Handicapped Child (First Annual Meeting), Chicago, 1963, 1–7.

Kronick, D. An examination of psychosocial aspects of learning disabled adolescents. *Learning Disability Quarterly*, 1978, *1* (4), 86–93.

Mann, L., Goodman, L., & Wiederholdt, L. (Eds.), *Teaching the learning-disabled adolescent*. Boston: Houghton Mifflin, 1978.

Meyen, E., & Deshler, D. The Kansas Research Institute in Learning Disabilities. *Learning Disability Quarterly*, 1978, *1* (1), 73–74.

McGinnis, M. *Aphasic children*. Washington, DC: Alexander Graham Bell Association for the Deaf, 1963.

Morgan, W. P. A case of congenital word-blindness. *British Medical Journal*, 1896, *2*, 1378.

Mulligan, W. Dyslexia, specific learning disability and delinquency. *Juvenile Justice*, 1972, 20–25.

Myklebust, H. Aphasia in children. *Journal of the Exceptional Child*, 1952, *19*, 9.

Myklebust, H. *Auditory disorders in children*. New York: Grune & Stratton, 1954.

Myklebust, H. *What do we mean by learning disorders*? Proceedings, Conference on Exploration into the Problems of the Perceptually Handicapped Child (First Annual Meeting), Chicago, 1963, 87–92.

Myklebust, H. Nonverbal learning disabilities: Assessment and intervention. In H., Myklebust (Ed.), *Progress in learning disabilities* (Vol. 3). New York: Grune & Stratton, 1975.

National Advisory Committee on Handicapped Children. *Special education for handicapped children* (First Annual Rep.), Washington, DC: Department of Health, Education and Welfare, 1968.

National Joint Committee for Learning Disabilities. *Learning disabilities: Issues on definition.* c/o The Orton Dyslexia Society, 724 York Road, Baltimore MD, 21204, 1981.

Nettleship, E. Cases of congenital word-blindness (inability to learn to read). *Ophthalmology Review*, 1901, *20*, 61–67.

Office of Education. Procedures for evaluating specific learning disabilities. Federal Register, 1977, *42*, 65082–65085.

Orton, S. Specific reading disability—strephosymbolia. *Journal of the American Medical Association*, 1928, *90*, 1095–1099.

Orton, S. *Reading, writing, and speech problems in children*. New York: W. W. Norton, 1937.

Pasternack, R., & Lyon, R. Clinical and empirical identification of learning disabled juvenile delinquents. *Journal of Correctional Education*, September, 1982.

Patten, B. Memory and mental images in verbal deficit modification. *Bulletin of the Orton Society*, 1978, *28*, 217–224.

Rawson, M. *Developmental language disability: Adult accomplishments of dyslexic boys*. Baltimore: Johns Hopkins Press, 1968.

Rawson, M. Dyslexia International—1971. *Bulletin of the Orton Society*, 1972, *22*, 106–116.

Rawson, M. Dyslexics as adults: The possibilities and the challenge. *Bulletin of the Orton Society*, 1977, *27*, 193–197.

Rogan, L., & Hartman, L. *A follow-up study of learning disabled children as adults*. Final Report. Evanston, IL: Cove School Research Office, 1976.

Silver, A. *The misunderstood child*. New York: McGraw-Hill, 1984.

Silver, A., & Hagin, R. Specific reading disability: Follow-up studies. *American Journal of Orthopsychiatry*, 1964, *34*, 85.

Simpson, E. *Reversals: A personal account of victory over dyslexia*. New York: Washington Square Press, 1981.

Strauss, A., & Lehtinen, L. *Psychopathology of the brain injured child*. New York: Grune & Stratton, 1947.

Strong, L. The Spanish-speaking dyslexic child. *Bulletin of the Orton Society*, 1972, *22*, 164–165.

Tarnopol, M. Reading problems worldwide. *Bulletin of the Orton Society*, 1977, *27*, 102–111.

Thomas, C. Congenital word-blindness and its treatment. *Ophthalmoscope*, 1905, *3*, 380–385.

Thompson, L. Language disabilities in men of eminence. *Bulletin of the Orton Society*, 1969, *19*, 113–120.

Wallin, J. Congenital word-blindness. *Lancet*, 1921, *1*, 890–892.

Wiig, E., & Semel, E. *Language disabilities in children and adolescents*. Columbus, OH; Charles E. Merrill, 1976.

Zigmond, N. A prototype of comprehensive services for secondary students with learning disabilities. *Learning Disability Quarterly*, 1978, *1*, 38–49.

# 2

# PRINCIPLES OF ASSESSMENT AND DIAGNOSIS

DORIS J. JOHNSON

Diagnosis in any field is a complex process that involves a search for patterns. It is a process that involves theory-driven assessment, ongoing hypothesis testing and decision making to determine the nature and scope of the problem. In Special Education it requires an understanding of both normal and atypical learning, an awareness of potential breakdowns, and the symptomatology associated with various handicapping conditions.

Our clinical study of adults is a two-day evaluation designed to respond to their concerns, obtain information about their overall ability, learning and achievement, and to investigate the impact of their problems on education, employment, social interactions, and daily living. Data also are used to implement remedial programs and suggest modifications for school or work. When necessary, referrals are made for medical, psychiatric, and/or vocational studies.

The procedures are based on the assumption that learning can be impeded for many reasons including sensory impairments, mental retardation, physical handicaps, emotional disorders, poor motivation, cultural factors, lack of instruction, or specific learning disabilities. Therefore, a differential diagnosis is needed (Myklebust, 1954).

Given the heterogeneous population and diverse symptomatology of adults with learning disabilities, the evaluation is designed to identify potential problems. It includes several broad measures of reasoning, auditory receptive and expressive language, reading, written language, mathematics, and nonverbal learning.

To further define the problems, studies of sub-skills and processes such as attention, perception, memory and conceptualization are included to examine possible correlates of poor achievement. These processes are not studied in

ADULTS WITH LEARNING DISABILITIES
ISBN 0-8089-1795-1

isolation. Rather, they are examined in conjunction with each area of symbolic behavior such as language or reading. Detailed error analyses often provide the bases for further hypothesis testing and informal assessment.

Whenever possible, strategy usage is examined. Observations of problem detection, problem solving, questioning behaviors, task comprehension, self-monitoring and organization are made throughout the evaluation.

Compensatory strategies also can be observed. Many adults spontaneously compensate for their disabilities by using intact skills. For example, many with word retrieval problems improve while reading because the visual symbol facilitates recall. Those with visual-motor problems may use verbal mediation while writing or problem solving. In contrast, some have the capacity to use such strategies but fail to evoke them spontaneously.

Because of our general interest in sub-types of learning disabilities we examine disorders that tend to co-occur. Problems rarely occur in isolation. Rather, patterns of performance and errors can be observed. For example, visual-spatial-motor problems frequently co-occur with disorders of handwriting, written spelling, and computation. Similarly, receptive language disorders typically interfere with reading comprehension and mathematical reasoning.

When analyzing test results, we note whether a problem in one area of learning masks performance in another. For instance, poor oral reading may be a reflection of an expressive language disorder rather than a decoding problem. Hence the *form* of representation and expression is as important as *level* of achievement.

The theories and schema used in assessment will be discussed later in this chapter, however, we emphasize at the outset that diagnosis is not simply a matter of administering a test battery. It is a process that begins with the initial referral and continues throughout all phases of the evaluation including the case history, testing, informal discussions, and diagnostic teaching. Efforts are made to study relationships between various symbol systems, learning processes, problem solving and strategies to understand the breadth and significance of their problems and to avoid fragmentation of services.

## PRIMARY REASONS FOR REFERRAL

Many adults in the clinic requested the evaluation themselves. Others were referred by employers, instructors, psychologists, vocational rehabilitation workers, or their families. Before scheduling an appointment, all adults were asked to write a letter describing the nature of their difficulties and reasons for wanting help. Even though the envelopes were often addressed by someone else, their personal statements indicated they were motivated to proceed with the evaluation. The letters also provided initial samples of their writing.

While the specific concerns of the adults varied somewhat, there were, in general, three primary reasons for referral. One-third of the group wanted to know if they had a specific learning disability. They were aware of their problems but did not know the reason for them. Many were concerned about their overall mental ability or the quality of their early schooling. For instance, a 26-year-old wrote that he "always had trouble learning new words and never knew what the English teachers were talking about." He wondered "whether this was due to some physical difficulty or bad teaching."

Another third of our population had been diagnosed as having learning problems during childhood, but had received no assistance for several years and were eager to gain a clearer understanding of their problems. Often they were considering college or a job change and wanted to know whether their goals were realistic. A few wanted to know if they should request modifications for school entrance examinations and, if so, what type.

A final third wanted an evaluation in order to obtain remediation or tutoring. Occasionally, employers stimulated the referral. For instance, a successful salesman had been promoted to a position that required considerable writing and the company had not realized his potential problems. They were willing to keep him on the new job if he could show progress in written language and organizational skills.

In general, the referrals indicated these adults were motivated and different, in some respects, from those with learning problems in correctional institutions, mental hospitals, or certain vocational programs. Nevertheless, we hope the description of assessment procedures and analyses of their disabilities will be useful to others working with similar populations. We also hope the descriptions of their persistent problems may guide future work with students in elementary and secondary schools.

## COMPONENTS OF THE DIAGNOSTIC STUDY

Our diagnostic studies incorporate data from four primary sources. These include (1) their chief concerns and present status, (2) previous history, (3) objective testing, and (4) clinical observations. From the initial contact through the final conference, the clinician observes behaviors, tests hypotheses, analyzes and synthesizes data, and makes inferences. Questions about the behaviors observed or reported are raised repeatedly. Data from one source of information are checked against others. Initial impressions gained from the case history are checked throughout the examination. Similarly, behaviors elicited during testing raise further questions. The reciprocity between these data sources is shown in Figure 2-1.

To illustrate the need for this type of study, consider the initial statement of a 30-year-old with a severe reading disorder who said, "I need to have you berify my absent from work today." Immediately, the clinician wonders whether he is concerned about his oral language or whether he is even aware of his errors. Further, one may wonder whether the man can discriminate the

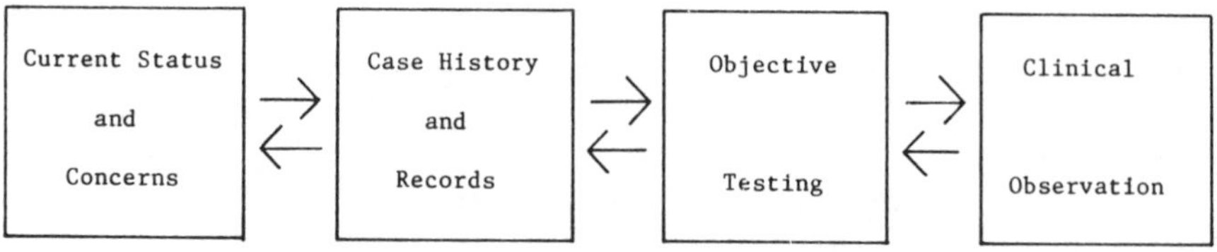


**Figure 2-1.** Components of the diagnostic process.

words, repeat, or read them correctly. We need to know if these are random or consistent errors and whether his problems will be evident on highly structured tests or only in natural settings that require the simultaneous processing of multiple bits of information. In terms of previous history, we would want to know whether he had speech and language therapy, and whether family members have similar problems.

## CLINICAL PROCEDURES

### Case History

The case history is one of the most important facets of the diagnostic process (Myklebust, 1954). From the history one obtains valuable information about the adults' perceptions of their problems, age when they first remember having difficulty, previous recommendations, special programs, and a description of the ways in which problems interfered with schooling, employment and daily living.

The initial questions are open-ended, but, to obtain pertinent information, the history includes many specific items (See Appendix). Generally we allow one and one-half to two hours for the history since most adults need ample time to discuss their concerns.

Because the history may evoke old memories, unhappy days in school or repeated problems at work, it can be a painful process. And yet the diagnostic study provides them with a unique opportunity to convey their concerns. Occasionally clients are slow to develop trust and reluctant to talk about certain topics. Consequently, background data may not be revealed until after the two days of testing or during the final consultation. In certain instances, they may not raise issues they feel are irrelevant. For example, some do not mention time orientation difficulties until prompted by specific questioning.

The history may not be totally accurate unless records from family, physicians and schools are available. However, the individual's perceptions of school and remedial programs are important for understanding attitudes toward learning and for data interpretation.

Developmental histories provide insights into parental expectancies and are useful in determining whether there are familial disabilities.

Medical records are important for those with histories of seizures, hospitalizations, or chronic illnesses that could have interfered with learning and school attendance. Previous psychological and psychiatric studies provide insight into their feelings about themselves and perceptions of the problems.

The occupational history gives an indication of the types of jobs held, length of time on each, and the degree of success. This information, together with current goals, is used to determine whether their objectives are compatible with overall ability and achievement. While some adults are reluctant to try new occupations, even if they have the ability to work at a higher level, others overestimate their potential, perhaps because they do not understand the demands of certain jobs in relation to their disabilities. For example, a student who wants to major in astronomy, but cannot multiply or divide, may not understand what is involved in the field. Similarly, those hoping to attend college are not always aware of the cognitive skills and physical endurance needed to complete the work.

Finally, information regarding leisure time is valuable for understanding the impact of certain disabilities on social life and recreation. If our objective is to understand their total quality of life, we should be concerned not only with schooling and work, but with friendships, interpersonal relationships, and the degree of satisfaction learning disabled adults experience with life in general.

## A Climate for Testing and Teaching

Clinicians should understand the range of potential problems in this heterogeneous group and be prepared for a variety of reactions during the testing-teaching situation. Despite their motivation and tenacity, these adults are quite vulnerable because of repeated failures and frustrations. Many have developed unique coping strategies to hide their problems. Hence, the hours of testing and questions that reveal disabilities can be very trying. As they reach their limits on various tasks they are constantly exposing their weaknesses. Yet, some feel the entire diagnostic process is therapeutic. Finding out they are not slow or bad—that the learning problems are not their fault—can be beneficial.

While one cannot avoid introducing tasks that are difficult, the clinician should be supportive without becoming overly emotionally involved with the client. Occasionally, the adults exhibit fear, tears, anger and depression, but generally these responses are realistic reactions to frustration and failure.

Throughout the history one must decide when to probe or limit the discussion. However, client concerns cannot be taken lightly. As a social worker said, "Feelings are facts." When the adults talk about their problems of overload, distractability, disorganization, or disorientation there is a temptation to say, "we all know people like that" or "I sometimes have difficulty with that, too." Yet the pervasiveness of the problems should be explored. Periodic overloads are one thing; it is quite another when persistent problems interfere with daily functioning.

Clinicians should be cautious in condoning excessive criticism of former teachers, employers, agencies, parents, and others. Some adults have a tendency to "blow up" or exaggerate minor incidents and perseverate on them. The verbally disinhibited also need to be kept "on track." Those who have not had anyone listen to them may talk endlessly. Others talk to avoid difficult tasks.

The examiner also must be prepared to work with individuals who have atypical social perception. Their infrequent or steady maintenance of eye contact can be rather disconcerting. Some tend to become overly familiar too quickly, particularly if they have few friends. In these instances the clinician needs to set the boundaries for discussion and maintain a professional relationship while being warm and understanding.

Most learning disabled adults are sensitive, resilient people who have spent years in environments that often were less than responsive. However, many had the support of one or more caring adults who helped them develop a certain amount of self respect. As a result of our work with this group we have profound respect for them and their desire to become an integral part of society.

## THEORIES AND PROCEDURES

Prior to testing, the client is told about the nature of the procedures and rationale for assessing each area. Since we are interested in obtaining information about learning strategies as well as level of performance, the adults are asked to describe their problem solving approaches. When testing procedures allow for questioning, they are asked to evaluate their performance and indicate whether they think their responses were correct or incorrect, since self-monitoring is an important part of achievement (Bos & Filip, 1982; Capelli & Markman, 1982).

### General Issues Related to Assessment

The evaluation of any exceptional learner requires an understanding of ways potential problems may interfere with performance and achievement. For example, when testing the deaf, blind or physically handicapped, it is obvious, that intact sensory systems, modes of response, and appropriate symbols must be used. Although learning disabilities are less obvious, the subtlety of the problems and heterogeneity of the population warrant careful selection of tasks and interpretation of results for both diagnosis and research. Consequently, several tests in each area of learning may be needed to determine whether processing deficits interfere with achievement. For instance, picture interpretation problems can reduce the level of performance on a language or reading comprehension test. Similarly, visual motor deficits may interfere with written spelling; hence, recognition and oral spelling tests may be needed. While "scatter" of performance has long been recognized with regard to the study of intelligence (Strauss & Lehtinen, 1947), it is equally important when evaluating oral language, reading, writing, and mathematics.

Most tests assess multiple functions and usually require more skills than they purport to measure. Even a relatively simple test such as Digit Span requires auditory perception, memory, and articulation. Thus, task failure requires further investigation. For instance, poor reading comprehension could result from problems in decoding, oral language, conceptualization, monitoring, attention, as well as many other processes.

Because standardized tests yield rather global scores, error analyses may be needed to define specific difficulties, particularly when planning remediation. For example, vocabulary tests do not include the type of linguistic analysis done by Litowitz (Chapter 8). Similarly, many spelling tests do not differentiate error types. Furthermore, tests rarely have enough items to indicate the person's level of rule acquisition. That is, one cannot discern whether the person needs help in acquiring, applying, or automatizing a particular rule. Therefore, informal tasks and criterion reference measures are needed.

Occasionally, if the problems are very severe, tests not designed for adults are used. For example, even though phonemic discrimination is relatively well developed by age eight, it continues to be a problem for many adults. Thus, such a test might be used to investigate certain error patterns.

An evaluation can be strengthened by comparing performance on tasks with varying degrees of structure. Certain learning problems are less evident on highly structured tests than on those requiring spontaneous problem detection. For example many adults perform better on standardized spelling tests than when writing a letter. Others, however, are more successful in naturalistic settings because of redundant cues in the environment.

Studies of task comprehension, self monitoring, fatigue, attention, persistence, and frustration add pertinent data for vocational and educational planning. Observing learning disabled adults read or write a single paragraph is not unlike watching the physically handicapped walk down the street. They may reach their goal, but only with incredible effort, and perhaps, idiosyncratic strategies. Their lack of automaticity and erratic errors often are due to fatigue and overload.

Observations of time used to complete tasks are also useful for making recommendations. Research indicates that learning disabled subjects frequently use less time than the control group because of impulsivity or lack of problem detection, yet others are slower than their peers.

In general, tests are chosen and observations are planned to answer a series of questions—not simply to accumulate a series of scores. No single theory, however, will provide the basis for all questions. Rather, the assessment is strengthened by using theories and methodology from various fields. Our understanding of learning disabilities is enhanced by the investigations of experimental psychologists, audiologists, developmental psychologists, linguists, and others who have contributed chapters in this volume.

### Basic Prerequisites for Learning

The examination begins with a study of the primary integrities necessary for learning—that is, with an investigation of hearing, vision, and intellectual ability.

An assessment of auditory acuity is essential, since even a mild hearing loss can interfere with language comprehension, learning, and daily function. While adults with both hearing impairments and learning disabilities were evaluated, only those with normal hearing are discussed in this volume.

Vision screening is done in the clinic, but the major assessment of visual acuity is conducted by the family physician or visual specialist. Previous recommendations for glasses and/or ocular training are obtained from the history and medical records.

Tests of mental ability are needed, not only to rule out retardation, but to obtain general information about language and learning processes. Since a learning disability can interfere with either verbal or nonverbal functions, the WAIS is routinely administered (Wechsler, 1955, 1981). Although adults with varying degrees of mental ability are assessed, the focus of this volume is on those with specific learning disabilities who have at least average mental ability. An analysis of the intelligence test results is included in Chapter 4.

Emotional status is evaluated through case histories, records, and interviews. While several adults had previous therapy or were in counseling to cope with frustrations and feelings of failure, in general, they came for an evaluation of learning and achievement, not for psychiatric study. Those who were classified primarily as emotionally disturbed are not included in this discussion.

Motivation is a major area to consider in the study of learning problems. Adelman and Taylor (1983) say "there is no way to know what people are capable of unless they want to show us their best" (p. 168). These authors feel that intrinsic motivation particularly, has been ignored in the field of learning disabilities. While we recognize the diversity of the total population, the adults in this clinical sample were motivated to achieve. Their drive to be independent, contributing members of society sets them apart from those who show limited curiosity and motivation. It is clear, however, from many discussions that they need assistance in order to achieve. Trying harder is not enough.

## THE STUDY OF ACHIEVEMENT AND COGNITIVE PROCESSES

The assessment battery is designed to explore the person's ability to understand and use the basic symbol systems of the culture at a level commensurate with mental ability, years of schooling, and motivation to learn. These areas include auditory receptive and expressive language, reading, written language, mathematics and many aspects of nonverbal learning, communication, and reasoning.

The broad relationships between these areas of learning are illustrated in Figure 2-2. The diagram suggests that all symbol systems are based on nonverbal cognitive processes or inner language (Myklebust, 1954), and that many reciprocal patterns of learning need to be investigated. The processes at the base of Figure 2-2 are frequently called the "Hierarchy of experience" and, together, provide the essential meaning for most symbols. Without an accurate perception, understanding, and memory of basic experience, words and numbers have little meaning. For example, the significance of environmental signs is dependent upon the ability to perceive differences in color, shape, and design. Similarly, comprehension of symbols such as "hexagon" or "octagon" requires the abstraction and perception of criterial attributes of the figures as well as perception and memory of the words.

When applying this hierarchy to diagnosis and remediation, we attempt to investigate the person's attention and perception of various stimuli. Then, at the level of imagery we note whether the person can remember what was seen, heard, or felt. At the level of symbolization, we investigate comprehension—that is, the ability to understand "what means what." Some people can perceive, remember, and imitate what they see and hear, but cannot comprehend. Finally, at the level of conceptualization, the adult's ability to classify and categorize objects, experiences, words, and ideas, is examined. These same processes are examined with regard to each symbol system. Thus, we explore the person's ability to discriminate, comprehend, and remember spoken and written words, numerals and other symbols.

Obviously, there are many interactions between levels of processing on this hierarchy (Johnson, 1982). Typically, severe disturbances in perception interfere with higher level functions. For example, problems of phonemic discrimination may interfere with comprehension or production of words. However, higher level functions also facilitate lower level processes. That is, previously acquired language may facilitate phonemic discrimination. Similarly, conceptualization aids recall.

Recent studies indicate learning disabled individuals often have the ability to perceive, remember, and categorize, but fail to use their background language and knowledge for new learning or complex problem solving. Newman (1980) found school-age students did not use conceptualization to aid recall of pictures until specifically directed to remember groups of "foods, clothing or school supplies." Therefore, the *processes* and *strategies* used to acquire and retain new information, as well as the final *products* or level of achievement, are noted.

Both receptive and expressive components of each symbol system are explored. Since many handicapped learners have difficulty with one or more expressive processes, it is important to determine whether their oral or written responses reflect their level of understanding. Receptively, we explore the person's ability to perceive, abstract, understand, and retain the symbols. Expressive processes include retrieval, revisualization, sequencing, rule usage, organization, and production.

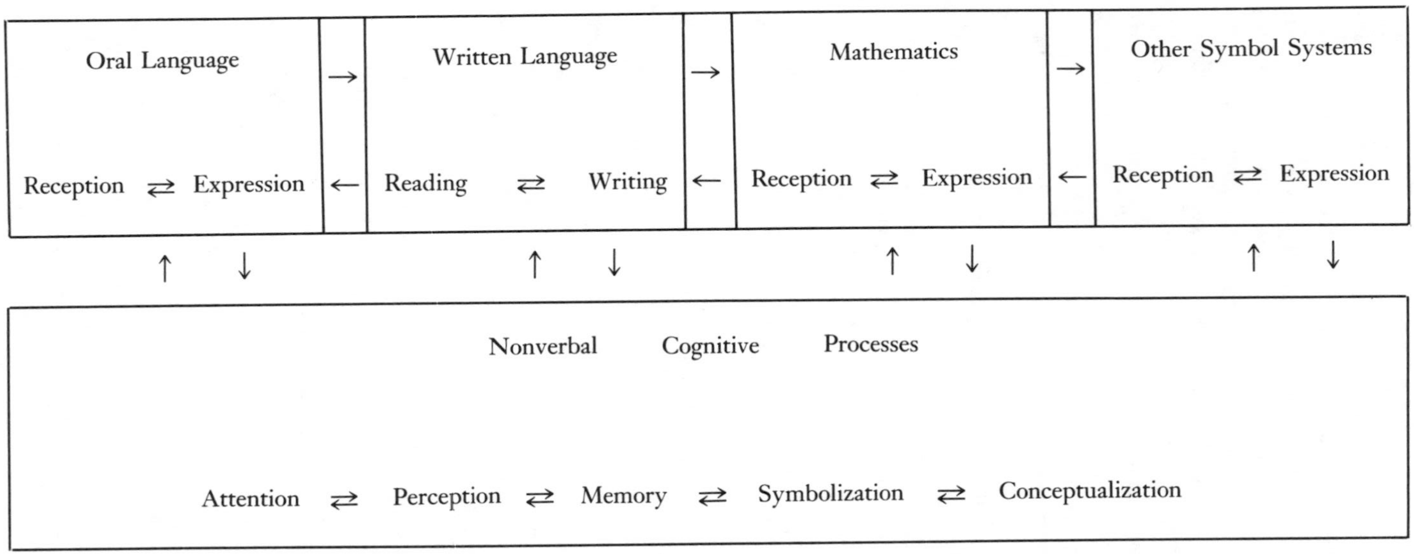


**Figure 2-2.** Relationships between language, achievement, and cognitive processes.

The relationships between these processes are exceedingly complex. For example, in learning the word "pen", one must abstract the concept of "pen-ness" from repeated experience with various writing instruments and objects of similar shape. Then, to use the spoken word, the listener must differentiate "pen" from similar words, comprehend the meaning, and execute the motor plan for speaking. In order to read and spell, the features of the orthography must be abstracted and integrated with the spoken word, and the writer must revisualize and reproduce the letters. In addition, one learns the multiple meanings for "pen".

The forms of representation also vary. Consider the meaning of the word "quarter." Making change requires the accurate perception of size and criterial attributes of the coin. However, the concept can also be represented visually by using the printed word *quarter*, 25¢, $.25, or twenty-five cents. In other contexts, the word "quarter" refers to spatial and temporal concepts in music, home economics, and other subjects. While it is impossible to fully analyze these relationships during the diagnostic study, some attempt is made to investigate learning across several areas of achievement.

Questions regarding the relationships between the components in Figure 2-2 have been addressed by faculty and students in the program for many years. Both clinical experience and experimental studies suggest that a problem is rarely restricted to a single area of symbolic behavior. Observations of children with auditory language problems (Myklebust, 1954; Johnson & Myklebust, 1967) indicated those with receptive disorders had comprehension problems that interfered with most symbol systems. In contrast, those with expressive disorders had problems with some aspects of reading and writing, but not all.

These observations were supported by McGrady's (1964) study of (1) normal children, (2) speech defectives, (3) receptive aphasics, and (4) expressive aphasics. (The latter two groups were developmental not acquired conditions.) Using an extensive battery which included measures for the components of Figure 2-2, McGrady found that children with auditory receptive language disorders had the most pervasive problems. They had difficulty with both verbal and nonverbal symbolic functions, with numerical concepts, and reasoning. In contrast, those with expressive disorders demonstrated more "scatter." As a group they performed below the controls on memory for sentences and written grammar. Thus, their oral expression problems interfered with written language, but not necessarily with reading. McGrady concluded that each of these disorders presents a different structure of abilities and that the groups varied in their overall behavioral organization and psychodynamics.

Later, Wren (1980) found children with severe oral expressive disorders had more receptive deficits than those with mild syntax disorders. They had more difficulty comprehending spatial and temporal concepts and discriminating morphological endings of words in context.

Most recently Friedman (1984) found preschool normal and deaf children performed better than those with receptive language disorders on most classification tasks. She concluded the latter group had a generalized deficiency in representational behavior and the findings supported a cognitive hypothesis of language impairment.

These studies emphasize the importance of studying relationships between verbal and nonverbal cognitive processes as well as relationships between various symbol systems. When planning programs it is helpful to note whether the individual has relatively generalized or specific deficits. However, the concepts underlying each symbol or code need to be considered. While spoken language, writing, numbers, pictures, graphs, maps, gestures, and music are all forms of representation, the rule systems to be abstracted are different. Music, mathematics, and reading all require auditory-temporal and visual-spatial integration, but the features and principles to be abstracted are not the same.

We make no generalizations about an adult's reading achievement from tasks requiring visual processing of nonverbal material. Rather, the analyses are done by using the symbols that are difficult for the individual. If the person is failing arithmetic, the tasks would be selected to study the perception, memory, symbolization, and conceptualization of numbers. Similarly, if the person were failing music, the evaluation would include discrimination of shape, color, size, and position of musical notations. Nevertheless, we are interested in the breadth of the problems and level of processing related to the acquisition or use of many types of symbols.

## A Systems Analysis

Several additional theoretical constructs guide the diagnostic study, and together, form the basis for a systems approach illustrated in Figure 2-3. These concepts derive from the fields of learning disabilities, language pathology, information processing, neuropsychology, and years of experience with atypical learners (Johnson & Myklebust, 1967). The figure suggests that an individual has multiple sensory systems for receiving and abstracting information from the environment, a vast network for processing information, and several modes for response.

The outer boundary of the figure indicates we need information regarding the types of stimulation provided by the family, school, or employer, and the person's ability to function in various settings.

### *Input-integration-output-feedback*

This broad schema is used to determine whether an individual has difficulty with the input, integration, output, or monitoring of information. This construct, together with others described below, constitutes a general plan for analyzing tasks and the individual's performance. When selecting tests, we consider the nature of the input, various cognitive processes, and mode of response for each. When analyzing results, we make hypotheses about the nature of the errors, and if necessary, construct additional tasks to check

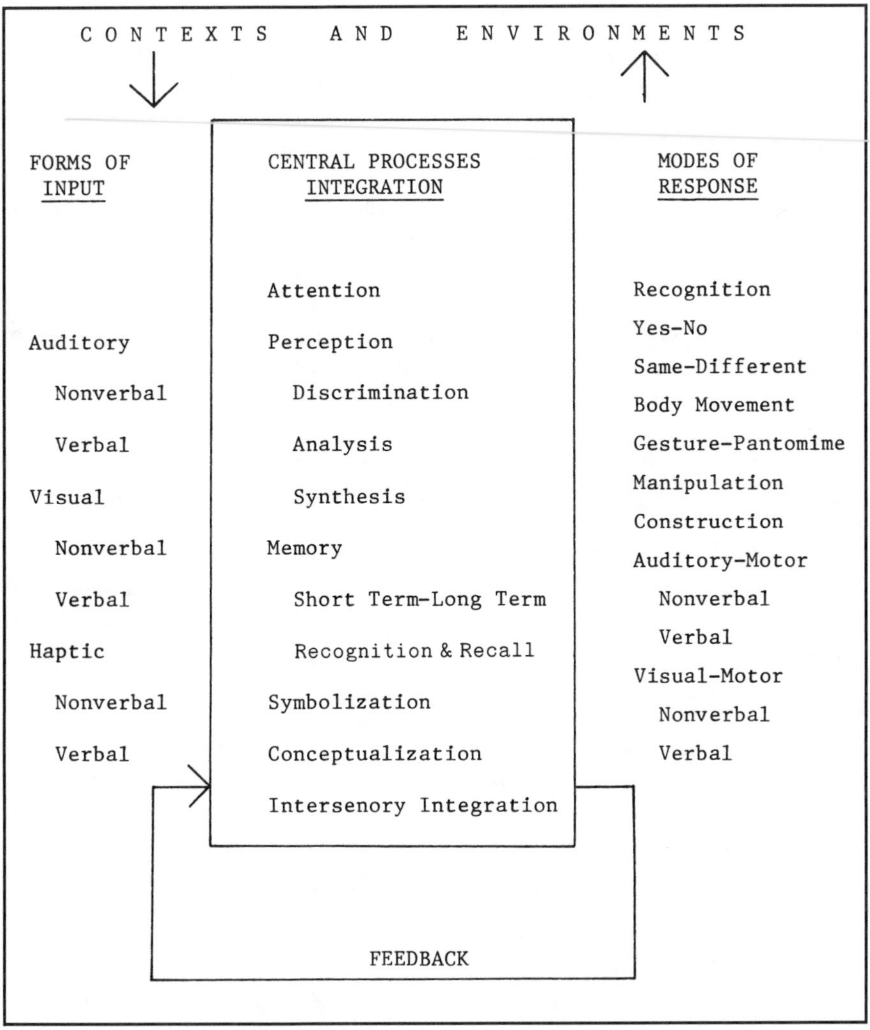


**Figure 2-3.** Schema for systems analysis.

hypotheses regarding a specific disturbance. For example, if a person mispronounces a word such as "pacific" for "specific" we want to know if the person can *monitor* the error (is aware of the mispronunciation), can *perceive* the difference between the two words spoken by the examiner, and can *repeat* the word immediately after the examiner. In addition, the person is asked to read the words to see if there is improvement when the visual symbol is present (Johnson, 1985). This objective is to determine whether problems are related to the "transmission" of a message (on either the input or output side), to storage and access of information, or integration and meaning. The data are used for planning remediation and for making modifications in school or at work.

### *Semi-autonomous systems*

Another theoretical construct derives from the work of Hebb (1963) who suggested that the brain is composed of systems that may operate semi-independently or together. Learning that requires the processing of information through only one sensory system is called "intrasensory"; that requiring two is "intersensory"; and that requiring more than two is "multisensory" (Birch & Belmont, 1965; Chalfant & Scheffelin, 1969; Johnson & Myklebust, 1967). Tasks are analyzed according to the number and nature of sensory systems needed. For example, phonemic discrimination tests requiring a comparison of two words (e.g., Do these sound the same?) involve only auditory verbal processing; whereas those requiring the subject to point to pictures (e.g., show me *face - vase*) require intersensory integration, since both auditory and visual processing are necessary. This does not mean that one test is preferred over another; rather this type of systems analysis may be used to explain differences in performance.

Intersensory integration typically requires more than *matching* or *associating* information from two or more sensory systems. Most learning, particularly verbal learning, requires intersensory *representation* and mapping of rules or concepts. For example, the auditory utterance "ay" can be represented by either upper or lower case manuscript or cursive letters of the alphabet (all of which may vary with type font and handwriting). The same sound can be represented by the orthographic units *ai*, *ay*, *eigh*, and *a-e*. In music the same utterance ("ay") refers to a particular tone or visual-spatial feature on a page of music. Thus, the problem for many learners is not just association rather it involves the abstraction of features and properties of the referrent as well as features of the symbol system. Without an understanding of these complex relationships, both diagnosis and remediation can be oversimplified.

The semi-autonomous systems construct also is relevant for remediation. For example, not all individuals profit from multisensory input. Some are confused by looking, listening, and writing simultaneously (Johnson & Myklebust, 1967). Therefore, during periods of diagnostic teaching we select various combinations of sensory input to facilitate learning (Johnson, 1979).

### *Verbal and Nonverbal Learning*

The ability to use language and other symbols typically requires both verbal and nonverbal processing as does the ability to function adaptively in the world. Some situations, however, require primarily verbal facility, whereas others require more nonverbal competence (e.g., recognition of faces or features of the environment). By adulthood, these processes are so interrelated and verbal mediation is used so frequently (even on nonverbal tasks) that it is sometimes difficult to differentiate the functions. Yet in pathological conditions such as acquired brain damage, the differences become more evident. Adults with acquired right hemisphere damage often have difficulty with facial recognition and orientation, whereas those with left hemisphere involvement have more verbal, temporal, and sequential difficulties.

Developmental learning disabilities are never quite so clear, but some children and adults do have problems that are primarily nonverbal or verbal. Therefore, we do not classify a person as having a modality specific disorder (e.g. auditory or visual) without specifying the type of content. In most instances, however, disturbance in either verbal or nonverbal processing results in a lack of integration. Hence, if an individual is asked to "point to the picture of the president", problems with either language comprehension or facial recognition could interfere with performance. Similarly, failure on a picture naming task could result from either picture interpretation or word retrieval difficulties.

If one incorporates concepts from the input-integration-output schema together with the semiautonomous systems, and verbal-nonverbal learning, many differences on test performance can be explained. In spelling, for example, writing words from dictation requires auditory-verbal input and a visual-motor response; whereas, writing the names of objects involves visual-nonverbal input and a visual-motor output. If inputs are held constant, but response modes are changed (e.g., oral spelling, manipulation of letter tiles, or writing), the processing demands are also different.

### *Simultaneous and Successive Processing*

The field of neuropsychology has generated considerable research regarding simultaneous and successive processing of information (Luria, 1966). Masland (1976) quotes Luria who said that there seemed to be two types of mental analytical processes—one for analysis of simultaneous events and the other for analysis of successive events which occur temporally. Recently these concepts were incorporated in the *Kaufman Assessment Battery for Children* (Kaufman & Kaufman, 1983).

This concept is relevant for diagnosis, since adults may be labeled as auditory or visual learners without noting whether material is presented simultaneously or successively. Because of the auditory memory and temporal disorders found among language impaired children and adults, it should be noted that information presented through the auditory system is sequential. Hence, there always is an element of temporal, sequential memory in oral language. In contrast, information from the visual system can be presented either simultaneously or successively. Words, pictures, or designs can be presented simultaneously for inspection or sequentially by using film strips, movies, or flashing lights. It is evident that the cognitive demands of these tasks vary. In a recent book entitled *Mind and Media*, Greenfield (1984) reviews several studies regarding children's responses to films, video presentations, and oral stories that highlight these differences.

Adults with auditory-temporal disorders sometimes perform better on reading than listening comprehension tasks because of the opportunity to review material. Similarly, some monitor written grammar better than oral because they can see their mistakes. Therefore, when analyzing diagnostic data, differences between successive and simultaneous presentations are noted.

## Rule Acquisition, Application, and Automaticity

Most forms of symbolic behavior and problem solving require the acquisition and application of multiple rules. Oral language, for example, has rules governing phonology (the sound system), semantics (meaning), syntax (grammar), and pragmatics (language usage). Similarly, writing requires knowledge of orthography (spelling patterns), grammar, punctuation, and discourse. Mathematics, music, and Morse Code all have rules.

Rules also are needed to function adaptively in most environments. On a daily basis one adheres to traffic rules, office rules, or disciplinary rules. During leisure time we follow rules of games either as spectators or participants. Generally, rule systems require several cognitive processes including perception, memory, sequencing, symbolization, or conceptualization. They also require organization and varying degrees of perceptual-motor skills.

In order to apply rules, one must know when to use a particular principle. For instance, one must "size up" a situation to know when a form of written discourse or level of verbal behavior is expected. In most instances *several* rules must be applied simultaneously and automatically.

Many adults with learning disabilities have problems with the acquisition and use of rules governing language, reading, writing, or mathematics. However, they are not totally lacking in the use of particular rules. That is, they do not always misuse particular plural forms or verb tenses nor miss the same arithmetic operation. Rather, their errors are random, inconsistent, and more frequent in situations that require multiple rule usage automatically. (Throughout this volume we have included many examples to illustrate these problems.) A major goal of our assessment is to determine whether the learner understands a rule or principle, can remember or apply it, and/or whether the rule is automatic. In diagnostic teaching, informal tasks are arranged to study levels of rule learning. For instance, if a person is suspected of having problems with plural rules, questions shown in Figure 2-4 might be used. The tasks incorporate concepts from schema described earlier in the chapter and are designed to determine whether there are problems of input, integration, output or feedback; and at the level of perception, memory, symbolization, and/or conceptualization.

Rule systems and symbols may be acquired either implicitly or explicitly. In early childhood most rules are learned implicitly, particularly those governing oral language. However, in school, rules are acquired both explicitly and

1. *Auditory Perception*
   "Do these sound the same?"—boy–boys; jump–jumped
   "Do these sound the same?"—The boy jumped–the boys jumped.
2. *Auditory Comprehension*
   "Do these mean the same thing?"
   —cat–cats; The cats eat.–The cat eats.
   —Show me the boy.–Show me the boys.
   —Show me the blocks are piled.–Show me the blocks are unpiled.
3. *Auditory Repetition* (Single words, phrases, sentences, questions)
   "Say these after me"—boy–boys; The boy jumped.–The boys jumped.
4. *Spontaneous Oral Production*
   From actions, pictures, or experiences attempt to elicit the correct form (e.g., hold up one boy doll figure—and then 2—then manipulate the doll figures and attempt to elicit a sentence).
5. *Visual Perception*
   "Do these words look the same?"—boy–boys; jumps–jump
   "Do these sentences look the same?"—The boy jumps.–The boys jump.
6. *Visual Comprehension*
   "Do these mean the same?"
   "Match the pictures with the sentences or questions."
   —The boy jumped.–The boys jumped.
7. *Auditory-Visual Recognition*
   "Point to"—boy–boys; The boy jumps.–The boys jump.
8. *Visual to Auditory Verbal Production*
   "Read these"—boy–boys; The boy jumps.–The boys jump.
9. *Visual-Motor Imitation*
   "Copy these words and sentences."
10. *Spontaneous Written Production*
    From actions, sentence completion, pictures, etc., attempt to have the student write grammatically correct sentences. Increase complexity of setting and ask the child to write stories. Note percentage of correct usage and rule patterns. Note random vs. systematic errors and automaticity.
11. *Application of Rule in Novel Situations*
    Nonsense pictures and nonsense words (oral and/or written)
    "Here is a wug.–Here are two ________."
    "This wug is troppy.–This one is troppier. This one is ________."
12. *Comprehension of Morphology at an Explicit Level*
    "Show me the part of the word that means more than one."—boy–boys
13. *Verbal Expression of Meaning of Morphology*
    "If I add an *s* to a word such as *cat*, what does it do?"
14. *Monitoring of Other Production—Auditory*
    "Listen; tell me whether this sounds correct."—The boys is jumping.
15. *Self-Monitoring—Auditory*
    "Did you say that correctly?" (tape-recorded)
16. *Monitoring of Other Productions—Visual*
    "Look; see if you can find any mistakes."—The boy are jumping.

**Figure 2-4.** Tasks for Studying Levels of Rule Acquisition and Application.

implicitly. Reading and spelling methods, for example, vary considerably with the theories of the authors.

Many learning disabled students have difficulty acquiring rules for complex syntax. This may be due, in part, to limited auditory memory and lack of opportunity to hear several instances of the same rule successively. Hence, they often acquire complex grammar through reading.

Many also have difficulty with morphosyntactic rules in spelling, particularly if the principles are not made explicit. For instance, as children acquire plural rules in English, they implicitly learn that "s" follows voiceless consonants as in "cats" and "cups", but that "z" follows voiced consonants as in "lads" and "cubs". Yet, in spelling, the letter s marks the plurals for all these words. Verb tenses are equally confusing. The person who writes "lookt" may be relying totally on phonological principles rather than the morpho-graphemic rule ed. In remediation we heighten awareness of these principles and provide structured exercises for rule application and automaticity.

Adults with oral language disorders also may have difficulty with explicit verbal rules because of memory and comprehension problems. They profit from opportunities to scan and observe patterns. Hence, both inductive and deductive learning is investigated.

In general, when an individual has difficulty with the acquisition and use of rules or principles we raise the following questions:

1. Did the person understand the task and various requirements of the assignment (e.g., understand what was expected)?
2. Did the person attend to all aspects of the task?
3. Did the person detect, perceive, and abstract features that are relevant for understanding the referrent for interpreting the symbols (e.g., discrimination of phonemes, letters, words, numerals, signs for arithmetic, etc.)?
4. Did the person comprehend the meaning of the symbols and relationships between symbols?
5. Did the person have short-term memory problems that interfered with the retention of information needed to solve various problems, follow directions, etc.?
6. Did the person have difficulty with long-term storage of information, principles, etc.?
7. Did the person have the perceptual-motor ability to imitate, repeat, or produce the symbols required (e.g., repeat words, copy, imitate movements.)?
8. If spontaneous expression was required, could the person access, retrieve (reauditorize, revisualize, and organize) the vocabulary, letters, words, numbers, etc.?
9. Could the person apply rules systematically and automatically? Could the person use multiple rule systems simultaneously (e.g., spelling, grammar, and punctuation)?

10. Could the person monitor his or her own performance? Did the person know performance should be monitored (e.g., proofreading, checking mathematics problems, etc.)?
11. Could the person process and integrate information and rules between two or more sensory systems?
12. Could the person process and integrate both verbal and nonverbal information?
13. Could the person spontaneously detect problems without direction? If problems were defined, could the person solve them?
14. What patterns of errors were present (Were there patterns of errors?) Were the mistakes random or consistent?

## Activity, Interaction and Learning

In order to better understand poor learning and performance, it is helpful to investigate the activity of the learner and type of instruction that has been provided (Johnson, 1981). We need to know something about *how* the individual tries to learn—that is, the degree to which he or she actively explores, questions, hypothesizes, searches for patterns, and tries to remember new information. It is also helpful to know if and how the individual preorganizes, organizes, and monitors performance.

Research and clinical observations indicate that learning disabled children may be less active learners than their nondisabled peers (Torgeson, 1982). We first observed limited activity in a study of haptic perception where the hands of both normal and learning disabled children were videotaped while exploring various objects and geometric figures. Whereas the normal children actively searched for distinctive features and tended to "edge" the entire figure, those with learning disabilities simply pressed, patted or squeezed the object. These observations lead us to conclude that at least some of the differential performance on the haptic perception tasks was related to lack of exploration. These findings are in agreement with those of Cable (1981) who found preschool learning disabled children showed less exploratory play than the normal group. Parents also said the learning disabled used less jargon, vocal play, and exploratory play than other children in the family.

At the upper age levels learning disabled students tend to ask fewer questions and fail to scan books for tables of contents, questions, and summaries. They read assignments only once without reviewing, underlining, or taking notes. And, research indicates that poor writers do less rereading and revising than good writers (Cooper & Odell, 1978). Thus, part of the reason for poorer performance may be related to limited activity or poor study habits.

Often this lack of activity results from ambiguous instructions, directions, or feedback. For example, overly general directions to "proof your paper carefully" are not specific enough to produce a change. Even a recommendation to proof for "punctuation, grammar and spelling" may need to be more explicit.

Without specific guidelines, models, and instructions, They may simply "spin their wheels." The instructions, cues, and reinforcement must be appropriate to foster independent work. Recommendations to "try harder" or "do it again" only exhaust and discourage the adults.

Occasionally, inactivity results from others having done too much for them. When the learner cannot perform in the expected manner, there is a tendency to reduce expectations or complete tasks for them, rather than providing structure and cues to foster independent cognitive control (Sammarco, 1983). Eventually this may lead to the behavior known as "learned helplessness" (Pysh, 1982).

Learning disabled students, however, are conscious of reduced expectations and are discouraged by this reaction. One man said, "the worst thing that happens is when no one expects anything of you anymore; then you really know you are hopeless." Instructors need to find ways of presenting assignments that are compatible with both intellectual and achievement levels so the learning disabled individual is neither over- nor under-stimulated.

## CLINICAL OBSERVATIONS

Throughout the two-day evaluation, there are many opportunities to observe verbal and nonverbal communication, organization, and problem solving and even more when the adults come for diagnostic teaching and remediation. During group sessions additional patterns of behavior and communication can be observed.

The importance of studying the adults in various contexts is illustrated by the diagram in Figure 2-3. Those who score low on standardized reading tests often use signs in the buildings, maps of the campus, and menus successfully. Others are more successful on structured tasks in a room free from distractions. The latter group often have many problems at work. For instance, they can compute and make change during testing but not in a busy, noisy environment.

White (1980), quotes Bronfenbrenner (1979), who believes that a relevant body of research will best be developed by studying children's natural environment and exploring the factors that play a role in their lives. White further says that we need to study the features of an environment that make it easy or hard for a child to show his or her best performance. Clearly, similar research is needed with adults who have learning disabilities. Vocational studies should not be limited to paper and pencil tasks but should include direct observation over time. These studies are necessary particularly for adults who are unaware of their errors that impact on schooling, work, and social interactions. Diagnosticians can help make them aware of their unintentional errors and behaviors that contribute to faulty performance.

## SUMMARY

The purpose of this chapter was to present principles and theories used in the assessment of adults with learning disabilities. The studies include measures of sensory acuity, intelligence, reasoning, various forms of symbolic behavior including oral language, reading, written language, and learning processes related to rule acquisition and application. The remainder of the volume is devoted to a description of the problems in the clinical population studied. While several group trends will be presented, we also have attempted to identify patterns of problems that tend to co-occur. Ultimately, however, diagnosis always requires a careful study of the individual in relation to his or her ability motivation and expectancies within the environment.

When diagnosing a learning disability we attempted to establish expectancy levels based on educational and family backgrounds, mental ability, and current life situations. Standardized tests, informal measures and diagnostic teaching were utilized in making decisions. Data from case histories, interviews, and previous records confirmed the chronicity of the problems. No diagnoses were made on the basis of a single test score; rather, they were based on patterns of problems and errors.

## REFERENCES

Adelman, H., & Taylor, L. Learning disabilities in perspective. Glenview, IL: Scott, Foresman, 1983

Birch, H., & Belmont, L. Auditory-visual integration, intelligence and reading ability in school children. *Perceptual and Motor Skills*, 1965, *20*, 295–305

Bos, C., & Filip, D. Comprehension monitoring skills in learning disabled and average students. *Topics in Learning and Learning Disabilities*. 1982, *1* (2), 79–85.

Bronfenbrenner, U. The ecology of Human Development: Experiments by nature and design. Cambridge, MA: Harvard Educational Review, 1979.

Cable, B. A study of play behavior in normal and learning disabled preschool boys. Unpublished doctoral dissertation, Northwestern University, 1981.

Capelli, C., & Markman, E. Suggestions for comprehension monitoring. *Topics in Learning and Learning Disabilities*, 1982, *1* (2), 87–96.

Chalfant, J., & Scheffelin, M. *Central processing dysfunctions in children: A review of research*. U.S. Department of Health, Education, and Welfare, National Institute of Neurological Diseases and Stroke, 1969.

Cooper, C., & Odell, L. *Research on composing: Points of departure*. Urbana, IL: National Council of Teachers of English, 1981.

Friedman, J. Classification skills in normally hearing/achieving, oral deaf, and language impaired preschoolers: A study in language and conceptual thought. Unpublished doctoral dissertation, Northwestern University, 1984.

Greenfield, P. *Mind and media*. Cambridge, MA: Harvard University Press, 1984.

Hebb, D.The semi-autonomous process: Its nature and nurture. *American Psychologist*, 1981, *18* (1), 16–17.

Jastak, J., & Jastak, S. *Wide range achievement test* (rev. ed.). Wilmington, DE: Jastak Associates, Inc., 1978.

Johnson, D. Design for individualization of language intervention programs. In J.

Miller, D. Yoder, & R. Schiefelbusch (Eds.), *Contemporary issues in language intervention*. Rockville, MD: ASHA Reports 12, The American Speech-Language Hearing Association, 1983.

Johnson, D. Factors to consider in programming for children with language disorders. *Topics in Language and Learning Disabilities*, 1981, *2* (1), 13–27.

Johnson, D. Programming for dyslexia: The need for interaction analyses. *Annals of Dyslexia*, 1982, *32*, 61–70.

Johnson, D. Psycho-educational evaluation of children with learning disabilities: Study ofauditory processes. In G. Millichap (Ed.), *Learning disabilities and related disorders*. Chicago: Year Book Medical Publishers, 1979.

Johnson, D. Using reading and writing to improve oral language skills. *Topics in Language Disorders*, 1985, *5*, 55–69.

Johnson, D. & Hook, P. Reading disabilities: Problems of rule acquisition and linguistic awareness. In Myklebust, H. (Ed.), *Progress in learning disabilities* (Vol. 4). New York: Grune & Stratton, 1978.

Johnson, D., & Myklebust, H. *Learning Disabilities: Educational principles and practices*. New York: Grune & Stratton, 1967.

Kaufman, A., & Kaufman, N. *Kaufman Assessment battery for children*. Circle Pines, MN: American Guidance Service, 1983.

Luria, A. *Human brain and psychological processes*. New York: Harper & Row, 1966.

Masland, R. The advantages of being dyslexic. *Bulletin of the Orton Society*, 1976, *26*, 10–18.

McGrady, H. Verbal and nonverbal functions in school children with speech and language disorders. Unpublished doctoral dissertation. Northwestern University, 1964.

Myklebust, H. *Auditory disorders in children*. New York: Grune & Stratton, 1954.

Myklebust, H. *The Psychology of deafness: Sensory deprivation, learning and adjustment*. New York: Grune & Stratton, 1960.

Newman, D. An investigation of learning disabled children's utilization of taxonomic organization to facilitate memory performance. Unpublished doctoral dissertation, Northwestern University, 1980.

Pysh, M. Learning disabled and normal achieving childrens' attributions and reactions to success and failure. Unpublished doctoral dissertation, Northwestern University, 1982.

Sammarco, J. Joint problem-solving activity in mother-child dyads: A comparative study of normally achieving and language disordered preschoolers. Unpublished doctoral dissertation, Northwestern University, 1984.

Strauss, A., & Lehtinen, L. *Psychopathology of the brain injured child*. New York: Grune & Stratton, 1947.

Torgesen, J. Psychoeducational aspects of learning disabled adolescents. In L. Mann, L. Goodman & J. Wiederholt (Eds.), *Teaching the learning disabled adolescent*. Boston: Houghton Mifflin, 1982.

Wechsler, D. *Wechsler adult intelligence scale*. New York: Psychological Corporation, 1955.

Wechsler, D. Wechsler adult intelligence scale-revised. New York: Psychological Corporation, 1981.

White, S. Cognitive competence and performance in everyday environments. *Bulletin of the Orton Society*, 1980, *30*, 29–45.

Wren, C. The relationship of auditory and cognitive processes to syntactic patterns in learning disabled and normal children. Unpublished doctoral dissertation, Northwestern University, 1980.

# 3

## Primary Concerns and Group Characteristics

JANE W. BLALOCK
DORIS J. JOHNSON

This chapter provides a general description of adults seen in the Learning Disabilities Center at Northwestern University and a summary of the problems that concerned them. Although several hundred adults have been evaluated, the information reported here was obtained from letters requesting an appointment, case histories, and records of 93 successive cases diagnosed as learning disabled.

In some respects their letters were as important for the diagnosis as the objective tests. Indeed, a compilation of their written statements could provide clearer statements about the significance of a learning disability than our summaries. Often, in reading their letters we saw obvious problems such as immature handwriting, faulty spelling and spacing of letters, and the results of repeated attempts to fold the paper to fit into envelopes. Similarly, their misuse of words, mispronunciations, lack of organization and word retrieval problems were sometimes evident, even at the time of the initial phone contact.

The content of their letters and discussions made it clear that a learning disability affects more than schooling and rarely affects a single area of achievement such as language or reading. The letters describing their performance as well as reactions from teachers, employers, and others were often very moving. A 26-year-old woman gave us permission to use her letter as an example. Her verbal IQ was 120 and performance was 116.

Dear Mrs. Blalock

You asked for a short background and what I hoped to gain form your tests I think the first thing I hope to gain is the knowledge of someone who knows what they are dealing with who can put a lot of litte pieces together and help me do something to over come a few abstacles.

ADULTS WITH LEARNING DISABILITIES
ISBN 0-8089-1795-1

In terms of learning I've always felt there was something amiss. One always notices how he/she is different than others but I kept coming up with different differences. I grew up in ______. I went to ______ School (K-6 grade then) where in kindegarden my one claim to notoriety was placing a gold fish under my teacher as she was sitting down. If I hadn't done that (she told my mother later) she never would have none I was around.

I learned from my folks that in 1st grade I was a terrific student but that somewhere between first and third the bottom fell out scholastically speaking.

Starting in forth grade my parents had me tutored in what ever was in dire need of it.

So it went all thru school. I could look at my homework in high school and it might as well have been greek. In High school (______) I took latin and Spanish so many times that they told me I could graduate without it-- I was hopeless. (I was also told "don't plan on making a career in the field.").

Math–there was another subject. It never made much sence until my tutors spent hours going painstakingly translating it. I's get an assignment and at night I'd work with my fahter for 3, or 5 hours on a 45 minute assignment. I had to sweat out every little math equasion. He would sit there giving me an example of what each could be used for so I could some how tie it together.

English & Combined Studies followed the same pattern. The teachers tutored me in study hall period.

My reports cards were a big joke . . . so were the conferences. They said I was always unmotivated . . . or not trying . . . or not giving a 100% effort. There were days I could have rammed those words down someone elses throat.

In my sophomore year in H.S. 2nd 6 week period (I think) I made a deal with my self to work harder than I had ever worked. I really worked a prayed over it all & when I got my report card I had raised my grade average to all passing. I was thrilled–no one else was. To them I had not put out enough effort. I went home after school and showed my parents my grades & they offered me 1.00 per A, 75¢ per B, 50¢ per C. Later After a good cry I felt better but nothing had changed.

I think the only thing I remember about my school (High School) years was one teacher who tutored me after school every day for 3/4 of my junior year and all my senior year in all my subjects. It was funny since he was from ______ [a foreign country] & we spent a great deal learning grammer & Conjigation as well as his love --Math. If it hadn't been for him I doubt I would have graduated. He was the only one who really honestly encouraged me and share joyously what little gain I made. He some how made me see things I never saw before.

I quit trying in my sophomore year and only with his help was I able to learn. in my last two years of H.S.

I did go to ______ College for two years. this may sound impressive but when you consider that I never read one text in school its rather amazing. All thru school I'd had a reading problem. I had a short attention span. I could not consentrate forlong periods of time. Reading was a pain–physically. I could only read for 35 min with out ending up with such a headache that all I could do is bury by head until it went away (with the help of an asprin or two.

I never graduated from ______. From there until year nothing really happened to me except I got married & had a family. . . .

. . .

I took a battery of tests down at ______ to see what I could learn. I took the

Wexchler (sp?) intelligent test and was given a 90% the rest of the tests I don't remember the results. In fact my memory all my life has been almost a haphazard thing its almost as if the information goes in and promply get tossed around until it accidently gets to the right space.

Back to what I was talking about. I was also tested by DVR to see what I would be best suited for for work. Here to I was again given the Wexchler test (though 1 year apart) this time I scored inthe 94%. So after 29 years I learned that I was intelligent even if scrambled off & on.

Now at the same time I was noticing things in my nine year old daughter that somewhere in the back of my mind I just couldn't forget. Because of this were having her testd learning disabilities . . .

I . . . received a listing of categories that Learning Problems are divided some what in. I'm going to use the Headinging and in outline form give examples from my life that I have over the years come to observe about myself (P.S. Im also doing this because Im tired of writing & your probably bored stiff reading)

I Language disorders

1. I stutter–not a lot but I go through periods that I can't get a sentence out in one piece
2. I don't mispronounce words much mainly because I've had to develope my ear since I learn thru hearing primarily
3. I quite often say a sentence in my mind and when it comes out several words are changed. I don't hear them when theyare wrong. I usually find I've goofed when I get a strange look or my family tells me (usually in an argument over what I've them to do do I find out what I said is not what I thought I said.)

II Coordination

1. I was never clutzy but awkward described me. Never quite up to par with my school friends in gym. except in Swimming.
2. Right or left handed–I'm right but I do a fast check to make sure with other things that are right and left oriented.

III Abnormal activity.

1. I was definitely NOT Hyperactive. I was nicknamed the turtle. My whole body make up seems to be running on 33 1/3 while everyone else is on 45 RP.M. Others get so much more done in a day then I do even though I work the whole time. I also find I'm sluggist in all that I do–I haven't been no matter what I weight–(which varies by quite a lot)

IV Attention Span.

1. Short–I find I have to really really consentrate to accomplish anything and do I hate to be interrupted and every little thing does interrupt me. An example would be my husband moving around the house out of sight but hearing his movement makes it hard to consentrate or the cat changing positions sleeping. I seem to be awear of everything that his going on any where in ear shot I just can't shut them out like I've always been told to do. they don't shut off

V Impulsive–

–that one I have a hard time supporting except to say I was always told not to be so impulsive by both teachers and parents for as far back as I can remember

VI Emotional instability

–I panic over anything from taking a trip to the museum in grade school to changing jobs, homes, situations. I have to have all my angles covered so I don't get caught short so I won't panic to the pit of my stomach.

VII Neurological signs

–Only my doctor knows for sure

VIII Immature developement

–Only my parents know and they don'treally remember.

IX Spacific learning difficulties

–My grades speak for themselves. out of a H.S. class of 800 I was 647. (#1 being the top)

With all this information I hope that I've given something to work with. I want so very much to go back to school but until these problems are worked out so to be handled at least I can't go to school. It's just wasing money.

Yours truly

Portions of other letters appear in subsequent chapters. They were not all this comprehensive. Some contained only one or two sentences as that in Figure 1 of Chapter 1. Most, however, provided the basis for making hypotheses about the problem and an understanding of their self perception and goals.

This group consisted of 65 men and 28 women ranging in age from 17 to 48 years with a mean age of 26.5 years. The distribution by age is shown in Table 3-1. Sixty-two were single and 31 were married. Socio-economic levels ranged from upper lower to lower upper class, with the majority being middle class. Six of the group were black, the others were white.

More than one-third (39 percent) of the adults reported a definite history of learning disabilities in their families. Of these, the majority indicated that the problems were in the immediate family (e.g., parents, siblings, grandparents, or their own children). A few, however, reported problems only among nephews, nieces, and cousins. An additional 10 percent indicated there might be familial learning problems but they were uncertain. For example, they remembered a parent, sibling, aunt, or uncle who "didn't read well," "never finished school like the others," or "didn't do very well in school." Thirty-eight percent reported no known history of learning problems in the family. No information was available on those who were adopted.

Many of this adult group might be considered special education "successes" since they were self-supporting, productive members of their communities. However, their learning disabilities continued to interfere with their schooling, work, and/or daily living. All were determined to improve some aspect(s) of

**Table 3-1**

Age Ranges of Adults Studied

| Age | 17–19 | 20–24 | 25–29 | 30–34 | 35–39 | 40–44 | 45–49 |
|---|---|---|---|---|---|---|---|
| Total No. | 14 | 30 | 16 | 19 | 10 | 3 | 1 |
| Male | 11 | 21 | 6 | 16 | 9 | 2 | 0 |
| Female | 3 | 9 | 10 | 3 | 1 | 1 | 1 |

**Table 3-2**
Chief Complaints

| Problem Area | Number of Adults |
|---|---|
| Attention | 7 |
| Oral Language | 26 |
| Reading | 62 |
| Written Language | 72 |
| Mathematics | 12 |
| Nonverbal Abilities | 6 |
| Conceptual Thinking | 4 |
| Organization, Planning | 15 |

their lives. Their initial complaints by area are summarized in Table 3-2. The following is a description of their educational, vocational, and social histories and their primary concerns.

## EDUCATIONAL BACKGROUND AND CURRENT PROBLEMS

### Educational History

The group, as a whole, had a relatively high level of education in terms of actual years in school; all but five had at least a high school diploma. Several who were not in school at the time of the evaluation planned to return, while others were being evaluated to obtain remedial help before reentering school. Their educational levels are summarized in Table 3-3.

Despite the fact that most of the group had remained in school, their histories revealed chronic, long-term educational problems. Eighty-six percent reported that their problems were noticed prior to or during elementary school.

**Table 3-3**
Educational Levels of Adults Studied

| Level | Total Number | Male | Female |
|---|---|---|---|
| Less Than 12 Years | 5 | 4 | 1 |
| 12 Years | 25 | 20 | 5 |
| Some College | 26 | 17 | 9 |
| College Graduate | 12 | 8 | 4 |
| Graduate Degree | 2 | 2 | 0 |
| Current Students | | | |
| Undergraduates | 18 | 9 | 9 |
| Graduates | 5 | 5 | 0 |

**Table 3-4**
Problems First Noted (Self Reported)

| Problem Noted | Number of Adults |
|---|---|
| Prior to School Entrance | 10 |
| Kindergarten-First Grade | 32 |
| Elementary-After Grade 1 | 37 |
| Junior High School | 3 |
| High School | 4 |
| Uncertain | 7 |

For specifics concerning when they *thought* their problems were first noticed, see Table 3-4.

One-third had been retained in school for at least one grade. Six had been retained two or more times. Their reactions to retention varied. Some felt it was beneficial, whereas others said they were still embarrassed by the fact that they had failed and could not remain in classes with their friends. Data on grades repeated are shown in Table 3-5.

Although many had remained in school, they were not always functioning independently at grade level. Often parents and tutors read their textbooks or summarized the content for them. More recently some had obtained tape recorded books and were given permission to take oral examinations. Occasionally academic requirements such as foreign languages were waived.

## Special Services

One-third had been evaluated previously for learning problems. Of the 93, 19 had been diagnosed as learning disabled. The others had been labeled "immature, dyslexic, reading disabled, language impaired, emotionally disturbed, or poorly motivated." Those who had not been evaluated always knew they had problems even though they had not been labelled.

The types of special services provided for the group while in school varied considerably, as shown in Table 3-6. As they advanced through school or after they graduated, some took speed reading courses, enrolled in adult education classes, and received counseling. When asked about the effectiveness of these

**Table 3-5**
Grades Repeated by Adults

| Grade | Number |
|---|---|
| First | 11 |
| Third | 7 |
| Fourth | 4 |
| Seventh | 3 |

**Table 3-6**
Services Provided to the Adult Group During Grades 1–12

| Service | Number |
|---|---|
| Learning Disabilities (Resource, Clinics) | 12 |
| General Tutoring | 20 |
| Remedial Reading | 12 |
| Speech Therapy | 10 |
| Special: Self-Contained Class | |
| Learning Disabilities | 4 |
| Educable Mentally Handicapped | 2 |
| Emotionally Disturbed | 2 |
| Noncategorical | 1 |
| Special School | |
| Learning Disabilities | 2 |
| Emotionally Disturbed | 2 |

special services, most reported that learning disabilities instruction had been helpful. They also found that counseling was useful for dealing with frustrations and other problems, but it did not aid their learning disability per se. Many said general tutoring was useful in helping them get through courses but they realized it did not help with specific problems. Speed reading courses were thought to be useless, since attempting to speed up a nonautomatic, faulty process only made things worse.

In general, we found very few had received long-term remediation, although their problems were of a chronic nature. This is in keeping with our findings regarding adolescents who were evaluated in our Center (Johnson, Blalock, & Nesbitt, 1978). The special services perceived to be of greatest value were those designed for specific learning disabilities.

## Current Educational Problems and Concerns

During the interview the adults were asked to describe the academic problems that were of greatest concern to them. The majority reported that they still had difficulty reading. Their word attack skills were poor or not automatic, and they had to reread material several times in order to comprehend. Some said it was difficult to learn new vocabulary from context. Most felt that their reading rates were slow so they did not have enough time to finish assignments. Reading for pleasure was a laborious process. Those in college said it took them so long to complete their work that they had little time for friends or for sleep.

Note-taking in class presented problems for many because they could not listen, comprehend, and write simultaneously. Some said they did not know what was important to write down and could not abstract what was relevant. Others did not try to take notes because they knew their notes would be incomplete or illegible. When reading assignments, those with comprehension disorders said they had no idea what material to underline. Therefore, they copied entire articles or attempted to memorize whole chapters, which made studying very inefficient and time consuming.

As expected, writing papers was difficult for most of the group. Several had taken incomplete grades in courses that required papers. They reported difficulties in using reference materials, in finding the information, summarizing main points, organizing their ideas, and planning the paper. The majority said they had problems with spelling, grammar, and punctuation. Often they expressed concern about their dependence on others to edit their work and wondered whether this was fair.

Although there were fewer complaints about oral language, many of the problems described above were related to thinking skills, verbal comprehension, and memory. Several adults hesitated to talk in class because they were afraid they might not be able to remember the information or pronounce words correctly. Others said they found it difficult to "make people understand what I mean." Some who had been offered tape-recorded books found the materials beneficial but time consuming when studying for exams. Those with auditory memory and comprehension problems said the tape recordings were often confusing and frustrating.

Students with mathematics disorders were concerned about passing required courses, but most said they simply avoided work in that area.

Time was a problem for many. They had problems planning and using time well, they could not estimate the time needed for completing assignments nor establish priorities. Most were simply unable to complete the work because of their disabilities.

Several adults reported a general uneasiness about their learning and wanted to know what was wrong. They felt "bad," "dumb," and/or "confused." Many said they had spent years trying to "try harder" (a typical recommendation) but it had not helped.

Despite these problems and frustrations many wanted to resume schooling or remain in school because they were interested in vocations that required reading and writing. The majority were intellectually curious and wanted to be able to function independently.

## VOCATIONAL BACKGROUND AND PROBLEMS

### Vocational History

At the time of the evaluation in our Center, 80 percent of the adults were either attending school or employed. They were generally independent, self-supporting members of the community. Some of those who were still living with their parents could have supported themselves outside the home.

**Table 3-7**
Vocations of Adults Employed

| Occupation Group Categories (Duncan, 1961) | Total | Male | Female |
|---|---|---|---|
| Professional, Technical, and Kindred Workers | 12 | 9 | 3 |
| Managers, Officials, Proprietors | 3 | 2 | 1 |
| Clerical, Sales, and Kindred Workers | 13 | 9 | 4 |
| Craftsmen, Foremen, and Kindred Workers | 4 | 4 | 0 |
| Operatives and Kindred Workers | 3 | 3 | 0 |
| Service Workers | 6 | 3 | 3 |
| Laborers | 8 | 8 | 0 |
| Unemployed | 18 | 11 | 7 |
| Students (including those entering school) | 26 | 16 | 10 |

Their occupations ranged from unskilled labor to professional, as shown in Table 3-7. Of those employed, some viewed their jobs as temporary while trying to acquire new skills, find a better position, or return to school. Others were satisfied with their occupations, but expressed concern over possible failure. A few were satisfied with their work and said they were doing well but wanted to learn new skills, particularly in the areas of reading and writing, for personal reasons.

Many older members of the group had histories of numerous job changes with periods of unemployment. Eleven had had seven or more jobs. Various reasons for the job losses were reported. Some with good social skills and verbal abilities, who appeared competent at the time of the initial interview, often accepted positions for which they were not qualified. After accepting jobs, they were unable to perform adequately, work under pressure, or handle several tasks simultaneously. Their inability to "keep up" with the demands, whether they were working on assembly lines, as clerks in supermarkets, or as tellers in banks only made them more anxious. Inconsistent performance from day to day also presented a problem.

At times, the adults were uncertain about what went wrong at work. When dismissed, they were often told, "Things just aren't working out—you are talented but this just isn't working." Occasionally they made mistakes that were costly to the company; in other instances they could not complete enough work for full-time employment. From these discussions it appears as though many need very explicit instructions, opportunities for rehearsal, and highly specific feedback (Hoskins, 1979) as well as assistance with "job keeping" behaviors.

## Vocational Services

Reports about the benefits of vocational assessment, counseling, and training varied. Some had never had any vocational education. Of those who had received services, many reported that interest and aptitude tests were not particularly helpful. Some had received lengthy reports that specified few aptitudes, or they had been given lists of their interests without regard for their mental ability or achievement levels. Occasionally, recommendations were made from less than comprehensive evaluations. For example, many with good verbal abilities were guided toward jobs in sales without an appropriate investigation of mathematics and nonverbal ability. After accepting a job they found they could not make change under pressure, write orders accurately, nor use cash registers and other machines quickly. Although they enjoyed selling in general, the discrepancies between potential, interests, and skills resulted in considerable frustration, and often dismissal.

It appeared that the most successful vocational programs included comprehensive evaluations and collaborative efforts on the part of all professionals such as psychologists, learning disabilities specialists, and vocational counselors. Unfortunately, these services are rarely available in the same setting. Thus, the adult was often responsible for getting the professionals together, a task frequently difficult and time consuming. As one man said, "It has taken me years to find all the professionals I needed and get them together. It should be easier."

## Current Problems and Concerns

Not all learning disabled adults need vocational counseling. Many understand their problems as well as the pros and cons of discussing their disabilities with employers and coworkers. For some, the constant fear of being "found out" added considerable anxiety to their lives. Several, who were successfully employed, had managed to "hide" their problems at work for years. Others said a few friends knew and helped them with difficult tasks. Several were reluctant to accept promotions because they felt they might not succeed, even though they had the mental ability to move on. Even those who made progress in reading and writing during remediation needed support when considering a job change. One man said, "I've always thought about all the things I would like to do if I could read and write better. Now that I can, it's sort of scary to think about trying something new." With support from a social worker and learning disabilities specialist he did leave his job as a stock boy in a store and accepted a position in sales. Later, after progressing from a seventh to an eleventh grade level in reading, he enrolled in junior college. With an intelligence quotient of 126, he clearly had the mental ability for college work.

Concerns about job performance were frequently related to a particular learning deficit. For example, secretaries with auditory disorders or spelling problems said they gave the phone to someone else when the message was very important. One woman, who could remember a message but knew she might misspell names, asked a coworker to write the memo and leave it for her boss. Many with auditory memory span problems carried note pads with them to write down instructions. Others were reluctant to write notes, realizing they might be asked why they had to write. As a result, they were reprimanded when they did not carry out instructions properly.

Low reading and writing levels created many concerns at work. Individuals who could not read manuals or write memos and reports, or perform at the expected rate, became quite anxious. Others with writing problems often omitted pertinent information because they failed to perceive what the reader needed to know.

Problems in planning, organization, and establishing priorities were reported frequently. Those with attention and memory problems forgot tasks or left work undone if they were distracted. A few in quite responsible jobs said they could not integrate various ideas, plans, or theories and often had difficulty summarizing material. They could not keep several ideas in mind simultaneously.

In summary, a variety of vocational problems related to both academic and nonacademic performance was reported by both the employed and unemployed adults. Although many were functioning at work, they still had problems. They needed elaborate compensatory strategies, time and energy to avoid or solve problems. Many were unaware of the reasons for failure and consequently repeated their mistakes.

When selecting vocations, adults need to consider variables such as the physical work setting, the amount of self-organization, planning, demand for speed, and various pressures. Although most of us have preferences for certain work environments, adults with learning disabilities have difficulty adapting to less-than-ideal situations.

## SOCIAL PROBLEMS

### Interpersonal Problems

The initial complaint of the adults usually related to academic learning; however, discussions during the interview, assessment, and remediation, indicated that social problems were often a concern. Twenty-five percent of the group mentioned social difficulties; however, the numbers are probably higher, since those with nonverbal disorders were not always aware of the reactions of people around them. Their problems ranged from general difficulties in making and keeping friends to specific disabilities associated with social functions such as dancing, playing cards, or word games at parties.

Many reported problems related to language and communication. Some said they could not follow conversations so they tried to "fake it." Others had difficulty with both rapid interchanges and comprehension of vocabulary, especially with jokes, teasing, and sarcasm. A few said they simply nodded and laughed with others even when they did not "get the point." Occasionally they asked friends or spouses to explain things, but, in general, their problems made them feel very unsure of themselves socially.

Many with expressive language disorders did not talk much in groups. A few with retrieval problems were afraid they would be unable to recall words, so they were reluctant to talk. Others said they could feel themselves "stuttering" or using filler words such as "oh, you know." Occasionally the adults were unaware they had misused a word until people "looked at them funny." Those who could not pronounce multisyllabic words tried to avoid using them. A young woman who worked for a florist requested remediation because she was embarrassed at being unable to pronounce the names of many flowers and plants. A few found older people were kinder and more understanding of their difficulties, so they tried to look for jobs where the employers would accept them and not laugh at their mistakes.

Although reading and writing problems obviously interfered with academic performance and certain vocations, they also limited social interactions. Poor readers often felt left out of their friends' conversations because they could not discuss the latest books or newspaper articles. One woman, who could read but not remember, tried to rehearse conversations at night so she could discuss the material in the lunch room at work the next day, but had so much difficulty she found it easier to make excuses to run errands at noon rather than joining the group.

Those with more severe disorders were concerned about reading menus, names of movies, or street signs if they went out with friends. Some dated a long time before telling their friends they could not read, occasionally not mentioning the difficulty until after they were married. In those instances, the spouse often referred them for evaluation and remediation. In a few cases, they dated or married people with learning disabilities.

Many poor readers tried to find out in advance if games were scheduled before accepting an invitation and avoided parties where word games were to be played. They disliked anything that involved "on the spot" reading and spelling.

Several could not participate in social activities that involved perceptual-motor or rhythmic skills. One woman found she could dance if she closed her eyes and concentrated on the rhythm and verbalized the steps, but nothing was automatic. Several reported they could not dance and talk at the same time and realized they were poor partners.

Some had no good friends and were concerned about meeting members of the opposite sex. Those in this group who had dated had difficulty maintaining relationships. In certain instances they were not aware of their behaviors that were turning people off.

In general, those with the greatest social problems had nonverbal thinking disorders difficulties. While those with language, reading and writing problems were somewhat limited socially, those with nonverbal communication disorders were among the most isolated. Until they can learn to observe others carefully, become more aware of their own behaviors, and acquire certain social skills, they may continue to have interpersonal problems.

## Problems of Daily Living, Independence, and Social Maturity

All learning disabilities interfere, to a certain extent, with independence and daily functioning. According to several in our group, the problem is always there, a "part of you," and "it never goes away." While they minimize the deficit by capitalizing on their strengths, they will, perhaps, always have educational, vocational, and social limitations. Even very bright people with specific reading disabilities have some reduction in social maturity (Doll, 1953). In an earlier study of 60 dyslexics we reported that the average social quotient was 85 (Johnson & Myklebust, 1965). To cite an example, poor readers may not pass an item on the *Vineland Social Maturity Scale* that requires them to look up telephone numbers in case of emergency. Even though they use the phone on a routine basis, they must be able to alphabetize and read to pass the item. Others fail items related to independent locomotion, either because they cannot read street signs or because of visual nonverbal disorders and orientation difficulties.

Oral language problems may interfere with following directions, recall of important information, and general communication. Adults with sequencing and reversal tendencies often have trouble with telephone numbers, addresses, and numbers on buses or trains. One woman said it took her 3 hours and 4 different trains to reach our campus (a trip that should have taken 45 minutes). A man said his car stalled and he tried to call his parents for help, but misdialed the phone so many times he used all of the change he had.

Reading and writing problems reduce independence in a number of ways. As expected, many are concerned about passing driving tests, and those who do, have developed strategies to compensate for slow reading ability. One woman said she pulled off the expressway periodically because she could not read the signs quickly enough while driving. Others asked people to fill out application forms and take care of their accounts. One man who held two jobs wanted to be able to write checks in case of emergency, but, because of his spelling difficulty, kept a copy of number words and the word "cash" in his wallet at all times.

Several wanted to write letters or thank you notes to friends but always worried about errors. At times, they dictated the message and asked someone to write it for them. One young man who wrote to his very supportive grandfather usually got the letter back with encouragement as well as suggestions for correcting word usage, grammar, spelling, and punctuation.

A rather serious problem was mentioned by adults whose handwriting and spelling was so poor that their signatures were not automatic. Three in the group had been embarrassed while cashing checks in the bank because their signatures did not match the original form. Others occasionally were unable to cash their own traveler's checks because of unstable signatures.

The impact of mathematics disorders also reduced overall social maturity. An inability to make change often put individuals at the mercy of sales clerks and waiters. Determining the price of sale items or calculating tips was impossible for most because they had not learned to figure percentages or use fractions or decimals. Similarly, they could not always follow recipes; nor double or reduce quantities. Those with mathematics and visual-spatial disorders also had difficulty using various measuring devices. Many could not read thermometers and gauges or use rulers. One woman said she had no idea how to hang a picture. Setting alarm clocks presented major problems for some. A very bright woman said she always had to arise on the hour until digital alarm clocks were available because of an inability to set the alarm.

Certain visual-spatial-motor problems interfered with even more basic functions. One man with high verbal and low nonverbal ability requested help in learning to tie a necktie, open milk cartons, use keys, and fold papers in thirds to fit in a business envelope. The latter task was a new requirement for his job and he could not master this skill using methods of trial and error or observation. With extensive verbal mediation techniques he learned how, but not without effort.

Others with visual-spatial disorders reported problems driving, riding bicycles, and even walking around the neighborhood. A few could not recognize familiar landmarks, and were apprehensive because they could not judge distance nor the speed of oncoming traffic. Reading maps was difficult for many. When told that a map would be sent to help them find our building, several responded that they could not read maps and it would be better if we simply told them what to look for.

Daily activities were major chores for those with low nonverbal abilities. They could not get things on hangers, pack boxes, wrap packages, arrange books on shelves, or get dishes back in cupboards in the same way each time.

Finally, problems of organization and planning were discussed by many adults. They wanted help in scheduling and deciding how to get important jobs done. Occasionally they forgot appointments or errands. One woman's husband worked with her each morning before he left for work to develop a list of activities that needed to be done in sequential order. Another woman said she knew that a routine was important but "if you can't organize in your head, then you have to do it externally, but then people say you are rigid."

Some tended to lose things as a result of their poor organization. When they opened briefcases or packets of materials brought to the evaluation, the papers, books, pencils, etc. were jumbled or in disarray. During the course of an interview it was not unusual for them to lose or misplace a paper several times. They said they also lost things at home.

## COPING

Throughout this discussion it should be evident that these learning disabled adults face many frustrations, not only in the academic world but at work, at home, and in social situations. They use a great deal of energy in managing their personal affairs. On the surface, the majority do not appear different, but their disabilities are always with them and their uneven abilities are evident in many levels of performance. While they demonstrate average to superior abilities in many ways, the deficits create a lack of harmony or poorly integrated performance. They have many strengths, but their specific disorders prevent them from actualizing their potential. For example, an artist may do a superior design, but reverse or transpose letters in the caption. A writer may have superior ideas and abstract thought, but the syntax and/or spelling is distorted. An individual may understand abstract vocabulary but be unable to pronounce the words. While the observer may be "taken aback" by these discrepancies, in the end, it is the learning disabled adults who have to live with the uneven performance. Their hopes and desires may not always be fulfilled unless they find ways of coping or obtain special services.

## REFERENCES

Doll, E. *The Vineland Social Maturity Scale*. Circle Pines, MN: American Guidance Service, Inc., 1953.

Duncan, O. Socio-economic status scale. In A. Reiss, O. Duncan, & C. North (Eds.), *Occupation and social status*. New York: The Free Press of Glencoe, 1961.

Hoskins, B. *A study of hypothesis testing behavior in language disordered children*. Unpublished doctoral dissertation, Northwestern University, 1980.

Johnson, D., Blalock, J., & Nesbitt, J. Adolescents with learning disabilities: Perspectives from an educational clinic. *Learning Disabilities Quarterly*, 1978, *1*, 24–36.

Johnson, D., & Myklebust, H. Dyslexia in childhood. In J. Helmuth (Ed.), *Learning disorders* (Vol. 1). Seattle: Special Child Publications, 1965.

# 4

# Intellectual Levels and Patterns

Jane W. Blalock

The assessment of intelligence is an important component in the psychoeducational evaluation of individuals with learning problems. An intellectual level is needed to exclude mental retardation as a cause of the learning deficit and to assist in determining levels of expectancy. In addition, the wide variety of cognitive tasks included in most intelligence tests provide the examiner with information about patterns of strength and weakness that can be explored during the evaluation.

The *Wechsler Adult Intelligence Scale* (WAIS) (Wechsler, 1955) and the *Wechsler Adult Intelligence Scale—Revised* (WAIS-R) (Wechsler, 1981) are widely used in assessing adults. The WAIS and the WAIS-R, like the other Wechsler tests, *Wechsler Intelligence Scale for Children—Revised* (WISC-R) (Wechsler, 1974) and *Wechsler Preschool and Primary Scale of Intelligence* (WPPSI) (Wechsler, 1967) yield individual subtest scores and separate Verbal and Performance IQs as well as the Full Scale IQ, making them particularly useful for testing people suspected of having specific rather than general cognitive deficits.

For many years, researchers have attempted to find patterns of scores on the Wechsler tests that are characteristic of particular conditions. Some have examined discrepancies between Verbal and Performance scores. In reviewing studies of Verbal-Performance discrepancies of special groups of adults, Zimmerman and Woo-Sam (1973) concluded that these differences were found in several groups and could be used only as an indication of the need for further evaluation. There have also been numerous studies of subtest patterns of learning disabled children on the WISC and the WISC-R (Wechsler, 1949; 1974). Results of these analyses have suggested that there may be characteristic subtest score patterns for learning disabled children as a group and for children with specific reading disabilities. For example, in a comprehensive study of 228 learning disabled and 228 normal children, Myklebust reported different

ADULTS WITH LEARNING DISABILITIES
ISBN 0-8089-1795-1

patterns of performance on the WISC for normal and learning disabled children (Myklebust, Bannochie, & Killen, 1971). He found that learning disabled children scored lower than normal children on several subtests including Information, Arithmetic, Vocabulary, Digit Span, Block Design, and Coding.

Specific patterns have also been described by Ackerman, Dykman, & Peters (1976), Bannatyne (1974), and Rugel (1974). Bannatyne (1974) suggested recategorizing WISC and WISC-R subtests into the following groups: Spatial, Verbal Conceptual, Sequential, and Acquired Knowledge. Using these patterns, several researchers have found groups of children with specific reading disabilities and groups of learning disabled children exhibit a characteristic pattern of Spatial > Verbal Conceptual > Sequential scores (Bannatyne, 1968, 1974; Rugel, 1974; Ackerman et al, 1976; Smith, Coleman, Dokecki, & Davis, 1977). A comparison of cognitive profiles of normal and learning disabled adults has suggested that some of these cognitive patterns are still evident in adulthood. The low Arithmetic, Coding, Information, and Digit Span scores frequently referred to as the ACID Pattern (Lutey, 1977) and the low Sequence Score (Arithmetic, Digits, Coding) described by Bannatyne (1974) have been reported in a group of young adults with learning disabilities (Cordoni, O'Donnell, Ramaniah, Kurtz, & Rosenshein, 1981). Currently, however, there is no evidence to suggest that these group patterns are sufficient for diagnosing individual learning disabilities or in planning remedial programs. Kaufman (1981a, 1981b) summarized the results of these studies and cautioned against using the group patterns in diagnosing individual cases. He also suggested further research regarding the analysis of specific patterns for planning remediation.

Ninety-one of the 93 adults with learning disabilities described in Chapter 3 were given the WAIS as a part of their evaluation. One of the remaining two was given the Stanford-Binet and the other had only the Verbal Scale of the WAIS (both of these scores were above 100.) The results of the intelligence testing were examined for the characteristic patterns that have been reported in children and adults with learning disabilities. To better understand the patterns seen, analyses of the scores of individuals exhibiting the patterns were done. The purpose of these analyses was to determine whether the group results reflect the performances of the individuals comprising the group. If so, these patterns might be useful in diagnosis and in establishing subgroups needing similar remedial programs.

## GROUP PATTERNS

The definition of learning disabilities specifies that the problem is not the result of mental retardation. In studying groups of learning disabled individuals it is important to determine that all of the individuals comprising these groups

**Table 4-1**
Intelligence Data for 91 Adults

| | Mean | SD | Range |
|---|---|---|---|
| Verbal IQ | 106.0 | 13.4 | 63–139 |
| Performance IQ | 103.7 | 13.8 | 71–136 |
| Full Scale IQ | 105.3 | 12.6 | 72–134 |

demonstrate average or above intelligence. Researchers have differed in their definitions of "average" and the lower limits for IQ levels have ranged from 70 to 90 across studies. In diagnosing the adults described here, only individuals with at least one score (Verbal or Performance) within one standard deviation of the test mean are included. This group of adults was of average ability having a mean Full Scale IQ of 105.3 with a standard deviation of 12.6. As a group, Verbal IQ (106) was slightly higher than Performance IQ (103.7). Means, standard deviations, and ranges are shown in Table 4-1. The standard deviations and ranges indicate considerable variability of scores within the group.

With four exceptions, everyone in the group scored within the Average Range (90–109) or higher on the Verbal and/or Performance scales of the WAIS. Specifically, the higher score for all but 4 individuals was 90 IQ points or better. The higher scores of the remaining 4 individuals fell within the upper end of the Low Average Range (80–89), between 85 and 89. Thus, everyone in this group diagnosed as "learning disabled" had at least one IQ score within one standard deviation of the test mean. Distribution of IQ scores by scale is shown in Table 4-2. Table 4-3 shows the distribution of the highest scores for the individual group members.

**Table 4-2**
Distribution of IQ Scores

| IQ Range | Full Scale IQ | Verbal Scale | Performance Scale |
|---|---|---|---|
| 130–139 | 2 | 3 | 1 |
| 120–129 | 9 | 8 | 10 |
| 110–119 | 23 | 27 | 20 |
| 100–109 | 30 | 25 | 26 |
| 90–99 | 17 | 20 | 19 |
| 80–89 | 8 | 5 | 10 |
| 70–79 | 2 | 2 | 5 |
| 60–69 | | 1 | |

**Table 4-3**
Distribution of Highest IQ Scores for 91 Cases

| Category of Scores | Verbal | Performance | Both Scores in Same Category |
|---|---|---|---|
| 130–139 | 3 | 1 | |
| 120–129 | 5 | 7 | 2 |
| 110–119 | 14 | 6 | 9 |
| 100–109 | 9 | 9 | 8 |
| 90–99 | 6 | 3 | 5 |
| 80–89 | | 2 | 2 |

## Verbal-Performance Discrepancies

Typically, groups of learning disabled individuals have exhibited higher mean Performance IQs than Verbal IQs. Lutey (1977) reviewed Verbal-Performance IQ differences reported in studies of learning disabled *children* tested on the WISC and found that 36 of the 42 samples reviewed (86 percent) had Performance IQs equal to or greater than Verbal IQs. The one WAIS study of learning disabled individuals she reviewed reported Performance IQs greater than Verbal IQs. Examination of the scores reported by Cordoni et al (1981) in their study of college students with learning disabilities also indicates a higher average Performance IQ than Verbal IQ.

The group of adults described here did not exhibit this profile. Although the number of individuals having Verbal IQs greater than Performance IQs (43) was the same as the number having Performance IQs greater than Verbal IQs, the magnitude of the differences was greater in the High Verbal group (5 individuals had Verbal IQs equal to Performance IQs). There are several possible explanations for the difference in this group. First, the nature of the population itself differs from most groups of children and adults with learning disabilities described in the research literature. This sample was not taken from a group in an academic setting. This was a group of self-referred adults (student and non-student) who were experiencing problems in educational, vocational, social, and self-help areas. Vogel (1981) reported that verbal deficits cause more academic problems for college students than nonverbal deficits. It would seem likely then, that more children and adults with verbal deficits would be referred for testing in academic settings. Second, it is possible that residual nonverbal deficits may be more debilitating in nonacademic than academic settings. Information obtained during the interviews suggested that residual nonverbal deficits did interfere more with the daily lives of these people than verbal disorders. This might account for a higher number of adults with nonverbal deficits requesting evaluations than might be referred in academic settings. Myklebust suggests that "nonverbal disturbances are more debilitating than the verbal" (Myklebust, 1975). If this is indeed the case, questions should be raised about the diagnosis and remediation of nonverbal deficits. The current federal definition of learning disabilities published in the Federal Register (August, 1977) does not include nonverbal problems. If these problems go undiagnosed and untreated they may interfere more than is necessary in adulthood. The question also must be asked as to whether nonverbal deficits are less remediable than verbal deficits. Behrens (1963), in a study of learning disabled children, found that after a period of remediation Verbal IQ improved significantly, but Performance IQ did not. Within the Verbal Scale, Similarities and Arithmetic showed significant improvement upon reevaluation. Behrens suggests that additional study is needed to understand why nonverbal behaviors did not show improvement comparable to that seen in verbal behavior. It is not possible to answer these questions with the data obtained from this group, but the problems described and the test scores provide evidence for the need to study the nature and impact of nonverbal deficits in both academic and nonacademic settings.

The Verbal-Performance discrepancies of individual group members also were examined. The mean discrepancy (in either direction) for the adults in this group was 10.98 points with a standard deviation of 8.18. The range of Verbal-Performance differences extended from 0 to 38 points. In addition, individual cases were examined for "significant" discrepancies. The 15 point "rule of thumb" recommended by Wechsler (1958) and Matarazzo (1972) was used. It should be noted, however, that despite the statistical "significance" of this discrepancy, differences of this magnitude are not unusual in the general population (Lutey, 1977; Zimmerman & Woo-Sam, 1973). Of the 91 cases examined, 29 (32 percent) had discrepancies of 15 or more points. Twenty-one had low Performance scores and eight had low Verbal scores. The Low Performance Group had a larger mean difference (21.7) than the Low Verbal Group (16.9). Means, standard deviations, and ranges for the two groups with significant discrepancies are shown in Table 4-4. Full Scale IQs and the average high scores for the two groups appeared to be similar.

Zimmerman and Woo-Sam (1973) suggest that the Verbal/Performance IQ discrepancy is of greater significance when the Full Scale score falls within the Average Range (90-109) than when it is either above or below Average. Thirteen adults with the Verbal/Performance discrepancy had Full Scale scores within the Average Range. Thus, some of the discrepancies may have been less significant than others.

High educational levels in combination with above average ability has been said to contribute to a Verbal/Performance discrepancy in favor of Verbal, so it is possible that this was a factor in a few of the Low Performance cases. Four of the five with Full Scale IQs above the Average Range were college graduates (one was a recent high school graduate). This suggests that the discrepancies observed could not be accounted for by the very bright, highly educated members of the group.

Although approximately one-third of this group did have a discrepancy

**Table 4-4**
Verbal/Performance Discrepancies

| | High Verbal/Low Performance | | |
|---|---|---|---|
| | $\overline{X}$ | SD | Range |
| Full Scale IQ | 102.6 | 11.7 | 86–133 |
| Verbal IQ | 111.9 | 14.0 | 94–139 |
| Performance IQ | 90.2 | 13.8 | 71–120 |
| V-P Difference | 21.7 | | 15–38 |
| | **High Performance/Low Verbal** | | |
| | $\overline{X}$ | SD | Range |
| Full Scale IQ | 100.6 | 16.6 | 72–116 |
| Verbal IQ | 94.0 | 15.7 | 68–107 |
| Performance IQ | 110.9 | 15.0 | 88–126 |
| V-P Difference | 16.9 | | 15–20 |

between Verbal and Performance scores, two-thirds did not. These findings are in agreement with the conclusions of many investigators that significant Verbal/Performance discrepancy should not be a primary criterion for diagnosing learning disabilities in individuals (Kaufman, 1981b; Zimmerman & Woo-Sam, 1973).

## Subtest Scores and Patterns

As would be expected of a group with slightly above average mean Verbal and Performance IQs, the mean subtest scores were generally average (Scaled Score = 10) or above. The means, standard deviations, and subtest scores are shown in Table 4-5. The highest scores were on Similarities (12.2), Comprehension (12.1), Vocabulary (11.3), and Information (10.9), while the lowest scores for the total group were on Digit Span (9.5), Arithmetic (9.6), Digit Symbol (9.9), and Picture Arrangement (10.0).

Studies of groups of learning disabled children frequently show lower mean scores in Arithmetic, Coding, Information, and Digit Span (Lutey 1977; Bannatyne, 1974). This pattern, often referred to as the "ACID" pattern, was also seen in the Cordoni et al (1981) study of IQ patterns in learning disabled college applicants. With the exception of the Information score, the same subtests were low in this group of learning disabled adults (Digit Symbol/Coding, Digit Span, and Arithmetic). The fourth subtest in the "ACID" pattern, Information, was among the top scores for this group. This may be a reflection of the educational level of the group and/or the large number of individuals in the High Verbal/Low Performance group. Despite the similar group pattern, it is important to note that only 11 individual cases had all 3 of these subtests (Arithmetic, Digit Symbol, and Digit Span) among their own 4 lowest subtest

**Table 4-5**
WAIS Subtest Scores of 91 Adults

| | Mean | SD | Range |
|---|---|---|---|
| Verbal Scale | | | |
| Information | 10.9 | 2.8 | 3–17 |
| Comprehension | 12.1 | 3.5 | 4–19 |
| Arithmetic | 9.6 | 3.0 | 3–16 |
| Similarities | 12.2 | 2.6 | 4–18 |
| Digit Span | 9.5 | 3.3 | 2–19 |
| Vocabulary | 11.3 | 2.9 | 5–19 |
| Verbal Mean | 10.9 | 2.3 | 3.8–16.0 |
| Performance Scale | | | |
| Digit Symbol | 9.9 | 2.8 | 3–19 |
| Picture Completion | 10.7 | 3.2 | 5–16 |
| Block Design | 10.6 | 3.1 | 3–17 |
| Picture Arrangement | 10.0 | 2.8 | 6–17 |
| Object Assembly | 10.8 | 3.7 | 2–18 |
| Performance Mean | 10.4 | 2.1 | 5.4–15.6 |

scores (An additional 5 had these subtests among the lowest 5 subtests and 2 individuals had Arithmetic, Digit Symbol, Information, and Digit Span as the lowest 4 subtest scores.) This suggests that these particular subtests are sensitive to a variety of processing deficits, but all types of deficits do not interfere with each of the subtests.

Bannatyne (1971, 1974) proposed the categorization of WISC and WISC-R scores into 4 groups: Spatial Ability (Picture Completion, Block Design, Object Assembly), Verbal Conceptual (Comprehension, Similarities, Vocabulary), Sequential Ability (Digit Span, Arithmetic, Coding), and Acquired Knowledge (Information, Arithmetic, Vocabulary) which have been widely used to study groups of learning disabled children. Bannatyne's research has shown that learning disabled children, as a group, typically score well below normal children on the Sequential Ability category. Genetic dyslexics were reported to have high Spatial scores and low Sequencing scores (Bannatyne, 1971). In a study to ascertain whether these patterns are also seen in young adults, Cordoni et al (1981) reported that a group of learning disabled college applicants scored significantly below normal college students in the Sequencing and Acquired Knowledge categories. They concluded that cognitive patterns of disturbance persist into adulthood.

WAIS subtests scores were combined into the Bannatyne factors to see if the characteristic pattern was also present in this sample of learning disabled adults. The highest score for the group was Verbal Conceptual (35.55) and the lowest score was in Sequential Ability (19.98). Means and standard deviations for the Bannatyne groupings are shown in Table 4-6. Thus, this group of adults

**Table 4-6**
Means and Standard Deviations of Bannatyne Categories for the WAIS

| | Mean | SD |
|---|---|---|
| Spatial Abilities | 32.20 | 7.5 |
| Verbal Conceptual | 35.55 | 7.7 |
| Sequential Abilities | 28.98 | 6.8 |
| Acquired Knowledge | 31.76 | 7.5 |

with learning disabilities appeared to have a low Sequential Ability score similar to that reported in groups of learning disabled children and college students. Unlike Bannatyne's dyslexics (1981), this group had a higher Verbal Conceptual score than Spatial score.

To determine whether the pattern of category scores might be related to the nature of the problems diagnosed, a subgroup demonstrating the Spatial > Verbal Conceptual > Acquired Knowledge > Sequential was examined. Ten adults clearly demonstrated this pattern. Learning problems differed among the group members, suggesting that the category scores may be affected by several types of processing deficits and are not specific enough to establish subgroups of individuals with similar needs. Analysis of this subgroup in relation to the others diagnosed as learning disabled confirms the cautions raised by Kaufman (1981) and Reynolds (1981) against using the subtest patterns for differential diagnosis. The variety of deficits in the group raises doubts as to whether the category patterns will provide useful information for teaching students to read, write, calculate or to perform various nonverbal skills.

## Scatter Among Subtests

Analyses of scatter among subtests of the WISC and WISC-R have not clearly demonstrated that learning disabled children consistently have greater scatter among subtest scores than normal children (Kaufman, 1979). Little has been done to study the "typical" scatter of abilities of normal adults on the WAIS. The intra-individual scatter of the group of young adults described here was examined in two ways. The difference between highest and lowest scaled scores (Range Score) and the number of scaled scores varying from the individual's mean subtest score were examined. The average range score for the Verbal Scale was 6; the Performance Scale average was 5.5; and the Full Scale average range was 8.1. The average number of scaled scores deviating from the individual's own subtest mean by 3 or more points was 2.5 with a range of 0–6. Table 4-7 shows the means, standard deviations, and ranges for the scatter analyses. These analyses indicate that while many of the adults do have considerable scatter, others do not. It would seem unlikely that significant

**Table 4-7**
Means, Standard Deviations, and Ranges for WAIS Scatter Analysis

| | $\overline{X}$ | SD | Range |
|---|---|---|---|
| Verbal IQ | 6.0 | 2.3 | 2–12 |
| Performance IQ | 5.5 | 2.3 | 1–12 |
| Full Scale IQ | 8.1 | 2.0 | 4–13 |
| Number of Scaled Scores ± 3 points from Mean | 2.5 | 1.5 | 0–6 |

scatter among subtest scores is "characteristic" of all learning disabled adults. Similar results were reported by Tabachnick (1979) who found significantly more subtest scatter in a group of learning disabled children than in normal children, but the overlap in the scatter of the two groups was substantial, making significant scatter unreliable as a single diagnostic indicator.

## Factor Analysis

Another method of examining patterns among the subtests of the Wechsler series is factor analysis. Cohen (1957) performed a factorial analysis of the standardization data of the WAIS and identified three significant factors: Verbal Comprehension, Perceptual Organization, and Memory (Freedom from Distractibility). Subtests making up the Verbal Comprehension factor were: Information, Comprehension, Similarities, and Vocabulary; subtests comprising the second factor, Perceptual Organization, were: Block Design and Object Assembly (and in some analyses: Picture Completion and Picture Arrangement); the third factor, Memory (Freedom from Distractibility), was comprised of Arithmetic and Digit Span. These same three factors have been reported in factor analyses of the WISC (Cohen, 1959) and the WISC-R (Kaufman, 1975).

Factor analysis was employed to ascertain whether the number and structure of factors in this sample of young adults were similar to those reported in the normal population. The SPSS subprogram FACTOR (Nie, Hull, Jenkins, Steinbrenner, & Bent, 1975) was used for the analysis. In order to determine the number of factors to be retained: (1) consider for retension all factors with eigenvalues greater than 1.0 (e.g., Kaiser-Guttman rule); (2) examine the slope of the plot of eigenvalues against the ordinal number of variables (e.g., the Scree Test, Cattell, 1966); and (3) the percent of overall variance accounted for. A varimax rotation procedure was applied to the unrotated factor pattern. Estimates of the subject to variable ratio needed for this type of analysis range from five per variable (Nunnally, 1970) to 10 or more per variable (Thorndike, 1978). The sample size employed in this study did not

**Table 4-8**
Varimax Rotated Factor Matrix for WAIS

| | Factor 1 | Factor 2 | Factor 3 |
|---|---|---|---|
| Information | .8054* | .0457 | .3998 |
| Comprehension | .7102* | .2427 | .0051 |
| Arithmetic | .4086 | .3389 | .5650* |
| Similarities | .6619* | .2575 | .2007 |
| Digit Span | .3152 | .0057 | .5107* |
| Vocabulary | .8395* | .1678 | .2464 |
| Digit Symbol | .0101 | .1723 | .4473 |
| Picture Completion | .3207 | .4647 | .1223 |
| Block Design | .1489 | .8220* | .2739 |
| Picture Arrangement | .2721 | .4489 | .3635 |
| Object Assembly | .0910 | .7724* | .0458 |

* Coefficient .50 or higher

meet the suggested 10 subjects per variable ratio, so results should be interpreted with caution. The factor analysis yielded two factors with eigenvalues greater than 1.0. The Scree Test indicated one inflection point (the three eigenvalues obtained were 4.3, 1.2, and .51). This first point was at 2 factors and accounted for 91.3 percent of the total variance.

The results of this analysis suggest some similarities and differences between this learning disabled adults sample and the normal population. The same general pattern reported by Cohen (1957) was seen. Specifically, both a Verbal Comprehension and a Perceptual Organization factor emerged from the analysis and accounted for 91 percent of the overall variance (see Table 4-8). Cohen's (1957) Memory factor, while visible in the factor pattern matrix, only had an eigenvalue of .52 and accounted for 8.7 percent of the variance. As such, this factor and its subtest loadings was not interpreted.

Because of the relatively small number of subjects, coefficients of .50 and above were interpreted as significant. A summary of the factors follows.

### *Factor 1—Verbal Comprehension*

The Verbal subtests Information, Comprehension, Similarities, and Vocabulary loaded on this factor. These are the same subtests Cohen found to load highly on this factor. The only other subtest with a loading approaching significance was Arithmetic.

### *Factor 2—Perceptual Organization*

The Performance subtests of Object Assembly and Block Design loaded on this factor. This is similar to the loadings described by Cohen with the exception of Picture Arrangement that loaded on this factor in all but one of Cohen's age groups (45–54). Picture Arrangement in this analysis did not load on any of the factors, but its highest loading was on this factor. In addition to

Picture Arrangement, Picture Completion approached significant loading on this factor.

## Memory Factor

The failure to confirm Cohen's Factor 3 has also been reported in other WAIS studies. Matarazzo (1972), for example, reported that some studies of brain-injured subjects failed to show this factor. The absence of this factor in this group of learning disabled adults could explain the variability in the "low sequence" group described above.

## Intertest Correlations

Researchers have also compared the intercorrelations of the subtest scores of normal and learning disabled groups. Myklebust, Bannochie, and Killen (1971) examined the intertest correlations (WISC) of a group of normal children, a group of moderately learning disabled children, and a group of severely learning disabled children. They found fewer significant (.01) correlations in both learning disabled groups than in the normal group. The fewest significant correlations for the learning disabled groups were those with the Coding subtest. Schiffman (1965) studied a group of learning disabled children with reading disabilities and reported that the 240 reading disabled children had lower intertest correlations on the WISC than those reported by Wechsler for the standardization sample (Wechsler, 1955).

Examination of the intercorrelation of the subtests helps to explain some of the results of the analyses of intelligence scores. The intercorrelations of the subtests for the learning disabled adult group are generally lower than those of the standardization sample reported in the WAIS manual (Wechsler, 1955). Table 4-9 shows the intercorrelations for the tests including the Verbal, Performance, and Full Scale scores. The correlation coefficients for Verbal subtests with Verbal IQ, Performance subtests with Performance IQ, and all subtests with Full Scale IQ are shown corrected for contamination (McNemar, 1949, p. 139).

Unlike any of the intercorrelations reported in the WAIS manual (Wechsler, 1955, p. 16), 17 of the correlation coefficients computed on scores obtained by the adults with learning disabilities were not significant at the .01 level (80 degrees of freedom). The subtests with the fewest significant correlations (including Verbal, Performance, and Full Scale), were Digit Symbol (3), Digit Span (7), and Object Assembly (9). The highest correlations among subtests were within the Verbal Scale with the exception of Block Design and Object Assembly (.67). The generally lower and nonsignificant correlations suggest that the learning disabled adults may not have some "assumed" abilities underlying the subtest tasks. There was, as a result of this, less commonality among the subtests.

**Table 4-9**
Intercorrelation of Subtests for the WAIS For LD Adult Sample

| | INF | COMP | ARI | SIM | DIG | VOC | DSY | PC | BD | PA | OA | V | P | FS |
|---|---|---|---|---|---|---|---|---|---|---|---|---|---|---|
| COMP | .576 | — | | | | | | | | | | | | |
| ARI | .574 | .421 | — | | | | | | | | | | | |
| SIM | .601 | .554 | .446 | — | | | | | | | | | | |
| DIG | .424 | .210* | .449 | .392 | — | | | | | | | | | |
| VOC | .81 | .612 | .519 | .635 | .386 | — | | | | | | | | |
| DYS | .23* | .039* | .329 | .122* | .202* | .11* | — | | | | | | | |
| PC | .357 | .350 | .312 | .371 | .08* | .366 | .215* | — | | | | | | |
| BD | .249 | .285 | .464 | .372 | .251 | .339 | .33* | .468 | — | | | | | |
| PA | .383 | .264 | .461 | .339 | .226* | .449 | .267 | .401 | .52 | — | | | | |
| OA | .124* | .264 | .383 | .282 | .018* | .209* | .151* | .349 | .679 | .347 | — | | | |
| V | .752 | .486 | .593 | .690 | .443 | .768 | .205* | .377 | .443 | .471 | .275 | — | .506 | |
| P | .376 | .358 | .561 | .41 | .197* | .428 | .308 | .547 | .717 | .522 | .514 | .506 | — | |
| FS | .599 | .446 | .613 | .593 | .270 | .639 | .163* | .433 | .536 | .502 | .315 | | | — |
| | | | | | | | Uncorrected Correlation | | | | | | | |
| V | .835 | .74 | .729 | .784 | .628 | .849 | | | | | | | | |
| P | | | | | | | .487 | .659 | .816 | .709 | .769 | | | |
| FS | .731 | .657 | .751 | .718 | .503 | .764 | .378 | .577 | .698 | .659 | .567 | .90 | .831 | — |

* Correlation not significant at .01 level

For example, lowered Arithmetic correlations and the fact that the Memory factor did not account for more variance might be explained by the presence of specific computational and/or language deficits as well as by problems in concentration, memory, and mental computation. Zimmerman and Woo-Sam (1973) state that by adolescence the ability to do these problems should be automatic and should not require paper and pencil. For this reason the test was thought to measure "attention and alertness." Despite the fact that the subtest involves computation at approximately a fifth grade level, many of the adults in this sample continued to make computational errors on paper and pencil tasks. Thus, computation problems may have been an added factor in the variability of scores. Examination of the subtest means for the Low Performance and Low Verbal groups reveals that Arithmetic scores are low for both groups. Performance on this subtest then may be affected by several problems, not just attentional and memory deficits.

Rank ordering correlation coefficients from highest to lowest and comparing this order to the order of the standardization sample coefficients reveals a different pattern of subtest scores. The highest correlation for both was Vocabulary/Information (.81 for both). For the learning disabled adults the next highest was Block Design and Object Assembly (.67). Other Vocabulary and Information correlations were much higher for the standardization group. Thus, we see several types of differences in this group: generally lower intercorrelations, a different pattern of correlations, and many nonsignificant correlations. All of these suggest different cognitive patterns in this sample of adults.

The limited number of significant intercorrelations for the Digit Symbol subtest is interesting. The Digit Symbol score correlated significantly (.01 level) only with Arithmetic (.33), Picture Arrangement (.27), and Performance IQ (.31). It was among the four lowest mean subtests scores for the group (9.9). In reviewing the performance of atypical groups on this subtest, Lutey (1977) reported low scores for the brain-injured, the mentally retarded, and psychiatric patients. WISC studies also report low scores on Coding in learning disabled children. Myklebust, Bannochie, and Killen (1971) reported similar intercorrelational patterns with Coding in WISC studies of normal and learning disabled children, with significant (.01) correlations occurring primarily for the normal control groups.

Several reasons for the lower mean score and the nonsignificant correlations between the Coding subtest and other tests might be proposed. Analysis of protocols revealed few errors, just fewer items completed. High scores on this test require learning an unfamiliar task and rapid execution of marks. This subtest is the only learning task on the WAIS. Thus, if learning is a problem it is expected this would be among the lower scores. Several problems may interfere with performance on this subtest: including visual scanning, visual memory, visual-motor-integration, verbal mediation, attention, and organization. Studies using this subtest have shown lowered performance among individuals with brain-damage. Wechsler (1958) reported that those with organic problems did very poorly on this subtest (more than three scale score points below their subtest means).

The nonsignificant correlation between Digit Symbol and Digit Span may help explain the variety of problems seen in adults with the low Sequence Scores. People receiving low scores on one may not do poorly on the other, making the assumption of a generalized sequencing or attention problem erroneous.

## SUBGROUPS

### Educational Level

As indicated earlier, the educational level of this group was generally high. Only 5 of the group did not finish high school, 19 had college degrees, and 18 were enrolled in college at the time of the evaluation. Intellectual levels were examined by educational level. Means, standard deviations, and ranges for Verbal, Performance, and Full Scale IQs are shown in Table 4-10. The average IQ increased with the number of years of education; however, there was considerable variability within each group. The subtest means for each group shows some very different patterns. Not one of the three lowest subtests for the whole group (Arithmetic, Digit Span, and Digit Symbol) was among the lowest four subtests for all five groups, again suggesting that group characteristics cannot be applied to individual cases or even subgroups.

Examination of the reading, spelling, and arithmetic scores for high school versus college graduates revealed generally higher scores for the college graduate group than for the high school graduates; however, there was considerable variability within groups and overlapping scores between groups. Neither

**Table 4-10**
IQ Levels by Educational Level

| | Verbal | | Performance | | Full Scale | |
|---|---|---|---|---|---|---|
| | $\bar{X}$ | SD | $\bar{X}$ | SD | $\bar{X}$ | SD |
| Less than 12 years (N = 5) | 92.2 | 11.1 | 94.6 | 8.8 | 92.6 | 9.1 |
| High School Grad (N = 25) | 99.3 | 13.9 | 99.3 | 16.7 | 99.2 | 13.6 |
| Incomplete College (N = 25) | 107.7 | 8.2 | 105.8 | 11.9 | 107.3 | 7.4 |
| Current College (N = 18) | 107.6 | 13.9 | 107.0 | 13.5 | 107.8 | 13.9 |
| College Graduate* (N = 18) | 115.3 | 11.6 | 105.9 | 12.0 | 111.9 | 11.5 |

* Includes 2 with graduate degrees and 5 in graduate school

group demonstrated academic skills in keeping with educational or intellectual levels.

## Description of Groups with Verbal-Performance Discrepancies

The subtest patterns, achievement levels, and educational levels of the High Performance and High Verbal groups were also examined. Subtest means and standard deviations for each group are shown in Table 4-11. Within the Verbal Scale both groups had the highest scores in Comprehension, Similarities, and Vocabulary. The two lowest Verbal scores for both groups were Arithmetic and Digit Span. The same patterns were not seen on the Performance Scale. The lowest scores for the Low Performance group were Object Assembly and Digit Symbol. These two scores were the highest for the High Performance group. These patterns are shown in Figure 4-1, along with the pattern for the whole group. It appears, then, that both verbal and nonverbal problems interfere with performance on Arithmetic and Digit Span. On the other hand, Object Assembly and Digit Symbol may be related primarily to nonverbal deficits.

The patterns of standard scores (highest to lowest) for the two groups on the subtests of the *Wide Range Achievement Test* were compared and found to differ somewhat. The order of scores for the High Verbal/Low Performance group was Reading > Spelling > Arithmetic while the pattern for the Low Verbal/High Performance group was Reading > Arithmetic > Spelling. (It should be noted that within each group the individual patterns varied.) The

**Table 4-11**
Scaled Score Means and Standard Deviations for High Performance and High Verbal Groups

| | High Performance (N = 8) | | High Verbal (N = 21) | |
|---|---|---|---|---|
| | $\overline{X}$ | SD | $\overline{X}$ | SD |
| INF | 8.4 | 3.0 | 11.5 | 3.0 |
| COM | 10.4 | 4.0 | 13.4 | 2.9 |
| ARI | 8.3 | 2.8 | 9.5 | 3.5 |
| SIM | 9.1 | 2.8 | 12.8 | 2.4 |
| DIG | 6.8 | 3.2 | 11.3 | 3.4 |
| VOC | 9.4 | 2.7 | 12.4 | 3.4 |
| DSY | 11.5 | 3.7 | 8.1 | 2.1 |
| PC | 11.4 | 2.7 | 9.2 | 2.1 |
| BD | 10.5 | 2.1 | 8.3 | 3.4 |
| PA | 11.0 | 3.6 | 8.7 | 2.2 |
| OA | 12.1 | 2.6 | 7.4 | 3.1 |
| All Subtests | 9.9 | | 10.2 | |

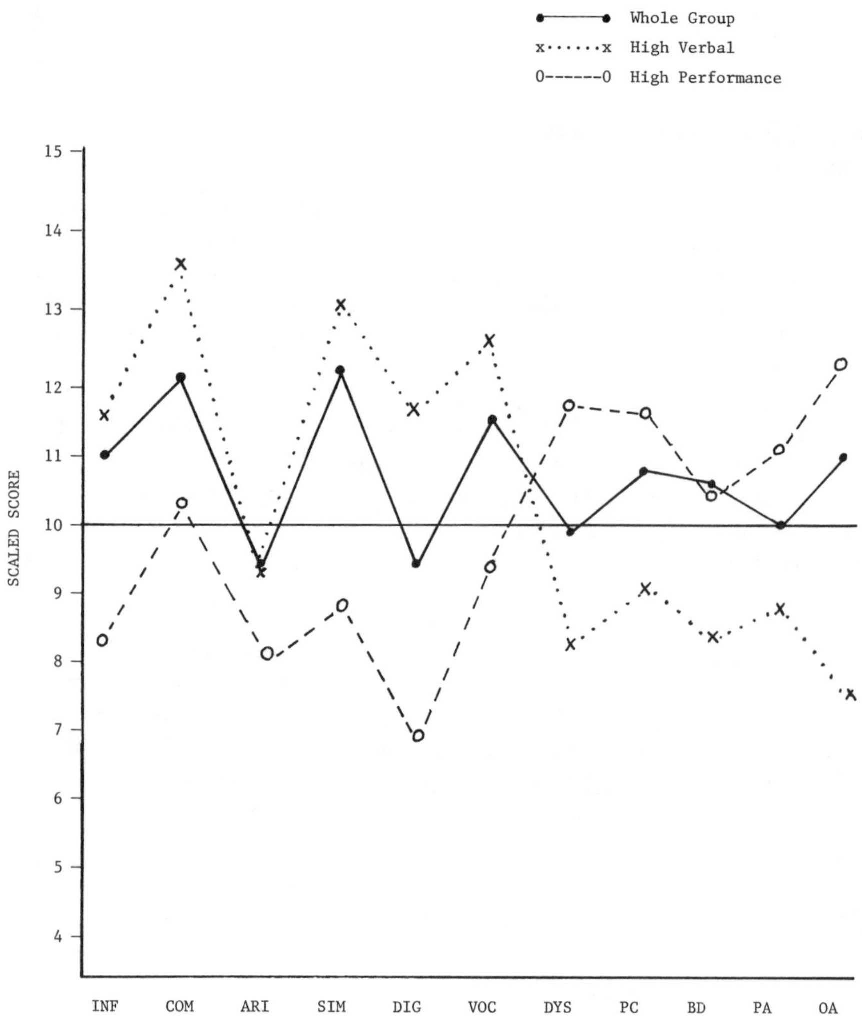


**Figure 4-1.** Intellectual profiles of the adults.

most significant difference was in the overall level of performance across subtests. The people with high Verbal scores as a group had a much higher mean Reading (decoding) standard score (106–88) and better Spelling (98–84) and Arithmetic scores (95–88) than those with low Verbal scores. Despite the small numbers, these results suggest that verbal deficits do indeed interfere with the acquisition of academic skills than nonverbal disorders.

Educational levels did not always reflect the academic skill levels. Every member of both groups had completed high school. Within the Low Performance group, seven had completed college and two were enrolled in college.

Decoding standard scores of the college graduates in this group ranged from 75 to 122. In the Low Verbal group there were no college graduates and no current students. Two of these were, however, planning to enter college.

## SUMMARY

The adults described in this volume are generally a bright group. Their learning difficulties in social, vocational, and educational situations cannot be attributed to limited mental ability. Examination of the patterns of scores revealed some similarities and some differences in comparison to other groups of learning disabled children and adults.

Like other groups of learning disabled individuals this group scored low on the Arithmetic, Digit Span, and Digit Symbol (Coding) subtests (the sequential cluster described by Bannatyne, 1974). Analysis of individual and subgroup scores, however, suggests that this pattern is *not* present in many individual cases. The nonsignificant correlation between Digit Span and Digit Symbol supports this. Thus, these results suggest an overall cognitive pattern difference in learning disabled persons, rather than a characteristic pattern that can be used in diagnosing learning disabilities in individuals. In addition, an examination of the learning problems and processing deficits seen in a subgroup exhibiting one of the patterns described by Bannatyne (1974) revealed many different deficits, rather than a consistent pattern. This suggests that these WAIS cluster scores will not be particularly useful in planning remedial programs.

Unlike other learning disabled groups described in the literature this group had a lower mean Performance IQ than Verbal IQ. This may be an indication that nonverbal deficits are more debilitating for daily living activities than verbal deficits since all of the individuals were self-referred and many were not in academic settings. Verbal deficits are reported to be more debilitating than nonverbal deficits in college settings, but the impact of nonverbal problems in other settings has not been examined as carefully. Information obtained from the case history interviews supports the notion that nonverbal deficits interfere with overall functioning more than verbal deficits, supporting the impressions of Myklebust (1975). It is evident that nonverbal deficits persist into adulthood. This could be because they are not as remediable or because they are less often diagnosed and/or remediated. Further examination of nonverbal deficits is indicated.

Group patterns were also compared with the reported patterns of the standardization sample. A factor analysis of the WAIS results yielded only two factors (Verbal Comprehension and Perceptual Organization) as compared to the three factors reported by Cohen (1957) and other researchers. Examination of the intertest correlations revealed lower correlation coefficients for this group; 17 of which were not significant at the .01 level. The intercorrelations reported for normals (Wechsler, 1955) are all significant at the .01 level. These findings suggest a different organization of the cognitive abilities assessed on the WAIS. Results of this analysis are similar to those reported by Myklebust, Bannochie, and Killen (1971) and support their conclusion of a different structure of mental abilities in learning disabled individuals. The results of these analyses also support the conclusions of Kaufman who states that the results of the many studies of characteristic patterns on the Wechsler Scales are "far from optimistic for differential diagnosis" (Kaufman, 1981, p. 397).

## REFERENCES

Ackerman, P., Dykman, R., & Peters, J. Hierarchical factor patterns on the WISC as related to areas of learning deficit. *Perceptual and Motor Skills*, 1976, *42*, 381–376.

Bannatyne, A. *Language, reading and learning disabilities*. Springfield, IL: Charles C Thomas, 1971.

Bannatyne, A. Diagnosing learning disabilities and writing remedial prescriptions. *Journal of Learning Disabilities*, 1968, *1*, 242–249.

Bannatyne, A. Diagnosis: A note on recategorization of the WISC scaled scores. *Journal of Learning Disabilities*, 1974, *7*, 272–274.

Cattell, R. The meaning and strategic use of factor analysis. In R. Catell (Ed.), *Handbook of multivariate experimental psychology*. Chicago: Rand McNally and Co., 1966.

Cohen, J. The factorial structure of the WAIS between early adulthood and old age. *Journal of Consulting Psychology*. 1957, *21*, 283–290.

Cordoni, B., O'Donnell, J., Ramaniah, V., Kurtz, J., & Rosenshein, K. Wechsler adult intelligence score patterns for learning disabled young adults. *Journal of Learning Disabilities*, 1981, *14*, 404–407.

Jastak, J. & Jastak, S. Wide range achievement test, revised edition. Wilmington, DE: Jastak Associates, Inc., 1978.

Kaufman, A. A new approach to the interpretation of test scatter on the WISC-R. *Journal of Learning Disabilities*, 1976, *9* (3), 160–168.

Kaufman, A. Assessment: The Wechsler scales and learning disabilities. *Journal of Learning Disabilities*, 1981, *14*, 397–398.

Kaufman, A. Factor analysis of the WISC-R at eleven age levels between 6½ and 16½ years. *Journal of Consulting and Clinical Psychology*. 1975, *43*, 135–147.

Kaufman, A. The WISC-R and learning disabilities assessment: state of the art. *Journal of Learning Disabilities*, *14*, 1981 (b), 520–526.

Lutey, C. *Individual intelligence testing*. Greeley, CO: Carol L. Lutey, Publishing, 1977.

Matarazzo, J. *Wechsler's measurement and appraisal of adult intelligence* (5th ed). Baltimore: Williams & Wilkins, 1972.

McNemar, Q. *Psychological statistics*. New York: 1949.

Myklebust, H., Bannochie, M., & Killen, J. Learning disabilities and cognitive processes. In H. Myklebust (Ed.), *Progress in learning disabilities* (Vol. 2). New York: Grune & Stratton, 1971.

Myklebust,, H. Nonverbal learning disabilities: Assessment and intervention. In H. Myklebust (Ed.), *Progress in learning disabilities* (Vol. 2). New York: Grune & Stratton, 1975.

Nie, N., Hull, C., Jenkins, J., Steinbrenner, E., & Bent, D. *Statistical Package for the Social Sciences, Second Edition*. New York: McGraw-Hill, 1975.

Nunnally, J. *Introduction to psychological measurement*. New York: McGraw-Hill, 1970.

Reynolds, C. A note on determining significant discrepancies among category scores on Bannatyne's regrouping of WISC-R subtests. *Journal of Learning Disabilities*, 1981, *14*, 468–569.

Rugel, R. WISC subtest scores of disabled readers: A review with respect to Bannatyne's recategorization. *Journal of Learning Disabilities*, 1974, *7*, 48–55.

Schiffman, G. *Particulars of 240 clinically retarded readers*. Presentation, International Reading Association Convention, Detroit, 1965.

Smith, M., Coleman, J., Dokecki, P. & Davis, E. Recategorized WISC-R scores of learning disabled children. *Journal of Learning Disabilities*, 1977. 10, 437–443.

Tabachnick, R. Test scatter on the WISC-R. *Journal of Learning Disabilities*, 1979, *12* (9), 626–628.

Thorndike, R. *Correlational procedures for research*. New York: Gardner Press, 1978.

Vogel, S. *College programs for young adults with learning disabilities*. Presentation, Conference on Young Adults with Learning Disabilities, Northwestern University, September, 1981.

Wechsler, D. *The measurement and appraisal of adult intelligence*. Baltimore: Williams & Wilkins, 1958.

Wechsler, D. *Wechsler adult intelligence scale*. New York: Psychological Corporation, 1955.

Wechsler, D. *Wechsler adult intelligence scale-revised*. New York: The Psychological Corporation, 1981.

Wechsler, D. *Wechsler intelligence scale for children*. New York: Psychological Corporation, 1949.

Wechsler, D. *Wechsler intelligence scale for children-revised*. New York: Psychological Corporation, 1974.

Wechsler, D. *Wechsler preschool and primary scale of intelligence*. New York: Psychological Corporation, 1967.

Zimmerman, I., & Woo-Sam, J. *Clinical interpretation of the Wechsler adult intelligence scale*. New York: Grune & Stratton, 1973.

# 5

# Abstract Reasoning and Problem Solving

C. ADDISON STONE

While use of the Wechsler Adult Intelligence Scale (WAIS) in a psychoeducational battery for adults provides valuable information concerning both general intellectual potential and specific strengths and weaknesses in basic verbal and nonverbal skills, one general area of functioning that is not well represented among the WAIS subtests is that of abstract reasoning and problem solving. Because of its importance in higher education and in many occupational settings, additional assessment in this area is useful. To gather such information about the learning disabled (LD) adults, a subset of the total sample was administered a task used in previous research on reasoning and problem-solving skills in normal-achieving and LD adolescents (Stone, 1980; 1981). This chapter includes a description of the task used in this portion of the assessment and a discussion of the additional information gained about the strengths and weaknesses of the adults in the areas of abstract reasoning and problem solving.

The task was a modification of Inhelder and Piaget's (1958) bending rods task. It has been argued that the rods task taps cognitive skills central to adolescent and adult problem solving (Case, 1974; Inhelder & Piaget, 1958; Stone & Day, 1978). Successful performance on the rods task involves the use of what has been called the "control-of-variables strategy." According to Inhelder and Piaget (1958), use of this strategy indicates that the individual has developed the cognitive structures characteristic of formal operational thinking, the highest stage in Piaget's developmental scheme (Ginsburg & Opper, 1969). While the details of Inhelder and Piaget's theoretical analysis of formal operational thinking have been questioned (Keating, 1980; Neimark, 1975; Stone & Day, 1980), it is now accepted that use of the control-of-variables strategy is a hallmark of adolescent cognitive development and that most

ADULTS WITH LEARNING DISABILITIES
ISBN 0-8089-1795-1

middle-class, normal-achieving adolescents have access to the strategy by age 15 (Neimark, 1980).

The control-of-variables strategy is essentially a method of scientific experimentation. In order to understand a given phenomenon, one goes through several steps: first, one identifies all of the factors that might play a role in the phenomenon; then, one proceeds to construct tests of each of these factors by varying only one factor at a time; and finally, one draws conclusions concerning the role of each factor in the phenomenon from the results of all of the tests. Such skills are involved in the critical thinking required in secondary and post-secondary education and in such everyday activities as choosing a new car or determining the source of an allergic reaction. In the case of the rods task, one needs to identify those factors that might play a role in the differential bending of the rods, choose pairs of rods that differ on only one dimension to test each factor, and draw appropriate conclusions from the resulting effects. Thus, successful performance on the rods task requires the integration of traditionally distinct abilities, i.e., nonverbal organizational skills and verbal reasoning skills.

The rods task has the added advantage of being relatively free of confounding with specific eduational skills, and of providing information about problem-solving skills in an unstructured situation similar to those confronted in higher-level educational and occupational settings. Finally, in the adaptation used here, the task allows the examiner to assess potential for improvement in problem solving as a function of the imposition of increased task structure. Thus, the task provides a useful complement to the standard diagnostic battery. (See Stone, 1980; 1981, for further discussion of these issues.)

The performance of the LD adults on the rods task will be discussed from two different levels of analysis. First, a summary score will be used to determine whether or not each adult is able to use the control-of-variables strategy in the session. Second, more specific questions will be asked concerning those components of the strategy that present difficulties to the adults failing to meet the quantitative criterion. In addition, the information obtained from the task will be related to the diagnostic information gathered with the standardized tests described in the following chapters.

## PROCEDURAL DETAILS

The subset of the total sample to which the rods session was administered consisted of 23 of the 93 adults (14 males and nine females). This group consisted of all of the adults who were evaluated, or who were receiving remediation services, between January and August of 1981. In terms of demographic variables and standardized ability, the 23 adults are fairly representative of the total sample (see Table 5-1). Mean verbal, performance, and Full Scale WAIS IQs are all within one point of the sample means. The sample is also comparable in terms of age and years of education. The means from the

**Table 5-1**
Characteristics of the Adults Participating in the Rods Session

| Variable | Mean | Standard Deviation | Range |
|---|---|---|---|
| Age | 29.0 | 6.4 | 18–40 |
| Years of Education | 13.3 | 2.2 | 8–17 |
| WAIS Intelligence Scores | | | |
| Full Scale | 105.3 | 13.1 | 84–133 |
| Verbal | 106.3 | 13.7 | 84–139 |
| Performance | 103.4 | 15.5 | 74–129 |
| Subscale Discrepancy | 12.3 | 8.9 | 0–32 |
| WRAT Grade Equivalents | | | |
| Reading (N = 19) | 8.4 | 2.4 | 4.1–12.2 |
| Spelling (N = 20) | 7.2 | 2.7 | 2.7–12.5 |
| Math (N = 19) | 6.0* | 1.6 | 3.0–9.2 |

N = 23 unless indicated.
* This score is significantly lower than that for those subjects not receiving the rods, $t$ (48.8) = 2.15, p = .036.

Wide Range Achievement Test (WRAT) indicate that the word recognition and dictation spelling skills of the smaller sample are similar to those of the larger sample; however, the mean computational performance is significantly lower. On the whole, these data suggest that the findings to be reported below can be generalized to the larger sample.

The rods session was structured so that the task was actually presented to the adults two times in succession (Parts I and III of the session), with an intervening task designed to focus attention on the crucial need for controlling variables (Part II). This double presentation allowed evaluation of the spontaneous use of the control-of-variables strategy (during Part I) and elicited use of the strategy (during Part III) following the structured experience with the task provided in Parts I and II. In this way, information about each individual's *potential* for complex problem-solving given task familiarity and structured presentations could be obtained. (For an interesting discussion of the value of such "double assessment" procedures, see Campione, Brown, Ferrara & Bryant, 1984.)

The materials for the task consisted of two sets of ten rods each, a pair of rods used for demonstration, a wooden stand into which two rods could be inserted (such that the rods extended horizontally above the table surface), and a pair of identical weights that could be attached to a rod pair to test the differential bending of the two rods. Each set of rods consisted of instances of three different lengths, three different diameters, and three different materials (plastic, wood and steel). In addition, each rod had three tabs spaced at equal intervals along its length (1/3, 2/3, and 3/3 of the length) for attachment of the weights. Thus, there were four variables that might affect relative bending: material, length, diameter, and place of weight attachment.

The task was presented to each adult in an individual, subject-paced session of 20–25 minutes. The subject sat at a table with the rods displayed in a prearranged order in front of him. The examiner used the demonstration rods (constituting a controlled test of the role of length) to show the subject that "some of these rods bend more than others do." He then asked the subject to use pairs of rods in order "to find out for sure what makes some rods bend more than others." The subject was told to work as long as he wished and that he was free to use each rod as often as necessary. The session was tape-recorded. As the session progressed, the examiner kept notes about the rods selected for each test and asked questions as necessary in order to determine why the subject was making each test and what conclusions he was drawing. If necessary, the examiner pointed out untested variables and requested additional tests in order to reach a judgment concerning the global strategy being used by the adult (see below).

This entire procedure constituted Part I of the session. Part III was identical to Part I except that the instructions were abbreviated and the second set of rods was used. Part II (which immediately followed Part I) consisted of a set of questions intended to focus the subject's attention on the need to control all other variables during the test of a specific variable. For each question the subject was presented with two alternative tests of a given variable and asked which test was "better." In each case, one test was controlled while the other was confounded by a second variable. The examiner asked the subject to justify his choices but did not give any feedback concerning performance. (For additional details concerning the rods task procedures used here, see Stone, 1981.)

The session as a whole provided two sources of potential data: (1) the actual rods chosen for each test (which allowed a determination of the consistency of any preference for controlled tests and an indication of the sequencing of tests) and (2) a transcript of the session, which allowed an anlysis of the subjects' observations and conclusions during the testing. This information was used to obtain both quantitative measures of ease of use of the control-of-variables strategy and qualitative indices of any reasoning and organizational difficulties evidenced by those subjects failing to use the strategy consistently.

## INCIDENCE OF STRATEGY USE

In order to assess the incidence of successful use of the control-of-variables strategy during the rods session, a quantitative index of the preference for unconfounded tests was tallied for each part of the session. Since subjects do occasionally choose rod pairs differing in only one dimension by chance, and since the need to control for some variables (such as length) might be more perceptually salient, the decision about whether or not a given individual had a clear preference for uncontrolled tests in Parts I and III was based on that individual's performance across each part of the session as a whole. For each of these parts, a subject received a score ranging from 0 to 4, depending on the number of variables that were tested in a predominantly unconfounded manner. For Part II, subjects also received a score from 0 to 4, based on the number of rod pair choices for which he chose the pairs constituting an unconfounded test of the target variable *and* provided a justification for that choice that made reference to the confounding variable in the rejected pair. A single measure of preference for unconfounded tests was then created by summing the scores for Parts I, II, and III. Thus, each subject received a score from 0 to 12 for the session as a whole.

This summary score is useful in relating performance to other areas of functioning. Table 5-2 contains Pearson correlations between this summary score and scores on the WAIS and the WRAT. Six of the 11 WAIS subtests are significantly ($\alpha = .05$) related to rods performance, as are the three IQ scores.

**Table 5-2**
Pearson Correlations Between the Rods Summary Score and WAIS and WRAT Scores

| Test | Correlation with Rods |
|---|---|
| WAIS (scaled scores) | |
| Full Scale IQ | .55* |
| Verbal IQ | .48** |
| Information | .11 |
| Comprehension | .40** |
| Arithmetic | .31 |
| Similarities | .42** |
| Digit Span | .44** |
| Vocabulary | .40** |
| Performance IQ | .46** |
| Digit Symbol | −.07 |
| Picture Completion | .30 |
| Block Design | .50* |
| Picture Arrangement | .26 |
| Object Assembly | .59* |
| WRAT (grade equivalents) | |
| Reading | .08 |
| Spelling | .01 |
| Arithmetic | .44** |

* $p < .01$
** $p < .05$

However, all of the correlations are moderate in size (.40 to .59), indicating 16–35 percent common variance. Thus, while rods performance is related to intelligence as assessed by the WAIS, the rods task also taps skills not shared with the WAIS. It should also be noted that rods performance is related to both Verbal and Performance subtests; this is consistent with the assumption that, although the task requires manipulation of nonverbal materials, successful performance also requires a component of verbal reasoning.

Of the three WRAT subtests, the rods summary score is significantly related only to Arithmetic. The correlation with Arithmetic may reflect a common relationship to visual-spatial skills. The failure to find a relationship with word recognition or spelling is hardly surprising given the nature of these tests.

In addition to the information provided by the rods summary score, it is useful to have a global index of the approach taken to the task as a whole, that is, an indication of whether or not each subject has access to the control-of-variables strategy. This information provides a qualitative indication of each subject's status with respect to the reasoning and problem-solving skills tapped by the task. Strictly speaking, genuine use of the strategy would involve consistent construction of unconfounded tests throughout the session. To allow for subject and measurement error, however, a criterion of consistent unconfounded tests of 3 of the 4 variables was chosen. Any subject meeting this criterion during Part I of the session was said to use the strategy *spontaneously*. For a subject who met this criterion during Part III, but not during Part I, the strategy was said to be *elicitable*. The strategy was said to be *absent* in the subjects who failed to meet the criterion in either part.

Using these criteria of strategy use, 11 of the 23 adults fell in the strategy-absent category, 4 in the elicitable category, and 8 in the spontaneous category. Thus, 48 percent of the sample (11/23) failed to show consistent evidence of use of the strategy, even after the structured experience with the task provided during Parts I and II. While there are no comparable data from a group of normal-achieving adults, this figure is considerably higher than that found in normal-achieving adolescents (15 percent) or in a group of LD adolescents seen at Northwestern over the last several years (22 percent) (Stone, 1981).

The high incidence of strategy absence is indicative of potentially serious difficulties with problem-solving skills. In order to gain some understanding of the nature of these difficulties, it is necessary to explore the subjects' performance more closely. As would be expected, given the heterogeneous nature of the sample, the performance of the strategy-absent adults during the session evidenced several types of difficulties. An initial indication of this fact comes from cataloging the primary areas of processing deficiencies evidenced by the subjects in the strategy-status groups. Table 5-3 contains such a breakdown.

As can be seen in this table, strategy status is not independent of area of primary disability. Subjects in whom the strategy is either spontaneous or

**Table 5-3**
Relationship Between Strategy-status and Primary Area of Processing Deficiencies

| | Strategy Status | |
|---|---|---|
| Primary Area of Deficiency | Spontaneous or Elicitable | Absent |
| Oral Language Comprehension and Formulation | 1 | 4 |
| Visual Nonverbal Perceptual and Representational Processes | 2 | 4 |
| Auditory- and Visual-Verbal Perceptual and Representational Processes | 9 | 3 |

Note. $\chi^2$ on 2 degrees of freedom = 5.30, p = .06.

elicitable are most likely (9/12) to have primary weaknesses in the areas of auditory- or visual-verbal perception, imagery, or memory. In contrast, only 3 of the 11 subjects in the strategy-absent group fit this pattern; the primary problems of this group are more likely to be in the areas of oral language or visual nonverbal functioning. These findings are similar to those reported elsewhere (Stone, 1981) for an adolescent LD sample. Thus, the difficulties seen in the rods session are related to difficulties in other areas of functioning.

## QUALITATIVE ASPECTS OF THE ADULTS' PERFORMANCE

In order to explore these difficulties more fully, informal analyses of the session transcripts were undertaken. The transcripts were first annotated with notes concerning rod selection and other nonverbal activity. The annotated transcripts were then analyzed for recurring patterns of difficulties. The goal of these analyses was the identification of those components of the control-of-variables strategy that presented difficulties for each individual, and the characterization of those difficulties in terms of the skills presumed to be necessary for successful execution of that component. Questions concerning strategy components were organized around two related dimensions of activity: *abstraction* and *organization*. Questions of abstraction referred to the appropriateness of the conceptual level at which a task component was conceptualized (e.g., the understanding of the overall goal of the task and the decomposition of the rods into component dimensions of variation, such as length and material). Questions of organization referred to the sequencing of behaviors during the execution of a subgoal (e.g., the order and efficiency of both verbal and nonverbal actions during the construction of tests and the explanation of any conclusions drawn).

With these issues in mind, the transcripts of each session were examined, with particular emphasis on recurring patterns of behavior. Because of the small sample size and the heterogeneous nature of the problems evidenced, these analyses were necessarily informal in nature. They did, however, provide some insight into the problem-solving difficulties of the adults failing to show evidence of consistent use of the control-of-variables strategies. To aid in this analysis, each session was divided into episodes. An episode was defined as all of the verbal and nonverbal behaviors centered around the selection of a pair of rods. This analysis highlighted the repeating patterns of behavior throughout the session.

The results of this analysis pointed to two general patterns of difficulties corresponding to the two diagnostic subgroups of adults composing the majority of the strategy-absent group; adults with oral language disabilities and adults with visual-nonverbal disabilities. Each pattern involved instances of difficulties in both abstraction and organization, but the exact nature of the difficulties and the relationship between the two components differed in the two patterns. In the following paragraphs, examples from the transcripts will be used to demonstrate how these difficulties are manifested in the subjects' behavior.

## Oral Language Cases

In the case of adults with oral language problems, difficulties of abstraction appeared to be fundamental while difficulties in organization appeared to be derivative. Problems of abstraction in these cases took several forms. One common form involved a concrete conception of the variables to be examined. This problem precluded a systematic approach to the task despite occasional signs of a more sophisticated understanding. For example, one subject whose performance was generally good insisted, when asked to choose the better of two alternative tests of material during Part II, that it was not possible to test the role of material without using instances of all three types of rods present in the array (steel, wood, and plastic):

> (1) *You have to have three (rods) in each group.* You need another one that's wood that's the same length as these and then you could figure it out. Metal would most likely be the best (i.e., bend the least), *but you still need another one.*

This response, while not strictly incorrect, is inappropriately concrete since a decision about whether or not the type of material matters for bending can be determined by comparing only two materials. An insistence that one make additional comparisons suggests that one is not investigating the role of a variable but rather the role of particular instances of a variable.

Another subject's concrete conception of the variables was evident in his inconsistent use of verbal labels in referring to the rods.

> (2) These are the things that are necessary, that you take into consideration: the material that is used, *the length of the material. . .*

(3) The longer it is and *the thinner the material*, the more it's going to bend.
(4) Examiner: What's making one (rod) bend more than the other? Subject: *The metal.*

In (2) and (3), this subject evidences confusion of the labels for the rods themselves with labels for the variables into which they could be decomposed ("material"). In (4), he confuses labels for the variables with labels for particular instances of the variables ("metal"). This behavior, as well as that of the first subject, suggests an unstable distinction between surface appearances (perceptible characteristics of the rods) and conceptual frameworks applied to those appearances (i.e., dimension of variation). The maintenance of such a distinction is essential to adequate use of the control-of-variables strategy.

At the the most general level, problems in abstraction in the oral language cases led to a difficulty in grasping the overall goal of the session: that one was supposed to attempt to "explain" the differential bending of the rods. For example, one subject asked following the examiner's initial demonstration and instructions: "Am I supposed to figure out as many combinations of even [bending]?" and then chose as his first pair two identical rods, for which he said:

(5) They bend equally as much, they're equally as long. Looks like equally as much, the same material, the same weight. So they're going to bend. Is there more information, more observation you'd like, or *should I go on to the next problem*?

His final question, ("Should I go on to the next problem?") suggests that, for him, each pair examined constitutes a discrete phenomenon. Despite repeated efforts on the part of the examiner, this subject never achieved an appropriate understanding of the need to explore differential bending, or to do so by integrating information across tests.

Problems of abstraction in the oral language cases led to subtle, but disruptive problems of organization. These problems took the form of loosely focused reasoning, which may have resulted from the influence of the concrete context on the sequencing of thought. In one case, a subject who was asked to conduct tests of specific variables by the examiner (in an effort to obtain more evidence concerning the type of tests preferred), quickly lost sight of the target variable at issue (despite his selection of a rod pair constituting an unconfounded test) and talked at length about other characteristics of the pair chosen. Thus, when asked to conduct a test of diameter, he chose a pair that constituted an unconfounded test of diameter, but, in his narration, ended by focusing on the length and material of the thinner rod:

(6) OK, here we had two that look the same and appear the same. Here are two the same material, the same length and before we've added one weight just because of the circumference, one is already, just by its own weight, due to the weight, due to the length, it's starting to curve.

These statements suggest that this subject had difficulty maintaining focus on the appropriate level of generality with respect to the goal at hand and lapsed into a discussion of irrelevant characteristics of the rods used to investigate a general hypothesis concerning diameter.

### Nonverbal Cases

In contrast to the oral language cases, problems of organization were more evident and more varied in the nonverbal cases and appear to be more fundamental, while difficulties in abstraction appeared to be derivative. One organizational difficulty took the form of choosing rods for tests on the basis of their position in the array rather than on the basis of criterial attributes. For example, one subject chose his tests by beginning at the left-most end of the array and using successive contiguous pairs of rods until the array had been exhausted. This subject allowed the physical structure of the task to govern his behavior rather than imposing his own goal-directed structure on his rod selection. Subjects with oral language problems often demonstrated a conceptually inadequate basis for rod selection, but in those cases their rod selection appeared to be random or attribute-governed, rather than governed by the task display.

Nonverbal organizational problems also occurred at a more superficial, but no less revealing level. Some subjects neglected to remove the weights from the rods and/or replaced the rods in the array upside down. These subjects evidenced inefficient action sequences that were often at odds with their expressed concern for conducting unconfounded tests. (For an interesting account of similar findings with younger "nonverbal" LD subjects using concrete operational tasks, see Schmid-Kitsikis, 1972).

Problems of abstraction in the nonverbal cases took a different form than those in the oral language cases. These subjects made attempts to conceptualize the objects and events in abstract terms, but the terms were often misused or inexact. For example, one subject used the word "flexibility" in a way which treated the quality of flexibility as a static event:

> (7) Examiner: When you say "More substance. . ." Subject: I mean the matter. I'm getting very scientific here. Of this whole glass thing. I mean there's just more to it than this. . . Examiner: Okay. I think I know what you mean. Subject: . . .and because of that, it has more ability, you know, not be so flexible. And for this one *the flexibility is just beginning*.

Based on the evidence from the sessions, these subjects appeared to have an adequate conception of the goal of the task but brought to bear sophisticated concepts that were not well-grounded in concrete experience and were therefore inexact. Such "detached" concepts can result in unusual conclusions when used in causal reasoning.

## CONCLUSIONS AND IMPLICATIONS

The above examples provide an indication of the range of difficulties with reasoning and problem-solving skills evidenced by the strategy-absent adults during the rods session. Successful reasoning of the type tapped by the rods task is a complex activity requiring intact functioning in several areas. Difficulties in these areas manifest themselves in different ways in individuals with different types of learning disabilities, but the impact of the problems is equally severe. In most cases, these problems were serious enough to preclude the subject's benefiting from the experience and task structure provided during Parts I and II of the session. As can be seen in Table 5-2, however, there were a few subjects in the language and nonverbal disability groups who showed evidence of consistent strategy use. In all but one case, these subjects still evidenced occasional difficulties similar to those described above. Such less-pronounced difficulties might interfere in less-structured, everyday problem-solving situations; however, these subjects' overall strong performance on the rods task suggests that they are capable of overcoming their difficulties in at least some situations.

In looking at such detail at the difficulties manifested by some of the LD adults, it is easy to lose sight of the strong performance of many other adults. As mentioned above, one-half of the adults tested (12 of the 23) were able to use the control-of-variables strategy consistently, either spontaneously or after some experience with the task. This fact attests to the strong reasoning and problem-solving skills of many LD individuals (Stone, 1981) and points to one of the reasons why they are often able to compensate for their severe difficulties in other areas.

This final point raises the issue of the relationship of rods performance to "real world" activity. The reasoning and problem-solving behaviors highlighted by the rods session are related to those that exist in certain academic and everyday problem situations. Thus, one would expect the behaviors evidenced in the rods session to be representative of a subject's functioning in other situations as well. While it is not possible to predict such situations with certainty, it is possible to highlight some possibilities. (See Kuhn, 1979, for a more detailed discussion of the role of formal operational skills in educational and everyday contexts.)

At the most general level, similar situations would be likely to involve one or both of two key components: (1) the adoption of an abstract, decontextualized perspective and (2) the conscious organization of a sequence of subgoals. An abstract perspective is required when one must reorganize information that is presented verbally or perceptually, as, for example, in conceiving of rods as composed of separate dimensions of variation. The sequencing of subgoals is required when one must carry out a series of discrete actions or steps in a particular order as determined by a given goal (e.g., the steps in the selection and testing of a rod pair).

Two naturalistic situations that require these components are (1) troubleshooting and (2) evaluating the assertions or conclusions of others. Troubleshooting involves identifying the possible sources of difficulty with a machine and investigating each in turn so as to isolate and repair the troublesome component. For example, no sound is coming from the speaker of your record player, but the sound returns momentarily when you jiggle the speaker wire. Checking the connections at each end leads to the conclusion that there is a break along the length of the wire.

Evaluating another person's assertion or conclusion involves thinking of other possible explanations or other factors to consider and of deciding whether or not one's current information is consistent with any other of the possibilities. For example, if a neighbor announces that his grass is greener since he switched to a different brand of fertilizer, you might want to point out that there has been a long-needed rain since the purchase.

Situations such as these occur frequently at home or on the job in more and less complex versions, and they might present considerable difficulties to individuals with weaknesses similar to those seen in the rods task. The reader may note that some of the adults in the larger sample reported problems similar to these during the initial interviews (see Chapter 3). One benefit of including a task such as the bending rods in an assessment is that an analysis of the subjects' performance during the session may help to highlight any such problems and to provide an estimate of strengths and weaknesses with such everyday thinking skills.

## REFERENCES

Campione, J. C., Brown, A. L., Ferrara, R. A., & Bryant, N. R. The zone of proximal development: Implications for individual differences and learning. In B. Rogoff & J. V. Wertsch (Eds.), *Children's learning in the "zone of proximal development."* (No. 23 in the series of *New directions for child development*). San Francisco: Jossey-Bass, 1984, (pp. 77–91).

Case, R. Structures and strictures: Some functional limitations on the course of cognitive growth. *Cognitive Psychology*, 1974, *6*, 544–573.

Ginsburg, H., & Opper, S. *Piaget's theory of intellectual development: An introduction.* Englewood Cliffs, NJ: Prentice-Hall, 1969.

Inhelder, B., & Piaget, J. *The growth of logical thinking from childhood to adolescence.* New York: Basic Books, 1958.

Keating, D. P. Adolescent thinking. In J. Adelson (Ed.), *Handbook of adolescent psychology.* New York: John Wiley, 1980.

Kuhn, D. The significance of Piaget's formal operations stage in education. *Journal of Education*, 1979, *161*, 34–50.

Neimark, E. D. Intellectual development during adolescence. In F. D. Horowitz (Ed.), *Review of child development research* (Vol. 4). Chicago: University of Chicago Press, 1975.

Neimark, E. D. Intellectual development in the exceptional adolescent as viewed within a Piagetian framework. *Exceptional Education Quarterly*, 1980, *1*, 47–56.

Schmid-Kitsikis, E. Exploratory studies in cognitive development. In F. J. Monks, W. W. Hartup, & J. deWit (Eds.), *Determinants of behavioral development*. New York: Academic Press, 1972, (pp. 51–63).

Stone, C. A. Adolescent cognitive development: Implications for learning disabilities. *Bulletin of the Orton Society*, 1980, *30*, 79–93.

Stone, C. A. Reasoning disorders in learning-disabled adolescents. *The Exceptional Child*, 1981, *28*, 43–53.

Stone, C. A. & Day, M. C. Levels of availability of a formal operational strategy. *Child Development*, 1978, *49*, 1054–1065.

Stone, C. A. & Day, M. C. Competence and performance models and the characterization of formal operational skills. *Human Development*, 1980, *23*, 323–353.

# 6

## Auditory Language Disorders

Jane W. Blalock

Disturbances of oral language have been of concern for many years to professionals in neurology, in learning disabilities, and in speech and language pathology. Early, research in language disorders focused on the acquired problems of adults and on the failure to develop language of young children (Eisenson, 1972; Myklebust, 1954; Wepman, 1962). More recently, clinicians and researchers in learning disabilities, speech- language pathology, psychology, and psycholinguistics have become interested in the auditory language/ auditory processing problems of older children and adolescents (Wiig & Semel, 1976; Wren, 1983). In part, this interest has been stimulated by a renewed interest in pragmatics (uses of language) and by research in metalinguistics, that is, the individual's knowledge about language.

There is increasing evidence to suggest that facility with spoken language continues to develop well into the school-age years (Asch & Nerlove, 1960; Chomsky, 1969; Karmiloff-Smith, 1979a; Loban, 1976). Evidence suggests that competency in oral language is important, not only because of its relation to the acquisition of higher levels of language learning, but also for effective, efficient oral communication in social, academic, and vocational situations (Bryan, 1978; Bryan & Bryan, 1983; Bryan, Donahue, & Pearl, 1981a; Ochs & Schieffelin, 1979).

Problems of auditory language and linguistic awareness have been observed in many learning disabled students with disorders of reading and written language (Bryan, Donahue, & Pearl, 1981b; Hook, 1976; Hook & Johnson, 1978; Spekman, 1981; Vogel, 1975; Wiig & Semel, 1976). Current research on sub-types of reading disabilities indicates a high incidence of auditory language problems including poor sentence repetition, word retrieval, and speech sound discrimination.

While there have been few studies of oral language in learning disabled

ADULTS WITH LEARNING DISABILITIES
ISBN 0-8089-1795-1

adults, there is clinical evidence to suggest many have persistent problems (Blalock, 1981; Johnson, 1980).

## CONSIDERATIONS IN THE ASSESSMENT OF SPOKEN LANGUAGE

Language, like other areas of learning, must be considered in relation to the individual's background, to current educational levels, and academic skills. This is particularly important when assessing adults because their daily experiences are more varied than those of children who are in school every day. Fewer assumptions can be made about adult's exposure to information than about that of children. Language performance should be considered in relation to socio-economic status, educational levels of the family and the individual, and reading ability. People who do not read may have: (1) smaller vocabularies, (2) less exposure to complex sentences, and (3) less general information than those who read effortlessly. Communication problems also may result from conceptual deficits, difficulty interpreting non-linguistic context, failure to utilize stored knowledge.

It is important to have a framework for assessing oral language in order to select, organize, and interpret information obtained from standardized tests. Methodology and theories from psycholinguistics, developmental psychology, aphasia, and other fields contribute to an understanding of language disorders. Because of our interest in learning processes that might impede rule acquisition and application, we attempt to look at both receptive and expressive components of the rule systems for phonology, semantics, and syntax. (See Chapter 2) The receptive processes in the evaluation include perception, comprehension and memory (Span and Sequence). Expresive processes include retrieval, vocabulary, rule usage, and pronunciation.

Tests with adult norms were selected as often as possible, however, some for adolescents were used to explore error patterns. Decisions about language problems were made on the basis of standardized test performance, oral language samples, diagnostic teaching, and observation.

## GENERAL NATURE OF ADULT LANGUAGE PROBLEMS

Seventy-eight percent of the adults (73 of the 93) were found to have some oral language, auditory processing, or metalinguistic problems. Their language was characterized by frequent misperceptions, misunderstandings, incorrect word usage, mispronunciation, faulty syntax, and poor organization. One striking feature was the unevenness of their language. They did not exhibit generalized low level language but showed scatter of abilities. As noted in the previous chapter, many had good verbal intelligence, but their misperceptions, misinterpretations, and expressive problems interfered with communication. All of the adults had ideas, information, and the desire to communicate, but for many, understanding and using spoken language seemed to require conscious effort. Demands for specific vocabulary or syntax made problems even more noticeable.

In general, the adults with auditory disorders could be described as inefficient language learners and users. They had neither the depth of word meanings nor the linguistic flexibility of the average adult. In particular they appeared not to have the same semantic and syntactic "options" and linguistic knowledge as their peers with comparable backgrounds and intellectual levels. One woman said, "I know I talk it, but I really don't know my language." She attempted to learn more about language by reading grammar books which she could not understand.

In many cases, thinking and conceptual problems, attention deficits, and nonverbal disorders contributed to poor communication. Their difficulty in selecting, retrieving and organizing relevant information resulted in faulty explanations, long pauses, and poor conversational skills. Lack of confidence in their communicative abilities was acknowledged by many who made comments such as "I have a hard time making people understand what I mean" or "Sometimes I don't understand what other people mean."

## AUDITORY RECEPTIVE PROCESSES

Most language processes are interrelated. Thus, a deficit in one area may affect performance in another. For example, words must be accurately perceived to be understood; however, perception is facilitated when the vocabulary is familiar. Similarly, comprehension facilitates retention. The interdependence of these abilities must be considered when interpreting test performance and in developing remedial programs. Adults with the most noticeable language problems often had deficits in all aspects of auditory reception assessed (perception, comprehension, memory).

### Auditory Perception

Current theories of speech perception describe it as an "active process" that involves more than analysis of incoming stimuli. In a review of perception theories Kuhl concludes that, in addition to the analysis of the phonetic content of a message, the listener uses knowledge about "language, the world, and the specific circumstances to restrict the set of possible hypotheses concerning what the talker actually said" (Kuhl, 1982, p. 288). Research has supported this notion, demonstrating that both children and adults perform best on perceptual tasks when the possibilities are limited by context (Elliott, 1979; Kulick,

Wiedmier, & Kuhl, 1979; Miller & Isard, 1963) They also perform best when the material is familiar to the listener (Atchison & Canter, 1979).

Several aspects of auditory perception have been studied in relation to the acquisition of oral and written language. Deficits in rate of processing, perception of sequence, speech sound discrimination, and auditory analysis or segmenting have been reported in children with language and learning disorders (Aten & Davis, 1968; Blalock, 1982; Elliott & Busse, Chapter 7 Hasbrouck, 1983; Hook, 1976; Johnson, 1980; Johnson & Myklebust, 1967; Lowe & Campbell, 1965; McReynolds, 1966; Tallal, 1976; Tallal & Piercy, 1978). The emphasis here is primarily on phoneme discrimination and auditory analysis. Additional information regarding auditory perceptual abilities is discussed by Elliott and Busse in Chapter 7.

### *Phoneme Discrimination*

Menyuk and Menn (1979) report that young children use meaning rather than phonological comparison when asked to discriminate words. These researchers state that a similar lexical "look-up" is used by adults prior to making phonological comparisons. Thus, the phonological aspects of language are integrated with the semantic and syntactic components. It is important, then, to assess the ability to make phonological distinctions with both familiar and unfamiliar material. Most tests of phoneme discrimination, however, use only familiar monosyllabic words.

Many standardized tests do not have norms beyond 7–8 years of age and children are expected to receive near-perfect scores at the upper age levels. Those tests that have adult norms (i.e., Goldman-Fristoe-Woodcock, 1970) indicate performance improves until about age 10 and begins a gradual decline at approximately age 34. During the young adult years near-perfect performance is expected, and a very few errors result in a low percentile score. Despite the expected early development of speech discrimination ability, persistent problems in auditory discrimination have been reported in language and learning disabled children and adolescents (Johnson, 1980; Katz & Ilmer, 1972; Lubert, 1981; Wepman, 1960; Wiig & Semel, 1976). Thus, the assessment of auditory discrimination is important in the evaluation of adults.

The standardized measures used to assess phoneme discrimination included Test of Auditory Discrimination Quiet and Noise (Goldman-Fristoe-Woodcock, 1970), Auditory Skills Battery: Tests of Discrimination (Goldman-Fristoe-Woodcock, 1974), and Auditory Discrimination Test (Wepman, 1958). Fourteen adults scored well below average on one or more of the measures used. Eight scored 1 standard deviation or more below the mean for 8-year-olds on the Wepman.

Informal tasks were also used to assess auditory discrimination. These included pairs of unfamiliar words, nonsense syllables, and words they had mispronounced. For example, a person who said, "I want to find out what my pacific problems are." was asked whether the following word pairs were the same or different: pacific—pacific, specific—pacific. Discrimination errors were most frequent on multisyllabic words, affixes, and tense markers. Typical errors included the following: dish/ditch, responds/response, inprove/improve, vicker/bicker, edifice complex/Oedipus Complex, elimit/eliminate, encumbered (president)/incumbent (president).

Using the results of both standardized measures and informal tasks, 36 percent (33 adults) were judged to have phonemic discrimination problems. These were most evident with decontextualized content and unfamiliar material. These findings, together with those of Elliott and Busse (Chapter 7), indicate many adults have difficulty making phonological distinctions. The adults perceived words better in high predictability context than in low predictability sentences.

Their discrimination problems interfered with learning new vocabulary in school and at work, with taking accurate telephone messages, especially names, with understanding spoken language in noise, with spelling; and, with pronunciation. Adults who had difficulty shifting conversational topics were frequently those with perceptual deficits.

### *Auditory Language Analysis and Linguistic Awareness*

The ability to isolate and manipulate words in sentences, syllables in words, and phonemes (sounds) in words was described as "metalinguistic" by Cazden (1973) since it involves the ability to analyze spoken language consciously. Others state this ability requires "linguistic awareness" and is not a simple perceptual task (Liberman, 1983; Mattingly, 1972). With the exception of segmenting sentences into individual words, auditory analysis has not been considered an essential process in oral language development. Linguistic awareness, however, is important for decoding and spelling (Bruce, 1964; Gibson & Levin, 1975; Liberman, 1973, 1983; Liberman, Shankweiler, Fisher & Carter, 1974; Menyuk & Flood, 1981; Savin, 1972; Zhurova, 1973).

The ability to segment words into syllables and sounds develops later in life than other auditory perceptual skills. Cazden (1973) states that the awareness of the phonological units of speech involves special cognitive demands that are not acquired as easily as spoken language. Segmenting by sound is difficult because meaning is destroyed. Thus, like discriminating nonsense syllables, segmenting by sound requires phonological analysis without benefit of meaning. Gibson and Levin (1975) reported a sequential pattern in the development of segmenting abilities. Children first acquire the ability to isolate words in sentences, then syllables in words, and finally, sounds in words. Liberman (1973) found that by age 6, 90 percent of the children she tested could identify the number of syllables in a word, but only 70 percent could identify the number of phonemes.

Several researchers found relationships between decoding and segmenting. Savin's (1972) findings indicated first grade poor readers had difficulty with tasks such as rhyming and Pig Latin. Hook (1976) found that 9 and 10–year-old dyslexic and normal readers differed on a variety of metalinguistic awareness

**TABLE 6-1**
Auditory Analysis: Segmenting by Syllable and Phoneme Performance by Normal and Learning Disabled Young Adults

| Task | N | $\overline{X}$ Raw Score | SD | t Value |
|---|---|---|---|---|
| No. of Syllables (12 words) | | | | |
| Normal | 65 | 11.75 | .98 | .523* |
| LD | 69 | 10.51 | 1.69 | |
| No. of Phonemes (25 words) | | | | |
| Normal | 65 | 21.14 | 5.90 | – 10.68† |
| LD | 63 | 13.39 | 6.00 | |

* N.S.
† p .001.

tasks and that Pig Latin-type manipulation of sounds was the best differentiator between the 2 groups. While there is evidence to support the notion that auditory analysis abilities are related to decoding and spelling in elementary-aged children little is known about these skills in older children and adults. Savin and Bever (1970) reported that segmenting by phoneme is more difficult for adults than segmenting by syllable, but adults can do both.

Since there are few standardized tests designed to study these skills, 4 segmenting tasks were developed at the Learning Disabilities Center for use with the adults. We were aware of potential differences associated with various modes of response and units of analysis (Chapter 2). Therefore the following tasks were developed: (1) *give the number* of syllables heard in 2, 3, 4, and 5 syllable words, (2) *say the syllables* heard in 2, 3, 4, and 5 syllable words, (3) *give the number* of sounds heard in words of 2 to 6 sounds, and (4) *say the sounds* heard in words of 2 to 6 sounds.

All segmenting tasks were administered to the adults. Two of the tasks (counting syllables and counting phonemes) were also administered to 65 normal 17 to 20 year olds for comparison with the learning disabled. The normal adults made only occasional errors in counting syllables, but several had difficulty counting phonemes. Some learning disabled adults had difficulty with both counting tasks, but phoneme segmentation was more difficult for the learning disabled as well as the normal group.

The learning disabled and normal group means on the 2 segmenting tasks were compared using the t-test. Means, standard deviations, and t-values are shown in Table 6-1. There was not a significant group difference on the syllable counting task, but the normals performed significantly better than the learning disabled on the phoneme counting task. It is important to note that some learning disabled adults did have difficulty segmenting by syllable. Seventeen scored 2 or more standard deviations below the normal adult mean.

When asked to *say* words syllable-by-syllable and sound-by-sound, the problems of the learning disabled adults were more evident. Errors involved (1) addition, omission, or substitution of sounds or syllables, (2) failure to separate consonant blends and (3) failure to separate the vowel from the preceding consonant.

Sixty percent of the adults (56) had difficulty with auditory language analysis (linguistic awareness).

A comparison of Reading and Spelling scores obtained on the *Wide Range Achievement Test* (WRAT) (Jastak & Jastak, 1978) with performance on the syllable and phoneme segmenting tasks indicated no clear pattern. The poorest segmenters were not the poorest decoders (standard scores below 85); in fact, some were among the best decoders. Most poor decoders, however, were among the worst segmenters. Most of the poor segmenters were among the worst spellers (standard scores below 85), but not all poor spellers had problems segmenting. Some had monitoring and visual memory deficits.

## Auditory Comprehension

Understanding spoken language is a complex linguistic-cognitive process that involves more than interpreting the linguistic code. Both situational and verbal context influence comprehension (Bransford & Johnson, 1972; Chapman, 1978; Donalson, 1978; Duchan, 1980; Huttenlocher, 1974; Lund & Duchan, 1983; Strohner & Nelson, 1974). Stored knowledge provides a framework for interpreting new information; missing details are provided, inferences are made, and ambiguities are resolved by this knowledge base (Markman, 1981). The failure to integrate incoming information with previously acquired knowledge results in superficial processing (Perfetti, 1977) or literal translation (Stark & Wallach, 1980). Hoffman and Honeck (1980) suggest that all language comprehension is a problem solving task, but the ease and rapidity with which most people comprehend masks the complexity and enormity of the task.

Despite increased research in language comprehension, little has been done to study systematically the nature of oral language comprehension deficits in adults with learning disabilities. Comprehension problems, however, have been reported in older children and adolescents with learning disabilities (Johnson & Myklebust, 1967; Menyuk & Looney, 1972; Semel & Wiig, 1975; Wiig & Roach, 1975; Wiig & Semel, 1976, 1984) and in adults (Blalock, 1982; Johnson, 1980).

The language of learning disabled adults included evaluation assessment of comprehension of vocabulary, connected language, discourse, and prosody.

### *Vocabulary Comprehension*

The development of word meanings has been of interest to researchers for many years. Studies of language acquisition have shown that word meanings continue to develop long after a vocabulary item is first used (Bloom & Lahey,

1978; Clark & Clark, 1977; deVilliers & deVilliers, 1978). New, as well as refined, meanings are acquired for existing vocabulary well into adulthood. The diagnostic study of vocabulary comprehension included content words (lexical meanings), function words (abstract relational meanings), and multiple meaning words (contextual meanings).

The assessment of vocabulary is a routine part of most learning disabilities evaluations. The Peabody Picture Vocabulary Test (PPVT) (Dunn, 1965; Dunn & Dunn, 1981) is used for this purpose. While the PPVT is a very useful instrument, it does not provide for the study of all classes of words or depth and flexibility of word meanings. Therefore, additional information regarding word meanings was obtained from definitions, from spontaneous use of words in context, and from use of specified words in sentence building tasks.

The adults' scores on the PPVT ranged from 75 to 135. The mean score for the group was 107.2, generally in keeping with the mean Verbal IQ of 106 on the Wechsler Adult Intelligence Scale (Wechsler, 1955). Sixteen adults exhibited receptive vocabularies on the PPVT, obtaining scores that were not in keeping with their Verbal and/or Performance abilities.

In addition to those with reduced vocabularies some adults had vague, associational, or context specific meanings for words. These meaning problems were more evident in oral language samples and in definitions than on multiple choice tests. For example, *fabric* was defined as "a clothing, something to do with clothing." Word meanings were also incorrectly derived from context. *Haste* was said to mean "take your time," probably an association with "Haste makes waste." Those with imprecise or associational word meanings made inconsistent errors in word usage, depending on the context.

Comprehension of relational words was difficult for many adults. Function (relational) words include prepositions, conjunctions, auxiliary verbs, articles, and pronouns. Problems were identified on a sentence building task and from errors on oral, read, and written language tasks. The most difficult words for the adults to use in sentences were conjunctions and prepositions. Numerous errors on cloze tasks occurred on the words *except*, *although*, *or*, *because*, and *but*. Failure to comprehend the relational words significantly affected understanding of directions.

Many adults had difficulty understanding common prefixes and suffixes. Frequently they had learned various forms of words as separate vocabulary items and were completely the common meanings. For example, an adult in a health-related field asked her clinician for help in learning to spell *arrhythmia*, a word she used in reports. When the clinician told her to begin with the word *rhythm*, she said *rhythm* was not what she wanted. *Rhythm* was only related to music, while *arrhythmia* referred to irregular heartbeats. Problems of this type make the acquisition of new vocabulary an arduous, time-consuming task.

On the basis of the PPVT, definitions, sentence building, and follow-up of word usage errors, 35 percent of the adults (33) were found to have receptive low vocabulary and/or problems learning new vocabulary.

### *Comprehension of Grammar*

Prior to the late 1960s there was general acceptance of the notion that by age 5, a child has mastered the syntactic structures of his native language. Since that time numerous studies have shown that syntax continues to develop beyond this age (Cambon & Sinclair, 1974; Chomsky, 1969; Cromer, 1970; Karmiloff-Smith, 1979a, 1979b; Kessel, 1970). Those aspects of syntax that develop between the ages of 6 and 8 years include understanding and use of relational terms, relative clauses, and reversal of temporal order, as well as an awareness that the grammatical subject is not always the agent. Additionally, children become less reliant upon extralinguistic cues as they understand specific linguistic forms (Karmiloff-Smith, 1979b). The continued development of syntax and morphology is in large part the result of improved understanding of complex structures, logical relations, and the functions of language structures.

Problems comprehending grammar have been reported in learning disabled children and adolescents (Wiig & Semel, 1976) and were considered in the adult evaluations. Assessment included formal measures such as *Clinical Evaluation of Language Function* (Semel & Wiig, 1980) and the *Test of Adolescent Language* (Hammill, Brown, Larsen, & Wiederholt, 1980), as well as informal tasks to follow-up on problems observed during testing and in conversation.

Twenty-two percent of the adults (20) had difficulty comprehending complex grammatical constructions. Problems were observed in understanding complex syntax, question forms, inverted order of words and clauses, and parenthetical expressions.

Often they did not consider the meanings of sentences to be the same if clauses were inverted or changes were made in the syntax. They frequently had difficulty with the Listening Grammar and Reading Grammar subtests of the Test of Adolescent Language (Hammill, et al, 1980). Their spoken language reflected their limited language skills since they used simple, correct constructions with little variation. Attempts to encourage them to use more complex constructions on sentence completion, sentence building, and/or sentence combining tasks resulted in grammatical errors and numerous reformulations.

### *Comprehension of Directions*

Perhaps the demand for precise understanding is greatest in oral directions. Directions are particularly difficult because they contain relational words for which there is often only limited context to facilitate comprehension.

Markman (1977) suggested that failure to comprehend directions might result from difficulty in comprehension monitoring. She reported that children were most likely to notice inadequate directions if they mentally executed the instructions (Markman, 1977, 1979, 1981). Failure to monitor for understanding was evident among adults who said they did not attempt to understand as they listened, but simply took notes or tried to memorize directions. Failure to mentally execute directions, however, could result from inability to comprehend the words, to visualize, or to utilize a strategy. In the group of adults having difficulty with directions, it did not appear that their problems comprehending directions could be accounted for by strategy deficits alone.

### *Comprehension of Ambiguous, Figurative, and Abstract Language*

The detection and resolution of ambiguous language (words and sentences with multiple meanings) is a "subtle" language skill that has been described as metalinguistic (deVilliers & DeVilliers, 1978). Difficulty with both multiple word meanings and ambiguous sentences is common among learning disabled children and adults (Johnson, 1980; Johnson & Myklebust, 1967; Groshong, 1980; Klees & Lebrun, 1972; Wiig & Semel, 1976, 1984; Wiig, Semel, & Abel, 1981).

Understanding figurative language (similes, idioms, irony, metaphor, poetry, and proverbs) is also problematic for learning disabled children (Jones, 1984; Nippold, 1985; Nippold & Fey, 1983; Wiig & Semel, 1976, 1984). Since figures of speech are common in everyday communication (Pollio, Berlow, Fine, & Pollio, 1977), adults with these difficulties may have problems socially.

Comprehension of ambiguous and figurative language was studied by using specific items on tests such as the *Clinical Evaluation of Language Function* (Semel & Wiig, 1980) (Processing Relationships and Ambiguities). The Understanding Ambiguous Sentences and Understanding Metaphoric Expressions subtests of the *Test of Language Competence* (Wiig & Secord, 1985) was used with several adults. An informal measure that required explanations of figures of speech such as "hit the ceiling" and "greeted with icy stares" was also used. Other information was obtained from the adults' misuse of idioms, metaphors, and similes.

In general, the adults who had comprehension problems experienced difficulties with most aspects of figurative language. They had trouble thinking of more than one meaning for words (i.e., *bark*, *check*, *left*, *bill*, *run*, *charge*) and in explaining figures of speech. One adult explained that the *bark* in "*barking up the wrong tree*" referred to "the stuff that grows on the trees." Proverbs were very difficult for those with thinking disorders. Many simply said they had "never heard that".

Adults with language comprehension problems also had difficulty with jokes and teasing. Jokes are frequently based on ambiguous language and require more than one level of interpretation. Inability to understand jokes was embarrassing; many hurt feelings resulted from inability to detect teasing. Knowing when people are teasing involves more extralinguistic information than comprehension of figurative language. Interpretation of intonation, facial expression, and situations, as well as knowledge of the speaker, are important in understanding when one is being teased. Consequently, adults with nonverbal comprehension deficits also described problems with teasing.

### *Comprehension of Prosody*

According to Crystal (1969, 1979) the term *prosody* typically is used to refer to "nonsegmental phonology" or "contrastive sound effect" which is not related to specific segments or phonemes. This includes variation in pitch, loudness, duration, rate, and rhythm. Intonation is an important factor in obtaining meaning from language. Attitudes, feelings, and emphasis, as well as grammatical information, are provided by intonation. The role of intonation in language comprehension and production has been emphasized by several researchers (deVilliers & deVilliers, 1978; Lahey, 1974).

Little has been done to examine comprehension of prosody in the learning disabled. However, problems have been observed among children with language disorders (Johnson & Myklebust, 1967). In a comparison of syntactic abilities of normal and dyslexic children Vogel (1975) found dyslexics had more difficulty differentiating between question and statement intonation than the normals on Recognition of Melody Patterns, a task that involved listening to nonsense sentences and reporting whether the speaker was "asking" or "telling".

Thirty adults suspected of having difficulty were given the Recognition of Melody Pattern developed by Vogel. Results were compared to the performance of her normal readers (mean raw score of 5.35 with a range of 4–6 correct; Vogel, 1975, p.47). Seven of the 30 passed fewer than 5 items and 4 of these had raw scores of 3 or less. While this task is not a comprehensive assessment of intonation, evidence suggests that problems comprehending intonation do persist into adulthood and should be considered in assessing adults who are having difficulty understanding language. Failure to understand the information conveyed by tone of voice, stress, loudness, etc. can result in significant communication problems. Failure to *use* the appropriate prosody can also result in communication difficulty.

### *Comprehension of Discourse*

The comprehension of extended utterances or discourse has been of interest to researchers in the areas of both oral language and reading comprehension (Danner, 1976; Kintsch, 1977; Nahmias, 1981; Stein & Glenn, 1979; Weismer, 1985; Wiig & Semel, 1984). Discourse comprehension involves understanding across sentences, ongoing integration and monitoring, understanding reference to previous information, and making inferences. Research indicates that most adults readily and automatically make use of context to facilitate comprehension and to construct inferences (Kintsch & Van Dijk, 1978). Deficits in any process might result in difficulty with discourse comprehension. These include thinking and organization, comprehension of vocabulary rate of comprehension and memory.

There are no standardized tests for comprehension of extended discourse without an oral response. Techniques for assessment, however, such as story retelling and inferential questions following a story, have been recommended

(Lund & Duchan, 1983). Adults in this group were asked to summarize material read to them and to answer questions about the material. Additional information regarding comprehension of extended utterances was obtained in the initial interviews and during conversation. Failure to comprehend was followed up with questions to determine the source of confusion. Although we have little specific information about problems comprehending discourse, some observations were made.

Those adults with comprehension problems typically had difficulty with discourse. Some seemed unable to use context to resolve confusion and appeared to "give up" when they encountered difficulty. Several interrupted saying, "I don't know what you are talking about!".

Comprehension monitoring problems described by Markman (1981) were observed. Several adults appeared unaware that they did not comprehend until they attempted to retell the material. Many adults with language and thinking problems had difficulty identifying the source of their confusion. They were unable to ask specific questions to resolve the problem. Typically, they asked for repetition or simply said, "I don't get it." When questioned they could not isolate the specific information or term that was not comprehended until questions were asked about each component of the material.

The ability to comprehend and making inferences from rapidly presented oral material was a significant problem for many adults, especially the students. They were "overwhelmed" by large amounts of orally presented information and sometimes *expected* not to understand. Their concern or anxiety about possible failure to comprehend seemed to exacerbate the problem.

## Auditory Memory

Retaining an appropriate amount of auditory information in the correct sequence long enough to act on it, repeat it, or commit it to intermediate or long-term memory is an important auditory "receptive" ability. Studies of memory development in children suggest that the ability to retain an increasing number of units in a specified sequence improves with age up to a point. Much of the developmental change in memory can be accounted for by children's acquisition of effective strategies to attain conscious or voluntary retention of information (Kail, 1979). However other factors can affect performance such as familiarity with the material, meaning, and complexity of the syntax. (Johnson & Myklebust, 1967; Wiig & Roach, 1975).

Problems with auditory memory span have been observed frequently in both learning disabled children and adults (Blalock, 1981; Johnson 1980; Johnson & Myklebust, 1965, 1967; Torgeson, 1980; Wiig & Semel, 1976, 1984). These memory span difficulties are often related to problems with strategy use (Torgesen, 1980; Torgesen, Murphy & Ivey, 1979; Wong, Wong & Foth, 1977). Newman (1980a) studied learning disabled and normal children's spontaneous utilization of clustering by category and found learning disabled

**Table 6-2**
Auditory Memory Tests

| Test | N | X | SD SS | Range |
|---|---|---|---|---|
| WAIS Digit Span | 91 | 9.5 | 3.3 | 2–19 |
| Detroit Tests | | Age Score in Years | | |
| Unrelated Words | 35 | 10.2 yrs. | 3.5 yrs. | 3.7–16.5 yrs. |
| Related Syllables | 46 | 12.1 yrs. | 3.1 yrs. | 4.3–17.0 yrs. |

children to be less efficient in using the organizational strategy and less knowledgeable about their own strategies than were normal peers. Although strategy use is a significant factor in the memory span problems observed in the learning disabled, Torgeson (1980) cautioned that we not assume all problems result from difficulty in strategy use. He reported that some learning disabled children do have strategy deficits.

Maintaining the order or sequence of information is also problematic for some learning disabled individuals. Burns (1975) found that a group of learning disabled poor readers had difficulty sequencing digits, both auditorily and visually, and suggested they might have generalized problems that were not sensory specific.

Assessment of auditory memory in the adult group was done by using a variety of formal measures, observation, and history. The *Auditory Skills Battery: Memory Tests* (Goldman, Fristoe, & Woodcock, 1974) and the *Woodcock-Johnson Psychoeducational Battery: Cognitive Abilities Tests-Sentence Memory Subtest* (Woodcock & Johnson, 1977) were used occasionally. However, the most frequently used tasks were the Digit Span subtest of the Wechsler Adult Intelligence Scale (WAIS) (Wechsler, 1955) and two subtests of the *Detroit Tests of Learning Aptitude* (Detroit) (Baker & Leland, 1958): Auditory Attention Span for Unrelated Words and Auditory Attention Span for Related Syllables. See results in Table 6-2. The Detroit subtests were not judged to be low if they were at or above 12 years, 6 months. As mentioned in the Intelligence chapter, the group score on Digit Span was the lowest mean subtest score on the WAIS with scaled scores ranging from 2-19. Examination of scores on the Digit Span subtests of the WAIS included inspection of digits forward and digits reversed separately. Adults repeating *fewer than* 5 digits forward were considered to have problems in auditory memory span and/or sequence.

Forty-three percent of the adults (40) were found to have short term auditory memory problems that were evident on at least 2 measures. While no specific studies on strategies were completed, Newman tested several adults with her experimental task and found problems similar to those seen in children. Some, however, appeared to have limited memory, particularly on digit span. More research is needed to explore strategy use and memory problems in adults.

## AUDITORY EXPRESSIVE PROCESSES

Auditory expressive processes included in the assessment of language were: retrieval, vocabulary, pronunciation, syntax and morphology, and discourse.

### Word Retrieval

Reauditorization and auditory recall problems have frequently been reported in children and adults with language and learning disabilities (Denckla & Rudel, 1976; German, 1979; Jansky & deHirsch, 1972; Johnson, 1980; Johnson & Myklebust, 1967; Wiig & Semel, 1984). Rutherford (1977) described the social impact of such deficits on an adult with a history of childhood language disorders.

Word retrieval problems among the adults were diagnosed from information provided in the case history, from observation in various communication situations, and from performance on tasks requiring specific, single-word responses such as Information and Picture Completion on the *WAIS*, Picture Vocabulary on the *Woodcock-Johnson Psychoeducational Battery* (Woodcock & Johnson, 1977), and the Producing Names on Confrontation subtest of the *Clinical Evaluation of Language Functions (CELF)* (Semel & Wiig, 1980). *The Word Latency Test* (Rutherford & Telser, 1971) was used in some instances.

Twenty-eight percent (26) of the 93 adults had significant problems with word retrieval, while several others had less noticeable difficulty. The problems were manifested in various ways including extended latencies, pauses, and circumlocutions. Some substituted words (chair/table, hot/cold) or used non-specific words such as "thing" or "whatchamacallit." Those exhibiting long latencies, numerous pauses, reformulations, and self-corrections had somewhat dysfluent oral language and said speaking was "difficult." Several indicated they actually avoided talking because of these problems, and most thought the problem interfered with their communication.

Despite the fact that retrieval problems are still evident in adults, follow-up studies have indicated that considerable improvement may occur (Johnson, 1980). None of the adults tested had problems as severe as those seen among children. It appears that word recall problems, like other auditory deficits, improve with remediation and vocabulary growth.

### Pronunciation Problems

Twenty-three percent (21) of the adults had difficulty pronouncing multisyllabic words. Very few had consistent sound substitutions, omissions, or distortions. Rather, problems in discriminating, retaining, recalling, or rapidly producing a sequence of sounds resulted in faulty pronunciation. These conclusions were drawn from general language sampling procedures and from the Echolalia Test Level C of the Slingerland Screening Tests for Identifying

Children with Specific Language Disabilities (Slingerland, 1969). This task involves repeating words several times. Of the 46 persons given the Echolalia Test, only 7 repeated every word correctly on all 3 trials. Errors included: bastkets/baskets; donimoes/dominoes and apostofee/apostrophe. Errors were also evident in spontaneous speech and on the Picture Vocabulary subtest of the Woodcock-Johnson Psycho-Educational Battery (Woodcock & Johnson, 1977).

Many of the pronunciation difficulties were related to auditory perceptual problems. As mentioned above, they were often unaware that they misperceived and mispronounced words. Those with sequencing disorders however tended to be more aware of their problems. They frequently avoided "long" or "hard" words and so made fewer errors in spontaneous speech. A few adults exhibited mild motor planning problems that were most evident in connected speech.

Three adults whose pronunciation errors occurred because of sound substitutions (sh/ch, f/th, etc.) were among those scoring below one standard deviation of the mean on the Auditory Discrimination Test (Wepman, 1958).

## Syntax and Morphology

The assessment of oral syntax and morphology included sentence repetition, sentence completion, sentence building, sentence combining, as well as spontaneous language sampling and analysis. Spontaneous samples were obtained from the case history interview, from explanations, and from responses to difficult questions on tests.

There were few consistent errors in syntax and morphology during spontaneous conversations. However, many adults used rather simple, declarative sentences. When required to define words, to give explanations of difficult problems, to complete sentences, and to use specific words in sentences, more errors were observed. They included omission of words and/or word endings, incorrect words and/or word forms, and frequent reformulations and self-corrections. Long pauses were apparent while they planned or reformulated their ideas.

Oral Sentence Building, a task we have used with children provided the most evidence of syntax problems. Subjects are instructed to use 22 familiar words in complete sentences. The words include different forms of the same noun (*cat*, *cats*), the same verb (*walks*, *walking*, *walk*, *walked*), complex verb forms and auxiliary verbs (*might have*), and relational words (*although*, *than*, *because*, *if*). Sentences are judged to be correct if the target word is used in a complete, grammatically acceptable sentence.

The sentence building task was administered to 36 normal 17–20-year-olds for a comparison with the performance of learning disabled adults. Twenty-five normal adults made perfect scores on the task, while 11 made at least one error. Of the 67 learning disabled adults who were given the sentence building task, only 9 made perfect scores. Thirty-six of the learning disabled adults scored

**Table 6-3**
Oral Sentence Building: Performance by Normal and Learning Disabled Adults

| | N | Range | $\overline{X}$ | SD |
|---|---|---|---|---|
| Normal | 36 | 20–22 | 21.6 | .6 |
| Learning Disabled | 67 | 6–22 | 18.6 | 2.9 |

below the range of the normal adults. Performances of both groups are summarized in Table 6–3.

The words on which the most errors were made and the nature of the errors differed for the learning disabled and normal groups. The most difficult words for the learning disabled to use appropriately were the relational words: *of*, *although*, *than* and *but*. Errors in the normal adult group were most often made in the second clause of complex sentences using *might have* (6 of 11 people). Errors on the target word accounted for most of the incorrect sentences in the learning disabled group. A list of the words with the number of errors made by learning disabled adults on each word (including omission) is shown in Table 6–4. Examples of incorrect sentences are shown in Figure 6–1.

Accuracy was not the only difference seen between the learning disabled and normal group. The length of time needed to complete the task was greater for the learning disabled group than the normals. The clinical population required 15–20 minutes to formulate the sentences (40 minutes in one case), whereas the normal groups typically took between 5 and 11 minutes. Learning disabled adults also had many more reformulations and self-corrections than did normals. False starts revealed problems with subject-verb agreement, incorrect

**Table 6-4**
Oral Sentence Building: Analysis of Error Frequency on Each Word

| Word | No. of Errors | Word | No. of Errors |
|---|---|---|---|
| boy | 7 | do | 3 |
| walking | 6 | when | 5 |
| walks | 7 | not | 4 |
| walked | 3 | of | 23 |
| walk | 8 | but | 22 |
| big | 5 | if | 12 |
| bigger | 4 | and | 13 |
| biggest | 4 | quickly | 6 |
| might have | 12 | because | 15 |
| had | 6 | although | 22 |
| in | 17 | than | 23 |

| | |
|---|---|
| *of* | Of what does he want?<br>What happened of the candy?<br>I never made a word with *of.* I can't do it.<br>I don't know. . . of. . . of. . . of what? What of? |
| *than* | the boat came than I said goodbye.<br>T-H-A-N? I don't know.<br>Than is not now it is later.<br>Often than there should be different types.<br>I like ice cream than cake.<br>At seven o'clock we will than adjourn the meeting.<br>Than I walked. . no. . . I went to school, than I ran home. No. I don't know the meaning of than so I use it in same terms. |
| *walked* | He *walked* so slow a tortoise could win him in a race. |
| *walk* | You *walk* well, very straight you stand up. |
| *quickly* | I walk *quickly* to class for I was late.<br>*Quickly* move when you are in emergency. |
| *walks* | Theologians often takes *walks* along Riverside Drive. |
| *might have* | I *might have* stopped at the corner if I saw the stop sign. |

**Figure 6-1.** Examples of oral sentence building errors.

use of target words, and difficulty with complex constructions. Normal adults typically used more words, greater syntactic variability, and more complex constructions than did the learning disabled. These observations are similar to those reported by Donahue, Pearl, & Bryan (1982).

The *Berry-Talbott Language Test: Comprehension of Grammar* (Berry, 1966) was also very difficult for many adults. This test, similar to the one developed by Berko (1958), assesses the application of morphological rules to nonsense words and is similar to grammatic completion tests. It is discussed with expressive language tasks because an oral response is required. While Berry found that children 8 or 9 years old could pass all items, Vogel (1977) reported that some college-age students did not respond correctly to every item. Her more lenient scoring key and norms were used in the adult evaluations. Of the 56 adults who were given this 36–item test, 24 scored more than 1 standard deviation (3.9) below the mean of 29.1 reported by Vogel (1977) for college undergraduates. No one responded correctly to all items. Errors included omission of word endings, incorrect word endings, and mispronunciation of the nonsense words. People with discrimination problems frequently mispronounced the nonsense words. Fourteen people *omitted* word endings on the test, but rarely did so in conversation. They did, however, omit word endings in their written language (See Chapter 10.)

## Oral Communication

The assessment of language is incomplete without some consideration for usage in context—i.e. pragmatics. There are no standardized tests to assess language usage in context although guidelines for analysis of pragmatic problems have been proposed by several researchers and clinicians (Gallagher & Prutting, 1983; Lund & Duchan, 1983; Wiig & Semel, 1984). As indicated previously, problems in many areas can result in faulty communication problems including receptive and expressive language, thinking and conceptual abilities, attention, and nonverbal.

Evidence of difficulty with oral communication was obtained throughout the evaluation process, particularly in the following situations: telephone conversations, explanations of problems, job descriptions, the re-telling or summarizing of material, and conversations. The use of extended utterances and conversational interchange were problems for many adults.

Introducing and maintaining a topic to completion was difficult for many adults. Failure to introduce a topic appeared to result from failure to select the most relevant information to convey, poor knowledge of listener needs, and/or inaccurate assumptions about shared knowledge. Particular difficulties included use of pronouns without referents, ambiguous statements, and failure to place events in time. In some cases the missing information was provided when the speaker was told "I'm not sure what you are talking about." For others, this type of cue was not helpful; specific questions were needed to elicit the necessary information. This suggests that some adults do not know what listeners need while others know but do not automatically provide or select the appropriate information.

Failure to maintain a topic to completion was also difficult. Attention, memory and organizational problems disrupted the flow of conversation and tangential topics or associations often intruded into explanations. It was not unusual for some adults to lose a topic completely, having to ask the clinician to remind them what they were talking about. Some "lost" information they intended to convey, saying "I forgot what I wanted to say." It was often difficult for the listener to follow discussions or reports because they presented information out of sequence and omitted transitional words. Questions from clinicians were often necessary to maintain the topic and resolve confusion. This need for structure was also found in learning disabled children (Spekman, 1981).

Timing was a problem for several adults. This observed in their gestures, actions and speech and in the timing of their speech with that of other speakers. "Turn-taking" was a *noticeable* problem in conversation, especially in telephone interviews. This was evident in "uncomfortable" pauses, interruptions, or simultaneous talking. Not all interruptions and pauses were the result of "timing" difficulties. Some adults said they had to interrupt because "if I don't,

I'll forget what I need to say." Poor word and information retrieval also disrupted the flow of conversation.

## SUMMARY AND CONCLUSIONS

Language disorders were observed in more than two-thirds of this population. Some of the problems appeared to be the residue of severe childhood disabilities for which they had received remediation. Others, however, were not previously diagnosed. The communication problems varied, but all made verbal interactions more difficult than expected for people with their overall ability. Minor difficulties that appeared subtle on tests often became quite troublesome in life situations. Lack of confidence in their communicative abilities was expressed by many during the interviews. Because of these persistent problems in oral language they also had difficulty with reading and writing.

## REFERENCES

Asch, S., & Nerlove, H. The development of double function terms in children. In B. Kaplan & S. Wagner (Eds.), *Perspectives in psychological theory*. New York: International University Press, 1960.

Atchison, M., & Canter, G. Variables influencing phonemic discrimination performance in normal and learning disabled children. *Journal of Speech and Hearing Disorders*, 1979, *44*, 543–556.

Aten, J., & Davis, J. Disturbances in the perception of auditory sequence in children with minimal cerebral dysfunction. *Journal on Speech and Hearing Research*, 1968, *11*, 236–245.

Baker, H., & Leland, B. *Detroit tests of learning aptitude*. Indianapolis: Bobbs-Merrill, 1967.

Berko, J. The child's learning of English morphology. *Word*, 1958, *14*, 150–177.

Berry, M. *Berry-Talbott language tests:1. Comprehension of grammar*. Rockford, IL: Berry Language Tests, 1966.

Blalock, J. Persistent problems and concerns of young adults with learning disabilities. In W. Cruickshank & A. Silver (Eds.), *Bridges to tomorrow: Vol. 2, The best of ACLD*. Syracuse, NY: Syracuse University Press, 1981.

Blalock, J. Persistent auditory language deficits in adults with learning disabilities. *Journal of Learning Disabilities*, 1982, *15*, 604–609.

Bloom, L., & Lahey, M. *Language development and language disorders*. New York: John Wiley, 1978.

Bransford, J., & Johnson, M. Contextual prerequisites for understanding: Some investigations of comprehension and recall. *Journal of Verbal Learning and Verbal Behavior*, 1972, *11*, 717–726.

Bruce, D. Analysis of word sounds by young children. *British Journal of Educational Psychology*, 1964, *34*, 158–169.

Bryan, T. Social relationships and verbal interactions of learning disabled children. *Journal of Learning Disabilities*, 1978, *11*, 107–115.

Bryan, J. & Bryan, T. The social life of the learning disabled youngster. In J. McKinney & L. Feagans (Eds.), *Current topics in learning disabilities*. New York: Ablex, 1983.

Bryan, T., Donahue, M., & Pearl, R. Studies of learning disabled children's pragmatic competence. *Topics in Learning and Learning Disabilities*, 1981a, *1* (2), 29–39.

Bryan, T., Donahue, M., & Pearl, R. Learning disabled children's peer interactions during a small group problem solving task. *Learning Disability Quarterly*, 1981b, *4*, 13–22.

Burns, W. *An investigation of the relationship between sequential memory and oral reading skills in normal and learning disabled children*. Unpublished doctoral dissertation, Northwestern University, 1975.

Cambon, J., & Sinclair, H. Relations between syntax and semantics: Are they 'easy to see'? *British Journal of Psychology*, 1974, *65*, 133–140

Cazden, C. *Play with language and metalinguistic awareness: One dimension of language experience*. Paper presented at Second Lucy Sprague Mitchell Memorial Conference at Bank Street College of Education, 1973.

Chapman, R. Comprehension strategies in children. In J. Kavanagh & W. Strange (Eds.), *Speech and language in the laboratory, school, and clinic*. Cambridge, MA: M.I.T. Press, 1978.

Chomsky, C. *The acquisition of syntax in children from 5 to 10*. Cambridge, MA: M.I.T. Press, 1969.

Clark, H., & Clark, E. *Psychology and language*. New York: Harcourt Brace Jovanovich, 1977.

Cromer, R. 'Children are nice to understand': Surface structure clues for the recovery of a deep structure. *British Journal of Psychology*, 1970, *61* (3), 397–408.

Crystal, D. *Prosodic systems and intonation in English*. Cambridge, England: Cambridge University Press, 1969.

Crystal, D. Prosodic development. In P. Fletcher & M. Garman (Eds.), *Language acquisition: Studies in first language*. Cambridge, England: Cambridge University Press, 1979.

Danner, F. Children's understanding of intersentence organization to the recall of short expository passages. *Journal of Educational Psychology*, 1976, *68*, 174–183.

Denckla, M., & Rudel, R. Naming of object drawings by dyslexic and other learning disabled children. *Brain and Language*, 1976, *3*, 1–15.

deVilliers, J., & deVilliers, P.. *Language acquisition*. Cambridge, MA: Harvard University Press, 1978.

Donahue, M., Pearl, R., & Bryan, T. Learning disabled children's syntactic proficiency on a communicative task. *Journal of Speech and Hearing Disorders*, 1982, *47*, 22–28.

Donalson, M. *Children's minds*. New York: W. W. Norton, 1978.

Duchan, J. The effect of cognitive bias on children's early interpretations of locative commands. *Language Sciences*, 1980, *2*, 246–259.

Dunn, L. *Peabody picture vocabulary test*. Circle Pines, MN: American Guidance Service, 1965.

Dunn, L., & Dunn, L. *Peabody picture vocabulary test-revised*. Circle Pines, MN: American Guidance Service, 1981.

Eisenson, J. *Aphasia in Children*. New York: Harper & Row, 1972.

Elliott, L. Performance of children aged nine to seventeen years on a test of speech intelligibility in noise using sentences with controlled word predictability. *Journal of the Acoustical Society of America*, 1979, *66*, 165–753.

Gallagher, T., & Prutting, C. (Eds.), *Pragmatic assessment and intervention issues*. San Diego: College Hill Press, 1983.

German, D. Word-finding skills in children with learning disabilities. *Journal of Learning Disabilities*, 1979, *12*, 176–181.

Gibson, E., & Levin, H. *The psychology of reading*. Cambridge, MA: M.I.T. Press, 1975.

Goldman, R., Fristoe, M., & Woodcock, R. *Goldman-Fristoe-Woodcock test by auditory discrimination*. Circle Pines, MN: American Guidance Service, 1970.

Goldman, R., Fristoe, M., & Woodcock, R. *Auditory skills battery*. Circle Pines, MN: American Guidance Service, 1974.

Groshong, C. *Ambiguity detection and the use of verbal context for disambiguation of language disabled and normal learning children*. Unpublished doctoral dissertation, Northwestern University, 1980.

Hammill, D., Brown, V., Larsen, S., & Wiederholt, J. L. *Test of adolescent language*. Austin, TX: Pro-Ed, 1980.

Hasbrouck, J. Diagnosis of auditory perceptual disorders in previously undiagnosed adults. *Journal of Learning Disabilities*, 1983, *16*, 206–216.

Hoffman, R., & Honeck, R. A peacock looks at its legs: Cognitive science and figurative language. In R. Honeck & R. Hoffman (Eds.), *Cognition and figurative language*. Hillsdale, NJ: Lawrence Erlbaum, 1980.

Honeck, R., Voegtle, E., Dorfmueller, D., & Hoffman, R. Proverbs, meaning and group structure. In R. Honeck & R. Hoffman (Eds.), *Cognition and figurative language*. Hillsdale, NJ: Lawrence Erlbaum, 1980.

Hook, P. *A study of metalinguistic awareness and reading strategies in proficient and learning disabled readers*. Unpublished doctoral dissertation, Northwestern University, 1976.

Hook, P., & Johnson, D. Metalinguistic awareness and reading strategies. *Bulletin of the Orton Soceity*, 1978, *27*, 62–78.

Huttenlocher, J. The origins of language comprehension. In Solso (Ed.), *Theories in cognitive psychology*. Potomac, MD: Lawrence Erlbaum, 1974.

Jansky, J., & deHirsch, K. *Preventing reading failure*. New York: Harper & Row, 1972.

Jastak, J., Bijou, S., & Jastak, S. *Wide range achievement test*. New York: Harcourt Brace Jovanovich, 1976.

Johnson, D. Psychoeducational evaluation of children with learning disabilities: A study of auditory processes. In G. Millichap (Ed.), *Learning disabilities and related disorders*. Chicago: Yearbook Medical Publishers, 1977.

Johnson, D. Persistent auditory disorders in young dyslexic adults. *Bulletin of the Orton Society*, 1980, *30*, 268–276.

Johnson, D. Consideration in the assessment of central auditory disorders in learning disabled children. In R. Keith (Ed.), *Central auditory and language disorders in children*. San Diego, CA: College Hill Press, 1982.

Johnson, D., & Myklebust, H. Dyslexia in childhood. In J. Hellmuth (Ed.), *Learning Disorders* (Vol. 1). Seattle: Special Child Publications, 1965.

Johnson, D., & Myklebust, H. *Learning disabilities: Educational principles and practices*. New York: Grune & Stratton, 1967.

Jones, J. *Metaphor comprehension in learning disabled and normally achieving adolescents*. Unpublished doctoral dissertation, Northwestern University, 1984.

Kail, R. *The development of memory in children*. San Francisco: W. H. Freeman, 1979.

Karmiloff-Smith, A. *A functional approach to child language: A study of determiners and reference*. Cambridge, England: Cambridge University Press, 1979a.

Karmiloff-Smith, A. Language development after five. In P. Fletcher and M. Garman (Eds.), *Language acquisition*. Cambridge, England: Cambridge University Press, 1979b.

Katz, J., & Ilmer, R. Auditory perception in children with learning disabilities. In J. Katz (Ed.), *Handbook of clinical audiology*. Baltimore: Williams & Wilkins, 1972.

Kessel, F. The role of syntax in children's comprehension from ages six to twelve. *Society for the Research in Child Development Monographs*, 1970, *35*(6).

Kintsch, W. On comprehending stories. In M. Just and P. Carpenter (Eds.), *Cognitive processes in comprehension*. Hillsdale, NJ: Lawrence Erlbaum, 1977.

Kintsch, W., & Van Dijk, T. Toward a model of text comprehension and production. *Psychological Review*, 1978, *85*, 363–394.

Klees, M., & Lebrun, A. Analysis of the figurative and operative processes of thought of 40 dyslexic children. *Journal of Learning Disabilities*, 1972, 5, 389–396.

Kuhl, P. Speech perception: An overview of current issues. In N. Lass, L. McReynolds, J. Northern, & D. Yoder (Eds.), *Speech, language and hearing* (Vol. 1). Philadelphia: W. B. Saunders, 1982.

Kulick, M., Wiedmier, B., & Kuhl, P. Children's detection of mispronounced words in fluent speech. *Journal of the Acoustical Society of America*, 1979 ( Supple. 1).

Lahey, M. Use of prosody and syntactic markers in children's comprehension of spoken sentences. *Journal of Speech and Hearing Research*, 1974, *7*, 656–658.

Liberman, I. *Segmentation of the spoken word and reading acquisition. Bulletin of the Orton Society*, 1973, *23*, 65–77

Liberman, I., Shankweiler, D., Fisher, F., & Carter, B. Explicit syllable and phoneme segmentation in the young child. *Journal of Experimental Child Psychology*, 1974, *18*, 201–212.

Liberman, I. A language-oriented view of reading and its disabilities. In H. Myklebust (Ed.), *Progress in learning disabilities* (Vol. 5). New York: Grune & Stratton, 1983.

Loban, W. *Language development: Kindergarten through grade twelve*. Urbana, IL: National Council of Teachers of English, 1976.

Lowe, A., & Campbell, R. Temporal discrimination in aphasoid and normal children. *Journal of Speech and Hearing Research*, 1965, *8*, 313–314.

Lubert, N. Auditory perceptual impairments in children with specific language disorders: A review of the literature. *Journal of Speech and Hearing Disorders, 1981*, *46*, 3–9.

Lund, N., & Duchan, J. *Assessing children's language in naturalistic contexts*. Englewood Cliffs, NJ: Prentice-Hall, 1983.

Markman, E. Realizing that you don't understand: A preliminary investigation. *Child Development*, 1977, *48*, 986–992.

Markham, E. Realizing that you don't understand: Elementary school children's awareness of inconsistencies. *Child Development*, 1979, *50*, 643–655.

Markman, E. Comprehension monitoring. In W. Dickson (Ed.), *Children's oral communication skills*. New York: Academic Press, 1981.

Mattingly, I. Reading, the linguistic process, and linguistic awareness. In J. Kavanaugh & I. Mattingly (Eds.), *Language by ear and by eye*. Cambridge, MA: M.I.T. Press, 1972.

McReynolds, L. Operant conditioning for investigating speech sound discrimination in aphasic children. *Journal of Speech and Hearing Research*, 1966, *9*, 519–528.

Menyuk, P., & Flood, J. Linguistic competence, reading, writing problems and remediation. *Bulletin of the Orton Society*, 1981, *31*, 13–28.

Menyuk, P., & Looney, P. Relationships between the components of the grammar in language disorders. *Journal of Speech and Hearing Research*, 1972, *15*, 395–406.

Menyuk, P., & Menn, L. Early strategies for the perception and production of words and sounds. In P. Fletcher & M. Garman (Eds.), *Language acquisition: Studies in first language*. Cambridge, England: Cambridge University Press, 1979.

Miller, G., & Isard, S. Some perceptual consequences of linguistic rules. *Journal of Verbal Learning and Verbal Behavior*, 1963, *2*, 217–228.

Myklebust, H. *Auditory disorders in children: A manual for differential diagnosis*. New York: Grune & Stratton, 1954.

Myklebust, H. Childhood aphasia: An evolving concept. In L. Travis (Ed.), *Handbook of speech pathology and audiology*. Englewood Cliffs, NJ: Prentice-Hall, 1971.

Myklebust, H. Disorders of auditory language. In H. Myklebust (Ed.), *Progress in learning disabilities* (Vol. 5). New York: Grune & Stratton, 1983.

Nahmias, M. *Inferential listening and reading comprehension of discourse in normal and reading disabled children*. Unpublished doctoral dissertation, Northwestern University, 1981.

Newman, D. *An investigation of learning disabled children's utilization of taxonomic organization to facilitate memory performance*. Unpublished doctoral dissertation, Northwestern University, 1980a.

Newman, M. Unpublished clinical project on taxomonic organization and memory in adults. Northwestern University, 1980b.

Nippold, M. Comprehension of figurative language in youth. *Topics in Language Disorders*, 1985, *3*, 1–20.

Nippold, M., & Fey, S. Metaphoric understanding in preadolescents having a history of language acquisition difficulties. *Language Speech and Hearing Services in Schools*, 1983, *14*, 171–180.

Ochs, E., & Schieffelin, B. *Developmental pragmatics*. New York: Academic Press, 1979.

Perfetti, C. Language comprehension and fast decoding: Some psycholinguistic prerequisites for skilled reading comprehension. In J. Guthrie (Ed.), *Cognition, curriculum and comprehension*. Newark, DE: International Reading Association, 1977.

Pollio, H., Berlow, J., Fine, H., & Pollio, M. *Psychology and the poetics of growth: Figurative language in psychology, psychotherapy, and education*. Hillsdale, NJ: Lawrence Erlbaum, 1977.

Rutherford, D. Speech and language disorders and M.B.D. In G. Millichap (Ed.), *Learning disabilities and related disorders*. Chicago: Yearbook Medical Publishers, 1977.

Rutherford, D., & Telser, E. *Word latency test*. Presentation, Association for Children with Learning Disabilities, Chicago, 1971.

Savin, H. What the child knows about speech when he starts to learn to read. In J. Kavanagh, & I. Mattingly (Eds.), *Language by ear and by eye*. Cambridge: M.I.T. Press, 1972, 319–326.

Savin, H., & Bever, T. The nonperceptual reality of the phoneme. *Journal of Verbal Learning and Verbal Behavior*, 1970, *9*, 295–302.

Semel, E., & Wiig, E. Comprehension of syntactic structures and critical verbal elements by children with learning disabilities. *Journal of Learning Disabilities*, 1975, *8*, 53–58.

Semel, E., & Wiig, E. *Clinical evaluation of language functions*. Columbus, OH: Charles E. Merrill, 1980.

Slingerland, B. *Screening tests for identifying children with specific language disabilities.* Cambridge, MA: Educators Publishing Service, 1964.

Spekman, N. Dyadic verbal communication abilities of learning disabled and normally achieving fourth- and fifth-grade boys. *Learning Disability Quarterly*, 1981, *4*, 139–151.

Stark, J., & Wallach, G. The path to a concept of language learning disabilities. *Topics in Language Disorders*, 1980, *1*, 1—14.

Stein, N., & Glenn, C. An analysis of story comprehension in elementary school children. In R. Freedle (Ed.), *New directions in discourse processing* (Vol. 2). Norwood, NJ: Ablex, 1979.

Strohner, H., & Nelson, K. The young child's development of sentence comprehension: Influence of event probability, nonverbal context, syntactic form, and strategies. *Child Development*, 1975, *45*, 567–576.

Tallal, P. Rapid auditory processing in normal and disordered language development. *Journal of Speech and Hearing Research*, 1976, *19*, 561–571.

Tallal, P., & Piercy, M. Defects of auditory perception in children with developmental dysphasia. In M. Wyke (Ed.), *Developmental dysphasia*. New York: Academic Press, 1978.

Torgesen, J. *Current trends in research in learning disabilities.* Presentation, Northwestern University Learning Disabilities Center, 1984.

Torgesen, J. The use of efficient task strategies by learning disabled children: Conceptual and educational implications. *Journal of Learning Disabilities*, 1980, *13*, 364–371.

Torgesen, J., Murphy, H., & Ivey, C. The effects of an orienting task on the memory performance of reading disabled children. *Journal of Learning Disabilities*, 1979, *12*, 396–401.

Vogel, S. *An investigation of syntactic abilities in normal and dyslexic children*. Baltimore: University Park Press, 1975.

Vogel, S. Morphological ability in normal and dyslexic children. *Journal of Learning Disabilities*, 1977, *10* (1), 41–49.

Wechsler, D. *Wechsler adult intelligence scale*. New York: Harcourt Brace Jovanovich, 1955.

Wechsler, D. *Wechsler intelligence scale for children–revised*. New York: Harcourt Brace Jovanovich, 1974.

Weismer, S. Constructive comprehension abilities exhibited by language-disordered children. *Journal of Speech and Hearing Research*, 1985, *28*, 175–184.

Wepman, J. *Auditory discrimination test*. Chicago: Language Research Associates, 1958.

Wepman, J. Auditory discrimination, speech and reading. *Elementary School Journal*, 1960, 325–333.

Wepman, J. Childhood aphasia. In R. West (Ed.), *Proceedings of the Institute on Childhood Aphasia*. San Francisco: Society for Crippled Children and Adults, 1962.

Wiig, E., & Roach, M. Immediate recall of semantically varied "sentences" by learning disabled adolescents. *Perceptual and Motor Skills*, 1975, *40*, 119–125.

Wiig, E. & Secord, W. *Test of Language Competence*. New York: Harcourt Brace Jovanovich, 1985.

Wiig, E., & Semel, E. Comprehension of linguistic concepts requiring logical operations. *Journal of Speech and Hearing Research*, 1973, *16*, 627–636.

Wiig, E., & Semel, E. Logico-grammatical sentence comprehension by learning disabled adolescents. *Perceptual and Motor Skills*, 1974, *38*, 1331–1334.

Wiig, E., & Semel, E. *Language disabilities in children and adolescents*. Columbus, OH: Charles E. Merrill, 1976.

Wiig, E., & Semel. *Language assessment and intervention*. Columbus, OH: Charles E. Merrill, 1984.

Wiig, E., Semel, E., & Abel, E. Perception and interpretation of ambiguous sentences by learning disabled twelve-year-olds. *Learning Disability Quarterly*, 1981, *4*, 3–12.

Wong, B., Wong, R., & Foth, D. Recall and clustering of verbal materials among normal and poor readers. *Bulletin of the Psychonomic Society*, 1977, *10*, 375–377.

Woodcock, R., & Johnson, M. B. *Woodcock-Johnson psycho-educational battery*. New York: Teaching Resources, 1977.

Wren, C. (Ed.), *Language learning disabilities: Diagnosis and remediation*. Rockville, MD: Aspen Systems, 1983.

Zhurova, L. Y. The development of analysis of words into their sounds by preschool children. In C. Ferguson & D. Slobin (Eds.), *Studies of child language development*. New York: Holt, Rinehart & Winston, 1973.

# 7

# Auditory Processing by Learning Disabled Young Adults

LOIS L. ELLIOTT
LU ANN BUSSE

The general notion that learning disabilities may be associated with auditory processing disorders is not new; a number of investigators have reported that children with speech-, language-, and/or learning-disorders have poorer-than-normal auditory perception (Eisenson, 1972; Lubert, 1981; Monnin & Huntington, 1974; Strange & Broen, 1981; Tallal, Stark, Kallman, & Mellits, 1981; Zlatin & Koenigsknecht, 1976). The tasks employed in many of these studies were experimental procedures and differences occurred even though the auditory sensitivity of the learning-disabled subjects was thought to be normal.

During the past six years, the first author and her associates have reported major age-related, developmental changes in auditory performance of normal listeners. Information about learning-disabled adults is much more sparse than information about children with learning disabilities. Thus, the questions addressed in this chapter concern whether or not members of the learning-disabled young adult population that is described in this book demonstrate auditory perception that matches performance typical of normal young adults.

All subjects were administered a number of conventional audiologic tests to assess their hearing and to rule out auditory pathology. They then participated in several experimental procedures. The discussion of experimental procedures is organized so that each task is first described, results expected for normal listeners are given, and then the results for young adult, learning-disabled listeners are presented. Because experimental auditory testing of LD individuals has been initiated quite recently, information is available for only a limited group of subjects.

ADULTS WITH LEARNING DISABILITIES
ISBN 0-8089-1795-1

## CONVENTIONAL AUDIOMETRIC TESTS

The conventional audiologic tests will not be outlined here since they are commonly used in clinic and hospital settings. Descriptions of each procedure are available in a number of sources (e.g., Katz, 1985; Rintleman, 1979).

### Conventional Pure Tone Sensitivity

Air conduction and bone conduction thresholds in both ears were obtained for the octave frequencies from 150- through 8K Hz using standard clinical procedures. Of the 10 subjects, 7 exhibited pure tone thresholds within the normal range in both ears (i.e., 20 dB HL (re Ansi, 1969), or better, at all test frequencies). One subject (DR) had a mild acquired left ear loss associated with Ménière's Disease and PE had a mild high frequency left ear loss of unknown etiology. Both had thresholds of 10 dB HL or better for all frequencies for the right ear. FL had an apparently congenital, bilateral loss of 30–40 dB HL from 250–4000 Hz with poorer hearing at 8K Hz. Bone conduction thresholds and acoustic impedance measures indicated that the three cases of hearing loss were sensorineural. The test ear was the right ear in all subjects who were all right-handed. In summary, the test ears of all subjects except FL exhibited normal pure tone sensitivity, according to conventional audiometric standards. Figure 7-1 displays results for normal young adults (filled circles). Compared to the normal control Ss, all of the LD Ss' conventional pure tone thresholds were higher (i.e., poorer) at 500 Hz. Conventional thresholds at 2000 Hz were more sensitive than the average threshold for normals for three of the LD Ss, whereas the other LD Ss had 2000 Hz thresholds that were poorer than normal.

### Middle Ear Impedance Tests

To rule out the possibility of slight conductive hearing loss, tympanograms were obtained for all subjects. This was done for both ears on the day that conventional pure tone thresholds were measured and for the test ear each time the subject reported for further testing. All subjects had normal tympanograms on every test session.

### Conventional Speech Understanding Tests

Audiologic speech testing typically begins with measuring the intensity required for 50 percent correct repetition of spondaic words (e.g., "railroad," "icecream," "football"). This "speech reception threshold" (SRT) was determined for each subject in the test ear. The SRT is usually followed by presentation of 1 or more lists of monosyllabic words (usually 50 words per list) presented at an intensity greater than the individual's SRT. This intensity increment is called the "sensation level" (SL) and was 30 dB in this project. The

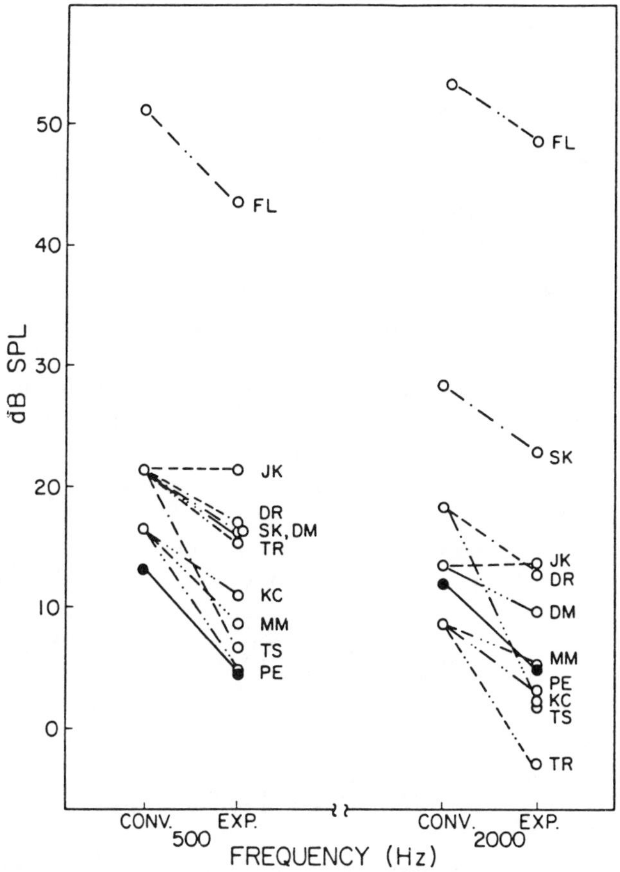


**Figure 7-1.** Pure tone detection thresholds. Audiometric results are shown in dB SPL for 500 and 2000 Hz for both conventional (CONV) and experimental (EXP), adaptive procedures. Individual LD subject data are shown by open circles and dashed lines. Mean performance of ten normal adults is shown by filled circles and solid lines.

word lists are "phonetically balanced" (PB lists) in the sense that they contain phonemes in approximately the same proportions that occur in everyday speech. Two different PB tests were used. One was a recording (Auditec of St. Louis) of the W-22 word lists, which were designed for adults, and require the listener to repeat each word. The other was NU-CHIPS (Elliott & Katz, 1980a,b). NU-CHIPS has a vocabulary level suitable for children as young as three years and requires a picture pointing response.

The SRTs of all subjects were in good agreement with their conventional pure tone thresholds. Also, all subjects demonstrated good speech understanding on the conventional speech tests. Performance on NU-CHIPS was 100 percent correct for all Ss while performance on the W-22 ranged from 92 to 98 percent correct. Thus, all scores were within the normal range for conventional speech testing.

### Acoustic Reflexes, Loudness Balance Procedure, and Tone Decay Tests

As a precautionary measure to rule out any possible auditory pathology that did not present on the conventional pure tone and speech tests, three "special tests" that are often used for assessing auditory pathology were administered. The loudness balance test is used to detect cochlear pathology, and both the tone decay test and measurement of acoustic reflexes are used to detect pathology that is located central to the auditory periphery (i.e., "retrocochlear"). Performance of all subjects on these three procedures suggested no retrocochlear pathology.

To summarize results of the conventional audiologic test procedures, seven LD subjects showed completely normal auditory behavior, two exhibited a mild peripheral unilateral loss, but the experimental procedures were administered to their normal ear, and a tenth subject exhibited a mild bilateral peripheral hearing loss. No other auditory problems were detected *using conventional, clinical audiologic procedures.*

## EXPERIMENTAL TEST PROCEDURES

The experimental procedures addressed pure tone and syllable detection, syllable identification, syllable discrimination, and understanding of sentences.

### Experimental Pure Tone Detection

A psychophysical procedure commonly employed in experimental investigations of sensory processes was used to measure pure tone detection. A storage-oscilloscope was positioned in front of the subject. The stimulus was presented during one of three time intervals, each of which was marked on the oscilloscope by displaying the numbers, "1," "2," "3," in succession (see Elliott & Katz, 1980c; Elliott et al., 1981a for further discussion). The subject's task was to decide during which interval the tone occurred and to respond by pressing one of three buttons corresponding to the three time intervals. Correct responses were reinforced by displaying a smiling face on the oscilloscope under the number of the correct response; absence of a smiling face informed the subject of an incorrect response. Each test run began well above threshold. Every time the subject made a correct response the stimulus intensity was decreased 2 dB. After every incorrect response the intensity was increased 2 dB. The test run was terminated after 20 reversals (i.e., after 20 changes from increasing intensity to decreasing intensity—or vice versa) and the mean of the last 15 reversals was taken as the threshold. This simple, up-down adaptive (Levitt, 1971) three-interval, forced-choice task has been used in other studies and both normal and learning-disabled children as young as 6 years of age have been found to learn it easily and to enjoy it (Elliott & Katz, 1980c; Elliott, Longinotti, Clifton, & Meyer 1981a; Yoneshige & Elliott, 1981). Experimental detection thresholds were obtained at 500 Hz and 2000 Hz, in the test ear, at 2 different test sessions (in reversed order at the second test session.)

Pure tone thresholds for the adaptive experimental procedure, at 500 and 2000 Hz, are shown in Figure 7-1. Normal college-aged adults (filled circles and solid lines) had lower thresholds for the experimental detection procedure than for the conventional clinical method. This occurred for a number of reasons. The experimental procedure used 2-dB step sizes as compared to the 5 dB step size used in conventional pure tone audiometry. The experimental procedure provided trial-by-trial feedback that enabled listeners to improve their performance. Finally, the detection threshold for the experimental task was the *mean* of the last 15 reversal-points of the adaptive procedure whereas the conventional audiometric threshold was the *lowest* intensity at which the listener responded correctly to 2 out of 3 trials when intensity was increased in ascending steps. Thus, the difference in thresholds between conventional and experimental test procedures was expected.

Figure 7-1 shows that all of the LD subjects except JK had more sensitive pure tone thresholds for the experimental task than for the conventional procedure. Exactly why JK's performance did not improve on the experimental procedure is not known; one possibility is that JK did not use the feedback and reinforcement provided in the experimental procedure and maintained the same internal criteria for responding to both tasks. However, even though all except one of the LD Ss exhibited better pure tone sensitivity for the experimental procedure, some did not improve as much as the normal young adults and one (TS) improved remarkably more.

## Synthesized Syllables

Computer-generated synthetic speech stimuli were used in several tasks to allow precise control of the acoustic characteristics of the stimuli and, in the discrimination task (described later) to permit testing of more "fine grained" discriminations that may be achieved when natural speech tokens are used as stimuli. A stimulus continuum of consonant-vowel (CV) syllables that varied in the place of articulation feature for the consonant and that were perceived as "ba"-"da"-"ga" was employed. Figure 7-2 diagrams this continuum and demonstrates that the major differences among the syllables were the starting frequencies of the second and third formants. (In speech science, a formant is a

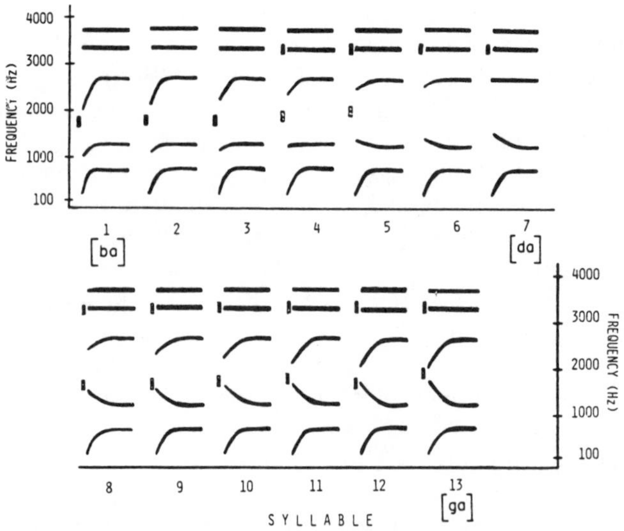


**Figure 7-2.** Continuum of 13 synthesized syllables. Duration for each consonant-vowel syllable is shown on horizontal dimension. Frequency of the formants is on the ordinate. The frequency of the initial consonant bursts is also noted. Stimulus #1 is the best exemplar of [b*a*], #7 of [d*a*], and #13 of [g*a*].

region of concentrated acoustic energy. In natural speech, voiced sounds may be characterized as having five formants.) Since the formants of the vowel sound [*a*] have a characteristic acoustic signature, regardless of the consonant that precedes [*a*], the second and third formants associated with the consonant sound may change to higher or lower frequencies depending upon the starting formant frequency for the initial consonant. (See Borden & Harris, 1980 or Picket, 1980) for further discussion of this point.) A 5-formant, 13-item continuum was used. All stimuli were 300 milliseconds in duration and were equalized in total (RMS) energy. Previous research showed that normal 6- and 10-year-old children and normal adults perceived stimulus items #1, #7, and #13 of this continuum as good exemplars of [b*a*], [d*a*], and [g*a*], respectively (Elliott et al., 1981a,b).

## Open-Set Response

Before the LD subjects were given instructions on any task that used the synthesized syllables they were given 5 presentations, in random order, of syllables #1, #7, and #13 at levels well above threshold and were asked to report what they heard. The open-set responses to CV syllables, for many of these LD subjects, were aberrant in ways that were never observed in the performance of normal children or adults. SK correctly identified stimuli #1 and #7, but consistently identified #13 as "da." TS also identified #1 and #7 correctly, but identified #13 as "ya," "ja," or "da." KC consistently identified #1 as "ba," was incorrect only once for #7 ("a"), and was correct 3 times for #13 while failing to respond to the other 2 presentations of #13. DR correctly identified #1 and was correct 4 of 5 times for #7 and 3 of 5 times for #13; DR's errors were "ga" for #7 and "da" for #13. DM correctly identified the initial phoneme of every syllable. However, DM added a final consonant to every response. For #1, DM consistently responded "bab," but for the other two syllables, the added consonant varied across "t," "f," "n," and "s." PE correctly and consistently reported the initial consonant for #1 and #13 and made only one initial consonant error for #7 ("glob" for [d*a*]); however PE also added a final consonant for every response, turning the CV into a CVC. TR also added a final consonant—a nasal—to every response and heard all vowels as [ə]. TR correctly perceived the consonant of #13 as "g" but reported "n" as the initial consonant of #7 and "m" as the initial consonant for 2 presentations of #1. JK heard no voiced stops in this free response task and reported "ah," "la," and "ya" indiscriminantly to all three syllables. FL reported "now," "da," and "ga" for #1; "ba," "ga," "fa," and "da" for #7; and "ba," "fa," and "ga" for #13. In summary, only MM gave free responses to these CVs in a completely normal manner. These results indicate that many of these LD listeners have auditory perception problems that were not identified by the conventional audiologic speech tests.

## Syllable Detection

The three-interval forced-choice adaptive procedure that was used for pure tone detection also was used for measuring syllable detection. The stimuli were syllables #1, #7, and #13, with 1 syllable presented throughout an entire test run. As in the experimental pure tone detection task, the subject pushed a button to indicate the interval during which he or she thought the stimulus occurred. Separate detection thresholds were obtained for each syllable; the order of syllables was counterbalanced across subjects; and all subjects performed the task a second time in a later test session.

Performance on the syllable detection task is shown in Figure 7-3. All LD subjects (open circle) except PE had syllable detection thresholds that were poorer than those of normal adults (filled circles); PE's thresholds for [b*a*] and [d*a*] were on the border of the normal range. Since the greatest amount of acoustic energy in the CV stimuli is in the vowel, and is concentrated at low frequencies, it is not surprising that detection of syllables was poorer than normal, since all the LD Ss had poorer-than-normal pure tone sensitivity at 500 Hz (Fig. 7-1) even though they exhibited "normal hearing" according to conventional audiometric standards.

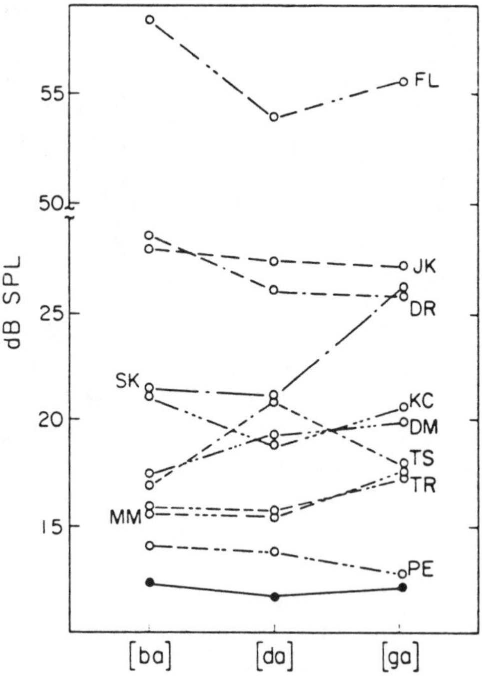


**Figure 7-3.** Thresholds for 3-interval, forced-choice procedure. Results are shown in dB SPL for three CV syllables. Data for individual LD subjects are shown by open circles and dashed lines. Mean performance of 12 normal adults is shown by filled circles connected by solid lines.

## Syllable Identification Thresholds

The same 3 CV stimuli (#1, #7, and #13) were used in another procedure where the subject's task was to identify which syllable was presented. The method of constant stimuli was employed; on each trial a circle on the storage-oscilloscope marked the presentation of one stimulus. The subject pressed one of three response buttons to identify the stimulus as "ba," "da," or "ga." Positive feedback was given for each correct response by the circle merging into a smiling face. For incorrect responses the circle disappeared. The three syllables were presented in random order and at different intensities. A preliminary run enabled the experimenter to approximate the range of stimulus levels where the subject's identification of syllables varied from below 50 percent to nearly 100 percent correct. In the subsequent test run, each of the three CV syllables was presented at five different intensities that differed in 5 dB steps; ten trials per stimulus per level were given in a computer-controlled, intermixed random order. Figure 7-4 illustrates the resulting points of the

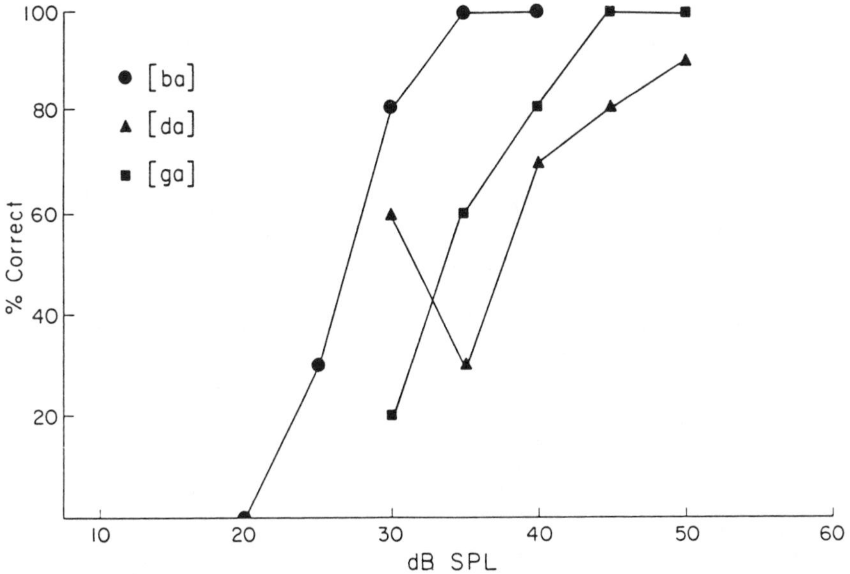


**Figure 7-4.** Performance intensity functions for [b*a*], [d*a*] and [g*a*] for one listener. Intensities at which the stimuli were presented are plotted along the abscissa in dB SPL, and performance (in percent correct) is on the ordinate. Logistic functions were plotted to data such as these to derive the 50 and 90 percent points shown in Figure 7-5.

performance-intensity functions for one subject at the end of one complete test run. Logistic curves were fitted to individual data sets to estimate the intensity required for 50 and 90 percent correct identification and to determine the slope of the performance-intensity function. $\chi^2$ tests were run to be certain that the individual fitted functions did not differ significantly from the data points.

Figure 7-5 shows that, except for DM's threshold for [g*a*], the 50 percent identification thresholds for the 3 syllables were considerably poorer (i.e., higher intensities were required) for all LD Ss than the identification thresholds of normal adult listeners. Only TS had 90 percent identification thresholds for all 3 CVs that approximated normal control values, although PE and DM had values close to normal for [b*a*], while MM, PE, and TR had near-normal 90 percent identification thresholds for [g*a*]. In general, the ordering of individual identification thresholds was similar to the ordering of the syllable detection thresholds of Figure 7-3. For example, JK had the poorest identification thresholds just as JK's performance was poorest for two of the three syllable detection thresholds. An exception concerned PE who had normal syllable *detection* thresholds for all 3 syllables but poorer than normal 50 percent *identification* thresholds for the same 3 syllables.

Normal listeners showed significant differences in the identification thresholds for the three syllables, with best thresholds for [b*a*] and poorest for [g*a*].

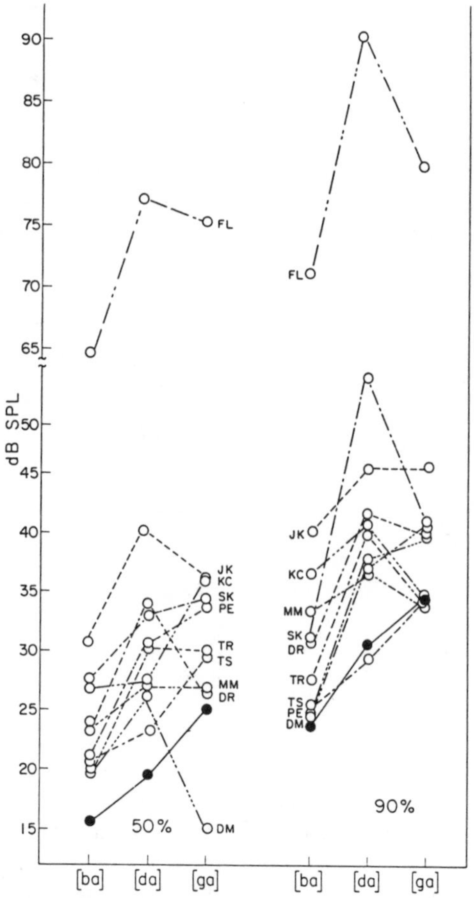


**Figure 7-5.** Identification thresholds (50 and 90 percent) for CV syllables. Mean performance of 12 normal adults is shown by filled circles and solid lines. Data are plotted for individual LD subjects (open circles) and shown in dB SPL.

Elliott et al (1981a) proposed that this was due to the acoustic characteristics of the three stimuli. At the beginning of the syllables, when the formants were changing in frequency, [b*a*] had the highest RMS-dB level and [g*a*] had the lowest, as occurs in natural speech. (The difference in RMS-dB levels for the full durations of stimuli was less than 0.2 dB.) Thus, Elliott et al (1981a) proposed that the higher intensity required by normals for the identification threshold of [g*a*], as compared to [b*a*], reflected RMS-dB differences for the initial portions of these syllables. In contrast to normal performance, many of the LD listeners showed higher 50 and 90 percent identification thresholds for

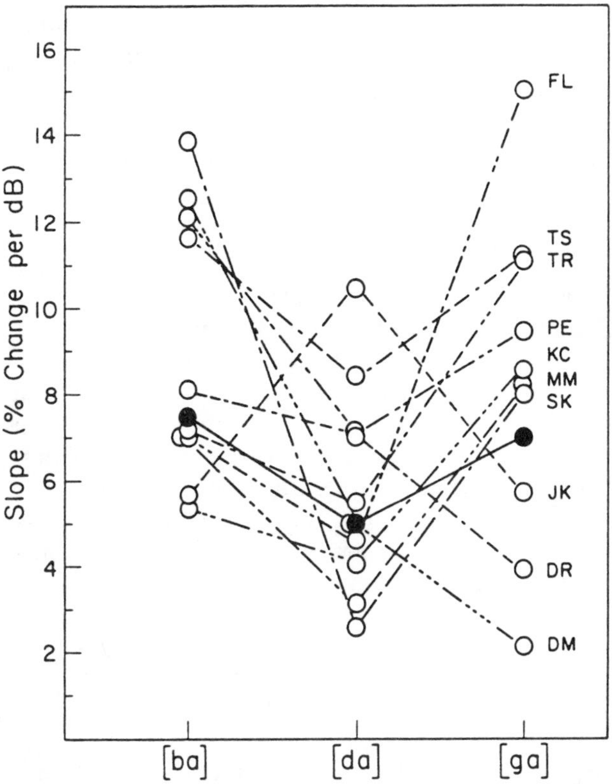


**Figure 7-6.** Slopes of identification functions of [b*a*], [d*a*] & [g*a*]. Plotted in terms of change in percent correct per dB change. Other features are similar to Figures 7-1 and 7-3.

[d*a*] than for the other 2 stimuli. This may be related to the difficulties that the LD listeners experienced in discriminating [d*a*] from the other two stimuli (see later discussion).

Figure 7-6 displays the slopes of the individual performance intensity functions and compares them to normal slopes. The configuration of slopes for the three CVs was similar to the normal pattern for several LD Ss (TS and PE), but was elevated (i.e., their slopes were all steeper than for normals). Other LD Ss showed larger differences, with relatively more shallow slopes for [d*a*] than for [b*a*] or [g*a*]. This probably reflects the fact that the LD listeners required higher intensities to identify [d*a*] correctly. In other words, once these Ss could identify [d*a*] correctly 50 percent of the time, the additional intensity required for 90 percent detection was not too great. JK's configuration of slopes was aberrant in that his steepest slope was for [d*a*]. This is not easily explained on the basis of his other test results.

To summarize this section, most of the LD listeners required higher intensities than normals to identify the [b*a*], [d*a*], and [g*a*] syllables and, for most, their patterns of results differed from normals'. Since one may presume that correct identification of speech sounds is a skill that is associated with speech understanding, these results suggest that these LD listeners are likely to experience difficulty when the listening conditions are less than optimal.

## Adaptive Syllable Labelling

It is well documented that when individual members of a continuum of synthesized stimuli, such as the one used here, are presented and listeners are asked to name "label" each stimulus, there are precipitous shifts in the labels that are applied. For example, items 1, 2, 3, and 4 of the 13-item continuum may be labelled "ba" nearly 100 percent of the time but item #5 may be labelled "da" consistently. Such rapid changes in the labelling functions are described as indicating "categorical perception" of the stimuli.* The point where two labelling functions (such as for "ba" and "da") cross (i.e., the point where a single stimulus is labelled "ba" 50 percent of the time and "da" on the remaining trials) is referred to as the "phoneme category boundary." Raz and Wightman (1984) developed a simple, adaptive procedure to estimate the phoneme boundary and Elliott et al. (1981b) demonstrated that the adaptive procedure produces results equivalent to those obtained using the original method of constant stimuli. When the adaptive, labelling procedure was used in testing LD adults, syllables were presented at a comfortable listening level that was well above threshold (specifically, 90 dB SPL). One stimulus was presented on each trial and the subject pushed one of three response buttons to label the stimulus as "ba," "da," or "ga." Syllables were presented according to their order in the continuum (9, 10, 11 or 11, 10, 9) with the direction of the sequence of stimuli changing each time the listener's response shifted from one phoneme label to another. In other words, the computer program oscillated between stimuli identified as "ga" and "da," or between stimuli identified as "ba" and "da." This procedure, which bracketed the 50 percent points of the labelling functions, had the advantage of directly estimating the phoneme boundary. For each test run, stimuli were presented until eight reversals (responses changing from "ga" to "da" or vice versa) occurred; stimulus numbers of the last six consecutive reversals were averaged to determine the estimated phoneme boundary.

Results showed that seven of the ten learning-disabled Ss had both phonemic boundaries (between "ba" and "da" and between "da" and "ga") within the normal range. Both boundaries for SK and TS fell outside the normal range while DR's results were outside the normal range for "ba"–"da"

*"Categorical perception" is a topic of much recent research and debate. The terminology is used here descriptively.

but within the normal range for "da"–"ga." These outcomes will be discussed further in comparison to these listeners' performances on the syllable discrimination task.

## Syllable Discrimination

This task was designed to provide a more fine-grained measure of auditory discrimination than is obtained with the conventional PB speech discrimination test scores. The purpose was to determine the smallest acoustic differences, among the CV syllables, that could be discriminated. The same 13-item continuum was used, with stimuli presented at about 90 dB SPL. Just noticeable differences (JNDs) were determined in relation to stimulus #7, which was expected to be perceived as "da." JNDs were measured separately in the direction of stimulus #1 and in the direction of stimulus #13. Two stimuli were presented sequentially on every trial and the listener's task was to judge them as "same" or "different" by pushing one of two response buttons. Trial-by-trial reinforcement was given in the form of a smiling face that appeared on the storage oscilloscope immediately after every correct response. A transformed up-down adaptive procedure was used. For example, stimuli #7 and #6 and then stimuli #5 and #7 might be presented and the subject might respond "same" to each pair. If stimuli #4 and #7 were next presented, the subject might respond "different." This stimulus pair was presented again, and a response of "different" was again required before the computer program would "reverse" and present stimuli #5 and #7. Although stimulus #7 occurred on every "test" trial, its position (first or second of the two stimuli) was randomly varied. "Catch trials" in which both stimuli were identical (and could be any stimulus close to or including #7) were inserted randomly by the computer so as to have equal numbers of "test" and "catch" trials. (For example, the exact sequence described above would have been unlikely; stimulus pairs such as #6 and #6, #7 and #7, or #8 and #8, would have been interspersed in that sequence.) Pairs of stimuli were presented until the subject gave eight response reversals; the numbers of the comparison stimuli for the last six reversals were averaged to provide a measure of the JND. Two measures of each JND were obtained at two different sessions for all Ss.

Results on the syllable discrimination task are shown in Figure 7-7 where performance of normal adults is displayed at the bottom with the stipled area representing average normal adult performance ± 1 SD. JNDs for DM and FL fell within the range expected for normal listeners for both the "ba–da" and "da–ga" discriminations. JNDs for the "da–ga" discrimination were also within normal limits for MM, PE, and JK. The JNDs for the other LD listeners were outside the range of results expected for normal adults and closer to the results expected for normal children who were shown by Elliott et al. (1981b) to have larger JNDs than adults. SK was unable to discriminate between "da" and "ga."

The larger-than-normal JNDs that occurred, in part, corresponded to the

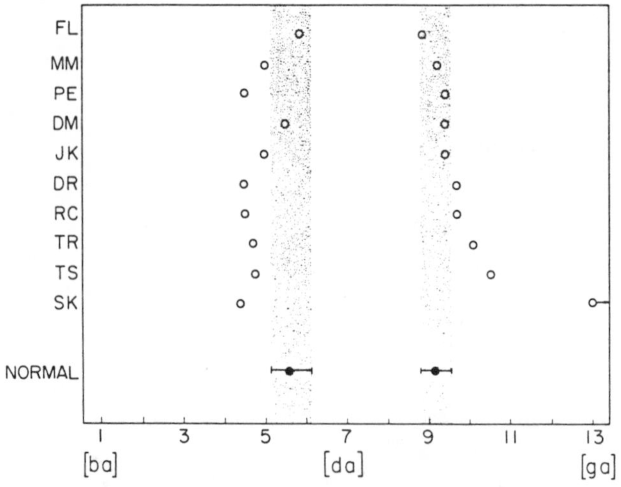


**Figure 7-7.** Mean JNDs for 10 normal adults and individual (LD) JNDs for LD listeners. Mean JNDs, relative to stimulus #7, for normal adults are shown at the bottom with the horizontal bars and stipling representing ±1 SD. Individual JNDs are shown for the LD subjects; the symbol above #13 for SK (with the arrow pointing to the right) indicates that SK could not make the "da–ga" discrimination.

open-set responses of several of these listeners (see previous discussion). For example, just as SK consistently identified syllable #13 as "da" in the open-set situation, SK was unable to hear the difference between [d*a*] and [g*a*] on the discrimination task. TS, who also could not identify [g*a*] correctly, had difficulty discriminating between [d*a*] and [g*a*]. DR showed some confusion errors between [d*a*] and [g*a*] on the open-set, identification task and DR's JND, measured in the direction of [g*a*] was at the border of normal performance. It is not clear why JK, who heard no initial voiced stop consonants on the "open-set" labelling task, had [da-ga] JNDs within the range expected for normal listeners. This may have occurred because the task demands of the labelling task were quite different from those of the JND task, which required a different type of analysis and a response of "same" or "different."

Of the Ss who performed best on the Syllable Discrimination task, FL, MM, PE, DM, and JK also had phonemic boundaries within the normal range for the Adaptive Syllable Labelling task. Only RC and TR, who showed normal phoneme boundaries, had larger-than-normal JNDs. It is known that discriminations can be made "within" phoneme categories. Thus, the JNDs for RC and TR were simply not as small as those of some of the other listeners. The overall interpretation of these several sets of data is that the performance of many of the LD Ss was quite consistent from task to task.

## Sentence Perception Test

Kalikow, Stevens, and Elliott (1977) described the development of a sentence test of speech understanding in noise (SPIN), which was developed to assess "everyday" speech reception in English-speaking adults. In addition to measuring word intelligibility, the SPIN test measures a cognitive component of speech understanding in that two different scores are derived—one for "high predictability" (HP) sentences that contain two or three "pointer" words that provide semantic links to the key words, and one for "low predictability" (LP) sentences that contain no semantic clues.† HP and LP sentences are randomly intermixed, with 25 of each comprising each SPIN test list. Sentence length does not exceed eight syllables and the listener's task is to repeat only the final word, which is always a monosyllabic noun. The tape-recorded sentences are spoken by a male talker and the test is presented against a babble of 12 voices.‡ When normal adults listen to these materials at a signal-to-noise (S/N) ratio of 0 dB (i.e., both signal and noise at the same intensity) or +5 dB (i.e., the signal is 5 dB greater than the noise) with the signal level at 70 dB SPL, their performance on the HP sentences is considerably better than on the LP sentences (filled circles and solid lines, Figure 7-8). This performance difference between the two sets of sentences *for normal Ss* is thought to be attributable, in large part, to the listener's ability to make use of the linguistic context of the HP sentences.

Four different SPIN lists were used in testing the LD subjects of this study. The subject's task was to repeat back the last word of the sentence. Subjects were tested at S/N ratios of 0, +4−, and +10 dB. After completion of testing against the noise background, each subject was also given a SPIN list in quiet to determine performance in the absence of competing noise.

Figure 7-8 shows performance, in percent correct, as a function of S/N for the LD subjects (open circles). When tested at the favorable S/N ratio of +10 dB, 8 of the LD Ss achieved scores on the HP sentences that were within 4 percent (1 word error) of normal young adult performance. However, only 3 of the LD Ss (DR, MM and TS) achieved near normal performance for the LP sentences at +10 dB S/N.

When tested at S/N = +4 dB, 5 of the LD Ss achieved HP scores that approximated normal performance but only JK's and DM's LP scores were close to the normals'. Indeed, at +4 dB S/N, TR, TS, SK, and KC achieved poorer LP scores than normal listeners achieved on the more difficult 0 dB S/N condition. All of the LD Ss performed much poorer than normals on *both* HP and LP sentences at 0 dB S/N.

When the SPIN sentences were presented in quiet, all LD subjects showed

†Examples of SPIN test sentences are: (HP) "The watchdog gave a warning growl;" (LP) "I am thinking about the knife."

‡The SPIN test is being evaluated and revised (Bilger et al., 1984) prior to commercial distribution.

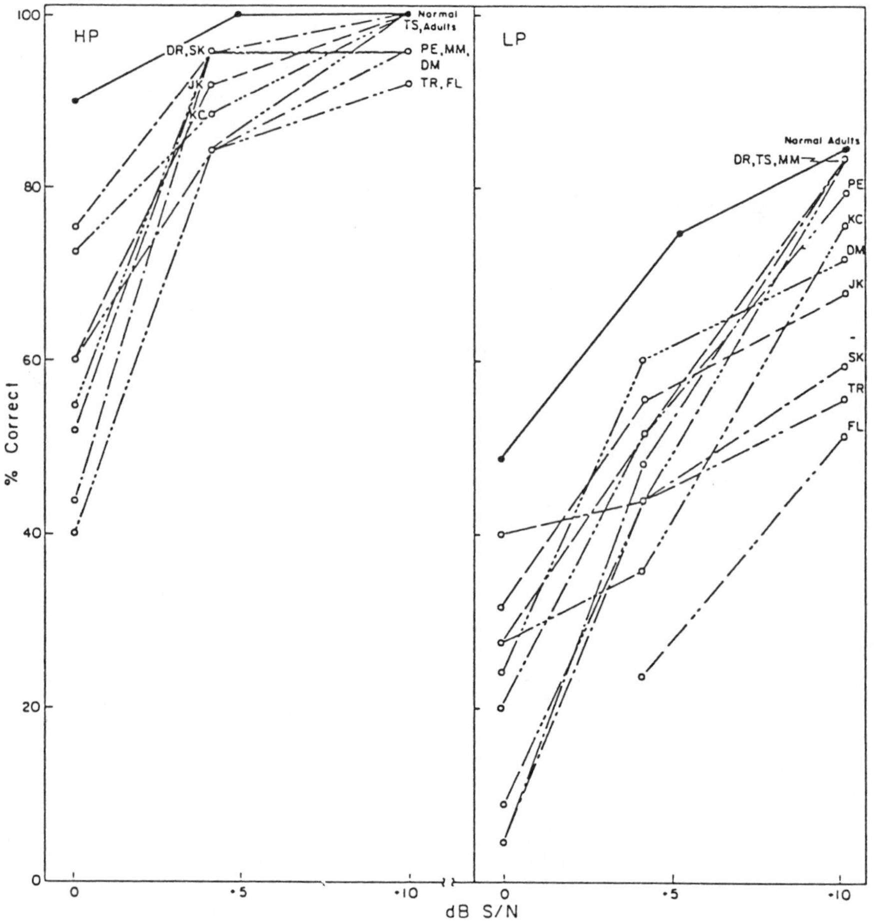


**Figure. 7-8.** Performance on the SPIN test. Performance for 10 normal adults is shown by filled circles and solid lines for High Predictability (HP) sentences (left side) and for Low Predictability (LP) sentences (right panel). Performance in percent correct is displayed on the ordinate and the abscissa notes signal-to-noise ratio in dB. Performance of individual LD subjects is shown by open circles. LD listeners were tested at S/N ratios of 0, +4 and +10 dB, while points for normal young adults represent testing at 0, +5 and +10 dB S/N.

normal performance, either achieving 100 percent correct or missing, at most, one word per HP or LP half list (i.e., 96 percent). In other words, they had no difficulty perceiving the sentence materials when tested under optimal listening conditions.

It is interesting to compare performance on the syllable discrimination task (Fig. 7-7) and LP sentences of the SPIN test (Fig. 7-8). FL had the best JNDs, but performed poorly on SPIN, presumably because of his hearing loss. (Competing noise is known to produce severe speech-understanding problems for many hearing-impaired listeners.) DM was the only other LD subject to have both JNDs within ±1 SD of the means for young normal adults. At S/N = +10 dB, DM ranked sixth in performance on the LP sentences. However, for the more difficult S/N = +4 dB condition, DM showed the highest performance among the LD listeners for the LP sentences. The other three Ss (MM, JK and PE) who had "da"–"ga" JNDs within ±1 SD of the mean for normals ranked fourth, seventh, and tied for first position when performance on LP sentences at +10 dB S/N was considered. However, these three Ss, at +4 dB S/N, had performance on the LP sentences that ranked just below DM. Thus, the JND measure appears to be predictive of performance on the low predictability (LP) SPIN sentences when the task is difficult—but not overly difficult.

The SPIN test results may be examined from a different perspective. In Figure 7-9, the *difference* between performance on HP and LP sentences is plotted (on the ordinate) against performance on the LP sentences (on the abscissa). The diagonal line sloping from the lower right toward the upper left establishes the region of possible data points. For example, if a listener scores 80 percent correct on LP sentences (at a given S/N), the maximum possible (HP-LP) *difference* score is 20 percent, since one may not score higher than 100 percent on either type of sentence. The filled circles connected by the solid lines represent average performance of normal young adult listeners at four S/N ratios—from left to right: −5, 0, +5, and +10 dB. A listener who did not make use of the contextual cues of the HP sentences would be expected to obtain equal scores on both HP and LP sentences and, hence, the function for this listener, in this type of plot, would be a horizontal line close to the abscissa. Thus, this type of plot illustrates the contributions of language knowledge and ability to utilize the redundancy of the HP sentences (i.e., "top down" processing) to understanding speech.

Note that data points for the LD listeners (shown by open circles) do not fall *directly* above the data points for normals. This is because LP performance is plotted on the abscissa and different listeners attained different LP scores. The line for each individual LD listener represents the (HP-LP) difference scores, plotted against that person's LP scores, for S/N ratios of 0, +4, and +10 dB (from left to right).

It is clear in Figure 7-9 that the contextual information of the HP sentences made the greatest contribution to the performance of young normal listeners at 0 dB S/N (where LP performance = 47 percent and (HP-LP) = 42 percent). The striking feature of Figure 7-9 is that performance of 5 of the LD listeners (TS, PE, JK, DR, and SK) fell on the diagonal line *when they were tested at the relatively favorable listening condition of S/N = +10 dB*. The remaining Ss performed quite well at the +10 dB S/N level. As the listening conditions became more difficult, many of the LD listeners made very good use of the contextual information. However, it must be remembered that this type of plot

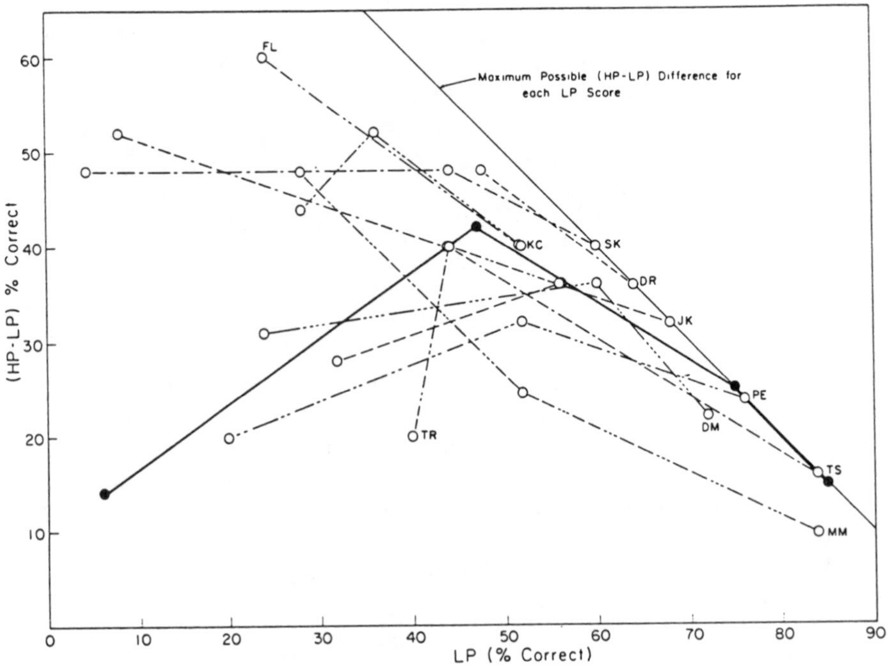


**Figure 7-9.** Data of Figure 7-8 redrawn as follows: Difference between HP and LP performance is plotted on the ordinate as a function of LP performance at the same S/N ratio. The left-most point for normal young adults (filled circles) represents testing at S/N = −5 dB, and the other points for normals are at 0, +5 and +10 dB S/N. The left-most points for the LD listeners (except for FL and DR) represent performance at S/N = 0 dB. The lowest S/N level at which FL and DR were tested was +4 dB. The points in the upper left quadrant indicate that some of the LD listeners, who exhibited very poor performance on the LP sentences at S/N = 0 dB, nevertheless utilized "top-down" processing to perform relatively well on the HP sentences.

does not emphasize the S/N ratios associated with the data points. For example, the left-most points for FL and DR represent S/N = +4 dB, while the left-most points for all other LD listeners represent 0 dB S/N. In contrast, the left-most point for normals (filled circle) is −5 dB S/N. While all of the LD listeners had poorer LP performance than normals at 0 dB S/N and (with the exception of JK and DM) at 4 dB S/N, they made relatively good use of "top down" processing and language skills. This type of plot suggests that the primary problem of the LD Ss, on this task, is basic discrimination of the acoustic speech signal.

It might be noted that Figure 7-9 presents a rather different picture from that obtained when SPIN test data for normal children (Elliott, 1979) are plotted in the same manner (Figure 7-10). In Figure 7-10, the data points for Ss aged 11 years and older, from left to right on each function, represent testing at −5, 0, and +5 dB S/N. Nine-year-olds were tested at 0 and +5 dB S/N. The

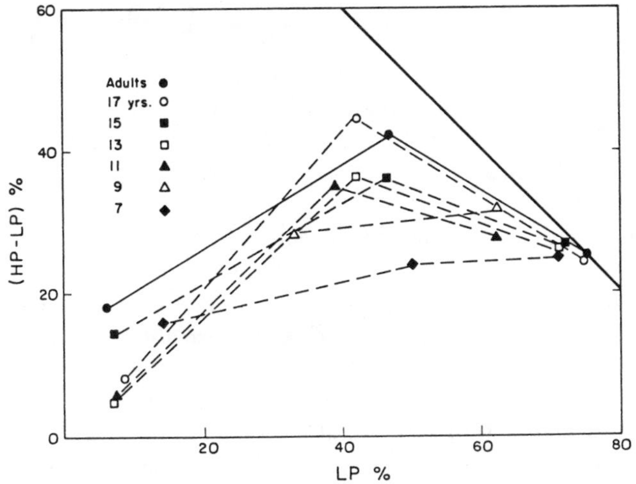


**Figure 7-10.** Performance of normal 7–17-year-olds compared to performance of normal young adults (filled circles). Same format as Figure 7-9. Children 11 years and older and adults were tested at S/N = +5, 0 and −5 dB. Nine-year-olds were tested at S/N = 0 and +5 dB; seven-year-olds were tested at S/N = 0, +4 and +8 dB.

7-year-olds were tested (from left to right), at S/Ns of 0, +4, and +8 dB. In the plot for children, except for the data point for 17-year-olds at S/N = 0 dB, which is slightly higher than the point for normal adults (filled circles and solid lines), the maxima of the functions all fall under the curve for adults. The performance of 9-year-olds (open triangles) falls considerably below the older Ss' at S/N = 0 dB, and scores of the 7-year-olds are remarkably poorer than those of older Ss even though the "middle point" for 7-year-olds represents testing at a S/N ratio 4 dB higher than the level for older Ss. The presumed explanation for these differences is that young normal children have less mature language skills and are not able to utilize the linguistic redundancy of the HP sentences as well as more experienced language users.

Comparison of Figures 7-9 and 7-10 emphasizes the performance differences between normal children aged 11–17 years, the 7–9-year-old normal children, and the LD young adults. The data points for normal 11- to 17-year-old children, tested at S/N = 0 dB, fall approximately in vertical alignment with performance of normal adults (Fig. 7-10). This indicates that performance on the low predictability sentences, where auditory discrimination of the target word is paramount, is approximately equal for these groups. The S/N = 0 dB data point for 9-year-olds falls to the left, and for 7-year-olds is displaced to approximately the same left-side location as occurred for LD adults (Fig. 7-9). This poorer discrimination of speech sounds, when contextual redundancy does not enable the listener to utilize "top down" processing, is in consonance with what one would expect on the basis of performance on the

Syllable Discrimination task (Fig. 7-7) and Elliott et al, 1981b). The *lowered* (HP-LP) points for children (Fig. 7-10) at S/N = 0 dB, as previously mentioned, are interpreted as reflecting poorer "top-down" processing—probably because of less experience with the linguistic contingencies of everyday types of speech due to their younger age. The LD Ss (Fig. 7-9), on the other hand, made good use of "top-down" processing *provided that they perceived a sufficient portion of the acoustic speech signal.*

A note should be added about the extent to which the SPIN test mimics real life listening circumstances. Just as there are many occasions when linguistic redundancy provides clues to words of conversational speech, there are also many situations where no such clues are available (i.e., when the subject of conversation is changed, when a new term is introduced, etc.). A S/N ratio of +10 dB is *much* more favorable than occurs in many everyday situations; S/Ns of approximately 0 to 4 dB are likely to be found during activity periods in school classrooms, on the school playground, in many home environments when music or TV is being played, and in many work environments. One would, therefore, anticipate that there are many situations encountered in daily life where contextual redundancy is not high and these LD listeners misperceive speech messages.

## SUMMARY OF EXPERIMENTAL TEST DATA

Many of the learning-disabled listeners showed poorer-than-normal performance for detection of pure tones and syllables, for syllable identification thresholds, for discriminating differences between syllables, and in sentence understanding. The only test procedure in which LD subjects, in general, performed in a near-normal manner was the one that measured boundaries between phoneme categories. On most of the syllable tasks, their performance was more like that expected of younger listeners. On the SPIN Test, at favorable S/N levels, some had performance that was near-normal on high predictability sentences but poorer than normal on low predictability sentences. When the sentence-understanding task was made more difficult (i.e., 0 dB S/N ratio), the LD listeners performed much poorer than normals for both LP and HP sentences. The pattern of SPIN test performance was *not* the same one that had been seen in children. The problems of these LD listeners appeared to be directly associated with their poor auditory discrimination skills. These outcomes occurred even though all except one of the test ears of the LD listeners exhibited normal hearing according to conventional audiologic tests. Therefore, identification of the type of auditory discrimination difficulties exhibited by these individuals will require development of new, more fine-grained diagnostic test procedures.

## DISCUSSION

These results indicate that learning-disabled adults need more acoustic information, or larger acoustical contrasts, than normal adults to achieve equivalent performance levels on speech understanding tasks that utilize synthesized CV syllables. It seems likely that the work and social activities of these LD adults are handicapped in subtle ways by their auditory perceptual problems. Rees (1973) emphasized that the simultaneous occurrence of poor auditory discrimination and poor communication skills does not necessarily imply a "cause and effect" relation. A major question that must remain unanswered *for these individuals* concerns their auditory performance at a younger age. The physiological bases for auditory discrimination and for developmental changes in discrimination are not well understood. Thus, it is not clear why auditory discrimination is poor in these listeners. It is possible that their childhood auditory performance (had it been measured) would have been poorer than performance observed for normal 6-year-olds, and that their rate of auditory development has paralleled the rate for normals (i.e., their auditory performance improved as they grew older, but remained poorer than normal). This possibility is intuitively attractive since abnormal auditory discrimination during their early childhood years might help explain some of these individuals' learning problems. Another possibility is that, had these LD adults been tested at an early age, they would have shown auditory perceptual performance comparable to that of normal children, but their auditory perceptual performance failed to improve as they grew older. Under this alternative, one might conjecture that some aspect of their learning disabilities prevented the expected developmental improvements.

Available data do not permit selection between these hypotheses concerning the time course of auditory perceptual development in these LD listeners. Only longitudinal study in which the same individuals are tested periodically can answer these questions—and it is possible that the situation differs across LD individuals. Research is presently underway to test these hypotheses.

To take a "devil's advocate" stance, one might argue that the auditory perceptual processing of these LD adult listeners actually followed a normal course, but that it was attentional difficulties that prevented them from performing normally on these tests. This hypothesis cannot be rejected on the basis of these data, but there are several arguments against it. At the level of voluntary cooperation, all LD adult subjects readily learned the tasks, gave evidence of deep concentration, and expressed a desire to perform well. Attentional difficulties could not explain, for example, why the "ba–da" JND for SK was within the range of values expected for normal 6-year-olds while SK was unable to discriminate [d*a*] and [g*a*]. Furthermore, the high predictability and low predictability sentences of the SPIN test are randomly intermixed. Thus, it is unlikely that attentional problems could explain the results for subjects who performed with 96–100 percent accuracy on the HP sentences but very poorly on the LP sentences at S/Ns of +4 and +10 dB.

Another question that is not presently answerable is whether or not training in auditory discrimination skills, using stimuli with small acoustic differences (such as the continuum of synthesized syllables used here) would enhance auditory perception of words and sentences for learning-disabled persons. Furthermore, it is not known whether training would need to be accomplished during childhood years or whether it could also be helpful to learning-disabled adults.

These data represent initial study of learning-disabled subjects and raise more questions than they answer. Research is continuing and it is hoped that, within several years, additional information pertinent to these issues will be available.

## ACKNOWLEDGMENT

Appreciation is expressed to the learning-disabled young adults who participated in these experiments and to Laura Lyons Bailet who assisted in collecting some of the data. This research was funded, in part, by grants from NSF and NIH (NINCDS). The manuscript was completed in 1982.

## REFERENCES

Bilger, R.C. Nuetzel, J.M., Rabinowitz, W.M., & Rzeczkowski, C. Standardization of a test of speech perception in noise. *Journal of Speech and Hearing Research*, 1984, *27*, 32–48.

Borden, G.J., & Harris, K.S. (Eds.), *Speech science primer*. Baltimore: Williams & Wilkins Co., 1980.

Eisenson, J. *Aphasia in children*. New York: Harper & Row, 1972.

Elliott, L.L. Performance of children aged nine to seventeen years on a test of speech intelligibility in noise using sentences with controlled word predictability. *Journal of the Acoustical Society of America*, 1979, *66*, 651–753.

Elliott, L.L., & Katz, D.R. Children's pure tone detection. *Journal of the Acoustical Society of America*, 1980c, *67*, 343–344.

Elliott, L.L., & Katz, D.R. *The Northwestern University-Children's Perception of Speech (NU-CHIPS) test*. Auditec of St. Louis, 1980a.

Elliott, L.L., & Katz, D.R. *Development of a new children's speech discrimination test*. Auditec of St. Louis, 1980b.

Elliott, L.L., Longinotti, C., Clifton, L., & Meyer, D. Detection and identifiction thresholds for consonant-vowel syllables. *Perception and Psychophysics*, 1981a, *30*, 411–416.

Elliott, L.L. Longinotti, C., Meyer, D., Raz. I., & Zucker, K. Developmental differences in identifying and discriminating CV syllables. *Journal of the Acoustical Society of America*, 1981b, *70*, 669–677.

Kalikow, D.N., Stevens, K.N., & Elliott, L.L. Development of a test of speech intelligibility in noise using sentence materials with controlled word predictability. *Journal of the Acoustical Society of America*, 1977, *61*, 1337–1351.

Katz, J. (Ed.), *Handbook of clinical audiology* (3rd Ed.). Baltimore: Williams & Wilkins, 1985.

Levitt, H. Transformed up-down methods in psychoacoustics. *Journal of the Acoustical Society of America*, 1971, *40*, 467–477.

Lubert, N. Auditory perceptual impairments in children with specific language disorders: A review of the literature. *Journal of Speech and Hearing Disorders*, 1981, *46*, 3–9.

Monnin, L.M., & Huntington, D.A. Relationship of articulation defects to speech-sound identification. *Journal of Speech and Hearing Research*, 1974, *17*, 352–366.

Pickett, J.M. (Ed.), *The sounds of speech communication*. Baltimore: University Park Press, 1980.

Raz, I., & Wightman, F.L. Adaptive estimation of phoneme boundaries and selective adaptation for speech. *Perception and Psychophysics*, 1984, *36*, 21–24.

Rees, N.S. Auditory processing factors in language disorders: The view from Procrustes' bed. *Journal of Speech and Hearing Disorders*, 1973, *38*, 304–315.

Rintleman, W.F. (Ed.), *Hearing assessment*. Baltimore: University Park Press, 1979.

Strange, W., & Broen, P.A. The relationship between perception and production of /w/, /r/ and /l/ by three-year-old children. *Journal of Experimental Child Psychology*, 1981, *31*, 81–102.

Tallal, P., Stark. R., Kallman, C., & Mellits, D. A reexamination of some nonverbal perceptual abilities of language-impaired and normal children as a function of age and sensory modality. *Journal of Speech and Hearing Research*, 1981, *24*, 351–358.

Yoneshige, Y., & Elliott, L. Pure-tone sensitivity and ear canal pressure at threshold in children and adults. *Journal of the Acoustical Society of America*, 1981, *70*, 1272–1276.

Zlatin, M.A., & Koenigsknecht, R.A. Development of the voicing contrast: A comparison of voice onset time in stop perception and production. *Journal of Speech and Hearing Research*, 1976, *19*, 93–111.

# 8

# Problems of Conceptualization and Language: Evidence from Definitions

Bonnie E. Litowitz

Problems of language and conceptualization are prevalent in young adults with learning disabilities. The exact nature of these problems, however, is often elusive and difficult to characterize. This chapter addresses one point of interface between language and conceptualization in this population, namely, definition-making. The following questions are raised: Do young adults with learning disabilities know how to define words? Do they differ in this ability from the non-learning disabled? If so, what is the nature of the differences? Before addressing these questions, however, some shared background information on semantics and on definitions will need to be established.

We assume that to know a language is to have acquired the particular phonological, lexical, and syntactic subsystems of one's linguistic community and to be able to use this knowledge in appropriate ways. We may say, then, that both linguistic structures and functions are involved. The acquired linguistic structures, if they are not vacuous imitations, convey meanings between members of the language community. When we speak of meanings, it is necessary to distinguish several kinds of different aspects. There are utterance meanings, sentence meanings, and lexical or word meanings (Lyons, 1977). In considering definitions, we will focus on lexical or word meanings (i.e., vocabulary), although how words function in sentences and utterances cannot always be easily separated from other aspects of meaning.

The questions arise: How can we assess meaning? How can we determine how this verbal, semantic knowledge is organized? Since we cannot simply look into the mind, we must judge knowledge on the basis of behavioral responses to specific tasks. Popular paradigms used in the research literature have been

ADULTS WITH LEARNING DISABILITIES
ISBN 0-8089-1795-1

sorting tasks and verbal explanations, word association tasks and definitions.* Each type of task makes a different demand on the underlying semantic information; that is, the same verbal knowledge may be used differently depending upon the task (Anglin, 1977; Litowitz & Novy, 1984; Nelson, 1978). Therefore, it is important in every case to understand the specificity of the task requirements in order to see how these affect responses. We will return to the specific demands of the task of defining, which is our concern here, after a brief discussion of the underlying semantic organization.

Many theorists hypothesize that semantic knowledge is organized in large networks that are partitioned into semantic domains or fields and connected by relations. For example, animals form one such domain in which *tigers* and *lions* are related to *animals* by the relation of taxonomy (or superordination); *tigers* and *lions* are related to each other as coordinates (or cohyponyms), and so forth, until all information is interconnected. Researchers propose as few as 3 and as many as 50 possible semantic relations (Evens, Litowitz, Markowitz, Smith, & Werner, 1980). Much current research in developmental semantics consists of studies in the order and sequence of acquisition of these relations and their interface with other aspects of logical, cognitive thought (Heidenheimer, 1978; Litowitz, 1981; Sordon, 1980; Steinberg & Anderson, 1975).

For the purpose of the present discussion on definitions we will be most interested in the following semantic relations:

1. Taxonomy—"a ball is a kind of object"
2. Synonymy—"work is labor"
3. Antonymy—"Black is the opposite of white"
4. Modification†—"Bread is soft, white, edible"

The first three of these, taxonomy, synonymy, and antonymy, have been called logical relations by Riegel (1970) who suggests that they follow developmentally such infralogical relations as modification, parts and wholes, locations, and others.

The definitional task is a purely verbal, metalinguistic task that requires that language be used (the definition) to talk about language (the cue word) in the following, very specific form: (1) only verbal responses are appropriate, e.g., not gestural or ostensive responses; (2) language used must be neither semantically empty, i.e., "thing," "stuff," nor deictic words such as "this," "that," "there," which rely on the real world situation for interpretation; and (3) only socially shared information is appropriate, e.g., not idiosyncratic, personal associations to the cue word. In addition, the prototype of good definitional form in western culture is that of an Aristotelian definition: genus plus differentiae. For example:

*For discussions of these methods as they apply to learning disabled school-age children (7 and 9), see Harris, 1979; Novy, 1981. For a general discussion of conceptualization and memory, see Litowitz, Harris & Newman, 1981.

†For the purposes of the present discussion, distinctions within modification will not be drawn, such as between perceptual attributes and functions (see Bruner, 1973; Novy, 1981).

**Table 8-1**
Range, Mean, Median scale Scores of 20 Young Adults from WAIS

| | Range | Mean | Median |
|---|---|---|---|
| Full Scale IQ | 86–127 | 106.5 | 108.5 |
| Performance IQ | 76–124 | 105.2 | 106.5 |
| Verbal IQ | 88–127 | 107.1 | 108.0 |
| Vocabulary | 8–16 | 11.7 | 12.0 |
| Simularities | 8–16 | 12.4 | 13.0 |
| Comprehension | 6–19 | 12.3 | 12.0 |
| Information | 7–14 | 10.8 | 10.5 |

a lion is an animal (genus) that roars, has a mane, lives in Africa, etc. (differentiae) (Litowitz, 1977). The differentiae may include perceptual, functional, or other modifying information, which alone comprises younger children's definitions. What distinguishes adult, more mature, "better" definitions is the use of a genus (or superordinate or class) name before the modifying information.

In terms of the semantic relations mentioned earlier, definitions provide semantic information organized by taxonomic (genus) and modification (differentiae) relations. Other logical relations, such as synonymy and antonymy, are also used in adult definitions. Adept definers possess a set formulaic approach to defining which older children in acquiring, approach with "pseudo-Aristotelian" definitions. For example, "*X* is something that Y or "*X* is a thing that *Y*." As we shall see, these forms can come perilously close to semantic emptiness (see (2) above), which is averted only by including additional modifying information. "Something"/"thing"/ etc. can serve as place holders for future superordinates in children whose semantic knowledge is not fully elaborated (Litowitz, 1977) or, equally, as we shall see, as circumlocutionary devices when retrieval of more specific terms is blocked.

With the above shared background, we can now turn to look at the definitions of some young adults with learning disabilities. The data came from 20 young adults (ages 17 to 35; mean 23.7; median 22.5) who were chosen from a total of 93 persons seen in the Northwestern University Learning Disabilities program. Standardized test score information for this group is shown in Table 8-1.

Table 8-1 indicates full scale WAIS scores, performance and verbal WAIS scale scores, as well as the following subtests scale scores; similarities, comprehension, and information. It is interesting to note that full scale scores on the WAIS are consistent with both performance and verbal scale scores. In addition, there is great uniformity across subtest scores for this group, with only the information subtest scale scores being slightly lower. Comparisons of these scores with those of the total clinical young adult population (N = 93) reveals that these young adults are quite typical of the total population seen at the Northwestern clinic. In sum, they are at least of average, and often higher, intelligence. They have at least average, and often better, verbal abilities as measured across several subtests. The vocabulary subtest involves definitions that have already been discussed. In contrast, verbal similarities offer a more controlled, structured task where semantic relational information is specifically focused. Studies with children have shown that this form is relatively easy even when children do not have superordinate information (Litowitz, 1981; Sordon, 1980). Interestingly, although the range on the similarities subtest is the same as on the vocabulary subtest that involved definitions (8–16), the mean and median are slightly higher. Scale across on the information and comprehension subtests corroborate the other scores, indicating that this population has considerable, and certainly adequate, verbal knowledge.

In addition to the standardized tests, these 20 young adults were asked to define 10 words both orally and in writing. (Presentations in the two modes were separated in time.) The ten words in Figure 8-1 were chosen as being common working vocabulary, available to even young children. All words are among the most common on the various measures found in the Teacher's Word Book (Thorndike & Lorge, 1972), and are suggested as appropriate for grades 1 and 2. Unlike the words on the WAIS vocabulary subtest, which are distinguished partially by their decreasing frequency in the adult vocabulary, the ten words on this list were selected to represent linguistic dimensions such as count versus mass noun, deictic versus nondeictic verbs, gradable adjectives and so forth. These differences among words will not be discussed here; rather, the definitions to all ten words will be analyzed.

Unlike the vocabulary subtest on the WAIS, which is scored on a three-point scale (0, 1, 2) according to such criteria as "good synonym" or "major function," definitions on the ten word list were scored as to the semantic relations evidenced in the definitions: taxonomy, modification, synonymy, and antonymy. Additional analyses of the responses were made, which will be explained in the discussion below.

Results of looking at semantic relations in these definitions are summarized in Table 8-2. By far the most common semantic relation used was taxonomy. The rank orders of percentages of use show that written responses were "better" in that more logical relations were used. In oral responses, the second most frequent (but only 7 percent) type of definition used a general noun as place holder (θ) such as "thing," "that." The θ response category is differentiated from more specific taxonomic responses (T) such as "food." "Wh" responses to definitions provide a whole experience, e.g., "when you do *x* or *y*," "Where *x* or *y* is." These forms, which I have called one type of hypothetical definition (Litowitz, 1981), are common in young children but are usually supplanted by the more preferred formulae in adults. X indicates defeat responses, e.g., "I don't know." Gestures, defeat responses and those responses that, although they use a semantic relation, are nonetheless wrong, were totalled; these comprise the

NAME ______________________ AGE ______________________
DATE ______________________ GRADE ______________________

I am going to ask you to define some words. I'll say a word to you and then you tell me what the word means.
"What is the definition of ______________?
"What does ______________ mean?"

1. ball ______________________________________________
2. break ______________________________________________
3. give ______________________________________________
4. thumb ______________________________________________
5. sell ______________________________________________
6. black ______________________________________________
7. work ______________________________________________
8. milk ______________________________________________
9. dirty ______________________________________________
10. think ______________________________________________

**Figure 8-1.** Words for Litowitz definition task.

**Table 8-2**
Percentages of Responses of Semantic Relations on Definitions—Oral and Written

| Oral | | Written | |
|---|---|---|---|
| Taxonomy | 73 | Taxonomy | 77 |
| Errors | 7 | Antonymy | 7 |
| θ—Placeholder | 7 | Synonymy | 6 |
| Synonymy | 5 | Modification | 5 |
| Modification | 5 | Errors | 5 |
| Wh—Experience | 5 | θ—Placeholder | 4 |
| Antonymy | 4 | Wh—Experience | 3 |
| X—Defeat | 2 | | |
| Gesture | 1 | | |

ERRORS percentage. Superimposed on the rank orderings of Table 8-2, there were more errors than all nontaxonomic responses in oral definitions, but less than several nontaxonomic relations for written responses. Note that these written definitional responses tended to use fewer general nouns or hypothetical forms.

In general, one can say that the written definitions are an improvement over their oral counterparts in terms of both relations used and diminished frequency of errors. This same direction of improvement is seen in the non-learning disabled population. In response to one of our primary questions—Do young adults with learning disabilities know how to define words?—we can answer affirmatively, essentially reiterating in a different manner what the vocabulary subtest scores would suggest. Furthermore, many of the responses from the young adults show considerable metalinguistic awareness and abilities. For example, in these data there are self-corrections and metastatements (Clark, 1978): "____, no ____," "I want to say opposite of receiving but that's not a definition," "a verb/adjective ____." Some definitions begin by naming the part of speech (grammatical class) to which the cue word belongs: "Do you mean the noun or the verb ____?" The taxonomic relation is lexically noted for nouns by "____ is a kind/type of ____" ("____ is a *part* of ____" for *thumb*) and for verbs by "*to* ____" or "an action/state/process/act of ____." Antonyms are marked by "not ____" or "opposite of ____." Verb superordinates used included "do," "use," "make," "give," "get," and "present." As one would predict noun superordinates are even more diversified (Miller, 1978): substance, object, liquid, nutrient, beverage, digit, protein, finger, dough, toil, product, food, trade, secretion, effort, endeavor, labor, appendage, drink, exchange, absence, presence, phalanges.

One would expect that the answer to the second of our initial questions, then, would be that the definitions of young adults with learning disabilities do not differ from those of their peers. But that is not the case. They do differ and it is necessary to explore our third question—What is the nature of those differences?—to illustrate the problems.

First of all, adults with good verbal skills should be able to use those skills to define adequately all of the words on a list as simple as this one. Certainly, there should be no errors, let alone defeats or gesture responses. Even "wh" hypothetical responses are surprising. Of the 7 percent oral errors, 3 percent are the result of gestures or defeat but the other 4 percent are due to errors when semantic relations are provided. Of the 5 percent errors in written definitions, all are due to those with semantic relations, since there were no gestures or defeat responses. The following examples illustrate this type of error:

sell—to sell something, sold at a price
dirty—a thing which is full of dirt
dirty—something dirty
give—to give is a gesture of friendship to someone
give—to give someone something is to give someone something

give—do good, receiving; to do good for someone
give—to forfeit an object or feeling
work—the opposite of lazy
dirty—is a substance that stain (sic) temporarily (sic) or permanently. It is a substance that does not belong where it lies.
dirty—an object covered with earth

How shall we interpret these errors? It seems as if, for some of these young adults, knowledge of the definitional formulae is very strong so that the form is present even when the correct content cannot be supplied. Verbs may be formally marked by "to ____" but no useful information is given; the word is simply put into a sentence or phrase or the wrong information is given. For example: To forfeit is *to give* over (or lose) but *to give* is not to forfeit; one sense of earth is dirt but not necessarily what is implied in *dirty*. In some cases the definitional form is stiffly imposed, yielding a stilted response reminiscent of bureaucratese. For example:

sell—a verb for promoting products to other persons
dirty—a state of having a foreign substance present that discolors article of central interest
work—the effort used to produce or destroy something in accordance with one thoughts (sic)
milk—the food whereby babies are fed
dirty—something dirty is some material that either stain or damage (sic) which doesn't belong in the place or environment

Support for the interpretation that these definitions may signal retrieval problems comes from the frequency in oral definitions of general nouns (θ). These generic nouns ("thing") keep the place in definitions without providing necessary, specific information. These do not necessarily result in wrong definitions but, rather, in too poorly specified or overly general content. The following examples illustrate definitions that are underspecified:

work—somewhere you go in the morning
bread—you eat it with food
work—something which must be done, being helpful
work—doing something
black—a color
bread—starch food
bread—cooked dough
bread—an eatable made of dough
work—labor
work—toil

Such unelaborated responses do not differentiate the cue word adequately from other words, e.g., bread from cake or cookies, black from white, work from other things one does. Equally poor are the overly specific or personal definitions that one would expect to have been long since given up by this age group. For example:

dirty—when you roll around in mud
give—when you hand a kid something

It is not clear if these definers do not appreciate the degree of detail needed in definitions or if these overly general or too specific responses are due to word-finding and other retrieval difficulties.

It seems, then, that some definers have information but cannot easily retrieve it. Within this general problem type, responses may vary. There may be no information given (dirty—something dirty), the wrong information (dirty—a thing which is full of dirt), or information at an inappropriate level of organization (dirty—an object covered with earth). The definitional form, if it is known, can become a circumlocutionary device that allows the definer to answer in an appropriate form even when appropriate content cannot be retrieved.

This group of responses that suffer from good form but lack of specificity, lack of information, or too specific information can be contrasted to another group of responses that lack form but provide information in spurts and starts often interrupted by pauses. These responses seem to spill out information about the cue word without selecting among the bits and pieces and without imposing a definitional formula as an organizational strategy. For example:

work—is . . . can be in your job, any type of—if it could be mentally or physically
milk—all types of milk, it's not man . . . Well, I think it's man-made now, a liquid
black—a . . . a shade . . . isn't a color, that is very dark, that is made by a mixture of . . . that's grey . . . I forgot how you get black.

Some definitions of this type are merely lists of attributes without any attempt at connections. Information is given but any organization must be provided by the listener or reader. For example:

ball—throw, bounce, play with
bread—eat, money, flour, it takes flour
milk—drink, vitamins
bread—it's got crust, it's got white in the middle and it's edible. You can eat it. It's made out of whole wheat.
bread—food, flour
dirty—unclean, not washed, stinky, smelly—has odor or appearance on the object.
bread—is made of wheat. It can vary in color from dark to light. It has to be baked.

Some responses are recipes:

bread—materials are needed to make bread such as milk, honey, wheat from flour, butter. Mix things together and bake—will result into (sic) bread.

Some definitions start with the beginning of a definitional form but seem to lose their way in a jungle of associations without clearly marked pathways:

give—to have with your possession to hand or physically or to relate verbally to another person.
give—to give um to . . . oh wow . . . to take something and bring it to someone as a present.
think—to-uh-is to uh . . uh . . . oh man . . to think is to uh. . . I'm thinking. I can't think of a different word for it. To think is to think. To delve into your mind. To get different feelings—emotions. To think is to think—I can't do it.

Whether these responses result from retrieval or organizational difficulties is not clear from these data alone. It does seem to be the case, however, that these definers, unlike the others above, cannot use the definitional form to present even inappropriate information. They seem overwhelmed by information without specified connections such as those between what an object is made of, looks like, is used for, is a kind of, and so forth. Both kinds of problems can lead to circumlocutions, but these may be of different origins.

A third difference between these definers and the non-learning disabled are evident on the written definitions. While, as stated earlier, the written definitions are semantically better (i.e., have higher-order relations and less errors), they are almost all filled with writing errors. When one looks at the written definitions, it is hard to believe most are written by adults. Handwriting is poor and there are many spelling errors.

In the definitions shown in Figure 8-2, as actually written for this task, spelling errors are mixed with word substitutions, e.g., "manual" for "mammal," "flower" for "flour," which may be indicative of difficulties in retrieving lexical items from memory.

In examples shown in Figure 8-2, a verb replaces a noun, e.g., "laughed" for "liquid," "absents" for "absence," which may indicate problems with derivational morphology attributable to the retrieval of lexical items from memory.

Morphosyntactic inflectional markers are omitted or mistaken in many cases. For example, in Figure 8-3, "-ing" has either been contracted to an added "g" or part of a syllable has been omitted from "contain."

In other examples in Figure 8-3, "-ing" is used instead of "-en" (giving/given) and "-ed" is omitted (drop/dropped); inflectional endings may be cropped as in the loss of "t" on the superlative (-est) or third person (-s) verb agreement; prepositional errors, either too many or wrong usage, also occur.

Lastly, difficulties in starting and carrying through a written definition, which are similar to oral formulation problems, are evident in the final examples in Figure 8-3.

In general, then, while written definitions by this population display the availability of adequate semantic knowledge, they are characterized by mechanical and organizational errors.

| Word | |
|---|---|
| milk | WHITE EATTABLE LIguiED |
| give | oppicit of toke to prosent to- |
| ball | a round cirlclie shape |
| milk | In a kind of pratine we get from variou anmides |
| milk | nevuhmext given to most young manual |
| bread | A LOAF OF EATABLE FLOWER |
| milk | White Laughed from a cow OR other namol to feed thieR young |
| black | Black is the absents of color. |

**Figure 8-2.** Written definitions of learning disabled adults.

## SUMMARY

The ten common words on this list have been given to some graduate students in the Northwestern University Learning Disabilities Program, young adults whose responses can be compared to those of young adults with learning disabilities. Without presenting a detailed account of graduate student responses, the major differences are:

—there are no defeat, gesture, or erroneous responses.
—written responses were more similar to oral responses, although any disparity is in the written over oral direction (as it is for the clinical population).
—all responses, oral and written, are well formed, not overly general and supplying all the necessary information to relate the cue word to similar words and to differentiate it from others.

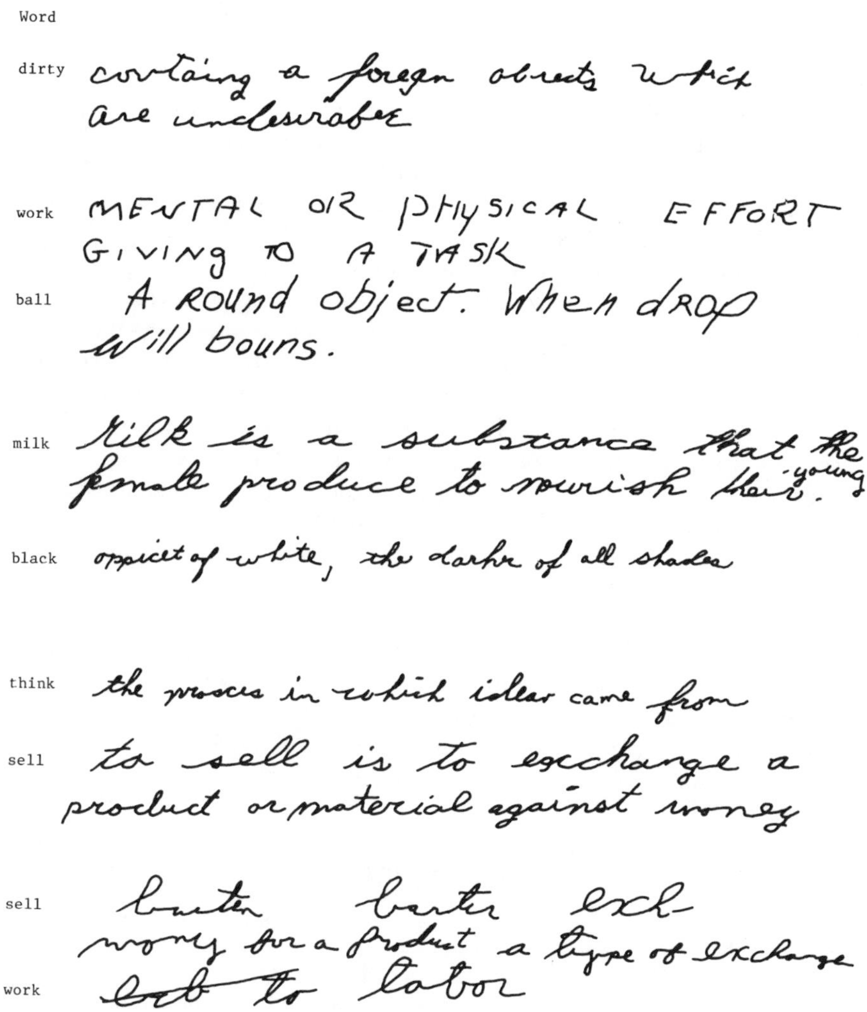

Word
dirty containg a foregn orbrets which are undesirabe
work MENTAL OR PHYSICAL EFFORT GIVING TO A TASK
ball A ROUND object. When DROP will bouns.
milk Milk is a substance that the female produce to nourish their young.
black oppicet of white, the darkn of all shades
think the proces in which ideas came from
sell to sell is to exchange a product or material against money
sell barter barter exch money for a product a type of exchange
work to labor


**Figure 8-3.** Written definitions of learning disabled adults.

Two further points need to be made. First, one cannot say that the responses of this learning disabled population are simply the same as younger, less mature definers, that is like the graduate students at an earlier stage. There are few purely functional definitions, so characteristic of early school-age definers (Al-Issa, 1969); the overwhelming percentage of definitions (82 percent oral; 90 percent written) utilize logical semantic relations. Secondly, one cannot predict poor performance on these definitions from standardized test scores. In other words, it is *not* the case that persons at the lower end of the standardized score ranges account for all, or even most, of the difficulties that have been described above.

The essence of a definition is to locate uniquely a particular word in semantic space by specifying its relations to other points in that conceptual map. The definitional form is a specific metalinguistic device whose function is to aid a speaker in accomplishing this task in order to transmit this information to another. The definitional task, therefore, can provide useful information for the assessment of language and conceptualization problems.

The population of young adults with learning disabilities discussed here had difficulties in extracting appropriate information from semantic memory to use in definitions and in using the definitional form to help structure semantic information for this task. In addition, while writing may provide a slower approach to this task as well as visual-motor feedback for monitoring performance, problems with writing per se may complicate this task for many in this population. Nevertheless, Olson (1977) has indicated the importance of definitions for written, versus oral, communication. And the use of definitions to improve organization and retrieval in both oral and written communication should be considered.

In summary, we can see that while these young adults have good verbal intelligence and knowledge, as evidenced on standardized test scores, these scores do not reveal subtle difficulties in both oral and written language performance. Only careful analyses of specific tasks that require retrieval and use of verbal knowledge can give us the necessary insights into these problems, which will enable us to provide meaningful assistance to these young adults.

## REFERENCES


Al-Issa, I. The development of word definition in children. *Journal of Genetic Psychology*, 1969, *114*, 25–28.

Anglin, J. *Word, object and conceptual development*. New York: Norton & Co., 1977.

Bruner, J. *Beyond the information given*. New York: Norton & Co., 1973.

Clark, E. Awareness of language: Some evidence from what children say and do. In Sinclair, Jarvella & Levelt (Eds.), *The child's conception of language*. New York: Springer-Verlag, 1978.

Evens, M., Litowitz, B., Markowitz, J., Smith, R. & Werner, O. *Lexical-semantic relations: A comparative survey*. Edmonton: Linguistic Research, Inc., 1980.

Harris, G. Classification skills in normally achieving and learning disabled 7- and 9-year-old boys: A study in conceptualization. Unpublished doctoral dissertation, Northwestern University, 1979.

Heidenheimer, P. A comparison of the roles of exemplar, action, coordinate and superordinate relations in the semantic processing of 4- and 5-year-old children. *Journal of Experimental Child Psychology*, 1978, *25*, 143–159.

Litowitz, B. Learning to make definitions. *Journal of Child Language*, 1977, *4*, 289–304.

Litowitz, B. Hypothetical speech: A developmental perspective. *Journal of Psycholinguistic Research*, 1981, *10*, 289–312.

Litowitz, B., Harris, G., & Newman, D. Studies of conceptualization and memory in learning-disabled children. *Learning Disabilties: An Audio Journal for Continuing Education*, (5), 1981.

Litowitz, B., & Novy, F. Expression of the part-whole semantic relation by 3– to 12-year-old children. *Journal of Child Language*, 1984, *11*, 159–178.

Lyons, J. *Semantics*. (1) (2), London: Cambridge Press, 1977.

Miller, G. Some relations among words. In Halle, Bresnan, & Miller (Eds.), *Linguistic Theory and Psychological Reality*. Cambridge, Mass: MIT Press, 1978.

Nelson, K. Semantic development and the development of semantic memory. In Nelson (Ed.), *Children's Language*, (1), New York: Gardner Press, 1978.

Novy, F. Categorical reasoning and semantic organization in learning-disabled and normal seven-year-old children. Unpublished doctoral dissertation, Northwestern University, 1981.

Olson, D. From utterance to text: The bias of language in speech and writing. *Harvard Educational Review*, 1977, *47*, 257–281.

Riegel, K. The language acquisition process: A reinterpretation of selected research findings. In Goulet & Baltes (Eds.), *Life-span-developmental psychology: Research and theory*. New York: Academic Press, 1970.

Sordon, S. Lexical relations, inference, and word meaning acquistion in four-, six-, and eight-year-old children. Unpublished doctoral dissertation, Northwestern University, 1980.

Steinberg, E., & Anderson, R. Hierarchic semantic organization in 6-year-olds. *Journal of Experimental Child Psychology*, 1975, *19*, 544–553.

Thorndike, E.L. & Lorge, I. *The teacher's word book of 30,000 words*. New York: Teacher's College Press, Columbia University, 1972.

Wechsler, D. *Wechsler Adult Intelligence Scale*. New York: The Psychological Corporation, 1955.

# 9

## Reading Disabilities

Doris J. Johnson

Problems related to reading have been noted for centuries. Indeed, whenever alphabets were developed and schooling was required, there were undoubtedly students who did not learn at the expected level or rate. There are, of course, many reasons for reading problems including mental deficiency, sensory impairments, poor instruction, limited motivation, and specific learning disabilities. It is the latter group that is our chief concern. Historically, this population has been labelled in various ways. Some professionals used the term "congenital word blindness" (Hinshelwood, 1900; Morgan, 1896). Others use "dyslexia" (Bender, 1975; Benton, 1980; Boder, 1973; Critchley, 1971; Hallgren, 1950; Mattis, French, & Rapin, 1975; Myklebust, 1954; Pavlidis & Miles, 1981; Vellutino, 1983). Yet many prefer more general terms such as specific reading disability (Bakker & Satz, 1970; Herman, 1959).

Although similar in many respects, disabled readers are a diverse group. They differ, not only in level of achievement, background knowledge, cognitive skills, and language proficiency but in their responses to instruction. While attempts have been made to isolate a single, underlying deficit such as perception or sequencing, it is unlikely one will be found because of the complexity of the reading process and the human mind. Therefore, the term "dyslexias" has been suggested to indicate the heterogeneity of the population (Wolf, 1984).

In our early studies of dyslexia we defined reading as a visual form of language used to represent oral language as well as underlying concepts, experiences, and ideas. We were interested in relationships between nonverbal cognition, auditory language, visual processes, integrative functions and reading. Language impaired children showed considerable variability in reading performance (Johnson & Myklebust, 1967). Those with auditory receptive problems often learned to decode but did not comprehend. Those with

ADULTS WITH LEARNING DISABILITIES
ISBN 0-8089-1795-1

expressive disorders could sometimes read silently but not orally because of word retrieval, sequencing or motor planning problems. Others with no obvious auditory disorders were unable to segment oral language into words, syllables, and phonemes. As a result, they learned whole words but could not generalize from familiar to unfamiliar words.

Some had visual-spatial problems and tended to reverse, invert, or transpose letters and words, particularly when writing. Many had difficulty learning sight words.

In addition, Myklebust described people with "inner language" and generalized meaning disorders (Myklebust, 1978). While their problems interfered with reading comprehension they were much more pervasive.

During the last decade many investigators have done extensive subgroup analyses with dyslexics. The results vary, however, with their theoretical orientation and test batteries. Several neuropsychologists identified subgroups on the basis of learning problems that co-occur with dyslexia (Denckla, 1977; Lyon, 1983; Mattis, French & Rapin, 1975; Petrauskas & Rourke, 1979; Satz & Morris, 1981). They assessed cognitive and linguistic processes such as phonemic discrimination, auditory memory, word retrieval, or visual perception and did factor or cluster analyses to identify readers with similar characteristics. Most found poor readers with more auditory language disorders than visual deficits. For example, of the three subtypes identified by Mattis, French and Rapin (1975), two groups had verbal disorders while a third had visual-spatial problems.

Other investigators focused directly on the reading errors of dyslexics. Boder, for example, identified three subgroups on the basis of reading and spelling mistakes (Boder, 1971, 1973). Her dysphonetic group included those with auditory problems whereas the dyseidetic group had visual difficulties that interfered with sight word recognition. The mixed group had both auditory and visual processing problems.

Researchers also analyzed good and poor readers' performance on simultaneous and sequential processing tasks (Das, Kirby, & Jarman, 1979; Kaufman & Kaufman, 1983; Leong, 1976–77). Most found both modes of information processing are needed for reading.

Doehring and Hoshko (1977) and Doehring et al. (1981) used a combination of both reading and nonreading tasks to identify subgroups. Since then, Doehring (1984) discussed several limitations of subtyping research and said we need more comprehensive models based on both theory and experience. Such models should highlight the complex interactions needed for reading. (Lesgold & Perfetti, 1981). Rumelhart (1977) also emphasized the simultaneous, interactive, parallel, perceptual cognitive processes involved in reading.

These multiple interactions were obvious when working with the slow, laborious processing of learning disabled adults. Most were unable to abstract the multiple rule systems needed for reading and could not monitor for phonology, syntax, and meaning simultaneously. They, like children we studied, seemed "overloaded". (Johnson & Myklebust, 1967).

Many had not automatized the rule systems for oral language and could not make good predictions while reading. Their lack of linguistic awareness and flexibility was very evident. Equally evident was their inconsistent performance. Unlike people who routinely substitute one verb form or plural rule for another, they made fewer rule governed errors. Their errors increased with task complexity reflecting a lack of automaticity and self regulatory skills. These difficulties are apparent in the written statements of their problems.

## PERSONAL DESCRIPTIONS OF READING PROBLEMS

Letters and discussions with the adults indicated reading disorders rarely occur in isolation. Many were conscious of difficulties with oral language, comprehension, or memory, and had remarkable insights into their problems and strategy use. They, like Miles' dyslexics (1983), had "plenty to say", but their faulty language and writing is illustrated in the descriptions below. Headings were selected to highlight patterns of problems they described.

### Generalized Language Problems

Although many requested help in reading, they were aware of other needs. For example, a 26-year-old woman wrote a 2 page letter filled with language errors and inconsistent use of upper and lower case letters. The following sentences capture the essence of her disability. Problems were noted in kindergarten.

> "I could Like to get iN NORTHwestern UNIV. LeARNINg disable SCHOOL. I tHINK that it WILL Help ME TO SPEAKER + READ BetteR."

She had problems with phonemic discrimination, comprehension, memory, syntax, articulation, and visual-spatial orientation. Despite her reading and communication disorders, she was holding two jobs. Both employers made accommodations because of her conscientious approach to work.

A man was equally concerned about his global language disorders, yet he achieved a Verbal I.Q. of 110 and a Performance IQ of 107. He wrote:

> "I have troubles with my speech, I have trouble saiding polsyllable words. I don't know how to make certain sounds, and I dont' say the endings, of words. I fined I have trouble hearing all the sound in works when some one speech to me. I also had trouble with my reading and writing. As I'm reading I nay but on a different endings on the words or I may said the wrong word altogether. This holds true for my writing as well, but I have a more trouble because of spelling and I seem to alway try to hurry through what every I am writing. I also lack confiness in my writing, but I feel this will past as I get better in it. One last thing is my menory.

In the short run my menory is very weak. I forget what has been said to me within the first few moments, but as time go by my memory become stable and I don't forget as much."

He had difficulty with phonemic discrimination, articulation, auditory analysis, memory, decoding, spelling, and linguistic awareness. His spelling errors, particularly those related to morpho-graphemic rules and revisualization, were more evident in context than on dictated tests.

## Problems Related to Oral Expressive Language

Several adults explained how their word retrieval and pronunciation problems interfered with oral reading. A woman with superior intelligence said, "I picture the meaning in my mind but sometimes I can't say the word." When looking at the word "squirrel" she said, "he's brown—he's going up a tree—he's got a nut—it's squirrel!" Occasionally she pantomimed an action to elicit a word.

People with auditory sequencing disorders often defined words they could not pronounce correctly. For instance, when shown the word "anonymous" one said, "it's when people give something without telling who they are".

Another with a history of severe expressive language and motor planning problems reported,

> "I never understood why teachers always made me read outloud. I can get the meaning from arkikles if I skim it and look for main words to get the gist. When I read aloud I can't hear things right and it mixes up the meaning."

Many had good comprehension despite their retrieval and phonological disorders.

## Problems Related to Visual Processing

While the majority had verbal disorders, several adults described their visual-spatial problems. A 21 year old wrote:

> "Since I have started school I have not been able to read or write. I have been told that I invert letter and mumbers I only know left from right from a scar on my right hand. I do some of the same things when I draw."

A man with a similar problem wrote:

> "I reverse words and letters. In writing I'll put hear as haer. In reading I reverse words in sentences."

Another wrote in a combination of mixed upper and lower case—manuscript and cursive letters:

> "My problem as i see it reading like reading Words Backwards or reading a paragraph over again once for twice and remembering what i read. Sometimes

When i Write i write i forget to put down a words or write same one twice. And i sometimes forget What i Write and Read."

His verbal intelligence was 103, performance 109 and full scale 106.

## Multisensory Processing Problems

Reading requires the abstraction and integration of multiple codes from both auditory and visual systems as well as monitoring for meaning, grammar, and phonology. Difficulty with intersensory processing was described in the following way by a college student:

"I think I might have a problem coordinating both my audio and my visual sences. It is very difficult for me to write notes and listen to a professor lecture at the same time."

Another student, concerned about his lack of integration, wrote:

"Sometimes my eyes, mind and mouth don't work together. Just today I noticed 'initiate' but before I thought I said invite."

These disruptions were apparent, particularly in remediation when he spelled words aloud correctly, but simultaneously wrote a different sequence of letters. (e.g. "first"/"frist"). The lack of crossmodal integration and synchrony between systems was also evident in reading, spelling, and mathematics.

## Primary Decoding and Spelling Problems

While most poor readers had some oral language problems others had primary decoding and spelling difficulties. They could not "unlock" the orthographic code. A bright 35-year-old wrote:

"I would like to let you know that I have a read and a spelling problem. I do not know how to sound the letter properly or how to deived a ward in silaboes. This is stoping me to go fether in school but I can not read the books."

Testing indicated difficulty with both syllable and phoneme segmentation as well as phonics. He made significant gains during remediation and eventually started his own business.

## Comprehension Problems

Although decoding problems interfere with comprehension, several adults were concerned specifically about their inability to understand. They learned phonological and orthographic rules but could not understand many words and ideas. As a result their writing reflected semantic errors as illustrated below:

"I have trouble in all my subjects in school. I found out that english is hard enough for me let alone any other language. I found out that comprehension is a big problem with me. My writing ability is not up to my expectations. I feel my math skills are not up too part infact I think I don't have many math skills at all. I can't grasp science at all. I just feel it's way over my head."

His reasoning problems were very obvious on the problem solving task described by Stone in Chapter 5; however, both his verbal and performance intelligence scores were within the average range.

A 29-year-old described his comprehension and memory problems in the following way:

> The more I learn about my problem the more parts of my life I see it affects from watching a movie to talking to a customer. Let me try to describe it to you. If I am reading an article. I subvocalize every word. Sometimes I read it through a few times before it makes sence if it ever does. I feel I can not extract the information from a sentence or paragraph. I do not know how to remember anything except word for word. If I read something to my wife, she can not understand what I am reading. If she reads it to me it makes more sense but it is still hard to understand.

These people are interesting because of their cognitive awareness and strategy use.

## Memory and Reading Speed Problems

Adults with the highest reading scores could decode and comprehend, but speed and retention were major problems. One man wrote:

> I am quite concerned about my inability to read at a good rate and to retain material that my occupation demands. In this area is my main concern. With the tremdous amount of mateiral I must read each daz I find it quite difficult to keep up with what I must know. In turn this reflects upon my professionalisum and may perhaps limit my true potential.

His spelling errors were related to self monitoring and fatigue. Like many others, he commented on the effort and concentration required to complete assignments.

## Coping Strategies

The psychological strain resulting from these problems left many adults feeling discouraged and frustrated. Yet the resilience and drive was clearly evident in a ten page letter from a woman who spent hours recopying it until she felt it was acceptable. The penmanship was excellent. Two paragraphs describing her reading deficiencies are printed below:

> I remember getting out of school still unable to read, determinded to be able to read I started on my own program, first it was a picture magazine and finally being able to read the captions or short sentences under the picture consistency and regularly. Then a regular magazine such as Time. Then all the way thru but slowly. I could give you numberous accounts of various steps and progress. Until fairly recently the dictionary was the most useless book anyone could hand me, now it is the most valuable book I have (I wouldn't think of taking a trip with out my paper back distionary so that when I send postcards their ledgibility are of higher contents besides Jane, Dick Spot and Puff version of the trip.)

> As a child I never was able to read a street sign, I simple got around by various landmarks I set up in my head; the pink house with purple shutters and if they painted the shutters a different color between the time I went and came I was in trouble. i.e. The other side of that coin is when I was in Europe alone I got around much begtter than most people who didn't speak that countries language, I simply reverted back to my childhood method, it was nothing new to me not to understand the language.

She also remembered the early concerns about her mental ability.

> I remember being taken in eight grade down to ______ to be tested for mentally retarded or *slow*. First I had to read paragraphs and underline the answer—my rating came out second grade. Then I had to look at pictures, bloxks or hear words and how are they related etc., I was so fast that they stopped me asking if I had take it before—I had not. All that came out of all that was that I was mentally alright.

And indeed she was. Her Verbal IQ was 126, and Performance 109; however, she had many problems related to auditory perception, reasoning, and linguistic awareness as well as reading.

## ASSESSMENT

The examples above illustrate the need for a comprehensive assessment of oral language, conceptualization, and writing as well as reading. As with all diagnoses, the clinician searches for patterns and bases for problems. Schreiner (1983) says the diagnostician is like a sleuth searching for clues and checking hypotheses. Samuels (1983) compared the clinician to a mechanic looking for defects in many systems when something goes wrong with the automobile. Our objectives were to determine whether the person had a reading problem, to describe the error patterns, and make recommendations for work, schooling, or remediation.

Four types of standardized reading tests and several informal measures were given. These included (1) oral reading of single words, (2) oral reading of context, (3) silent reading vocabulary, and (4) silent passage comprehension. Because of variability in reading levels, identical tests could not be used. However, all adults were given the Wide Range Achievement Test (Jastak & Jastak, 1976) to assess oral reading of single words. Then, depending upon levels of performance, they were given a test such as the Gray Oral (Gray & Robinson, 1967) and two or more comprehension tests listed in the appendix.

Informal tasks were included to assess decoding ability, since standardized tests rarely have enough words with particular orthographic patterns to study rule acquisition. Word lists were prepared to assess the role of organization and structure on performance (e.g., names of fruits, colors, CVC words with the same vowel, etc.). We were interested in the adults' spontaneous search for patterns, use of background knowledge, hypothesis testing, and monitoring. A major objective was to determine whether rules needed to be taught, applied or automatized.

When time permitted, the adults were given familiar and unfamiliar reading material to observe their use of background knowledge. Miscues were analyzed in a manner similar to that of Goodman and Burke (1972) noting which were graphically, semantically, and/or syntactically similar to the target words and which, if any, were self corrected.

The rationale for using both oral and silent reading tasks is based on experience with both children and adults. People with expressive difficulties often read better silently than orally, however, some read aloud to comprehend. Current investigations of brain function such as the brain electrical activity mapping (BEAM) studies of Duffy et al. (1980) may provide further insight into the cognitive and linguistic processing used for various reading tasks (Duane, 1983).

Studies of oral and silent reading have also been done by developmental reading specialists (Allington, 1984; Gilmore & Gilmore, 1968; Spache, 1976; Wells, 1950). Spache says oral and silent reading are similar processes during the first two years of school but later they diverge. When reading silently, we tend to skip words, use context clues, and work more quickly. Oral reading may not reveal either silent or oral comprehension at any school level. Therefore, comprehension is best measured following silent reading. Nevertheless, oral reading provides insights into differences between good and poor readers (Ackerman, Dykman, & Peters, 1977; Clay, 1969; Deno, Marston, Shinn, & Tindal, 1983). The latter group found learning disabled students read aloud more slowly and less accurately than other low-achievers. Ackerman et al. (1977) concluded those with reading disabilities lacked automatic word recognition skills.

Tests of both single words and context were given to observe decoding and use of background knowledge. Context allows more "top-down" or "inside-out" processing (Smith, 1979) whereas reading isolated words requires more specific attention to the orthography. While most daily reading is done in context there are times when individual words must be decoded (e.g., for using a telephone book or an index). Chall (1983) says guessing is appropriate at certain stages of reading development but good decoding is essential for reading specific names and new words.

Tasks were also chosen to study multiple strategy use. Gray (1947) said efficient readers need four basic strategies including (1) word recognition or sight vocabulary, (2) phonetic analysis, (3) structural or morphological analysis, and (4) context. Each of these requires slightly different, but overlapping, cognitive and linguistic skills. Stanovich (1983) defines word recognition as the process of extracting enough information from words so that a location in the mental lexicon is activated. He cites other theorists who suggest both visual and phonological access processes may be activated simultaneously. Phonetic analysis requires visual and auditory analysis and synthesis as well as linguistic awareness. Structural (morphemic) analysis requires more knowledge of the meaning units in language and the ability to identify root words, prefixes, word endings, and suffices. To use context, predictions are made on the basis of previous experience, conceptualization, or language.

Throughout the assessment, efforts were made to observe problem solving, self monitoring, and other strategic behaviors. (Garner, 1983; Markman, 1977; Masson, 1982; Wong, 1982).

Not all the answers to reading behavior lie within the boundaries of a clinic, laboratory, or a test battery. From naturalistic studies one can learn about the poor reader's coping strategies, use of background knowledge to infer word meanings from the environment, and psychological factors such as risk taking, persistence, and reaction to failure. The impact of problems on daily functioning, independence, and work is also apparent.

Reading strategies vary with the context and purpose. (Gibson and Levin, 1975). We read warning signs and directions, scan names in a directory, skim a newspaper or read it in detail; we read for pleasure and study new information to increase knowledge. Each requires slightly different cognitive and linguistic skills. Hence, test results yield limited insight into overall reading behavior.

Obviously we know more about adults who were seen for remediation and diagnostic teaching than those seen only for testing. Nevertheless, there were several opportunities throughout the two days to observe their ability to read signs in the building, follow directions, and use materials in the waiting room. When asked about their ability to acquire information from print the better readers said they read newspapers but the poorest said they skimmed a few ads, items from the sports page, and simpler columns. They guessed at words on signs and menus but the context was not always sufficient to reduce ambiguity. One woman said she knew where to look for meats or vegetables on a menu but still had difficulty identifying specific words such as "beans" or "peas" or "carrots" and "cabbage." A dyslexic businessman could not read the names of airlines on his ticket so he "matched" the words and numbers at the airport. These poignant stories revealed their constant struggles and reasons for wanting help.

## READING PERFORMANCE

### General Trends

As expected with a large, heterogeneous group, reading skills varied widely. On standardized tests, their performance ranged from first through twelfth grade, and standard scores ranged from 60 to 120. These findings might suggest their problems were not always severe enough to prevent them from obtaining employment or functioning independently. However, we agree with Chall (1979) who said, that in this era, in this society, an eighth grade reading level is barely sufficient. While in 1940 average adults read at the eighth grade level, Chall says the demands for higher achievement will increase as more people go to college.

Eighty-three of the total group (93) were classified as reading disabled. The diagnosis was based on chronicity of problems, below average performance on at least one standardized reading measure, and patterns of errors on many informal measures. We also noted discrepancies between their mental ability, years in school, overall goals, and reading levels.

The ten adults, not classified as poor readers consistently scored at an eleventh or twelfth grade level with standard scores above 110 on all reading measures used. Their primary problems were in written language, nonverbal processes, mathematics, organization, or attention.

Given the numerous auditory and conceptual problems described in previous chapters most adults did not have the oral language competence on which to base an orthographic code. Perceptual, memory, comprehension, and syntactic deficits all interfered with various aspects of reading. Their lack of linguistic awareness and flexibility was particularly evident. It might be argued that reading difficulties had prevented them from acquiring more complex vocabulary and syntax; however, this was not always the case. Occasionally, the poorest decoders had remarkable vocabularies. This was particularly true of a few college students who had gone through school with tape recorded books or assistants to read their texts. Perhaps they had to develop certain auditory skills and strategies to survive.

## Oral Reading and Decoding Patterns

### *Single Words*

Of the 83 classified as poor readers, thirty percent had standard scores below 80 (grade 5) on the Wide Range Achievement Test (Jastak & Jastak, 1976); forty percent scored between 80 and 90; and the remainder achieved scores of 90 to 110; None however, even in the latter group, could be considered skilled decoders. In fact, two people could not read any nonsense words.

An inspection of over 1400 WRAT errors indicated all except 54 substitutions began with the same sound as the target word and one-third had the same final sound. Hence, most errors occurred on the vowel and medial portions of words. This is in keeping with the findings of Shankweiler and Liberman (1972).

Further inspection of errors indicated the adults tried to use both phonetic and structural analysis but were not proficient with either. For example, an examination of errors on the word "tranquility" indicated they all substituted a form of "tranquil" but errors on "contagious" were never semantically related. They substituted words such as "connections, continents, or continuous."

Visual-spatial errors were less frequent. There was only one p/b and one d/p error on the WRAT (Jasktak & Jastak, 1976) but reversals and inversions were noted on other tasks. Numerous transpositions occurred on words such as "form, split, and aboard" even among better readers, but in general, these observations are in keeping with Vellutino (1977) who feels perceptual problems have been overemphasized.

A few errors on the WRAT resulted from retrieval, production, and pronunciation problems. Examples were "burn" for "scald", "mouth" for "lip" and "thumb" for "finger". Occasionally adults defined words they could not pronounce (e.g. "a list of books" for "bibliography"). They accessed meaning through a visual route even though they could not say the words. Several adults with oral expressive problems did not try to recode words they could not pronounce. Particular difficulty was noted with rhythm and accent.

Whenever possible, we observed monitoring for meaning and phonology. It was apparent, however, that monitoring is difficult unless one has a correct image against which to make a judgment. Thus, adults with poor discrimination, memory, and comprehension could not evaluate what they did not know. An inspection of WRAT errors indicated poor readers were generally effective in self correcting words up to the fifth or sixth grade level but, as the level of difficulty increased, many simply uttered a series of unrelated sounds and syllables. This was partly because they could not decode; however, vocabulary, memory, and pronunciation problems also limited their performance.

Children reading at the fourth grade level generally achieve 95 to 100% accuracy on these tasks. Twenty-five of the poorest decoders were given the following informal word lists to investigate rule learning and strategies:

1. A group of high frequency-high imagery nouns appropriate for children in grades one through three. They were told the words were "all names of things" to see if these instructions fostered prediction and self monitoring.
2. Groups of semantically related words (e.g., fruits) without the category label to explore their use of conceptual knowledge. The lists began with easy words such as "apple and orange" but increased in level of difficulty.
3. A list of CVC words with instructions to remember, "all of the words have /a/ in them." We were interested in decoding, maintenance of a mental set, and self monitoring with maximum structure.
4. A list of orthographically regular words with consonant clusters in the initial or final position (cast, clasp, strap).
5. A group of high frequency functor and relational words (e.g. this, these, there, which). We find, as Krieger did (1981), that these words are read more accurately in context.
6. To elicit possible reversals, inversions, and transpositions, a list similar to Shankweiler and Liberman's (1972) was given. (pat, bat, tab, saw, was).
7. Structural analysis was tested by using relatively simple base words (jump,

jumps, jumped, jumping, jumper) as well as words with more complex forms (destroy, destructive).

8. Finally, words were presented in random order.

In general, the poorest performance was on the randomized word lists. None of the 25 tested achieved a perfect score indicating word recognition skills were not automatic.

Orthographically regular words with consonant clusters in the initial and final positions were the next most difficult. Poor readers frequently transposed, omitted, added, or substituted letters. The reasons for errors varied. In some instances, the mistakes seemed to result from faulty scanning and impulsivity. Hence, further studies of visual search strategies may be beneficial (Coburn, 1983). Research on detection of various size perceptual units also is needed. Noell (1980) found both normal and learning disabled fifth graders responded more accurately and rapidly to single letter and whole word perceptual units than to syllables and letter clusters. Problems also may be related to faulty eye movements (Pavlidis, 1981) or difficulty with temporal-sequential and visual-spatial integration (Bakker, 1972; Orton, 1937). Phoneme segmentation was probably a major factor, since five of the poorest readers were totally unable to segment by phoneme.

Only 12 of the 25 adults achieved a perfect score on the structural analysis list. They did not miss simple plurals and verb tense, yet they frequently omitted them in context. Most errors occurred on words requiring a pronunciation shift (child-children destroy-destructive). These results are similar to those of Vogel (1975, 1977) who found poor readers had difficulty with complex forms on the Berry Talbott test. (Berry, 1966). Given the adults' poor performance on the Berry Talbott (see Chapter 6) these results are not surprising, since reading requires the application of rules in novel situations.

Although few reversals occurred on the WRAT, the adults made more mistakes on word lists designed to elicit errors (pat; tab; bat). There were a total of 29 letter reversals (most often in the final position) and twenty-three word reversals (saw-was). Each of the 25 adults made at least one error, but no one made more than six. While perceptual problems should not be emphasized, they cannot be overlooked.

Relatively good performance was observed on high imagery-high frequency nouns. Visual imagery seemed to aid performance. The mean score for 25 poor readers was 98 percent. Apparently they used holistic strategies but were unable to generalize to new words because of difficulties with auditory analysis, linguistic awareness, and decoding.

Performance on the CVC (short a) word list was the best. Sixteen of the 25 obtained a perfect score and no one made more than three mistakes. This was, perhaps, because the words were shorter and they were told to remember the specific vowel sound. Adults with good monitoring skills self corrected mistakes; others were unable to maintain the mental set or remember the sound.

**Table 9-1**
Patterns of Adults who scored at Fifth Grade Level on the WRAT

| | % Correct | | | |
|---|---|---|---|---|
| Word List Type | Case #1 | Case #2 | Case #3 | Case #4 |
| Randomized Words | 75 | 60 | 89 | 59 |
| Consonant Blends | 89 | 82 | 91 | 75 |
| CVC (short a) | 95 | 95 | 100 | 97 |
| Structural Analysis | 100 | 86 | 96 | 86 |
| Semantic Groups | 100 | 87 | 94 | 91 |
| High Frequency Functor | 100 | 94 | 100 | 94 |
| High Frequency Nouns | 100 | 98 | 97 | 95 |

While group trends are of interest, they do not reveal individual needs. The scores in Table 9–1 illustrate various error patterns of adults who had standard scores below 85 on the WRAT.

The results in Table 9–1 show how various cognitive and linguistic skills may interact with reading performance.

Case #1 had high average intelligence, good conceptual and oral language skills, but poor auditory analysis and decoding.

Case #2 had problems in all language skills discussed in Chapter 6.

Case #3 had a history of language problems but had received more remediation. Also his conceptual skills were higher than those of Case #2, but both had average mental ability.

Case #4 had many language and decoding problems.

In general, word recognition skills of the group were weak as demonstrated by their numerous, inconsistent errors. They were similar, perhaps, to the disabled readers in Elbert's study (1979). She concluded they performed fewer or less thorough feature tests than good readers and responded impulsively according to holistic properties of words. She found many were capable of phonological encoding, but when given the choice, the learning disabled subjects continued to use a visual coding strategy.

Performance on these reading tasks may also indicate poor readers fail to integrate the semantic, orthographic, and phonological codes as easily as good readers (Zecker, Tanenhaus, Alderman & Sequeland, 1986).

### *Oral Reading in Context*

Although adults rarely need to read aloud, performance was assessed to investigate their ability to predict words in context. A few requested help because they were in professions (e.g., ministry) requiring accurate oral reading.

As expected, performance varied widely. Some could not even read simple sentences whereas others managed passages at upper grade levels. Yet none were fluent. Their substitutions, hesitations, and repetitions indicated lack of automaticity, even on relatively simple paragraphs.

When reading of single words was compared with context, three broad patterns were observed. Nearly half of the poor readers read single words better than context. In most cases they were poor decoders with language disorders. In some instances, however, the structured word lists reduced impulsivity.

One fourth of the group read context better than single words. While they were not proficient decoders they had better receptive language, thinking skills, and auditory memory than the others. Another fourth read at approximately the same level on both single words and context. Decoding was frequently the primary problem though many had auditory disorders. These patterns are illustrated with the three examples below.

| Subject # | Words: Grade Level | Context: Grade Level |
|---|---|---|
| 1 | 5.6 | 2.3 |
| 2 | 5.6 | 7.2 |
| 3 | 5.6 | 5.4 |

Subject #1 had a long history of both oral language and reading disorders. He had problems with phonetic discrimination, pronunciation of multisyllabic words, syntax, auditory analysis and decoding. Subject #2 had fewer oral language problems and used background knowledge whenever possible. Subject #3 had both decoding and short term memory problems which prevented him from using context effectively. He could not remember the initial portion of a sentence while attempting difficult words. In his initial letter he wrote:

> "When I look at a word I can't figure out, I usually loose my train of thought. It has always been a victious circle for me."

Poor readers with limited short term memory often have problems monitoring for meaning. Not only do they have difficulty when decoding multisyllabic words but they read and re-read material so the material makes sense. Problems related to short term memory and reading have been well documented by Torgesen (1977), Torgesen and Goldman (1977), and others.

Analyses of oral reading passages revealed word substitutions were the most frequent type of error. The substitutions were often graphically similar to the target word (facility/faculty; alerting/altering; consistent/constant) indicating the adults were "tied to print." While many searched for meaning they did not succeed because of decoding or language problems. All occasionally made errors that altered both syntax and meaning. Even those with high conceptual ability inevitably made mistakes that distorted the text. Performance was noticeably better, however, when they were given familiar content. At times, their reading varied as much as three grade levels when they could use their background knowledge and read for confirmation. Learning from reading was a much more difficult task.

All poor readers periodically substituted semantically similar words that altered the syntax of the text (nature/natural; electric/electronic; mechanism/ mechanics). Their morphosyntactic rules were noticeably weak. Some disregarded word endings completely. Occasionally they converted entire passages from past to present tense. Similar behaviors were observed among learning disabled children (Henderson & Shores, 1982). Many altered the syntax in both reading and sentence repetition tests. They preserved meaning but changed the vocabulary and word order. For example, a 22 year old, asked to repeat the questions "Shoudn't children who aren't well go to sleep early?" said "Shouldn't the children go to sleep early when they aren't well?". An example from his reading is illustrated below:

> The morning routine of clearing the water and the saturated bedding from the raft was occupying more of our time as conditions worsened, and we were becoming slower in performing even small tasks.

Adult Reading:

> The morning routine of clearing the water and the soaked bedding from our raft occupied more of our time as con - condit—as things got worse, and we were slower in pre - preparing - even small tasks.

He abstracted the meaning and tried to monitor errors, but, like others, frequently had to abandon unsuccessful attempts.

Adults with primary comprehension disorders sometimes made fewer decoding errors but failed to monitor for meaning and often read passages that made no sense to the listener. For example, note this response to the passage above:

Adult Reading:

> The morning routine of clearing the water and the saturated bidding from the raft was occurring more than our time as conditions weakened and we were blowing slower in pretending even small takes.

In this case the reader substituted real words but was unconcerned about lack of meaning.

Many adults omitted or changed articles (a/n;a/the). On the surface, these mistakes appear insignificant, but ultimately, they make a difference, particularly in writing. The a/an error may indicate problems with phonological-orthographic rules and the a/the error may show lack of attention to linguistic features needed for appropriate referential communication.

While we have reservations about testing comprehension following oral reading, we compared the accuracy and comprehension scores of 40 subjects on oral reading tests. In over one-half of the cases, both accuracy and comprehension scores fell within the same grade level or standard score range. Eleven people, however, scored accurately higher on comprehension than accuracy. In most instances, their miscues did not affect meaning. Some readers however, seemed to process information accurately through the visual system, but said something different and failed to hear the mistake. For example, one person read a paragraph about an "engine", but substituted the word "energy" throughout. Later when asked questions about the passage, he used the word "engine" correctly. We observed this lack of synchrony among both learning disabled children and adults.

Twenty percent of the poor readers scored higher on oral reading accuracy than comprehension tests. Most had auditory comprehension problems; others could not read aloud and comprehend simultaneously.

During diagnostic teaching, adults were asked to re-read material before they were asked questions. As expected, on the basis of Samuels' research (1979) and others (Bos, 1982), repeated readings facilitated both comprehension and fluency, but it made less difference for those with generalized meaning disorders.

In general, these poor readers, like those described by Guthrie and Seifert (1978) had not integrated the many sub-skills needed for accurate oral reading. As a result, they had little mental energy for thinking about ideas while reading. Nevertheless, they continued to add to their background knowledge by observing, listening, using tape recorded books, or watching television.

### *Oral and Silent Reading Patterns*

An analysis of oral and silent reading indicated forty percent of the group scored at approximately the same level on both types of tasks. In most instances lack of automaticity as well as language disorders interfered with reading. Twenty-five percent of the group, however, scored considerably higher on silent than oral reading tests. They generally had difficulty with decoding, pronunciation, retrieval, and/or syntax. Thirty-five percent read better orally than silently. Most in this group had both listening and reading comprehension problems. A few, however, were impulsive and skimmed too quickly when reading silently.

## Reading Comprehension

Reading, according to Gibson and Levin (1975), is an active process that requires the extraction of meaning from print. Meaning is not in the text per se; rather, readers actively use their knowledge and language to determine meanings the writer intended. Smith (1975) says comprehension is often assumed to refer specifically to language, but it encompasses broader aspects of behavior including observation and knowledge about the world. Comprehension means relating new experience to that which is already known. In everyday language, "comprehension means making sense." As such, it is an elusive process that is somewhat difficult to measure, in part, because meanings are personal and change over time with experience.

Adults with learning disabilities present a particular diagnostic challenge, because of their varied experiences, occupations, levels of schooling and general background. The foreman in a factory may have different cognitive and linguistic experiences than the nurse, the artist, minister or social worker. Leisure time and compensatory strategies also vary. For example, the poor reader who listens to Shakespearian plays will hear more complex syntax and vocabulary than one who only watches comedy on television.

In general, poor reading comprehension may result from problems in conceptualization, imagery, oral language, reasoning, use of background knowledge, or decoding. As indicated in Chapter II, it is important to investigate relationships between cognition, language and reading (Carroll, 1977). Sticht and James (1984) stress the need for comparing both auding (listening) and reading when planning instruction. This need was noted by Nahmias (1981) who found reading disabled subjects had difficulty with both inferential listening and reading comprehension.

Failure to comprehend the language of instruction may also contribute to poor performance. For example, Downing (1979) found some children were confused by the terminology in phonics. The adults frequently misunderstood words such as "vowel, consonant, noun, or subject". A college student said he "never quite understood what the English teachers were talking about." Several had difficulty with phrases such as "mark all *except* ______", "mark *every other* letter in the series", or "mark the word that means the opposite of ______".

Poor performance on reading comprehension tasks may be related to types of responses required. Gibson and Levin (1975) listed several widely used procedures including (1) following directions, (2) supplying missing words, (3) answering questions based on a text, (4) report of truth or falsity of statements, (5) reproduction or recall of a passage, and (6) subjective report—that is, simply asking readers how well they understand. Each requires a different type of linguistic competence. While standardized tests often require only multiple choice responses, many diagnostic procedures (Goodman & Burke, 1972) and research tasks (Stein & Glenn, 1979) require verbal summaries. People with output disorders may often comprehend more than they can express.

Factors within the text may affect comprehension and retention (Gibson and Levin, 1975). These include clarity and style of writing, use of key words, topical sentences, summaries, and use of devices such as graphs to reduce uncertainty.

Length of passage and opportunities for rescanning material also need to be considered. Adults with memory disorders often comprehend short passages and respond correctly but are unable to summarize and recall material if it is removed.

Ideally, comprehension assessment should include a study of performance at the level of the word, sentence, and discourse (Pennock, 1979). An exemplary plan for evaluating decoding, vocabulary, sentence understanding, and text comprehension was designed by Calfee, Spector, and Piontowski (1979) to assist educators in planning instruction.

Comprehension monitoring, strategic behaviors, and metacognition (Brown, 1980; Capelli & Markman, 1982; Markman, 1977) should be explored by noting questioning behaviors, pre-planning, re-reading, note taking, and revising (Manzo, 1979; Masson, 1982; Pennock, 1979).

### General Reading Comprehension Patterns

On the basis of test performance and observations, it appears that adults with comprehension disorders have difficulty abstracting, inferring, and acquiring new word meanings. They pay too little attention to relationships between words and ideas and tend to search primarily for the "gist" or main idea. They use first letters of words, background knowledge and a bit of text to obtain general information. This cognitive style may be all some can manage but it also may be fostered by "main idea" questioning. More emphasis is needed on vocabulary, morphology, comprehension of complex sentences, and organizational patterns of discourse.

An inspection of single word and passage comprehension tests revealed three general patterns. Approximately one-half of the poor readers scored at the same level on both vocabulary and passage comprehension. Most were inefficient decoders but several had limited vocabulary. One-fourth of the group performed better on passage comprehension than on vocabulary. They used background knowledge or context to answer many questions but had difficulty with specific word meanings, synonyms, and opposites, even when they could decode words. Another fourth scored higher on reading vocabulary than passage comprehension. Typically they had difficulty with critical reading, reasoning, inferential thinking, and comprehension monitoring.

Hypotheses about the reasons for errors were made by studying entire test protocols, informal tasks, data from other language tests, and diagnostic teaching.

### Reading Vocabulary

Several factors contributed to low vocabulary scores including receptive language, attention, maintenance of a mental set, and monitoring. Even when they could decode words, many adults had vague word meanings and poor semantic organization.

For example, items on the Wide Range Vocabulary Test (Atwell & Wells, 1972) were arranged so the reader was to select a synonym for the underlined word:

| | | | | | |
|---|---|---|---|---|---|
| A *far* country is | away | near | beautiful | strange | rich |
| To *take* is to | send | please | carry | lose | give |

Several adults apparently had difficulty remembering they were to select a synonym. Hence, they periodically gave syntagmatic rather than paradigmatic responses; that is, they completed the sentence rather than selecting a synonym (e.g. a *far* country is *beautiful*). Erratic performance was observed on other tests as well. For example, their difficulty shifting or maintaining a mental set was also evident on arithmetic tests. They failed to attend to signs even though they were capable of calculating.

Their poor semantic organization and narrow word meanings were observed on many tasks. For example, several selected "immune" as a synonym for "exposed" rather than "protected." "Commence" to some meant—a gathering—like a commencement." "Consume" was defined as "take in—like groceries or knowledge." Others gave overly personal associative definitions. For example, some said "breakfast" was "bacon, eggs and toast" and "domestic" was defined as "help."

Several errors could have been related to perceptual disorders. For example, they indicated "rumple" meant "dance" rather than "wrinkle." Similar errors were noted on oral vocabulary tests when they focused on phonological features rather than meaning. For instance, some said "ponder" meant "wonder." Another said "cavern" is like "tavern."

The poor comprehenders often missed relatively simple items but answered more difficult ones correctly. For instance, a college student with a low vocabulary score defined fabric as "an item of clothing, usually a soft woolen substance" yet he defined "fortitude" as "inner strength." Another defined "sentence" as "a compound of word put into an organized phrase" yet she defined "tranquil" as "calm," and "tangible" as "something you can touch." On the Similarities subtest they often gave low, level concrete answers followed by abstract ones (e.g. "a cat and dog both have hair"; "air and water both have oxygen").

At times, the foils on vocabulary tests contributed to variation in performance. When the alternative selections all began with the same letter, items were more difficult for poor decoders but when the foils were semantically similar, those with comprehension difficulty failed more items.

Because many adults omitted morphological endings on both oral and written language tests, an informal task was prepared for those in remediation to determine whether they understood the significance of suffices and prefixes. Fifteen people were given a series of questions (both orally and in writing) such as the following: "*Pre*—what does *pre* mean in the words: *preheat*, *premature* and *prejudge*?" or "*Bi*—what does *bi* mean in words such as *biweekly*, *bifocal*, and *bicycle*?" While none of the adults missed all the items those with language comprehension disorders made frequent errors. For example, they, said "pre means after" or "bi means you do it every week." When asked how "ed" changed the meaning of a word, one man said, "I think it makes it past tent." Work on morphology is important not only for the oral reading accuracy, but for meaning.

### *Passage Comprehension*

Since many reading tests have only short paragraphs, informal tasks with longer and more varied discourse are needed, particularly, to evaluate adults interested in higher education. Frequently their own text books and term papers were used as a basis for diagnostic teaching.

A few adults had global comprehension disorders which were apparent in all forms of language. Problems of vocabulary, syntax, and discourse in both oral and written language, and are illustrated in the following examples from a twenty-three year old.

> "I want help to expand my achievment—could be personal or in the business sector. I would like to attain these achievement easier instead of harder. My abilities stop me. I'm ceased. It comes to a halt. In social situations I might say the wrong think—I can't remember words. I have trouble at work remembering the steps and following them. The steps have to be inserted millions of times".

In reading he often failed to understand the language of instructions, vocabulary, prefixes, suffices, and relational words. His written sentence building errors highlight the complex interactions between perception, comprehension, and expression.

> The baseball player *jumps* to evade the ball.
> I *myself* will not be subjective to this arrestment.

When asked about reading he said "I have difficulty forming a mental image of complex words. I can sound out words but I am blind inside." He reported a history of familial language disorders and felt his father had "no variety of words."

Others had a relatively good vocabulary, but could not understand relational words, cohesive ties and referential expressions. Their overall reading style was to search for general meaning without noting hierarchical relationships and structure of discourse. The lack of organization, subordination, and use of correct temporal relations was particularly noted in written language. Their class notes and papers indicated they had not understood key points or relationships between ideas.

Several missed comprehension questions related to time, space and number concepts. Adults with nonverbal disorders also missed questions requiring interpretation of figures, graphs, and pictures. We observed this same tendency among learning disabled children.

In remediation poor comprehenders had difficulty determining the class of words from exercises such as the following:

> A bletch flibbed the prat.
> Is the bletch a person, action, or thing?
> Is flibbed a person, action, place or thing?

These problems were noted particularly among adults who had a history of receptive language disorders. They had not learned how structural and syntactic features of language can guide comprehension (Morrison, 1979). Research like Sordon's should be done with these adults (1980). Her subjects were given sentences with nonsense words to assess their ability to infer semantic relations such as taxonomy, synonymy, antonymy and part-whole.

Whenever possible, we tried to investigate poor self-regulatory behavior. Problems of attention, impulsivity, holding several ideas in mind simultaneously, maintaining or shifting mental sets, and monitoring were observed frequently. Some adults who failed Stone's reasoning tasks (Chapter 5) were good decoders with poor comprehension monitoring.

Those who came in remediation were encouraged to ask themselves, "Does this make sense?" or "Is that right?". Whether the task involved reading, mathematics, or social skills, they had to be "activated" to think about meaning.

While oral language disorders were prevalent among the poor readers, Maria and MacGinitie (1982) emphasized that not all reading comprehension disorders can be explained by studying conceptualization and oral language. They feel that poor readers may over rely on their background knowledge when processing written language, and therefore have difficulty learning new information from print. Written language provides cues that differ from those in oral language and poor readers fail to attend to those cues. The differentiation of these problems often requires periods of diagnostic teaching.

### Reading Rate

Reading rate was a problem for all of the adults. Only three people performed above the fiftieth percentile on rate measures. All except five scored below the thirty-fifth percentile. This is in keeping with their own verbal reports at the time of the evaluation. Many were slow because of lack of automaticity and decoding problems (LaBerge & Samuels, 1974 Stanovich, 1983). In other instances, their general language difficulty probably interfered with reading (Menyuk & Flood, 1981). Slow rates also might reflect anxiety. (Spache, 1976).

## SUMMARY

In summary, reading is a complex process requring the integration of many cognitive skills and linguistic rule systems. As such, even a minor disruption can interfere with the ability to extract meaning from print.

We have tried to illustrate the need to analyze various strategies used during oral and silent reading of words and context. We also emphasized relationships between oral and written language. By including examples of spontaneous writing we have tried to demonstrate that the adults had much to say about their own cognitive processes, and, at the same time illustrate their problems with the integration of rules for phonology, morphology, semantics, syntax, and orthography. The examples highlight the type of scatter and uneveness discussed in Chapter II. Hence, we argue that their overall language patterns are not simply delayed but different. These differences and idiosyncratic patterns are more evident on tasks requiring multiple rule systems; however specific error patterns can often be detected on tasks with varying degrees of structure. Therefore, in remediation, we feel it is important to identify the problems associated with specific rule acquisition, application or monitoring but the ultimate goal is to achieve integration and linguistic flexibility.

The current research on subtypes (Masland, 1979) is very useful, but we agree with Doehring (1984) and Lovett (1984) who feel more complex, interactive models may be required to identify all possible variables (Johnson, 1982). While researchers continue to investigate learning disabilities, it is important for diagnosticians and educators to keep detailed records of test scores and observations so that future studies of brain-behavior relationships (Galaburda, 1983; Galaburda & Kemper, 1979) can be linked with psychoeducational data. Observations, tape recordings and video tapes will provide additional evidence into reading strategies used by both good and poor readers.

## REFERENCES

Aaron, P. G. The neuropsychology of developmental dyslexia. In R. N. Malatesha & P. G. Aaron (Eds.), *Reading disorders: varieties and treatments*. New York: Academic Press, 1982.

Ackerman, P., Dykman, R., & Peters, J. Learning disabled boys as adolescents: Cognitive factors and achievement. *Journal of the American Academy of Child Psychiatry*, 1977, *16*, 296–313.

Allington, R. Oral reading. In P. Pearseon (Ed.), *Handbook of reading research*. New York: Longman, 1984.

Atwell, C., & Wells, F. *Wide range vocabulary test*. Chicago: Psychological Corp., 1972.

Bakker, D. Temporal order in disturbed reading. *Bulletin of the Orton Society*, 1972, *22*, 80–83.

Bakker, D., & Satz, P. *Specific reading disability: Advances in theory and method*. Rotterdam: Rotterdam U. Press, 1970.

Bender, L. A fifty-year review of experiences with dyslexia. *Bulletin of the Orton Society*, 1975, *24*, 5–23.

Benton, A. Dyslexia: Evolution of a concept. *Bulletin of the Orton Society*, 1980, *30*, 10–26.

Berry, M. *Berry-Talbott language tests 1. Comprehension of Grammar*. Rockford, IL:1966.

Boder, E. Developmental dyslexia: Prevailing diagnostic concepts and a new diagnostic approach. In H. Myklebust (Ed.), *Progress in learning disabilities* (Vol. 2). New York: Grune & Stratton, 1971.

Boder, E. Developmental dyslexia: A diagnostic approach based on three atypical reading-spelling patterns. *Developmental Medicine and Child Neurology*, 1973, *15*, 663–687.

Bos, C. Getting past decoding: Assisted and repeated readings as remedial methods for learning disabled students. *Topics in Learning and Learning Disabilities*, 1982, *1*, 51–57.

Brown, A. Metacognitive development and reading. In R. Spiro, B. Bruce, W. Brewer (Eds.), *Theoretical issues in reading comprehension*. Hillsdale, NJ: Erlbaum, 1980.

Calfee, R., Spector, J., & Piontkowski, D. Assessing reading and language skills: An interactive system. *Bulletin of the Orton Society*, 1979, *29*, 129–156.

Capelli, C., & Markman, E. Suggestions for training comprehension monitoring. *Topics in Learning and Learning Disabilities*, 1982, *2*, 87–96.

Carroll, J. Developmental parameters of reading comprehension. In J. Guthrie (Ed.), *Cognition, curriculum, and comprehension*. Newark, DE: International Reading Association, 1977.

Chall, J. On reading: Some thoughts on the old and the new. *Bulletin of the Orton Society*, 1979, *24*, 6–16.

Chall, J. *Stages of reading development*. New York: McGraw Hill, 1983.

Clay, M. Reading errors and self-correction behavior. *British Journal of Educational Psychology*, 1969, *39*, 47–56.

Coburn, L. *An investigation of conceptual tempo and strategies of visual search in learning disabled and normally achieving children*. Unpublished doctoral dissertation, Northwestern University, 1983.

Critchley, M. Developmental dyslexia. *Pediatric Clinics of North America*, 1971, *15*, 669–676.

Das, J., Kirby, J., & Jarman, R. *Simultaneous and successive cognitive processing*. New York: Academic Press, 1979.

Denckla, M. Minimal brain dysfunction and dyslexia: Beyond diagnosis by exclusion. In M.E. Blaw, I. Rapin, & M. Kinsbourne (Eds.), *Topics in child neurology*. Jamaica, NY: Spectrum Publications, 1977.

Deno, S., Marston, D., Shinn, M., & Tindal, G. Oral reading fluency: A simple datum for scaling reading disability. *Topics in Learning and Learning Disabilities*, 1983, *2* (4), 53–59.

Doehring, D. Subtyping reading disorders: Implications for remediation. *Annals of Dyslexia*, 1984, *34*, 205–216.

Doehring, D., & Hoshko, J. Classification of reading problems by the Q technique of factor analysis. *Cortex*, 1977, *13*, 281–294.

Doehring. D.G. Trites, R.L., Patel, P]G], & Fiedorowica, C.A.M. (Eds.), *Reading disabilities: The interaction of reading, language, and neuropsychological deficits*. Academic Press, 1981.

Downing, J. *Reading and reasoning*. New York: Springer-Verlag, 1979.

Duane, D. Underachievement in written language: Auditory aspects. In H. Myklebust (Ed.), *Progress in Learning Disabilities* (Vol. 5). New York: Grune & Stratton, 1983.

Duffy, F., Denckla, M., Bartels, P., & Sandini, G. Dyslexia: Regional differences in brain electrical activity by topographic mapping. *Annals of Neurology*, 1980, *7*, 412–420.

Galaburda, A. Developmental dyslexia: Current anatomical research. *Annals of Dyslexia*, 1983, *33*, 41–53.

Galaburda, A., & Kemper, T. Cytoarchitectonic abnormalities in developmental dyslexia: A case study. *Annals of Nerology*, 1979, *6*, 94–100.

Garner, R. Correcting the inbalance: Diagnosis of strategic behaviors in reading. *Topics in Learning and Learning Disabilities*, 1983, *2* (4), 12–19.

Gibson, E., & Levin, H. The psychology of reading. Cambridge, MA: M.I.T. Press, 1975.
Gilmore, J., & Gilmore, E. *Gilmore oral reading test*. New York: Harcourt Brace Jovanovich, 1968.
Goodman, Y., & Burke, C. *Reading miscue inventory: Procedures for diagnosis and evaluation*. New York: Macmillan, 1972.
Gray, W.W. *On their own in reading*. Chicago: Scott Foresman, 1947.
Gray, W., & Robinson, H. *Gray oral reading tests*. Austin, TX: Pro-Ed, 1967.
Guthrie, J., & Seifert, M. Education for children with reading disabilities. In H. Myklebust (Ed.), *Progress in learning disabilities* (Vol. 4). New York: Grune & Stratton, 1978.
Hallgren, B. Specific dyslexia ("congenital word-blindness"): A clinical and genetic study. *Acta Psychiatrica Scandinavia*, 1950 (Suppl. 65).
Henderson, A., & Shores, R. How learning disabled students' failure to attend to suffices affects their oral reading performance. *Journal of Learning Disabilities*, 1982, *15*, 173–177.
Herman, L. *Reading disability*. Copenhagen: Munksgaard, 1959.
Hinshelwood, J. A case of dyslexia: A peculiar form of word-blindness. *Lancet*, 1900, *2*, 1451–1454.
Jastak, J., & Jastak, S. *The wide range achievement test*. Wilmington, DE: Jastak Associates, 1978.
Johnson, D. Programming for dyslexia: The need for interaction analyses. *Annals of Dyslexia*, 1982, *32*, 61–70.
Johnson, D., & Myklebust, H. *Learning disabilities: Education principles and practice*. New York: Grune & Stratton, 1967.
Kaufman, A., & Kaufman, N. *Kaufman assessment battery for children*. Circle Pines, MN: American Guidance Service, 1983.
Krieger, V. A hierarchy of "confusable" high-frequency words in isolation and context. *Learning Disability Quarterly*, 1981, *4*(2), 131–138.
LaBerge, D., & Samuels, S.J. Toward a theory of automatic information processing. *Cognitive Psychology*, 1974, *6*, 293–323.
Leong, C.K. Spatial-temporal information processing in children with specific reading disability. *Reading Research Quarterly*, 1976–7, *12*, 204–215.
Lesgold, A., & Perfetti, C. *Interactive processes in reading*. Hillsdale, NJ: Lawrence Erlbaum, 1981.
Lovett, M. The search for subtypes of specific reading disability: Reflections from a cognitive perspective. *Annals of Dyslexia*,l 1984, *34*, 155–178.
Lyon, G.R. Learning-disabled readers: Identification of subgroups. In H. Myklebust (Ed.), *Progress in learning disabilities* (Vol. 5). New York: Grune & Stratton, 1983.
Maria, K. & MacGinitie, W. Reading comprehension disabilities: Knowledge structures and nonaccommodating text processing strategies. *Annals of Dyslexia*, 1982, *s32*, 33–59.
Manzo, A. The ReQuest procedure. In C. Pennock (Ed.), *Reading comprehension at four linguistic levels*. Newark, DE: International Reading Association, 1979.,
Markman, E. Realizing that you don't understand: A preliminary investigation. *Child Development*, 1977, *48*, 986–992.

Masland, R. Subgroups in dyslexia: Issues of definition. *Bulletin of the Orton Society*, 1979, *29*, 23–30.

Masson, M. A framework of cognitive and metacognitive determinants of reading skill. *Topics in Learning and Learning Disabilities*. 1982, *2*, 37–44.

Mattis, S., French, J]H][ & Rapin, I. Dyslexia in children and young adults: Three independent neuropsychological syndromes. *Developmental Medicine and Child Neurology*, 1975, *17*, 150–163.

Mautner, T. Dyslexia—"My invisible handicap." *Annals of Dyslexia*, 1984, *34*, 299–311.

Menyuk, P., & Flood, J. Linguistic competence, reading, writing problems and remediation. *Bulletin of the Orton Society*, 1981, 31, 31–28.

Miles, T. Dyslexia: *The pattern of difficulties*. Springfield, IL, Charles C. Thomas, 1983.

Morgan, W.P. A case of congenital word-blindness. *British Medical Journal*, 1896, *2*, 1378.

Morrison, B. One route to improve reading comprehension: A look at word meaning skills. In C. Pennock (Ed.), *Reading comprehension at four linguistic levels*. Newark, DE: International Reading Association, 1979.

Myklebust, H.R. *Auditory disorders in children*. New York: Grune & Stratton, 1954.

Myklebust, H.R. Toward a sicence of dyslexiology. In H.R. Myklebust (Ed.), *Progress in learning disabilities* (Vol. 4). New York: Grune & Stratton, 1978.

Myklebust, H.R., & Johnson, D.J. Dyslexia in children. *Exceptional Children*, 1962, *29*, 14–25.

Nahmias, M. *Inferential listening and reading comprehension of discourse in normal and reading disabled children*. Unpublished doctoral dissertation, Northwestern University, 1981.

Noell, E. *An investigation of the utilization of multiple perceptual units as word recognition strategies in learning disabled and normally achieving children*. Doctoral dissertation, Northwestern University, 1980.

Orton, S. *Reading, writing and speech problems in children*. New York: W. W. Norton, 1937.

Pavlidis, G. Sequencing, eye movements and the early objective diagnosis of dyslexia. In G. Pavlidis, & T. Miles (Eds.), *Dyslexia research and its applications to research*. New York: Wiley, 1981.

Pavlidis, G., & Miles, T. (Eds.), *Dyslexia research and its applications to research*. New York: Wiley, 1981.

Pennock, C. (Ed.) *Reading comprehension at four linguistic levels*. Newark, DE: International Reading Association, 1979.

Perfetti, C. Language comprehension and fastdecoding: Some prerequisites for skilled reading comprehension. In J. Guthrie (Ed.), *Cognition, curriculum and comprehension*. Newark, DE: International Reading Association, 1977.

Perfetti, C.A., & Lesgold, A.M. Coding and comprehension in skilled reading and implications for reading instruction. In L. B. Resnick & P. A. Weaver (Eds.), *Theory and practice of early reading* (Vol. 1). Hillsdale, NJ: Erlbaum, 1979.

Petrauskas, R., & Rourke, B. Identification of subgroups of retarded readers: A neuropsychological multivariate approach. *Journal of Clinical Neuropsychology*, 1979, *1*, 17–37.

Rumelhart, D. Toward an interactive model of reading. In S. Dornic (Ed.), *Attention and performance*. Hillsdale, NJ: Erlbaum, 1977.

Samuels, S.J. The method of repeated reading. *The Reading Teacher*, 1979, *32*, 403–408.

Samuels, S.J. Diagnosing reading problems. *Topics in Learning and Learning Disabilities*, 1983, *2* (4), 1–11.

Satz, P., & Morris, R. The search for subtype classification in learning disabled children. In R. Tarter, (Ed.), *Neuropsychological and cognitive processes in reading*. New York: Academic Press, 1981.

Schreiner, R. Principles of diagnosis of reading difficulties. *Topics in Learning and Learning Disabilities*, 1983, *2*, 70–85.

Shankweiler, D., & Liberman, I. Misreading: A search for causes. In J. Kavanagh & I. Mattingly (Eds.), *Language by ear and by eye*. Cambridge, MA: M. I. T. Press, 1972.

Smith, F. *Comprehension and learning: A conceptual framework for teachers*. New York: Holt, Rinehart & Winston, 1975.

Smith, F. Conflicting approaches to reading research and instruction. In L.B. Resnick & P.A. Weaver (Eds.), *Theory and practice of early reading* (Vol. 2). Hillsdale, NJ: Erlbaum, 1979.

Sordon, S. *Lexical relations, inferences, and word meaning acquisition in four, six, and eight year old children*. Doctoral dissertation, Northwestern University, 1980.

Spache, G. *Diagnosis and correcting reading disabilities*. Boston: Allyn & Bacon, 1976.

Stanovich, K. Individual differences in the cognitive processes of reading: I. word decoding. *Journal of Learning Disabilities*, 1983, *15*, 485–493.

Stanovich, K. Individual differences in the cognitive processes of reading: II. Text-level processes. *Journal of Learning Disabilities*, 1983, *1*, 60–71.

Stein, N., & Glenn, C. An analysis of story comprehension in elementary school children. In R. Freedle (Ed.), *New Directions in discourse processing*. Norwood, NJ: Ablex, 1979.

Stricht, T., & James J. Listening and reading. In P. Pearson, R. Barr, M. Kamil, & P. Mosenthal (Eds.), *Handbook of reading research*. New York: 293–318, 1984.

Torgesen, J. Memorization processes in reading-disabled children. *Journal of Educational Psychology*, 1977, *22*, 375–385.

Torgesen, J., & Goldman, T. Verbal rehearsal and short-term memory in reading-disabled children. *Child Development*, 1977, *48*, 56–60.

Vellutino, F. Alternative conceptualization of dyslexia: Evidence in support of a verbal-deficit hypothesis. *Harvard Educational Review*, 1977, *47*, 334–354.

Vellutino, F. Childhood dyslexia: A language disorder. In H. Myklebust. *Progress in learning disabilities: Vol. V*. New York: Grune & Stratton, 1983.

Vogel, S. *Syntactic abilities in normal and dyslexic children*. Baltimore: University Park Press, 1975.

Vogel, S. Morphological ability in normal and dyslexic children. *Journal of Learning Disabilities*, 1977, *10*, 35–43.

Weaver, P., & Dickinson, D. Story comprehension and recall in dyslexic students. *Bulletin of the Orton Society*, 1979, *29*, 157–171.

Wells, C. The value of an oral reading test for diagnosis of the reading difficulties of college freshman of low academic performance. *Psychological Monographs*, 1950, *64*, 1–35.

Wiig, E., Semel, E., & Crouse, M. The use of morphology by high-risk and learning disabled children. *Journal of Learning Disabilities*. 1973, *6*, 457–465.

Wolf, M. Naming, reading, and the dyslexias: A longitudinal overview. *Annals of Dyslexia*, 1984, *34*, 87–115.

Wong, B. Understanding learning disabled students' reading problems: Contributions from cognitive psychology. *Topics in Learning and Learning Disabilities*, 1982, *1*, 43–50.

Zecker, S. G., Tanenhaus, M. K., Alderman, L., & Sequeland, L. Laterality of lexical codes in auditory word recognition. *Brain and Language*, 1986, In press.

# 10

## Disorders of Written Language

Doris J. Johnson

During the past decade there has been a surge of interest in the study of written language. This is due, in part, to the concerns of educators, parents, and employers who feel there has been a deterioration in the writing skills of American students. *Newsweek* Magazine even did a cover story on the "writing crisis" in our country (Sheils, 1975). Because of these concerns, many special projects and curriculum changes were initiated at the elementary, secondary, and post secondary levels.

In addition to these pragmatic developments, new theories regarding discourse (Frederiksen & Dominic, 1981; Nystrand, 1982), cohesion (Halliday & Hasan, 1976), syntax (Hunt, 1970, 1975) and spelling (Frith, 1980; Hanna, Hodges, & Hanna, 1971; Venezky, 1970) provided the impetus for extensive studies of writing. Tests for written language fostered research (Hammill & Larsen, 1981; Myklebust, 1965), and new instructional programs were designed (Britton, Burgess, Martin, McLeod, & Rosen, 1975; Larson, 1975; Lopate, 1975; Phelps-Gunn & Phelps-Terasaki, 1982).

Equally important were the contributions of theorists who developed complex models to study the writing *process*. Rather than analyzing the finished products of writers, they focused on processes such as preorganization, composing, and revision (Bereiter, 1980; Cooper & Odell, 1978; Emig, 1971; Flowers & Hayes, 1980; Gregg & Steinberg, 1980). To test their models, they observed writers at work, examined drafts to note types of revisions that were made with successive rewrites, or conducted interviews with writers and asked them to explain their activities at each stage. Humes (1983) provides a good overview of research methods on the composing process.

The study of written language has a relatively long history at Northwestern since Myklebust developed the Picture Story Language Test over 20 years ago (1965). This test, which includes scales for productivity, syntax, and levels

ADULTS WITH LEARNING DISABILITIES
ISBN 0-8089-1795-1

of abstraction provided a basis for comparing the writing of mentally retarded, deaf, emotionally disturbed, learning disabled, and other handicapped groups (Myklebust, 1973). It was also used in the clinical evaluation of learning disabled adults.

Many longitudinal studies of children with language disorders and dyslexia indicated that writing problems persisted into adulthood, even though significant gains were made in oral language and reading (Critchley, 1973; Rawson, 1968). Our clinical observations were similar. All the adults in this study had problems with one or more aspects of written language. Hence, it should be a major area of concern for diagnosticians and special educators.

## The Need for Writing

Writing is not simply an abstract symbol system used for school assignments; rather it is a means of communicating with oneself and others. Many people begin each day by writing lists for themselves to prioritize, remember, and organize activities. Throughout the day, writing for others may include phone messages, notes for children, messages to workmen, forms to be completed, envelopes to be addressed, and thank you notes or letters to family.

In school, writing instruction is often fragmented into sub-skills such as penmanship, spelling, and English composition. Unfortunately, this practice may interfere with a student's overall understanding of written language. In contrast, some educators recommend that writing be a part of every course, not a unique subject (Blake, 1975; Larson, 1975). In this way, students have an opportunity to practice and understand the functions of writing. They keep journals, record experiments in science, draw maps and label figures in social studies; they write story problems, recipes, and construct graphs in mathematics. They also write for school newspapers—editorials, cartoon captions, news summaries, etc. And, as they advance through school they learn more about note taking, outlining, and various forms of discourse. If writing is associated only with spelling, grammar drills and theme writing, many students, particularly atypical learners, may not acquire the skills needed for functional writing. Those in Special Education programs with little emphasis on writing may be even more deprived of a basic form of communication.

When working with learning disabled adults we emphasize writing for self as well as for others to aid memory and self-organization. Although some with severe disorders resist this recommendation, they soon realize they will worry less about remembering even if they write only a few notes to themselves. Those who are disorganized profit from writing a sequence of daily activities and assignments. Some learn spontaneously to use writing as a strategy for recall and organization.

The importance of writing for oneself was emphasized by Britton and his colleagues (1975) in their research on "sense of audience." They encourage students to write for self, as well as for trusted, familiar, and unfamiliar audiences. At times, writing can even be a form of therapy. By keeping a personal diary one can "try out" feelings, reflect, and contemplate ideas—and, if one chooses to do so—destroy the written product. Dagenais and Beadle (1984) suggest that to neglect written language is to ignore a buried treasure; those who facilitate its discovery may provide students with a special gift.

While some people say we need not worry about reading and writing to survive in modern society, our discussions with these adults indicate that written language disorders can limit educational, social, and vocational mobility. And because writing is so permanent and visible, their faulty products are embarrassing and a constant reminder of their problems.

## Oral and Written Language

Most developmental theorists and educators agree that oral language precedes written language and that the rudiments of comprehension precede expression. Children first develop auditory receptive language, then oral expressive language, visual receptive language (reading), and finally, visual expressive language or writing. This development is not all linear, however. Reciprocal patterns are evident during many phases of development. As children acquire interrogative forms they add to their receptive language by asking, "What's that?" or "What does _____ mean?." As they learn to read they acquire more complex syntax and abstract vocabulary. Similarly, reading is enhanced by writing. Graves (1983) says children begin to write even when they can make no more than a few letters. Spelling also increases linguistic awareness.

Because of both hierarchical and reciprocal patterns of development, we have emphasized the importance of studying relationships between all forms of language, particularly among exceptional learners (Johnson, 1982). We have found, for example, that reading may be used to aid oral language skills such as phonemic discrimination, memory, and syntax. Similarly, writing may foster strategies for memory and organization (Johnson, 1985).

The hierarchical pattern of language acquisition is evident in the proportions of problems observed among the learning disabled adults. All (N = 93) had difficulty with written language. Fewer (83) had difficulty reading, and fewer still had oral language problems (73). These numbers suggest that problems at lower levels interfere with higher functions, that writing problems persist, but relatively few adults have difficulty only with writing.

While certain aspects of language development can be studied hierarchically, writing is not simply talk written down. There are major differences between oral and written language (Litowitz, 1981; Nystrand, 1982; Olson, 1977; Stubbs, 1982; Vygotsky, 1962). First, the "vehicles" for conveying ideas are different. Oral expressive language requires an intact auditory-motor system whereas written expression requires visual-motor skills.

Another major difference according to Vygotsky (1962) is that in most instances, oral communication allows immediate feedback from the listener. Thus, ambiguity can be reduced if the listener looks puzzled or asks for clarification. Writing, in contrast, is done in isolation with an absent audience. Hence, it is thought that writing involves a greater awareness of audience needs—or "sense of audience." That is, the writer must take the perspective of the reader and develop a cohesive text.

On the other hand, oral communication also requires an awareness of audience needs. When speaking to a stranger, it is as important to introduce a topic and provide relevant details as it is when writing. Problems with sense of audience for both oral and written language were observed among adults in the clinic. For instance, secretaries who handled telephone inquiries reported that some adults did not introduce themselves or the topic. Therefore, more probes and prompts were needed to determine the reasons for the call. Likewise, self referral letters often arrived with missing information (e.g., the name of the city or state) and mixed levels of formality. Occasionally the salutations were very formal (e.g., Dear Dr. Doris J. Johnson) and the text very "chatty"—sometimes like a running stream of consciousness. ("I don't know what to write but I'll think of something.") In other instances, the salutation was informal even when I had never met the person (Hi, Doris) and the text relatively formal.

When comparing oral and written language, the types of instruction also should be noted. Children acquire the rules for phonology, semantics, syntax, and pragmatics implicitly in natural contexts. However, the rules for written language, particularly in the upper grades, are taught more explicitly. People who fail to learn implicitly may need more direct instruction, but the vocabulary used for teaching spelling rules and grammar may be difficult for students with language disorders.

Another major difference between oral and written language is the system for self monitoring. The ability to monitor one's own speech requires considerable auditory memory and temporal sequencing, since the speaker must remember what was said in relation to what is planned. In contrast, writing allows for more review of vocabulary, syntax, spelling, and organization. There is a greater opportunity for self correction. Because of these differences, students with auditory memory and oral language difficulties sometimes perform better when writing than speaking. For example, written definitions of the adults were slightly better than oral ones (see Chapter 8).

The type of feedback provided by others also varies. When communicating orally, the speaker needs to observe the listener for clues that indicate a lack of understanding. Adults with nonverbal disorders may be unable to detect these cues. Others are aware of listener needs but have limited language and, like Woolf's subjects (1983), are less able to respond to requests for clarification than their normal peers.

Feedback from written language is usually more permanent than oral but may not be specific enough to help the writer. An admonishment to "Proofread your paper" or "Watch your grammar" will be of little help to many.

Ambiguous, vague instructions are ill advised for any student, but are particularly ineffective for the learning disabled (Groshong, 1980; Hoskins, 1979).

## ASSESSMENT

A single sample of writing is rarely sufficient to define the breadth and depth of a problem, since written language may vary with the nature of the task, instructions, and stimulus. A story written about a single picture may yield different results from one about a series in overall productivity, number of temporal words (e.g., first, later), and use of verb forms. An autobiography may elicit more output than a picture from some writers, but restrict others. Sense of audience is more evident if writers are asked to convey an experience to both a stranger and a friend, and many aspects of writing, including spelling and syntax, vary with the degree of structure imposed by the clinician. These contrasts are useful for defining the problem and determining what needs to be taught, applied, or automatized.

Adults in the clinic were given the Picture Story Language Test (Myklebust, 1965), the spelling portion of the Wide Range Achievement Test (Jastak, Bijou, & Jastak, 1976), and a written sentence building task. In addition, all were asked to write a letter describing the nature of their difficulties. Some were given portions of the Test of Written Language (Hammill & Larsen, 1981) and several were asked to write an autobiography, a procedure recommended by Weiner (1980).

Those who came for diagnostic teaching and remediation were given tasks such as copying, spelling with various modes of response, writing to dictation, letter writing, note taking, and to complete forms. Those in college or vocational programs brought samples of their own writing projects. By observing, teaching, and talking with them, we gained additional insights into their problems. The remainder of this chapter is devoted to a general description of their difficulties in handwriting, spelling, syntax, formulation, and discourse.

## WRITTEN LANGUAGE PERFORMANCE PATTERNS AND TRENDS

Perhaps the most striking feature of the writing samples obtained from this group was the uneveness or "scatter" of performance. Within a single product one could observe adult vocabulary with atypical spelling, high levels of abstraction with defective syntax, or imaginative ideas with faulty letter formation. At times, the word usage and spelling errors created rather bizarre patterns. For example,

> "My math level only exceeds to addition" or "I need techniques in helping me curtail thes problem significantly."

While the concept of scatter has long been discussed with regard to the intellectual profiles of brain damaged children (Strauss & Lehtinen, 1947), it is equally relevant when studying complex processes such as written language. Often the uneven performance is lost if one examines only spelling, syntax, and handwriting on structured tests.

Inconsistency was evident in many writing samples. One does not expect a bright 30-year-old to periodically misspell his own name. Nor does one expect the gifted artist to reverse letters on a design, or the chemist to alternately write "PCB, PBC, BPC." This fluctuating performance often indicates that errors are not rule governed but result from attention disorders, faulty monitoring systems, or overload.

One had the feeling that many adults had not advanced beyond the stage of "talk written down." That is, they had not fully differentiated oral from written language. They wrote as they spoke with little regard for morphographemic or morphosyntactic rules. Even the punctuation was reminiscent of spoken language. Few used appropriate paragraph structure and their transitions between ideas were not well marked. Shaugnessy (1977) observed similar characteristics in college level basic writers.

Despite their problems with the written code, the adults did express ideas and feelings. Some even attempted poetry. They could not, however, communicate at a level commensurate with their mental ability. Thus, their writing conveyed two basic messages. On the one hand, the *content* of their letters, in particular, revealed their concerns, hopes, and fears. But the written *forms* and *structures* revealed their language disorders.

Often, their writing reflected their general approach to reading. As indicated in the previous chapter, poor decoders used the first letters of words and context to extract meaning. They did not—or could not—treat language analytically. Their failure to analyze words, note word endings, and understand certain relational words was evident in their writing.

Most adults were aware of their spelling and writing problems and mentioned them in their letters. Yet they could not independently produce or monitor a product that was totally free of errors. Although some had found ways to avoid writing at home or work, those in school or seeking higher levels of employment knew they needed help. When required to write, they had few alternatives. On the one hand, they could concentrate on ideas, ignoring spelling, punctuation, grammar or handwriting. Or, they could try to convey ideas by using only words they could spell. One man wrote,

> I have always had great diffulcality in spelling the words that I could spell, when knowing that full well that the word that I knew would fully express my fellings was never to be used because of my lack of knoeage of how to spell it.

## HANDWRITING

Since many adults use penmanship that is less than perfect, the diagnosis of a problem should be made with care. Nevertheless, some in our clinical population asked specifically for help with handwriting. Usually, however, they also were concerned about their inability to perform other tasks requiring visual-spatial-motor integration. At no time did we observe a handwriting disorder in isolation. Rather, we usually saw the same co-occurring problems we observed among children (Johnson & Myklebust, 1967). These included dysgraphia, mathematics problems, and left-right disorientation.

In order to determine whether an individual needs to be taught how to write letters, numbers and words, we recommend that copying tasks be used, since spontaneous writing requires additional memory, spelling, and language skills. For example, the man who wrote the sentence in Fig. 10-1 performed no better when asked to copy; however, the one who wrote the material in Figure 1-1 of Chapter 1 had no difficulty copying. His faulty writing was due to the fact that he could read and spell only a few words. Therefore, when he did not know a word he simply drew rather vague representations of letters.

During the evaluation, adults with poor handwriting were asked to copy upper and lower case manuscript, cursive letters and words, numerals, and geometric designs. Words for cursive writing were selected to examine connections between letters in words such as "on" and "no," since the letters are formed differently in words than in isolation.

Spontaneous handwriting was analyzed to investigate memory, spatial visualization, and consistency. Error patterns can be studied by using either a global or an analytic scale. The Test of Written Language (Hammill & Larsen, 1981) might be considered a global scale, since a sample is compared with examples in the manual. Often, however, the poorest writing of the adults was below the lowest level of the TOWL or so idiosyncratic they did not appear on the scale. Analytic scales direct the examiner to make judgments about letter formation, alignment, spacing, and other features (Mercer, 1983).

Throughout the evaluation, grasp, posture, position of the paper, and writing movements were observed. Some adults appeared to *draw* letters because they had no automatic motor plan. Occasionally they could produce intersecting lines (see the word explosion in Fig. 10-3).

### Visual-spatial-motor Integration

Thirteen adults had major problems in copying, visual analysis, and visual-motor integration. Performance was judged to be deficient when their faulty letter formation, spatial organization, alignment, or connections interfered with legibility or when their writing resulted in questionable spelling patterns.

The writing and drawing of the 30-year-old man whose work is shown in Figure 10-1 is a representative sample of the most severe disorders. He wrote,

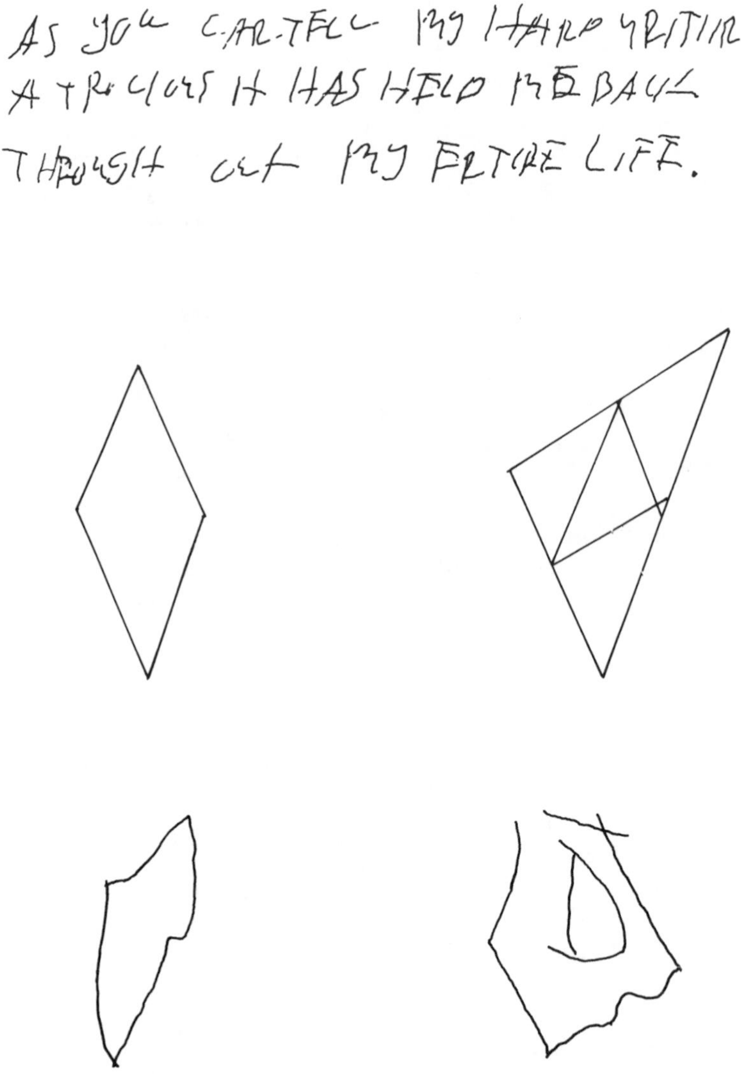

**Figure 10-1.** Writing and drawing of a 30-year-old man.

"My handwriting is atrocious—it has held me back throughout my entire life." This man, like others with this pattern of difficulty, had good verbal intelligence and low nonverbal ability. He had no difficulty with oral language or reading. Spelling was adequate, but he, like others with this disability, made occasional mistakes because of visual monitoring and fatigue associated with writing. His primary areas of underachievement were in handwriting, arithmetic, and nonverbal learning. He had difficulty tying a necktie, wrapping packages, opening

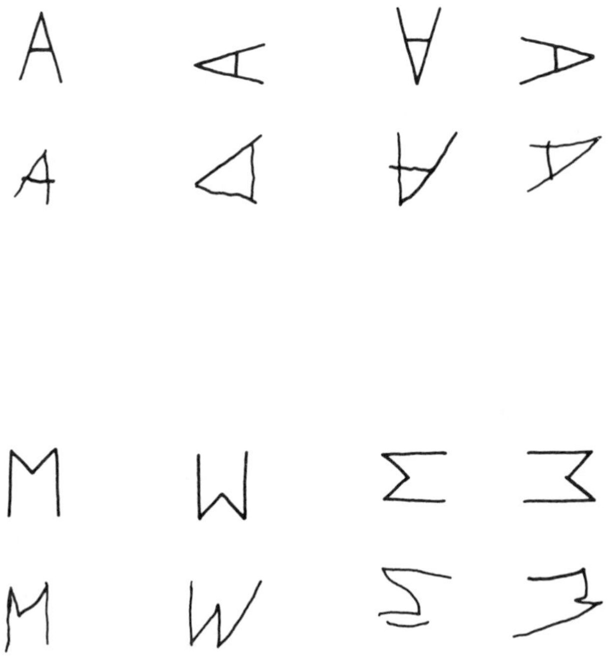

**Figure 10-2.** Copying rotated figures.

milk cartons, using keys in locks, and folding paper to fit into envelopes. Specific disabilities included visual analysis and synthesis, spatial visualization (Moyer, 1978), and visual-spatial-motor integration. These problems are reflected in his copying of two designs from the Beery Buktenica Test of Visual-Motor Integration (Beery & Buktenica, 1982) at the bottom of Figure 10-1. His difficulty with visual spatial orientation was evident when he was asked to print the capital letters M and A in different positions. (see Fig. 10-2) His scores from the Wechsler Intelligence Scale for Adults (1981) are given below.

| Verbal Intelligence | 108 | Performance Intelligence | 71 |
|---|---|---|---|
| Information | 12 | Digit Symbol | 8 |
| Comprehension | 12 | Picture Completion | 8 |
| Arithmetic | 8 | Block Design | 3 |
| Similarities | 12 | Picture Arrangement | 6 |
| Digit Span | 15 | Object Assembly | 2 |
| Vocabulary | 10 | | |

While not all were as severe as the case described above, their problems interfered with written communication because of poor letter closure (e.g., the cursive word day looked like clay), inappropriate letter heights (no differentiation between the cursive *e* and *l* or *f* and *b*), and faulty connections between

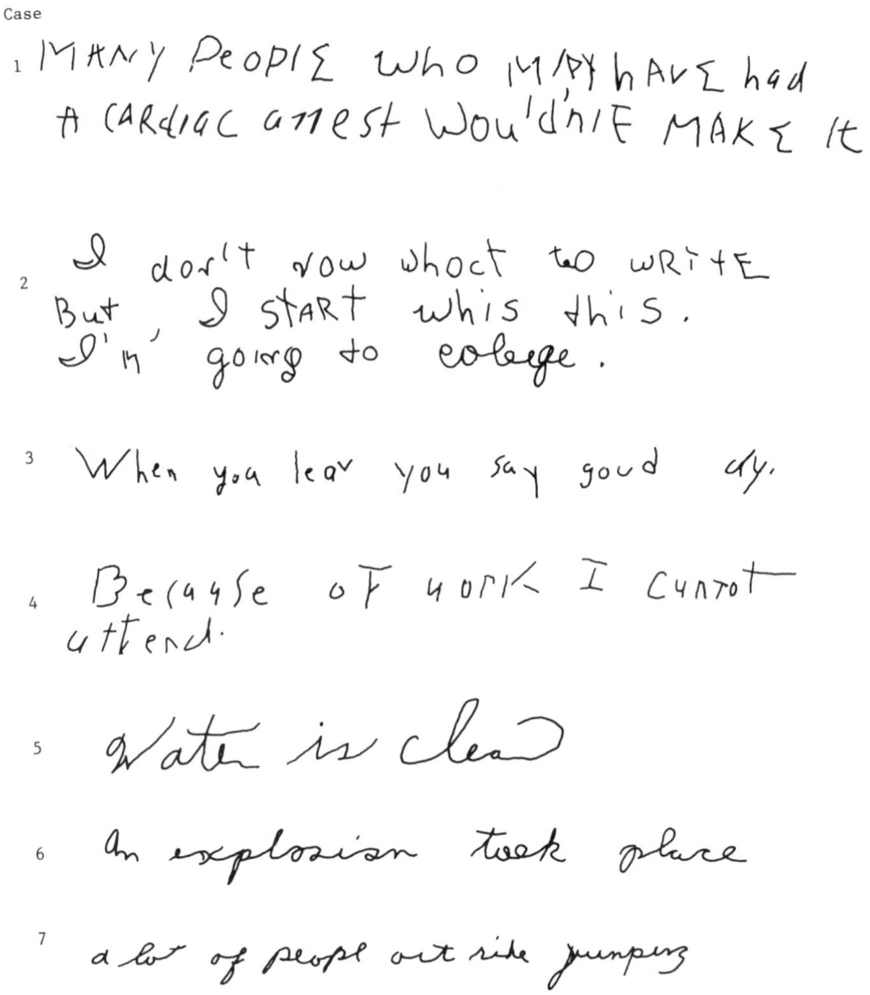


**Figure 10-3.** Examples of faulty handwriting.

letters (see Fig. 10-3), and spacing. Often it was difficult to determine the beginning and end of words. However, visual spatial problems were different from those related to linguistic awareness. Adults who wrote units such as *onceupon atime* had not established word meaning boundaries.

Uneven pressure was noted in several cases. This may have resulted from either faulty proprioception or fatigue. A few adults were aware of their inability to judge the amount of pressure to use, not only in writing, but in other tasks. Others, however, could not monitor their performance.

Lack of automatic motor planning was noted in three cases who had been diagnosed as apraxic during early childhood. One man who had a history of

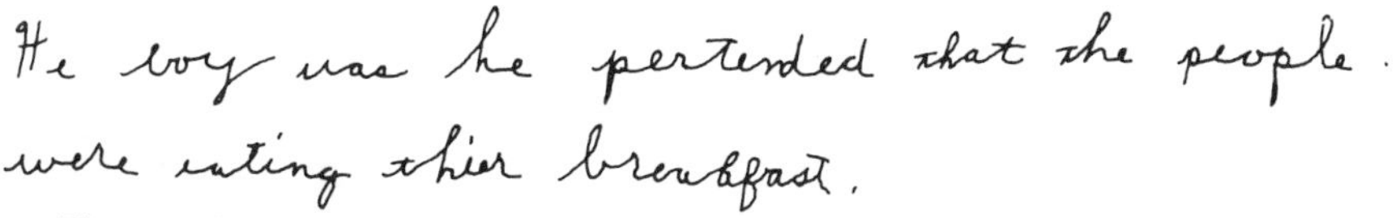


**Figure 10-4.** Writing of a man with apraxia and motor planning problems.

both speech and writing problems was concerned about the amount of time it took to complete papers. His difficulty was obvious when watching him slowly write the material in Fig. 10-4.

Often people with these disabilities are encouraged to type. While the final products are more legible and satisfying, it should be noted that typing also requires visual-spatial-motor integration, so instructions may need to be modified. Our experience with several children and adults has indicated verbal instructions are needed to direct the motor plan for both writing and typing. Verbal guides such as *up*, *down*, and *around* may be needed for handwriting. For typing, verbal cues such as a,s,d,f,g (order of letters on the typewriter) may be helpful.

Visual spatial problems may also prevent monitoring of typewritten work. This is evident in the spontaneous letter (Fig. 10-5) of a young man who had poor handwriting and visual-spatial disorders.

### Visualization and Related Memory Problems

Several adults could copy, but could not always revisualize letters. Similar problems were observed among children (Johnson & Myklebust, 1967). The person who wrote the sentence at the bottom of Figure 10-3 omitted part of the *t* in *lot* and the *u* in *out*. As a result, the legibility was decreased. Furthermore, the writing calls attention to itself because of the incomplete forms.

Ten adults had difficulty with spatial visualization. They could spell orally, but reversed letters or parts of letters as shown in Figure 10-3. The man who wrote *may* in the first example was inconsistent in printing the letter A, and the woman who wrote the second sentence in Figure 10-3 partially reversed the *n*.

Several people had both motor planning and visualization difficulties. The woman who wrote the sixth sentence in Figure 10-3 (*An explosion took place*) had problems copying and visualizing intersecting lines. Note her *x* in *explosion*, and connections between the two *o*s in *took*. In remediation, people with memory disorders are given models of the correct forms and, if necessary, directions for producing difficult letters. In other instances, they are given more time to complete their work since speed of access seems to be a problem.

### Mixed Forms and Automaticity

An inspection of all the writing samples of our 93 adults indicated that over $\frac{1}{3}$ (36 percent) used mixed manuscript and cursive or upper and lower case letters within a single product. This same tendency was noted among the basic writers

Dear Miss

I want t o thank you for the help you
have given me during these past years. Yo u have helped
me a great dael. It has been an enjoyablee time.

Thank you again,,

Yours truly

**Figure 10-5.** Typing of a man with handwriting and visual-spatial disorders.

described by Shaugnessy (1977). There are several reasons for these errors. In some instances they had never learned to make all the letters easily. Therefore, during spontaneous writing they used forms they could access easily. Some said they lost their train of thought if they stopped to think about letter formations.

Others avoided reversals by inserting capital or cursive letters even in the middle of a word. They were conscious of their directionality problems and tried to reduce errors. Some could spell words aloud correctly, but wrote the wrong forms.

In a few instances, writers used their own idiosyncratic rule systems. For example, the man who wrote the first sentence in Figure 10-3 used an upper case *E* at the end of words but a lower case *e* in the middle. He did not, however follow a rule for the upper and lower case *r*. He used an upper case *R* in *caRdiac* but a lower case *r* in *arrest*. Often these mistakes result from attention disorders or difficulty shifting from one code to another. The identification of upper and lower case letters in writing samples was a surprisingly difficult task for several adults and seemed to indicate lack of facility with various codes.

While most adults were inconsistent, one adult who used mixed manuscript and cursive had a clear, distinct rule. When asked why, he said he wrote all names in cursive because "you can't write anyone else's signature." In this case, the atypical writing resulted from a misunderstanding of the word *signature*. When told the real meaning of the word, he no longer had difficulty with the use of upper and lower case letters.

Most poor writers had multiple problems as evident in Figure 10-6. This 20-year-old had numerous problems in spelling, written syntax, handwriting, and visualization. When writing a story, all the subskills deteriorated because he could not think about ideas, spelling, and letter formation simultaneously.

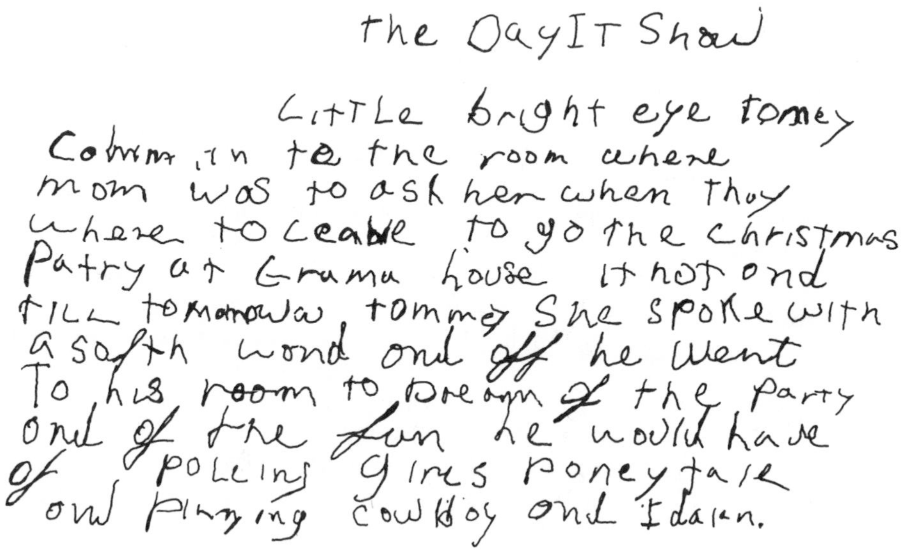

the OayIT Show
LitTLe bright eye tomey
Cobrin in to the room where
mom was to ask her when thoy
where to Leave to go the christmas
Patry at Grama house it not ond
till tomorrow tommy She spoke with
a softh word ond off he went
To his room to Dream of the Party
Ond of the fun he would have
of poleing gires poneytale
ow playing cowboy ond Idaian.


**Figure 10-6.** Writing of a 20-year-old man.

### Handwriting and Reading Disorders

The handwriting of dyslexics has been of interest to many researchers, particularly those interested in subtypes. Mattis, French, and Rapin (1975), for example, found one subgroup had difficulty with articulation and graphomotor skills as well as reading.

While it is assumed that poor readers will have difficulty with spontaneous writing, some copy letters quite easily and have few difficulties with analysis and synthesis. Others, however, write (almost draw) letters like young children. One severe dyslexic even used wide lined paper when she first began writing. In remediation it was several months before her letters lost their child-like characteristics. She and another man were pleased when they could finally write their names and addresses in adult-like script. As they were learning, it was evident why they had occasional problems in banking and cashing travellers checks.

While handwriting is only a minor part of written language, problems can interfere with communication and with the ability to proofread their own work.

## SPELLING

Spelling is a significant component of written language that requires the abstraction and use of multiple rule systems. It is not simply an isolated skill associated with weekly tests in school. The complexity of the process is evident from the research of Beers and Henderson (1980), Frith (190), Hanna, Hodges, and Hanna (1971) and Venezky (1967) who state that spelling requires knowledge about phonology, semantics, morphology, and syntax as well as the integration of these rule systems with the orthography. Venezky (1970) says children must treat language analytically in order to write efficiently. From our clinical work we concluded that spelling requires more auditory and visual discrimination, memory, sequencing analysis and synthesis, and integration than perhaps any other skill (Johnson & Myklebust, 1967). Given these processing demands, it is evident that most learning disabled adults will have problems.

The evaluation of spelling, like other aspects of language, should include both spontaneous and structured (elicited) samples. Comparisons provide information regarding motivation, generation of ideas, rule application, and strategies. Discrepancies between structured and spontaneous writing also may reflect processing deficits. Adults often make more spelling and syntax errors during spontaneous writing when they are expected to apply several types of rules simultaneously. Others, particularly those with sequencing and reauditorization disorders, spell better from dictation, since they profit from the auditory input of the examiner. Those with revisualization or visual-motor difficulties may perform better on multiple choice tests or when given the opportunity to type. During diagnostic teaching we may vary the forms of input and output as shown in Figure 10-7.

## Spelling from Dictation

All the adults in this project were given the Wide Range Achievement Test (Jastak, Bijou, & Jastak, 1976). As expected on the basis of their reading performance, spelling achievement levels and standard scores varied from below 46 to 120. As a group, their mean performance on spelling tests was below oral reading. These findings highlight the fact that reading is predominantly a receptive process, whereas writing involves recall and expression.

A more detailed analysis of individual records indicated, however, that both the size and direction of the discrepancy between reading and spelling varied. Eight subjects scored four grades higher on reading than spelling. In these cases, revisualization, rule application, and visual-spatial-motor problems contributed to the writing deficiencies.

In contrast, 13 percent of the group scored at least 1 grade higher on spelling than reading tests. These discrepancies may be related to differences in reauditorization and revisualization. Whereas oral reading requires the conversion of visual symbols to their auditory-motor equivalents, spelling from dictation requires the conversion of oral language to a graphomotor response. Thus, people with severe reauditorization deficits may spell better than they read.

This discrepancy also may be related to the theories of Bryant and Bradley (1980) who state that reading requires visual clustering strategies while spelling requires more phonemic analysis and linguistic awareness. Evidence from several studies support their hypotheses (Bradley & Bryant, 1985).

Scores from achievement tests provide limited data for detecting spelling

| INPUT | FORM OF RESPONSE |
|---|---|
| 1. AUDITORY DICTATION<br>"Write Basket" | WRITTEN<br>bukt |
| 2. AUDITORY DICTATION<br>"Spell the word basket" | ORAL<br>B-A-K-S-E-T |
| 3. SLOW AUDITORY DICTATION<br>"Write bas - ket" | WRITTEN<br>basket |
| 4. VISUAL VERBAL<br>"Make these letters say basket" | MANIPULATION<br>BAKSET |
| 5. VISUAL AND AUDITORY VERBAL<br>"Point to basket" | RECOGNITION<br>BASKET BAKSET |
| 6. VISUAL NONVERBAL<br>"Write the name of this object" | WRITTEN<br>bast |

**Figure 10-7.** Examples of systems study of spelling.

strategies or planning remediation (Cicci, 1983; Rourke, 1978) since words chosen only according to frequency of occurrence may not elicit patterns of errors. Thus, tests such as the Boder (1982) or the Test of Written Spelling (Larsen & Hammill, 1976), which includes predictable and unpredictable words, are used. Informal lists such as those described in the preceding chapter also can be used to study relationships between reading and spelling. Words with relatively consistent phoneme-grapheme correspondence, consonant clusters, morphological endings etc. provide further insight into strategy use.

With time constraints it is not always possible to give multiple lists. Therefore, specific error analyses are useful. For example, Temple, Nathan, and Burris (1982) classified the spelling patterns of young children as prephonemic, early phonemic, letter name, transitional, and correct. Miles (1983) and the researchers in Frith (1980) developed elaborate schema for studying error patterns of the deaf, aphasic, and reading disabled. Spache (1976) used categories such as omissions, substitutions, additions, and reversals found that good spellers tend to write words phonetically. That is, their mistakes do not alter the pronunciation of words (e.g., ommission, independance). Poor

| Correct Form | Phonetic | Nonphonetic |
|---|---|---|
| train | trane | train |
| institute | institoot | instut |
| anxiety | angziety | ansity |
| lucidity | loosidity | lacity |
| opportunity | oppertunity | optinty |

**Figure 10-8.** Examples of Phonetic and Nonphonetic Spelling Errors.

spellers, in contrast, omit, add, or substitute letters or syllables (e.g., inpenence). Rourke (1978) concluded that his phonetically inaccurate spellers had generalized linguistic deficits.

In a study comparing the mistakes of (1) good readers–good spellers, (2) poor readers–poor spellers, and (3) good readers–poor spellers, Frith (1980) found the poor reader–poor speller group made more phonetically unacceptable errors than either of the other groups.

The WRAT spelling errors of the adults were classified as phonetically acceptable or unacceptable (see Fig. 10-8 for examples). Results indicated that all except one person, who was a pure phonetic speller, made mistakes of both types. However, when the errors at each grade level were classified, the pattern in Table 10-1 emerged. Adults who were spelling at the fifth grade level or below made more phonetically unacceptable errors than those achieving at the upper grade levels. Seventy-seven percent of the mistakes made by the poorest spellers were phonetically unacceptable, whereas only 29 percent of the best spellers' mistakes were unacceptable. In order to compare this latter group with nondisabled adults, 35 high school graduates were given the WRAT. Those with standard scores comparable to the best adults made even a smaller proportion (24 percent) of phonetically unacceptable errors. They had difficulty with doubling rules, and morphological endings in which the vowels are not stressed (ance, ence).

The poorest spellers used primarily wholistic strategies. When they could not visualize whole words, they wrote nothing more than one or two letters. Generally, their performance reflected difficulties with auditory analysis and linguistic awareness. In a few rare instances their writing was nothing more than written jargon (See Fig. 10-9). Several words in this passage contained orthographically illegal patterns. Miles (1983) would have classified many as Impossible Trigrams because they contained three letters that are unacceptable in English (e.g., drpzong).

These observations support the hypothesis that poor spellers have problems related to linguistic awareness. (Blalock reported a high correlation between phoneme segmentation and spelling ability in Chapter 8.) There were exceptions, however. A more detailed inspection of phonetically unacceptable errors,

**Table 10-1**
Analysis of Spelling Errors on Wide Range Achievement Test

| Grade Level Score | # of Cases | % Phonetic | % Nonphonetic |
|---|---|---|---|
| 5 and below | 12 | 22 | 77 |
| 6 | 12 | 32 | 68 |
| 7 | 9 | 40 | 60 |
| 8 | 11 | 46 | 54 |
| 9 | 6 | 47 | 53 |
| 10 | 6 | 51 | 49 |
| 11 | 6 | 52 | 48 |
| 12 | 6 | 71 | 29 |

particularly at the upper levels, appeared to be due to faulty visual monitoring, memory, or spatial visualization. Some adults with relatively good segmenting skills reversed, transposed, or wrote incomplete letters that resulted in phonemically unacceptable words. Subtle disorders of attention and perseveration often created unacceptable patterns (e.g., rememember). A lack of synchrony between auditory and visual processing or between phonology and orthography was evident in several instances. Occasionally we heard an adult spell the word circle correctly while writing clrce. The latter would have been classified as an Unacceptable Trigram by Miles (1983).

While error analyses based on phonetic and nonphonetic patterns are useful, they are too limiting, since morphological rules can be overlooked. Both Cromer (1980) and Frith (1980) emphasized the need to look beyond the surface structure of language. If spellers focus primarily on the ways words sound in English (phonology), they fail to note derivatives and morphographemic rules. We saw many errors of this type in the writing of the adults (see Fig. 10-10). Results of research with learning disabled children are similar. Bailet (1985) found only 6 of her poor readers/poor spellers wrote all 6 exemplars of the ed ending, whereas 13 of 14 normal fourth graders spelled all 6 exemplars correctly. Even some of her sixth grade subjects wrote lookt. She concluded normal spellers had achieved greater mastery of morphophonemic-morphological rules than learning disabled children.

Morpho-graphemic spelling errors of the adults were not totally rule governed, since only a small proportion of the plurals or verb endings were incorrect. This may suggest lack of automaticity and/or differences in the way listeners perceive the morphemes in connected speech.

**Figure 10-9.** Spontaneous writing of a severe dyslexic.

| Correct Form | Error |
|---|---|
| notices | notices |
| earloer | earlier |
| oriented | oriented |
| belongings | belonginges |
| toys | toyes |
| enjoys | enjoyes |
| forties | fortys |
| calls | calles |
| cleaned | cleand |
| gotten | gotton |
| notices | notest |
| looks | lookes |
| having | haveing |
| bored | bord |
| pieces | piecus |

**Figure 10-10.** Examples of spelling errors related to morphological endings.

The errors also may result from lack of explicit instruction. When acquiring oral language, children learn implicitly to pluralize nouns that end with voiceless consonants by adding /s/ (cats, mops) but pluralize those ending with voiced consonants by adding /z/ ("bedz; bugz"). Yet the written plural for both is formed by adding "s." It is our impression that some people with language disorders fail to make these inferences and, therefore, need more specific instructions to highlight the orthographic rules. The morphographemic spelling errors also may be related to the adults' poor performance on the Berry Talbott test of morphology (1961) and their difficulty with structural analysis in reading.

## Spontaneous Spelling

While standardized tests allow for group comparisons, spontaneous writing provides additional data regarding rule application and strategies. One error type, found only in context, is related to segmenting and word boundaries (Fig. 10-11). While one might expect young children to make errors of this type (Downing & Oliver, 1973–74), there were 30 instances on the Picture Story Language Test (Myklebust, 1965) and even more in their letters.

More letter transpositions occurred in spontaneous writing than in spelling from dictation (see Fig. 10-12). It is hypothesized they resulted from an inability to retain a temporal sequence, reauditorization, or faulty attention and monitoring.

## Diagnostic Teaching and Strategy Use in Spelling

Many adults and children in our clinic are seen for diagnostic teaching following the two day assessment to explore possible reasons for errors and make recommendations. Modification of sensory inputs and directions often

| Correct Form | Error |
|---|---|
| into | in to |
| until | and till |
| instead | in stead |
| used to | ustedto |
| want to | wan to |
| forgot | for got |
| interaction | inter action |
| always | all ways |
| away | a way |
| however | how ever |
| upon a time | plontime |

**Figure 10-11.** Segmenting errors from the Picture Story Language Test.

provides useful information for the study of learning processes and spelling. In an investigation based on Luria's approach (1966), Trout (1973) completed five successive days of spelling tasks with a child to elicit information about auditory, visual, and kinesthetic processes and rule generalization. With this approach, subjects are given screening tests followed by a series of hypotheses and tasks to determine the basis for errors. Subjects are "forced" to use or inhibit certain responses. For example, they are required to say or visualize words before writing them. At other times, they are inhibited from reauditorizing or speaking by holding a pencil between their teeth. Clinicians then make inferences about deficient processes and compensatory strategies.

More recently Hoff (1985) completed a study in which normal and learning disabled children were asked to generate graphemic options for certain phonological units (e.g., /j/). She found learning disabled poor spellers generated fewer

| Correct Form | Error |
|---|---|
| party | patry |
| chair | chiar |
| from | form |
| etc. | ect. |
| because | becasue |
| involvement | invovlement |
| girl | gril |
| home | hmoe |
| pure | prue |
| self | slfe |
| pretends | pertends |
| guest | guset |
| waited | wiated |
| does | dose |

**Figure 10-12.** Transposition errors from the Picture Story Language Test.

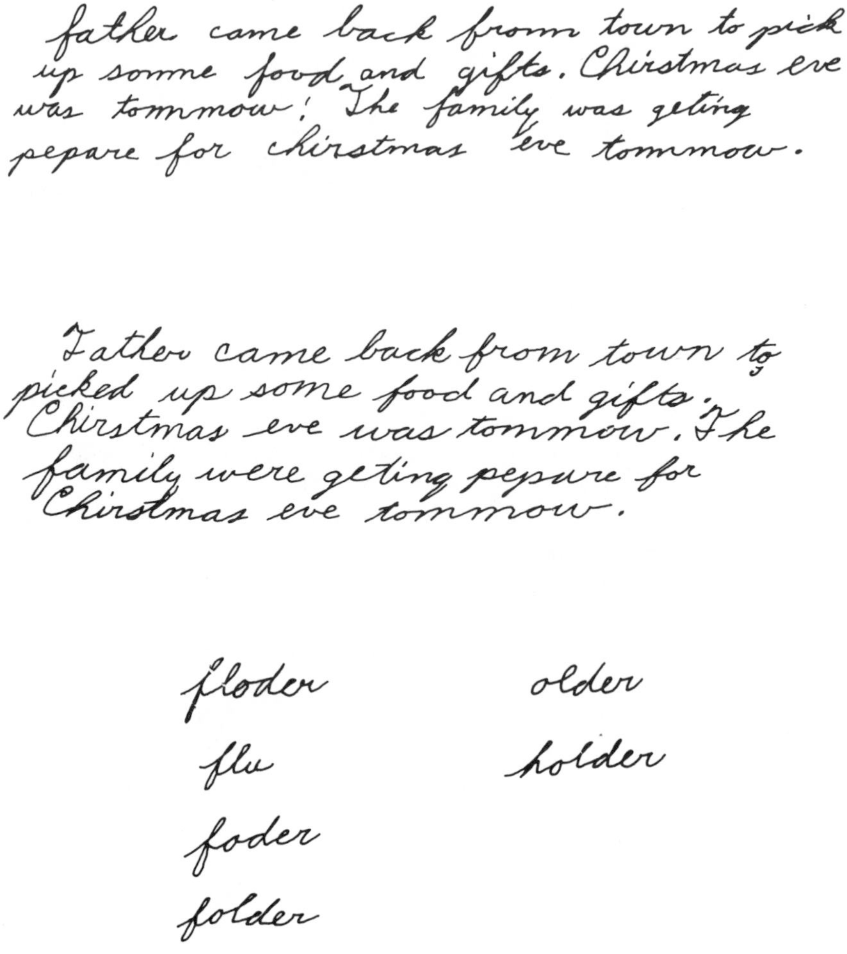

father came back from town to pick
up somme food and gifts. Chirstmas eve
was tommow! The family was geting
pepare for chirstmas eve tommow.
Father came back from town to
picked up some food and gifts.
Chirstmas eve was tommow. The
family were geting pepare for
Chirstmas eve tommow.
floder
flu
foder
folder
older
holder


**Figure 10-13.** Self monitoring of a man with oral language disorders.

options than their nondisabled peers and concluded they had less linguistic awareness than the control group. Her data also may suggest that poor spellers cannot "image" as many patterns as normals.

During diagnostic teaching, we frequently note whether we can heighten a person's awareness to certain patterns or rules by dictating several words of the same type. Bailet (1985) used this approach in her research and found both normal and learning disabled subjects improved with added structure.

Self monitoring is also explored. We are interested in knowing how many and which types of mistakes the writer can correct with and without probes. For example, the first three sentences at the top of Figure 10-13 were written by a

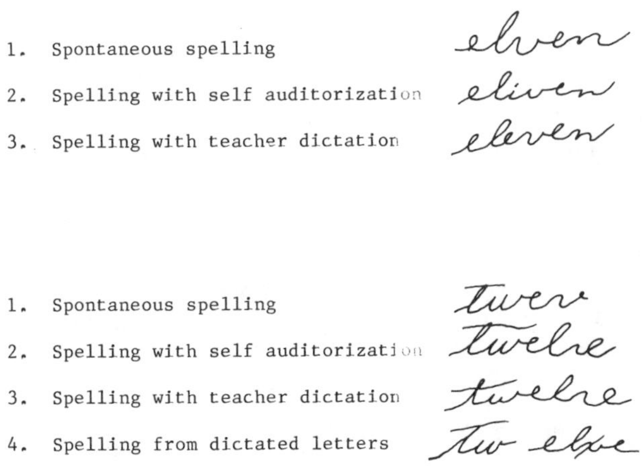


**Figure 10-14.** Spelling patterns of a dyslexic.

young man with severe oral language disorders. On the second day he was asked to proof and correct as many errors as possible. The material at the bottom of the figure indicates he detected letter formation errors but no spelling mistakes. He changed one sentence, presumably because of grammar, but it was also incorrect.

Following the self-monitoring activities, we dictated the words he misspelled and found he wrote 80 percent correctly. Thus, in remediation we tried to "induce" auditorization techniques. This was not always successful, however, because of his faulty pronunciations. For instance, he could not spell the word "folder" correctly until he was directed to "watch the speaker, raise your tongue for the *l*," and practice the pronunciation before writing. His performance and immediate transfer to similar words is shown in Figure 10-13. The examples in Figure 10-14 illustrate problems of auditorization as well as letter formation. By inducing certain strategies and varying forms of input and output, we also explore avenues that are available for independent learning.

## WRITTEN FORMULATION AND DISCOURSE

Multiple samples of written language are needed to investigate the writer's range of vocabulary, syntax, and use of various forms of discourse such as narration, argumentation and description (Phelps-Gunn & Phelps-Terasaki, 1982). While extensive samples were unavailable from all adults, we had at least a letter and a story from each, and in many instances we had autobiographies, essays, and themes from those in school.

## Productivity

Given the numerous language, reading, and spelling disorders of this group one would expect overall productivity to be limited. This hypothesis was confirmed when their Picture Story Language Tests were compared with those of 17-year-olds. The data in Table 10-2 show they used fewer words and sentences than high school seniors. The mean number of words per story was 126.98 with a range from 14 to 228. Stories of the poorest readers were below the thirty-fifth percentile for 7-year-olds.

Their letters, however, were often longer than their stories. They were apparently motivated to explain why they wanted help and found it easier to generate ideas from their own experience.

## Text Organization and Sense of Audience

An analysis of the stories and letters indicated problems of organization, cohesion, and sense of audience in 80 percent of the products. These were often reflected in the first sentences of the Picture Story Language Test, the opening paragraphs of themes, and salutations of letters. Note the examples of introductory sentences for the PSLT in Figure 10-15. Often the information was too specific or too vague for the introduction of a topic, character, or setting. Many of their products were filled with ambiguous pronouns and referents. These same characteristics were reported by Podhajski (1980) who investigated narrative skills in normal and learning disabled children. Similarly Cohen (1983) found sixth grade learning disabled students were less able to accommodate readers' perspectives and frequently failed to include relevant information. This same characteristic was noted in compositions of the adults. One man with a language disorder began a book report as follows:

> "Dan went down to check out the western. The Western was on the tip of the mountain. The Western was being to fall, dan was starting to have trouble. When dan went up the surface, he told the crew what happen. Jenkins didn't like the crew. Mr. Duncan wanted the motors from the western star.

His writing continued for six pages, leaving the reader wondering who the characters were, what the setting was, and the general plot of the story.

**Table 10-2**
Performance on the Picture Story Language Test

| | Mean Age | SD | Mean Stanine | Range |
|---|---|---|---|---|
| Total Words | 12.0 | 3.8 | 3.9 | 1-9 |
| Total Sentences | 10.7 | 4.1 | 4.3 | 1-9 |
| Words per Sentence | 14.2 | 3.0 | 4.5 | 1-9 |
| Syntax | 12.2 | 4.0 | 3.5 | 1-9 |
| Abstract/Concrete | 12.5 | 4.2 | 4.3 | 1-9 |

1. The mind of a child is a woundresss thing in that it has the ability to produce the missing parts.
2. Once upon a time a boy lived with his familyu on ashford Ave.
3. Jansen a young boy who was very lonely.
4. The is this little boy who lives down the block from me.
5. The child in the photograph is immiganiting what family life is like at dinner time.
6. One day in 1949, there was a little boy name John.
7. The white (Caucausian) boy (age about six) who is wearing a white shirt, with a sweater and jacket is sitting down at table with some toys.
8. This is a stoy of young boy about the age of Seven years old.
9. The little boy must find a way to happy by playing with all these objects.
10. A little boy makeing a go famliy house.
11. The boy is sitting trying to oput the man and chair into place where he want them to go.
12. A little boy playing house in what appears to be an office of some kind.
13. This is Johnny in the thirties, forties—have you seen children it a neat, trim, fitting jacket lately?
14. The little boy is seating at the table.
15. "Hey, come back here", dick says to Max.
16. Most of the children at the school love to play and fool around whenever they could.
17. This is the story about ayoung man of the age of 6.
18. A child can express what th word family mean to him in many different ways, such as his affection toward the family, through his own words or through play.
19. In this brief story I am going to give this young man the name of Dick.
20. As a boy grows up.

**Figure 10-15.** Examples of introductory sentences from the Picture Story Language Test.

Several letters began in equally abrupt fashion or in a manner characteristic of young children who have not yet differentiated oral from written language. For example, one wrote, "Hi, how are you today." I would like an antrance of your clinic." Twenty-three percent of the salutations were classified an inappropriate or incorrect. These included excessively informal openings such as "Dearest Jane," redundancies (e.g., "Dear Dr.Miss Doris Johnson"), and problems with word boundaries (e.g., "To whomit may consure"). Less obvious errors occurred in the placement and punctuation of the salutations.

## Level of Abstraction and Story Organization

The mean age level scores for the abstract/concrete scale of the Picture Story Language Test (Myklebust, 1965) were well below average (see Table 10-2). The majority wrote stories that were judged to be either concrete/descriptive or concrete/imaginative. This was probably due to poor vocabulary, reading level, spelling, and limited sense of audience.

In order to analyze their written organization we prepared a series of questions that were given to three raters who judged each of the stories. The questions included some used by Stein and Glenn (1979). First, we asked the raters to make a judgment as to whether the product was a story. Thirty-six percent were judged not to be stories because they had no clear beginning, middle, and end. None had a title. Twelve percent did not introduce the character or setting. However, 91 percent *did* have an initiating event. A relatively high percentage (24 percent) had no conclusions to their stories.

As expected from our initial observations, temporal organization was judged to be lacking in 70 percent of the stories. This was reflected in their failure to use temporal conjunctions and cohesive ties. It is interesting to note that Loban (1976) says children begin to use such connectives at about age 12. Some adults even misused the word "because." When the raters were asked to judge whether the writer had used a logical sequence of events, 14 were judged lacking in appropriate cause-effect relations. A few were similar to the "unfocused chains" described by Applebee (1978).

Because of the faulty introductory sentences, we asked whether the adults used excessive details in their stories, but raters found this tendency in only six instances. Nevertheless, in these cases it was significant enough to lead the reader astray and destroy the organization.

Finally, since the adults often expressed concern about the child pictured in the test we tabulated the number of instances in which feelings were expressed. Forty-one percent wrote about a boy who was disabled in some way. Perhaps the picture for the test lends itself to this theme. Nearly half wrote about a boy who was either learning disabled, mentally retarded, emotionally ill, or physically disabled. They expressed concern and thought the boy was in a special place to receive help or overcome his problems.

## Vocabulary

The relationships between problems of word meaning, conceptualization, spelling, and syntax were evident in many of their written products including definitions (see Chapter 8). Their misperceptions, misunderstanding of words, and lack of attention to morphosyntactic rules can be noted throughout this volume. A man with a generalized language disorder (see Chapter 9) wrote that "I lack confiness in writing—and I fined I have trouble hearing all of the sounds in works." Another wrote a note asking if we would "berify his prudentials." These examples and others raise many questions: Would they say the same thing? Do they talk that way? Could they detect their mistakes? and in some instances, What does he mean? The answers emerge only during periods of diagnostic teaching when one can follow-up on the errors. For example, a college student wrote that his "schooling had been pledged by his poor spelling ability and he never got dissent grades." In this instance both of the substitutions were correctly spelled real words. Follow-up discussion indicated that he knew "pledged" was wrong and was surprised that he had written it, yet he admitted he did not know how to spell plague. He could use the words "dissent" and "decent" correctly in oral sentence building tasks, but was not sure when to use each in writing.

In contrast, the man who wrote "berify prudentials" said what he wrote. He had misperceived the words but understood them. When asked to discriminate pairs of words (verify-berify), he was slow to detect the differences and even slower to repeat them correctly.

In general, their vocabularies were below expectancy because of language, reading, and spelling problems. Since many were relatively poor readers, they had not had an opportunity to expand their vocabularies.

## SYNTAX

Written syntax disorders of learning disabled adults have been reported by many researchers, Gregg (1982) and Weiner (1980a&b). Many findings are also summarized in Chapter 14 on college programs.

In our group, syntax was studied by using the Picture Story Language Test (Myklebust, 1965), their letters, and a written sentence building task. None of the 93 achieved a perfect score on either the PSLT or sentence building. The mean age scores shown in Table 10-2 indicate that as a group, their scores were comparable to sixth graders. Further analysis indicated errors of all types, but the most frequent were omission of words, word endings, and punctuation. These findings are similar to those of Gregg (1982) who studied normal college freshmen, basic writers, and learning disabled students.

Syntactic complexity was investigated by tabulating sentence types used in the PSLT. Forty-seven percent of all sentences were simple. Twenty-two percent were compound and the remainder were complex or compound-complex. There were many fragments and, as expected, from the lack of punctuation, many run on sentences.

The range of conjunctions used was very limited. The most frequent was "and" followed by 14 instances of "but" and eleven of "so." Only one person used "while" and another "thus." Their failure to use causal and temporal vocabulary resulted in a lack of cohesion and clarity.

None of the adults achieved a perfect score on written sentence building. The mean percentage of correctly formulated sentences was 83.7 (SD 13.1) and the mean percentage of correctly punctuated sentences was 63.8 (SD 29.9). In contrast, the mean percentage correct for a group of 35 nondisabled high school graduates was 98.3. Only seven made any errors and those were probably related to faulty monitoring since the mistakes often were omissions of an article or final letter.

The errors frequently distorted the meaning of the sentences, a finding similar to that of Gregg (1982) who used a sentence combining task with her college freshmen.

The most frequent errors on sentence building occurred with articles and conjunctions. For example, fifteen misused "an" and "and." (e.g., Joe an I like baseball). One person used *an* as a part of the word *another* (I had *an*other comb in my bag) or as a proper noun. (An lived next door). Often they seemed to be guided by phonology rather than meaning and orthography.

Problems related to the use of *if*, *because*, *since* etc. were related to conceptual difficulties, time disorientation, vocabulary, and monitoring. A vague notion of the writer's intent could be perceived, but the forms were wrong. A feeling of causal relations is apparent in the sentence, "I love doctors that alway have a because to disagree with you," but the writer substituted "because" for "reason." Some errors probably occurred because of syntax or visual monitoring, e.g., "The grass did not grow because it was not water."

All writers periodically make "slips of the pen" and misuse or misspell words they know. Wing and Baddelly (1980) collected a corpus of errors made by college students and hypothesized that they occur when the writer's thoughts exceed the rate of writing and motor movements. Memory also plays a major role.

While these factors might have contributed to the mistakes, others reflected primary language disorders and vague word meanings. Many in the group had been able to cope with oral communication, but the precision required for writting elicited many errors. Perhaps the language they hear in conversation or on television does not allow them to learn the vocabulary, syntax, and structures needed for writing. Greenfield (1984) provides an excellent review of the impact of media on various types of learning and expression.

## REVISION AND MONITORING

Recent studies on the revision process indicate poor writers reread their work less than good writers (Cooper & Odell, 1978). Murray (1978) feels good writers and teachers should discuss their own revisions, redrafting and struggles with students. We agree and often encourage adolescents to read *From Writers to Students* (Weiss, 1979) to help them understand more about the writing process. Adults also find it helpful to talk about their problems with people who have had similar experiences.

Many find it frustrating to reread their faulty spelling and handwriting, and may not even be able to decipher their own work. Hence, monitoring tasks must be presented carefully. Others can reread their work but are less aware of the need for revising. Most, however, cannot change their work without very specific assistance. Therefore, periods of diagnostic teaching are provided to explore the type of instruction that will foster independent learning.

The diagram in Figure 10-16 was used to help the person who wrote the material in Figure 10-13. Because of his language disorders he could not modify his writing with vague instructions, such as "Proofread your paper." Moreover, he did not fully understand the meanings of "punctuation" and "grammar." Therefore, it was necessary to highlight specific features of words and sentences.

## SUMMARY

The writing performance of the adults in this clinical population varied widely. Some, because of severe language and reading disorders, could only write a few words and sentences. Even in cases of emergency they could convey

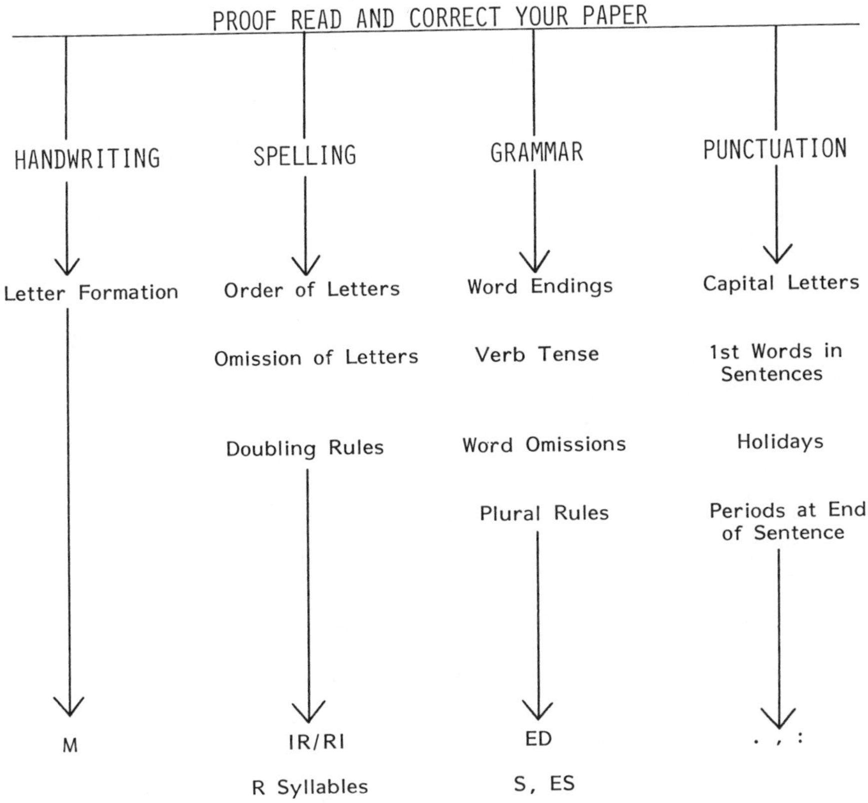


**Figure 10-16.** Examples of levels of instructions.

little through writing. Therefore, functional reading and writing for communication and independence is recommended.

The moderately impaired were often considering job changes that required the mastery of specific content as well as higher levels of reading and writing. Hence, the material from their trade books could be used for remediation.

Those at the upper levels who are still in school, college, or professions requiring higher level skills need work on spelling, syntax, organization and sense of audience. Many at all levels need guides for writing letters, thank you notes, applications, and other forms. Throughout all of the instruction, it is important to remember the multiple parallel processing required for writing. Litowitz (1981) says that writers must manage ideas, spelling, syntax, audience, and the text. It is essential to study the role of parents, teachers, and peers, as well as the activity of the writer.

Finally, we strongly recommend writing as an aid to memory. Since adults often complain about their disorganization, they should be encouraged to write for themselves even if they never write for others.

## REFERENCES

Applebee, A. *The child's concept of story*. Chicago: University of Chicago Press, 1978.

Bailet, L. *Spelling rule application skills among learning disabled and normal spellers*. Northwestern University dissertation, 1985.

Beers, J., & Henderson, E. *Developmental and cognitive aspects of learning to spell*. Newark, DE: International Reading Association, 1980.

Beery, K., & Buktenica, N. *Developmental test of visual-motor integration (Revised)*. Chicago: Follett, 1982.

Bereiter, C. Toward a developmentaltheory of writing. In L. Gregg & R. Steinberg (Eds.), *Cognitive processes in writing*. Hillsdale, NJ: Lawrence Erlbaum, 1980.

Berry, M. *Berry-Talbott language test: Comprehension of grammar*. Rockford, IL: 1961.

Blake, H. Written composition in English primary schools. In R. Larson (Ed.), *Children and writing in the elementary school*. New York: Oxford University Press, 1975.

Boder, E. & Jarrico, S. *The Boder test of reading-spelling patterns*. New York: Grune & Stratton, 1982.

Bradley, L, & Bryant, P. *Rhyme and reason in reading and spelling*. International Academy for Research in Learning Disabilities. Monograph Series, No. 1. Ann Arbor: The University of Michigan Press, 1985.

Britton, J., Burgess, T., Martin, N., McLeod, A., & Rosen, H. *The development of writing skills* (pp. 11—18). London: MacMillan Education, 1975.

Bryant, P., & Bradley, M. Why children sometimes write words which they do not read. In V. Frith (Ed.), *Cognitive processes in spelling*. New York: Academic Press, 1980.

Cicci, R. Disorders of written language. In H. Myklebust (Ed.), *Progress in learning disabilities, Vol. 5*. New York: Grune & Stratton, 1983.

Cohen, C. *Writers' sense of audience: Certain aspects of writing by sixth grade normal and learning disabled children*. Unpublished doctoral dissertation, Northwestern University, 1983.

Cooper, C., & Odell, L. *Research on composing: Points of departure*. Urbana, IL: National Council of Teachers of English, 1978.

Critchley, M. Some problems of the ex-dyslexic. *Bulletin of the Orton Society*, 1973, *23*, 7–14.

Cromer, R. Spontaneous spelling by language disordered children. In U. Frith (Ed.), *Cognitive processes in spelling*. London: Academic Press, 1980.

Dagenais, D., & Beadle, K. Written language: When and where to begin. *Topics in Language Disorders*, 1984, *5*, 59–85.

Downing, J., & Oliver, P. The child's concept of "a word." *Reading Research Quarterly*, 1973–74, *9*, 568–582.

Emig, J. *The composing processes of twelfth graders*. Urbana, IL: National Council of Teachers of English, 1971.

Flowers, L., & Hayes, J. The dynamics of composing: Making plans and juggling constraints. In L. Gregg & E. Steinberg (Eds.), *Cognitive processes in writing*. Hillsdale, NJ: Lawrence Erlbaum, 1980.

Frederiksen, C., & Dominis, J. (Eds.), *Writing: The nature, development and teaching of written communication* (Vol. 2). Hillsdale, NJ: Lawrence Erlbaum, 1981.

Frith, U. (Ed.) *Cognitive processes in spelling*. New York: Academic Press, 1980.

Graves, D. *Writing: Teachers and children at work*. Exeter: Heinemann, 1983.

Greenfield, P. *Mind and media*. Cambridge, MA: Harvard U Press, 1984.

Gregg, K. *An investigation of the breakdown in certain aspects of the writing process with college age learning disabled, normal, and basic writers*. Unpublished doctoral dissertation, Northwestern University, 1982.

Gregg, L., & Steinberg, R. (Eds.), *Cognitive processes in writing*. Hillsdale, NJ: Lawrence Erlbaum, 1980.

Groshong, C. *Ambiguity detection and the use of verbal context for disambiguation of language disabled and normal learning children*. Unpublished doctoral dissertation, Northwestern University, 1980.

Halliday, M., & Hassan, R. *Cohesion in English*. London, England: Longman Group, Ltd., 1976.

Hammill, D., & Larsen, D. *Test of written language*. Austin, TX: Pro-Ed, 1981.

Hanna, R., Hodges, R., & Hanna, J. *Spelling: Structure and strategies*. Boston: Houghton Mifflin, 1971.

Hoff, L. *An investigation of knowledge of graphemic options for spelling in normal and learning disabled children*. Unpublished dissertation, Northwestern University, 1985.

Hoskins, B. *A study of hypothesis testing behavior in language disordered children*. Unpublished doctoral dissertation, Northwestern University, 1979.

Humes, A. Research on the composing process. *Review of Educational Research*, 1983, *53*, 201–216.

Hunt, K. Recent measures in syntactic development. In R. Larson (Ed.), *Children and writing in the elementary school* (pp. 55–69). New York: Oxford, 1975.

Hunt, K. Syntactic maturity in school children and adults. *Monograph of the Society for Research in Child Development*, 1970, *35*, 1–44.

Jastak, J., Bijou, S., & Jastak, S. *Wide range achievement test*. New York: Harcourt Brace Jovanovich, 1976.

Johnson, D. Programming for dyslexia: The need for interaction analyses. *Annals of Dyslexia*, 1982, *32*, 61–70.

Johnson, D. Using reading and writing to aid oral language. *Topics in Language Disorders*, 1985, *5*, 55–69.

Johnson, D., & Myklebust, H. *Learning Disabilities: Education principles and practices*. New York: Grune & Stratton, 1967.

Larsen, S., & Hammill, D. *Test of written spelling*. Austin, TX: Pro-Ed, 1976.

Larson, R. *Children and writing in the elementary school*. New York: Oxford, 1975.

Litowitz, B. Developmental issues in written language. *Topics in Language Disorders*, 1981, *1*, 73–89.

Loban, W. *Language development: Kindergarten through grade twelve*. Urbana, IL: National Council of Teachers of English, 1976 (pp. 81–84).

Lopate, P. *Being with children*. New York: Doubleday, 1975.

Luria, A. *Higher cortical functions in man*. New York: Basic Books, 1966.

Mattis, S., French, J., & Rapin, I. Dyslexia in children and young adults: Three independent neuropsychological syndromes. *Developmental Medicine and Child Neurology*, 1975, *17*, 150–163.

Mercer, C. *Students with learning disabilities* (2nd ed.). Columbus, OH: Charles E. Merrill, 1983.

Miles, T. *Dyslexia: The pattern of difficulties*. Springfield, IL: Charles C Thomas, 1983.

Moyer, M. *An investigation of spatial visualization abilities in normal and learning disabled children*. Unpublished doctoral dissertation, Northwestern University, 1978.

Murray, D. Internal revision. In Cooper & Odell (Eds.), *Research on composing: Points of departure*. Urbana, IL: National Council of Teachers of English, 1978.

Myklebust, H. *Development and disorders of written language* (Vol. 1.). New York: Grune & Stratton, 1965.

Myklebust, H. *Development and disorders of written language* (Vol. 2.). New York: Grune & Stratton, 1973.

Nystrand, M., (Ed.), *What writers know: Language, process, and structure of written discourse*. New York: Academic Press, 1982.

Olson, D. From utterance to text: The bias of language in speech and writing. *Harvard Educational Review*, 1977, *47*, 257–281.

Phelps-Gunn, T., & Phelps-Terasaki, D. *Written language instruction: Theory and instruction*. Rockville, MD: Aspen, 1982.

Podhajski, B. *Picture arrangement and selected narrative language skills in learning disabled and normal seven year old children*. Unpublished doctoral dissertation, Northwestern University, 1980.

Rawson, M. *Developmental language disability: Adult accomplishments of dyslexic boys*. Baltimore: Johns Hopkins Press, 1968.

Rouke, B. Reading, spelling, arithmetic disabilities: A neuropsychologic perspective. In H. Myklebust (Ed.), *Progress in learning disabilities* (Vol. 4). New York: Grune & Stratton, 1978.

Shaugnessy, M. *Errors and expectations: A guide for the teacher of basic writing*. New York: Oxford University Press, 1977.

Sheils, M. Why Johnny can't write. *Newsweek*, Dec. 8, 1975, 58–65.

Spache, G. *Diagnosis and correcting reading disabilities*. Boston: Allyn & Bacon, 1976.

Stein, N. and Glenn, C. An analysis of story comprehension in elementary school children. In R. Freedle (ed.). *New directions in discourse processing*. Norwood, NJ: Ablex, 1979.

Strauss, A., & Lehtinen, L. *Psychopathology and education of the brain injured child*. New York: Grune & Stratton, 1947.

Stubbs, M. Written language and society: Some particular cases and general observations. In M. Nystrand (Ed.), *What writers know*. New York: Academic Press, 1982.

Temple, C., Nathan, R., & Burris, N. *The beginnings of writings*. Boston: Allyn & Bacon, 1982.

Trout, S. *A neuropsychological approach to the analysis of written spelling disorders*. Unpublished doctoral dissertation, Northwestern University, 1973.

Venezky, R. English orthography: Its graphical structure and its relation to sound. *Reading Research Quarterly*, 1967, *12*, 75–105.

Venezky, R. *The structure of English orthography*. The Hague: Monton Press, 1970.

Vygotsky, L. *Thought and language*. Cambridge, MA: M.I.T. Press, 1962.

Wechsler, D. *Wechsler Adult Intelligence Scale-Revised (WAIS-R)*. New York: Psychological Corporation, 1981.

Weiner, E. The diagnostic evaluation of writing samples. *Learning Disability Quarterly*, 1980, *3*, 54–59.

Weiner, E. The diagnostic evaluation of writing skills. *Journal of Learning Disabilities*, 1980, *13*, 48–53.

Weiss, M. (Ed.) *From writers to students: The pleasures and pains of writing*. Newark, DE: International Reading Association, 1979.

Wing, S., & Baddelly, A. Memory and spelling. In U. Frith (Ed.), *Spelling errors in handwriting: A corpus and a distribution analysis*. New York: Academic Press, 1980.

Woolf, C. *Responses to requests for clarification in normal and language disordered children*. Unpublished doctoral dissertation, Northwestern University, 1983.

# 11

## Problems in Mathematics

Jane W. Blalock

Mathematics is an abstract science that has been described as "a study of patterns and relationships, a way of thinking, a language, an art, and a tool" (Reys, Suydam, & Lindquist, 1984). Two aspects of mathematics taught to all school children are arithmetic, which is concerned with numbers, and problem solving. General intelligence, spatial ability, verbal ability, and approach to problem solving or reasoning are factors related to mathematical ability (Chalfant & Scheffelin, 1969). Most factor analytic studies also show a specific numerical ability involved in mathematical ability (Badian, 1983). Mathematics, is a complex symbol system that requires the integration of many abilities.

Piaget (1965) stated that logico-mathematical abilities are basic to learning mathematics. These abilities begin to develop very early in life. Logico-mathematical knowledge is constructed by the child through actions on objects and mental abstraction. This knowledge cannot be acquired through verbal transmission or observation (Copeland, 1984; Hendrickson, 1983; Piaget, 1965). Concepts thought to be necessary for understanding mathematics instruction are: concept of number, classification, and conservation or invariance (Copeland, 1984). Without basic knowledge or concepts, symbols and arithmetic skills are used by rote and are not readily available to solve "real" problems.

Mathematical skills and abilities are used in everyday living as well as in formal coursework. Adults who lack reasoning and problem solving abilities and/or basic computation skills are at a great disadvantage in society. Lack of basic competency or literacy in mathematics may result from several problems. These include inadequate instruction, emotional "blocks" or math anxiety, lack of "talent" or interest, lowered mental abilities, and learning disabilities.

ADULTS WITH LEARNING DISABILITIES
ISBN 0-8089-1795-1

## DISTURBANCES IN MATHEMATICS

Disorders of mathematics were first described in adults who lost the ability to calculate subsequent to cerebral damage or disease. The term *dyscalculia* was first used by Henschen to refer to these acquired deficits (Badian, 1983; Chalfant & Scheffelin, 1969). In 1937, Guttman suggested that some children had symptoms similar to adults with acquired deficits. Since that time many clinicians and researchers have described mathematics disabilities in children (Cohn, 1971; Fleischner & Garnett, 1979; Garnett & Fleischner, 1983; Johnson & Myklebust, 1967; Kaliski, 1967; Strauss & Lehtinen, 1947; Svien & Sherlock, 1979).

Investigators have attempted to delineate deficits in cognitive abilities associated with disturbances in learning mathematics. Cohn (1971), for example, suggested that language, memory, logical reasoning, and visual-spatial deficits were seen in conjunction with dyscalculia. In general, both verbal and nonverbal deficits have been found to affect functioning in mathematics (Aiken, 1971; Mardell, 1972).

Researchers have also attempted to identify subtypes of mathematical learning disabilities. Rourke (1978) identified two subgroups of children with poor computational abilities. The first subgroup was made up of children having low arithmetic, reading, and spelling performance associated with verbal deficits. The second group consisted of children having low arithmetic performance in conjunction with visual-spatial deficits without reading and spelling difficulty. Rourke cautioned researchers to examine patterns of achievement in studying arithmetic disorders and not to assume that all children with problems in arithmetic had the same deficits.

Kosc (1974, 1981) suggested six types of dyscalculia: practognostic (difficulty with manipulation of objects), verbal, lexical, graphical, operational (difficulty understanding operations), and ideognostical (difficulty understanding mathematical relations). Badian (1983) proposed subtypes based on a classification system used for adults with acquired dyscalculia; alexia-agraphia (problems reading and writing math symbols), spatial, anarithmetria (difficulty understanding operations), attentional-sequential (difficulty with facts, multiplication tables, inconsistency), and mixed. Groups having problems in mathematics that are related to verbal deficits and to visual spatial deficits have been identified most often.

Children with verbal disturbances may have problems in logical reasoning as well as difficulties relating to their particular language disabilities (Johnson & Myklebust, 1967 Mardell, 1972). Those with auditory comprehension problems may experience difficulty learning mathematical vocabulary and concepts. They may also have problems understanding oral and written word problems (Johnson & Blalock, 1982). In addition, limited vocabulary and inability to explain concepts and phenomena may result in poor performance on some Piagetian mathematical tasks (James, 1975; Silvius, 1974).

Nonverbal visual-spatial deficits may interfere with understanding the number system. Individuals with spatial deficits may have difficulty with place value, with understanding operations, and with learning cardinal and ordinal numbers. They may also have visual imagery problems (Moyer, 1978). Some people with visual-spatial perception and memory deficits misalign problems, forget what numerals look like, and have difficulty dealing with visually confusing worksheets and tests.

## CONSIDERATIONS FOR ASSESSMENT AND DIAGNOSIS

The determination of a disability in mathematics presents particular problems in the evaluation of adults. First, there is variability in educational backgrounds. The clinician cannot make assumptions based strictly on attained level of education, because some adults have not taken a math course since early in their high school programs. A second problem in the evaluation of adults is the differing demands for application of mathematics skills and knowledge among adults. Therefore, considerations in identifying math problems include: overall educational level, background in mathematics instruction (actual courses taken and reported performance); mental ability, and demand for use of skills since leaving school. In our adult evaluations, individuals lacking the skills needed for daily, independent living were more likely to be classified as having problems than were those who had difficulty with higher level mathematics.

A variety of instruments was used to assess basic arithmetic skills and quantitative concepts. The measures administered to the largest number of adults were the Arithmetic subtest of the *Wechsler Adult Intelligence Scale* (WAIS) (Wechsler, 1955) and the Arithmetic subtest of the *Wide Range Achievement Test* (WRAT) (Jastak & Jastak, 1978). These served as indicators of the need for additional testing. Additional measures used included: subtests from the *Woodcock-Johnson Psycho-Educational Battery: Cognitive Ability Tests* (Quantitative Concepts) and *Achievement Tests* (Applied Problems) (Woodcock & Johnson, 1977); *Stanford Diagnostic Mathematics Test* (Beaty, Madden, Gardner, & Karlsen, 1976); and *Test of Academic Skills* (Gardner, Callis, Merwin, & Madden, 1973). Occasionally, parts of the *Key Math Diagnostic Arithmetic Test* (Connolly, Nachtman, & Pritchett, 1976) were used informally to explore the extent of problems of people with low skill levels and/or poor concepts. An informal computation task developed in our Center was used with adults who had difficulty with the basic operations. In addition, routine questions were asked about making change, balancing checkbooks, determining sale prices, planning and budgeting, and estimating. Some diagnostic teaching was necessary for those who had difficulty with problem solving and/or basic quantitative concepts.

## NATURE OF ADULT PROBLEMS

Mathematics problems were observed in 54 percent of the adults (50). Although only 12 mentioned them among their major concerns, the adults with problems knew they had difficulty in this area. It is important to note, however, that "math" was often interpreted narrowly as "school subjects" rather than in the broader sense of skills necessary for daily living.

Very few adults had received remedial work in mathematics. Their relative lack of concern for this area of learning (despite a high incidence of problems) is consistent with a study of adolescents carried out in our program (Johnson, Blalock, & Nesbitt, 1978). Math problems were less concern to their parents than strictly verbal problems and were less likely to have been included in remedial programming. This suggests that socially it is more acceptable to say, "I'm not good in math." than "I don't read well."

A majority of the arithmetic difficulties were manifested in daily living. Lack of facility and automaticity with basic computational skills limited the independence and job opportunities of many in the group. Some adults also had difficulty with problem solving. The *significance* of their problems was not, however, always evident on structured paper and pencil arithmetic tests; the impact of problem solving difficulty was often revealed during the interview. Follow-up testing (formal and informal) and trial teaching were needed to analyze the nature of the specific problems.

### Problem Solving

Problem solving in mathematics requires the application of known information and knowledge to new situations. It involves problem analysis (or understanding) and development of a plan, followed by selection of relevant information, execution of the plan, and evaluation of the solution (Reys et al, 1984). While typically associated with number and mathematics, problem solving is critical to daily living and is a major component in "common sense." In the area of mathematics education, word problems are widely used to teach problem solving and to "practice" computation. In studying problem solving it is important to consider more than the solution to word problems and to examine the reasons for difficulty in the *process* of solving problems, both verbal and nonverbal. In our evaluations, word problems were used to assess problem solving. (See Chapter 5 for additional discussion of problem solving.)

According to Sharma (1981), word problems involve several types of "translation" that makes them more difficult than simple calculation. "Real-world" problems must be translated into familiar, acceptable language that has to be translated into "mathematical expressions." Finally, the solutions must be translated back into "real world" terms and results. Children and adults who dislike solving word problems often have had difficulty with the mathematical language necessary for these translations.

Learning disabled adolescents with deficits in language, reasoning, or organization, as well as computation, may have difficulty with word problems (Blankenship & Lovitt, 1976; Cawley, Fitzmaurice, Shaw, Karn, & Bates, 1979, Sharma, 1981). Variables that contribute to the difficulty level of word problems include: (1) complexity of syntax and vocabulary (Larsen, Parker & Trenholme, 1978; Sharma, 1979), (2) extraneous information (Goodstein, 1981), and (3) absence of cue words (Goodstein, 1981).

Some problem solving difficulties were evident on the WAIS Arithmetic subtest, which consists of orally presented word problems. Although it was not designed to be a comprehensive measure of arithmetical or problem solving abilities, this test often identifies people who have significant problems in either area. Levy (1981) suggested that the WISC-R (Wechsler, 1974) Arithmetic subtest identified children with arithmetical and mathematical learning problems. Both the WISC-R and WAIS Arithmetic subtests assess the ability to select the appropriate solution and to obtain an answer mentally.

Factors that contributed to low scores on the WAIS Arithmetic subtest included memory and attention deficits, computation problems, particularly in items containing fractions or percents, and difficulty in problem solving. The most frequently made errors were in selection of the operation or in procedures.

Additional evidence for problem solving deficits was obtained from the Applied Problems subtest of the *Woodcock-Johnson Psycho-educational Battery* and from informal assessment. Multi-step problems and those with extraneous information were the most difficult. Some adults were unable to answer or to "act out" problems presented during informal assessment (i.e., If I walk two steps in one second, how many will I walk in two seconds?).

Adults with generalized meaning deficits and those with reasoning problems usually had difficulty with mathematics. The math performance of adults who were given the control of variables test (see Chapter 5) was examined to study these relationships. Seventy-three percent of those performing poorly on the rods task were classified as having math problems. Forty-two percent of those who did well on the task had difficulty with math. The "good reasoners" had math problems related to recall of facts and procedures and to monitoring. The "poor reasoners" had more problem solving and conceptual difficulties.

## Computational Skills

Adults in our society are expected to have basic computational skills involving addition, subtraction, multiplication, and division with whole numbers and decimals. Adults also have to recognize and use percents and perform simple computations with common fractions (Reys et al, 1984). Both formal and informal measures were used to examine these skills.

The WRAT (Jastak & Jastak,1978) Arithmetic subtest was given to 80 of the 93 adults, and scores were interpreted using standard scores (1978 norms), mathematics educational background, and overall intelligence. Thirty-one

**Table 11-1**
WRAT Arithmetic Scores for 80 Adults

| | $\bar{x}$ | SD | Range |
|---|---|---|---|
| Grade Score | 6.68 | 2.23 | 3.0–14.1 |
| Standard Score | 94.84 | 14.63 | 71.0–137.0 |

adults were functioning below the expected levels using this method. Mean scores on the WRAT Arithmetic test are shown in Table 11-1.

Errors on the WRAT and on our informal computation test were analyzed to examine calculation problems. In general, errors were most frequent on multi-step problems. A variety of consistent and inconsistent errors on both algorithms and facts were observed. The majority were inconsistent errors on facts (particularly the multiplication tables) and in regrouping. The inconsistency of errors suggested problems in recall of facts, automaticity, and/or monitoring. Some adults performed the incorrect operation on one or more WRAT problems, failing to shift operations from the previous item. On the informal computation task where all the problems on a page required the same operation, fewer incorrect operations were performed.

Consistent computation errors were seen in division, multiplication, fractions, decimals, and percents across tests. These errors were similar to those reported by McLeod and Armstrong (1982) in their study of intermediate and secondary level learning disabled children. They found that the 7 most commonly reported problems were (in order of frequency) upper level skills of division of whole numbers, basic operations with fractions, decimals, percents, fraction terminology, multiplication of whole numbers; and place value.

### Addition

All adults tested understood the basic operation of addition. As a group, they made fewer "fact" errors on addition problems than on those requiring other operations. A few errors were due to uncertainty about procedures when adding figures with different numbers of digits (e.g., 327 + 29). Most errors were made on multi-digit addition problems, with the majority of them involving regrouping. Follow-up work indicated that, with a few exceptions, adults could correct errors that were called to their attention, thus suggesting a monitoring problem.

### Subtraction

Most adults also understood the operation and concept of subtraction, although they made more errors than in addition. Only isolated, inconsistent fact errors were made unless the problems required regrouping. When regrouping was required, some subtracted the smaller number from the larger number regardless of position. During informal assessment they were reminded, and most began to "borrow" correctly.

#### *Multiplication*

Many adults found multiplication difficult and generally made both consistent and inconsistent errors. Three could do only simple facts problems. Consistent errors were made by those who did not know the multiplication tables. When multi-digit problems requiring regrouping were presented, 14 individuals showed consistent errors with the algorithm. Only 34 adults correctly multiplied a 3-digit number by a 2-digit number on the WRAT.

#### *Division*

Division, the most complex of the basic operations, is typically the last taught. A study by Hoy (1982) revealed that normal sixth graders continue to have difficulty with some types of division problems. The way the problems were expressed symbolically ($8/2$ vs. $2\overline{)8}$) and the syntax of word problems affected the performance of normal children. McLeod and Armstrong (1982) also found division to be the most difficult operation for learning disabled adolescents. Since division problems are evident in normal children and learning disabled adolescents, it was not surprising that the adults had difficulty. Several adults could not divide at all. Many omitted all division problems after those with simple facts. Twenty-five people made errors on a problem involving the division of a 4-digit number by a single digit with no remainder. When zeros were required in answers as place holders, the errors increased greatly. Problems were seen with facts, the algorithm, and understanding the operation.

#### *Decimals, Percents, and Fractions*

Adults made many errors on problems involving decimals, percents, and fractions. Decimals were frequently omitted from otherwise correct answers. While a majority of adults understood percents, they often omitted percent problems. Fractions caused the most difficulties. Many adults appeared not to understand the relations expressed by fractions, and an even larger number did not understand relationships between decimals, fractions, and percents.

### Patterns of Mathematics Problems

An attempt was made to identify subtypes of math problems similar to those reported by Rourke (1978), Kosc (1974), and Badian (1983). The four subgroups described below are similar to those seen by others, but not identical. Because of limited testing, these groups must be considered tentative. Furthermore, there was considerable variability within the subgroups.

A visual-spatial group was clearly seen. People in this subgroup usually had an adequate "sense of number" and knew basic facts. Their errors included poor writing of numbers and faulty alignment of columns. A few had difficulty with regrouping and failed to use zeros as place holders in division. Some reversed multi-digit numbers (42/24). Others, perhaps because of attentional deficits, omitted decimals and dollar signs and performed incorrect operations because of a failure to shift from the previous problem. Errors were rarely corrected spontaneously. Several in this group had difficulty with spatial activities such as measuring to hang a picture, setting clocks, etc. They typically had higher Verbal than Performance IQs (not always significantly higher), adequate decoding skills, poor handwriting and spelling, and organizational problems in daily living and in paper writing. They had good oral language abilities, however. Adults in this group tended to have the "organization" problems on Stone's rods task. (See Chapter 5.)

A second group also had lower Performance than Verbal IQ scores. They, however, had poor logico-mathematical abilities. They exhibited deficits in nonverbal concepts, meaning, or inner language. For example, they had difficulty with class inclusion and conservation tasks. The group included those described by Kosc (1981) as not knowing when to calculate or which operation to use. Calculation skills were mostly rote but often accurate. They had poor understanding of time, money, and measurement. Calculators were not helpful to some because of their difficulty with basic concepts and understanding of operations. They also did not estimate well. Word problems were usually solved by "cue words", so they had difficulty when these cues were not present. Extraneous numbers in problems also resulted in errors. This group was typically good at decoding, but comprehension varied according to content. On Stone's task, several exhibited the "detached concepts" he describes.

A third group had difficulty with some math concepts because of language comprehension problems. Often they were confused by symbols and mathematical terminology (e.g., "Which is percent and which is decimal?"). Many had difficulty with word problems, particularly those without "cue words." If there was a discrepancy on the WAIS, Verbal IQ was lower. Problems of "abstraction" were seen in members of this group who participated in Stone's study.

The fourth group identified scored low on all subtests of the WRAT and was similar to Rourke's subgroup. They typically had no significant discrepancies between Verbal and Performance IQ scores. They made frequent, inconsistent fact errors and some inconsistent procedural errors. Several had difficulty with multiplication tables. Most would be considered dyslexic. They had no primary visual-spatial-perceptual deficits, but some had visual memory problems. While many had auditory perceptual and memory deficits they had relatively good comprehension. They had difficulty with practical aspects of math, such as making change, keeping checkbooks, calculating tips, etc. Math concepts were usually good. Adults in this group who did the rods task (Stone) performed well.

**Table 11-2**
Comparison of IQ Scores: Math Learning Disabled vs. Non-math Learning Disabled

| | N | x̄ | SD | Range | T-Value |
|---|---|---|---|---|---|
| Verbal IQ | | | | | |
| Math LD | 50 | 101.6 | 13.3 | 63–139 | t = 3.82* |
| Non-math LD | 42 | 111.0 | 11.0 | 84–136 | |
| Performance IQ | | | | | |
| Math LD | 50 | 99.8 | 14.5 | 71–129 | t = 3.05* |
| Non-math LD | 41 | 108.3 | 11.6 | 84–136 | |
| Full Scale IQ | | | | | |
| Math LD | 50 | 100.9 | 12.7 | 72–133 | t = 3.92* |
| Non-math LD | 41 | 110.5 | 10.3 | 85–134 | |

Note: WAIS not available for 1 subject and PIQ not available for another.
* $p < .01$.

### Mathematics Problems and Intelligence

Comparison of WAIS IQ scores revealed that the learning disabled adults who were found to have math difficulty had mean IQs significantly lower than the mean IQs of those without math problems. This was not accounted for by lower scores on either scale in particular, since both Verbal and Performance means were lower for the math learning disabled group. Means, standard deviations, ranges, and t-values for the two groups are shown in Table 11-2. The ranges of scores indicate these IQ differences do not exist in all cases.

Examination of math performance levels of the 30 individuals with significant discrepancies between Verbal and Performance IQs revealed that those with discrepancies in either direction were most likely to have problems in math. While only 54 percent of the total adult group had math difficulties, 73 percent of the 29 with significant Verbal-Performance discrepancies were found to have math problems (67 percent of the Low Performance group and 89 percent of the Low Verbal group). These findings support the conclusions of researchers who report that either verbal or nonverbal deficits result in math problems.

### Mathematics and Memory

Questions regarding the relation between digit span and arithmetic abilities have been raised by several researchers (Levy, 1981). In our study, the scaled scores of the math learning disabled and non-math learning disabled adults on the Digit Span subtest of the WAIS were compared using the t-test. The non-math disabled performed significantly better on memory for digits than the math disabled. The means, standard deviations, ranges, and t-values are shown

**Table 11-3**
Comparison of Digit Span Scaled Scores: Math Learning Disabled VS. Non-math Learning Disabled

| | N | x̄ | SD | Range | T-value |
|---|---|---|---|---|---|
| Math LD | 50 | 8.6 | 2.9 | 2–15 | 3.33* |
| Non-math LD | 42 | 10.7 | 3.2 | 2–19 | |

Note: WAIS not available for 1 subject and PIQ not available for another.
* $p < .01$.

in Table 11-3. Examination of the mean number of digits repeated, both forward and reversed, showed that the group without math disabilities did somewhat better on both aspects of the task. (See Table 11-4 for means, standard deviations, and ranges.) These analyses suggest that many adults with math deficits also had some memory problems that were related to their learning difficulties. Garnett and Fleischner (1983) also found that learning disabled children had difficulty with automatic recall of basic facts and procedures. It seems likely that strategy use problems affected performance on memory and arithmetic tasks.

## Incidence of Mathematics Problems by Sex

Since sex differences in mathematics abilities and disabilities have been suggested (Tobias, 1982; Badian, 1983), the incidence of problems was examined in this population. No evidence of sex differences in the incidence of math disabilities was found. The percentage of females in the math disabled group was essentially the same as in the total group of adults. Thirty percent of the total group was female and 28 percent of the math disabled group was female. Approximately one-half of the males and one-half of the females had math problems.

**Table 11-4**
Comparison of Digits Forward and Digits Reversed: Math Learning Disabled VS. Non-math Learning Disabled

| | Math Learning Disabled* | | | | Non-math Learning Disabled | | | |
|---|---|---|---|---|---|---|---|---|
| | N | x̄ | SD | Range | N | x̄ | SD | Range |
| # Digits Forward | 47 | 6.0 | 1.3 | 4–9 | 42 | 6.6 | 1.5 | 4–9 |
| # Digits Reversed | 47 | 4.0 | 1.1 | 3–7 | 42 | 5.0 | 1.3 | 2–8 |

* Number of digits repeated forward and reversed not available for 4 subjects.

## MATHEMATICS AND DAILY LIVING

Mathematical problems interfered with daily living in a variety of ways. The people with nonverbal conceptual or meaning problems were the most handicapped. Their problems interfered with reasoning and certain types of logical thinking as well as with math concepts. While many performed adequately on computation tests, they had difficulty applying computational skills to life problems. Much of their information about measurement and part-whole relations was rote; so it was not always applied correctly in problem solving.

Adults with generalized meaning problems and some with nonverbal deficits had day-to-day problems. They experienced difficulty in reading graphs and charts, in estimation and approximation, in prediction, and in use of calculation devices—skills that are thought to be necessary for daily living in our society (Alley & Deshler, 1979; Glenn, 1978; Reys et al 1984). Many adults had difficulty with money, especially making change. Some could work arithmetic problems with decimals on paper, but were unable to make change. As a result, they felt somewhat uncertain about their day-to-day functioning and were somewhat dependent on others. The incidence and impact of these deficits indicate a need for increased emphasis on mathematics (both problem solving and calculation) in Special Education.

## REFERENCES

Aiken, L. Verbal factors in mathematics learning: A review of research. *Journal of Research in Mathematics Education*, 1971, *2*, 304–313.

Alley, G., & Deshler, D. *Teaching the learning disabled adolescent: Strategies and methods*. Denver: Love Publishing, 1979.

Badian, N. Dyscalculia and nonverbal disorders of learning. In H. Myklebust (Ed.), *Progress in learning disabilities* (Vol. 5). New York: Grune & Stratton, 1983.

Beaty, L., Madden, R., Gardner, E., & Karlsen, B. *Stanford diagnostic mathematics test*. Cleveland, OH: The Psychological Corp., 1978.

Blankenship, C., & Lovitt, T. Story problems: Merely confusing or downright befuddling? *Journal of Research in Mathematics Education*, 1976, *7*, 290–298.

Cawley, J. Fitzmaurice, A., Shaw, R., Kahn, H., & Bates, H. Word problems: Suggestions and ideas for learning disabled children. *Learning Disability Quarterly*, 1979, *2*, 25–41.

Chalfant, J., & Scheffelin, M. *Central Processing dysfunctions in children: A review of research*. Bethesda, MD: U.S. Department of Health, Education and Welfare, 1969.

Cohn, R. Arithmetic and learning disabilities. In H. Myklebust (Ed.), *Progress in learning disabilities* (Vol. 2). New York: Grune & Stratton, 1971.

Connolly, A. Nachtman, W., & Pritchett, E. *Key math diagnostic arithmetic test*. Circle Pines, MN: American Guidance Service, 1976.

Copeland, R. *How children learn mathematics* (4th ed.). New York: Macmillan, 1984.

Fleischner, J. & Garnett, K. Arithmetic learning disabilities: A literature review.

Research Review Series 1979–1980, Vol. 4. New York: Teachers College, Columbia University, Research Institute for the Study of Learning Disabilities, 1979.

Gardner, E., Callis, R., Merwin, J., & Madden, R. *Stanford test of academic skills* (1st ed.). Cleveland, OH: The Psychological Corp., 1973.

Garnett, K., & Fleischner, J. Automatization and basic fact performance of normal and learning disabled children. *Learning Disability Quarterly*, 1983, *6* (2), 223–230.

Glenn, J. (Ed.). *The third R: Towards a numerate society*. New York: Harper & Row, 1978.

Goodstein, H. Error analysis in verbal problem solving. *Topics in Learning and Learning Disabilities*, 1981, *1*, 31–45.

Guttman, E. Congenital arithmetic disability and acalculia. *British Journal of Medical Psychology*, 1937, *16*, 16–35.

Hendrickson, A. Prevention or cure? Another look at mathematics learning problems. In D. Carnine, D. Elkind, A Hendrickson, D. Meichenbaum, R. Sieben, & F. Smith (Eds.), *Interdisciplinary voices in learning disabilities and remedial education*. Austin, TX: Pro-Ed., 1983.

Hoy, C. *An investigation of certain components of division with learning disabled and normal sixth-grade boys*. Unpublished doctoral dissertation, Northwestern University, 1982.

James, K. *A study of the conceptual structure of measurement of length in normal and learning disabled children*. Unpublished doctoral dissertation, Northwestern University, 1975.

Jastak, J., & Jastak, S. *Wide range achievement test*. Wilmington: DE, Jastak Associates, Inc., 1978.

Johnson, D., & Blalock, J. Problems of mathematics in children with language disorders. In. N. Lass, L. McReynolds, J. Northern, & D. Yoder (Eds.), *Speech, language and hearing* (Vol. 2). Philadelphia: W. B. Saunders, 1982.

Johnson, D., Blalock, J., & Nesbitt, J. Adolescents with learning disabilities: Perspectives from an educational clinic. *Learning Disability Quarterly*, 1978, *1*, 24–36.

Johnson, D., & Myklebust, H. *Learning disabilities: Educational principles and practices*. New York: Grune & Stratton, 1967.

Kaliski, L. Arithmetic and the brain-injured child. In E. Frierson & W. Barbe (Eds.), *Educating children with learning disabilities*. New York: Appleton-Century-Crofts, 1967.

Kosc, L. Developmental dyscalculia. *Journal of Learning Disabilities*, 1974, *7*, 165–178.

Kosc, L. Neuropsychological implications of diagnosis and treatment of mathematical learning disabilities. *Topics in Learning and Learning Disabilities*, 1981, *1*, 19–30.

Larsen, S, Parker, R., & Trenholme, B. The effects of syntactic complexity upon arithmetic performance. *Learning Disability Quarterly*, 1978, *1*, 80–85.

Levy, W. How useful is the WISC-R arithmetic subtest? *Topics in Learning and Learning Disabilities*, 1981, *1*(3), 81–87.

Mardell, C. *The prediction of mathematical achievement from measures of cognitive processes*. Unpublished doctoral dissertation, Northwestern University, 1972.

McLeod, T., & Armstrong, S. Learning disabilities in mathematics-skill deficits and remedial approaches at the intermediate and secondary level. *Learning Disability Quarterly*, 1982, *5* (3), 305–311.

Moyer, M. *An investigation of spatial visualization abilities in normal and learning disabled children*. Unpublished doctoral dissertation, Northwestern University, 1978.

Piaget, J. *The child's conception of number*. New York: W. W. Norton, 1965.

Reys, R., Suydam, M., & Lindquist, M. *Helping children learn mathematics*. Englewood Cliffs, NJ: Prentice-Hall, Inc., 1984.

Rourke, B. Reading, spelling, arithmetic disabilities: A neuropsychologic perspective. In H. Myklebust (Ed.), *Progress in learning disabilities* (Vol. 4). New York: Grune & Stratton, 1978.

Sharma, M. Language, vocabulary, and symbols in mathematics. Framingham, MA: Center for Teaching/Learning of Mathematics, 1979.

Sharma, M. Using word problems to aid language and reading comprehension. *Topics in Learning and Learning Disabilities*, 1981, *1*, 61–71.

Silvius, J. *A study of the comparative performance of learning disabled and normal children on Piagetian tasks of conservation*. Unpublished doctoral dissertation, Northwestern University, 1974.

Strauss, A., & Lehtinen, L. *Psychopathology and education of the brain-injured child* (Vol. 1). New York: Grune & Stratton, 1947.

Svien, K., & Sherlock, D. Dyscalculia and dyslexia. *Bulletin of the Orton Society*, 1979, *23*, 269–276.

Tobias, S. *Overcoming math anxiety*. Boston: Houghton Mifflin, 1978.

Wechsler, D. *Wechsler adult intelligence scale*. New York: Psychological Corp., 1955.

Wechsler, D. *Wechsler intelligence scale for children-revised*. New York: Psychological Corp., 1974.

Woodcock, R., & Johnson, M. B. *Woodcock-Johnson psycho-educational battery*. New York: Teaching Resources, 1977.

# 12

# Nonverbal Disorders and Related Learning Disabilities

Doris J. Johnson

Disorders of verbal learning are the most prevalent in the learning disabled population, but *nonverbal* problems are frequently the most debilitating because of their impact on social maturity and independence. (Johnson & Myklebust, 1967; Myklebust, 1975). Even in cultures where literacy is limited, people who cannot learn from observation, perform basic perceptual-motor skills, or acquire the "manners" of the culture may be identified. Verbal disorders typically impede the acquisition of oral language, reading, written language, and many aspects of mathematics whereas nonverbal problems interfere with spatial orientation, body image, facial recognition, interpretation of gesture and various visual-spatial-motor processes whereas nonverbal problems interfere with spatial orientation, body image, facial recognition, social perception, and various visual-spatial motor processes needed for writing and computation. There may be secondary effects on verbal comprehension.

Having had the opportunity to follow several individuals with nonverbal problems from the preschool years through young adulthood, we have concluded it is often easier to teach people to abstract patterns from the orthography (i.e., to read) than to abstract patterns from nonverbal experience. Perhaps printed codes are more stable and predictable than environmental features because the latter change if objects are moved, buildings are demolished, or repainted. Many environments look different with seasonal changes, which adds to the confusion and the uncertainty for people with nonverbal disorders. This was most apparent when one adult in the group asked to be guided home after it snowed because she knew the street signs would be covered and she consequently would not recognize her street.

Certain nonverbal disorders have been recognized for years in Special Education, Neurology, and other fields. For example, perceptual motor disor-

ADULTS WITH LEARNING DISABILITIES
ISBN 0-8089-1795-1

ders, problems of body image, left-right and spatial orientation were emphasized by authors in Cruickshank (1966), Frostig (1964), Kephart (1960) and Strauss and Lehtinen (1947). "Brain injured" children were frequently characterized by their poor visual-motor coordination, clumsiness, disorganization, and perceptual disorders. Occasionally these problems were observed together with dyslexia and other language disorders (Orton, 1937). Unfortunately, these problems were overemphasized in some remedial programs, thus limiting the amount of time devoted to reading, spelling, and other primary areas of underachievement (Benton, 1985). Yet, nonverbal problems cannot be ignored, particularly when they interfere with self-help skills and independence.

Less emphasis has been given to the symbolic and conceptual aspects of nonverbal thinking, social perception, and nonverbal communication although more studies have been completed in recent years (Bryan, 1977; Knott, 1974; Myklebust, 1975; Terris, 1985; Wiig & Harris, 1980). In order to appreciate the significance of nonverbal learning, it is helpful to consider the multitude of abstractions and inferences one makes throughout the day. For example, even before rising in the morning we hear countless sounds that provide information about time of day, season, and weather, all of which require discrimination, figure-ground perception, memory, and interpretation. I can differentiate the sound of rain from sleet on the windowpane and begin to make decisions about clothing for the day. Sometimes I am aware that it has snowed because the world seems quieter. I perceive traffic sounds and may hypothesize that I overslept if the patterns are different from what I expect. I also am aware of the absence of sound and wonder whether something is wrong with the refrigerator if I have not heard it running.

If I arise before dawn I can usually find my way to a light switch in the dark by using kinesthetic and tactual memory. I also can locate the cold or hot water faucet, turn it on and estimate how long the water should run before it reaches a particular temperature. I can pull up a shade and control the movement until it reaches the desired height. Looking out the window I see both familiar and unfamiliar people and infer who is tired by noting posture, speed of movement, and facial expression.

As I prepare breakfast I may lift the milk carton, visualize how much is left, and make a mental note to buy some more. Later, I select one piece of fruit over another because it looks riper.

Clearly many of these thoughts are verbally mediated and are possible because of previous intersensory experiences. Nevertheless, the observations, hypotheses, and conclusions I reached were formed without any verbal input from the environment.

Children and adults with nonverbal disorders frequently cannot or do not make these inferences spontaneously, nor do they always use verbal mediation and background knowledge to scan the environment or formulate hypotheses (Blalock, 1977). Hence, they may need verbal prompts or reminders from those around them.

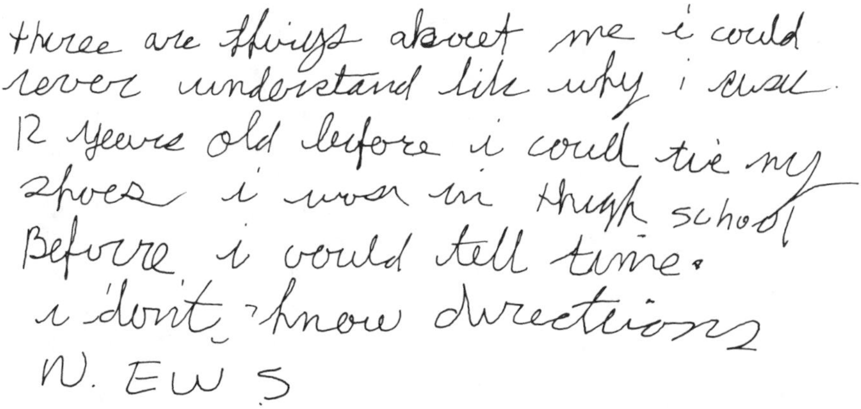

there are things about me i could
never understand like why i was
12 years old before i could tie my
shoes i was in high school
Before i could tell time.
i don't know directions
N. E W S


**Figure 12-1.** Concerns of a woman with nonverbal perceptual-motor problems.

Many people with these problems do not profit from their own exploration and activity. Unlike young children who acquire visual-spatial-motor generalizations by manipulating objects, these adults are still deficient in performing daily skills such as tying shoes, opening cartons, or using keys in locks. Some perceive what needs to be done but cannot execute the necessary motor plans.

The woman who wrote the sentences in Figure 12-1 said she was desperate for help and did not want to be a failure. Earlier she had been told the problems would go away—that "like a desises—it automaticaly cures when your an adult."

Unfortunately, the problems do not go away and many are unable to actualize their potential. Not only do they find it difficult to acquire basic knowledge from observation but because of their nonverbal disorders, they often do not know why they are reprimanded or rejected unless given explicit feedback.

Having observed many children and adults with nonverbal problems we have concluded they learn less well implicitly from observation and exploration than their nondisabled peers. Yet the knowledge acquired from this form of learning is very important in society. While most cultures provide explicit instruction for reading, spelling, and arithmetic, less is offered for nonverbal communication and observational skills.

When dealing with these problems, we feel complex interactive models such as those for reading are necessary. That is, we need to consider top-down, bottom-up, and parallel processing. We need to study how people use their background knowledge and language to guide their looking and scanning of the environment. And we need to consider the number of features or rule systems they can process simultaneously. Eisenberg and Smith (1971) say that multiple features must be noted to grasp messages in social situations. These include eye movement, gesture, tone of voice, prosody, posture, distance, and many other factors. The rapidity and number of symbols, together with language, create an overload for many adults.

Some in this population are not unlike people with acquired right hemisphere disturbances (Perecman, 1983) who have facial recognition, spatial orientation, and directionality problems. (Badian, 1983; Benton, 1979; Heilman & Valenstein, 1979; McFie, Piercy & Zangwill, 1950).

Two women were evaluated after right hemisphere aneurysms but are not included in the group of ninety-three. Both had difficulty recognizing faces. One had severe body image disturbance and constructional apraxia (Critchley, 1953) and could no longer put on her glasses or clothing. The other had fewer motor planning problems but more visual monitoring disorders. She failed to note which burners of the stove were on, made grilled cheese sandwiches without noting the lack of cheese, and lost her "innate" sense of measuring. In addition, she was unable to identify any objects from touch with her left hand. To compensate for her problems, she pasted reminders, recipes, and verbal guides on the walls.

In addition to her nonverbal disorders, she, like many of the congenital cases, made spelling errors because of visual monitoring failure. Often she repeated the same letter in words (e.g., threee; thiss).

While developmental disabilities are never as "clear cut" as acquired ones, it is helpful to investigate possible co-occurring problems. The adults with nonverbal problems were characterized by their relatively high verbal skills and their deficiencies in one or more aspects of visual perception, spatial orientation, nonverbal memory, and symbolization. Most could decode despite severe visual-spatial disorders, yet many had reading comprehension problems. Arithmetic and handwriting were typically low. Their overall language skills were good, but some did not understand words related to space, time, and number. They relied on verbal directions and cues. Nonverbal communication, problem solving, and organizational skills were frequently deficient. While their disabilities interfered with certain facets of writing, arithmetic, and language comprehension, their non-academic problems were more obvious.

In a book on comprehension, Smith (1975) says we learn by listening, observing, doing, and reading. Initially we learn how *to* listen, look, and read but later we learn *from* looking, listening, reading, and doing. This chapter is devoted to descriptions of adults who have learned to listen and read but learn less well from observing and doing.

## ASSESSMENT

In general, the constructs from Chapter 2 were used in the evaluation. Tasks were selected to determine whether problems occurred at the level of input, integration, output or monitoring. In addition, as in our work with children, we noted differences on social vs. nonsocial tasks and meaningful vs.

nonmeaningful ones (Johnson & Myklebust, 1967). Whereas some people have problems with nonmeaningful tasks such as Block Design, others have more difficulty with those that require the interpretation of symbols (e.g. Picture Arrangement).

The hierarchy of experience allowed for the differentiation of problems at the level of perception, imagery, symbolization, and conceptualization. A brief description of tasks at each level is provided below.

## Perception

Perceptual tasks involve the comparison or discrimination of stimuli that remain present such as color, form, or picture matching. At a slightly higher level, mid-way between perception and imagery, tasks require analysis and synthesis or some mental manipulation with the model present (e.g., Block Design).

Studies of brain-injured children indicated they often had difficulty with part-whole relationships (Strauss and Lehtinen, 1947). Birch and Lefford (1966) found writing or copying problems were related to disorders of analysis and synthesis. They observed many subjects, could discriminate forms but not copy them. In the Birch and Lefford studies perceptual analysis was studied by asking subjects to find parts of a figure within the whole (i.e. a particular oblique angle in a diamond). Synthesis was studied by asking them to select one of four sets of lines that could be used to construct a whole figure (e.g., a square, rectangle, or diamond). They found the neurologically damaged group was markedly atypical in perceptual analysis.

Analysis and synthesis skills of the adults were investigated by asking subjects to construct figures, letters, and numerals with wooden pegs or strips of paper.

## Imagery

Tasks at the level of imagery involve either partial or total recall. For example, Picture Completion requires more imagery than tasks requiring the identification of missing parts when a full model is present for comparison. Object Assembly requires more memory than Block Design because the subject is required to construct a picture from disassembled pieces without a model.

Spatial relations tasks vary according to the amount of visualization needed. The ability to draw figures as they would appear when rotated, flipped, or turned, necessitates more mental manipulation than tasks requiring the identification of a figure from an array.

Size estimation tasks require considerable visual imagery as well as proprioception. Some also require motor planning. We frequently ask people to show, with their hands, the length of a dollar bill or the size of an orange or quarter. Many cannot image or plan the motor movements to complete the task.

## Symbolization

Tasks at the level of symbolization require interpretation and the general idea that something stands for something else—that is, representation. All forms of nonverbal communication, signals, signs in the environment, and pictures are symbols.

While pictures of real objects are easily interpreted by most adults, drawings are often difficult because of insufficient detail or representational features. For example, certain lines represent movement or speed; others represent sound (such as the lines drawn around an alarm clock); others denote temperature (e.g., the wavy lines above a bowl of soup or frozen pond). Shading may designate time of day or a reflection from a mirror and color contrasts are used to define distance, temperature, and other attributes. Often these are difficult for children and adults with nonverbal disorders.

Picture series and films may be difficult because of relationships between objects. For example, time and space concepts are often illustrated by altering the size and distance between figures. Greenfield (1984) reported that young children and adults from certain cultures did not understand the visual cues on television. The panning and zooming in on specific objects led some to believe that the objects actually increased in size.

Siegel (1975) states that pictures may be defined by their level of structural organization, themes, and complexity. He further indicated they vary according to the amount of detail presented, the degree of approximation to the object or event depicted (i.e., representational level), and spatial organization. These factors should be considered when designing studies and selecting materials for instruction (Podhajski, 1980). Often people with language impairments have generalized disorders that interfere with the understanding of both nonverbal and verbal symbols.

All facets of nonverbal communication require symbolization. Facial expression, body language, and gesture also require perception and interpretation of movement (Allport & Vernon, 1933; Birdwhistle, 1970; Duncan, 1969; Ekman, 1978). According to Ekman and Friesen (1969) and Eisenberg and Smith (1971) gestures may be used either as symbols to represent words or to supplement verbal communication. The former, called *emblems*, are used when verbal communication is blocked. In adulthood, gestures are important for certain occupations. Policemen, the ground crew at an airport, and waiters often use signals or emblems on a routine basis. More often, gestures are used as illustrators for emphasis or to designate specific ideas such as size, location, and direction.

Proxemics, the study of space, has been studied extensively by Hall (1959) who found that all families, communities, and cultures have rules that are important for functioning within the group. Over time we learn which distances are acceptable to maintain relationships. Some learning disabled adults have not learned to use space appropriately. At times they "get too close" and, in addition, may not respond to the nonverbal "regulators" or feedback from people in the environment. Tactual communication also plays a powerful role in relationships.

Prosody, vocal inflection, rhythm, and voice set are equally important, (Crystal, 1969; Eisenberg & Smith, 1971). Even without hearing words, we frequently can determine the sex, approximate age, feelings, and emotional state of speaker. Studies indicate listeners even make inferences about occupation and socio-economic status.

### Conceptualization

While most conceptual tasks require some language or verbal mediation, certain tests and everyday activities require the ability to draw conclusions on the basis of observation. Often learning disabled students have difficulty with open-ended tasks that require spontaneous abstraction of criterial attributes (e.g., put things into groups). If told to sort them by "shape, size, function," etc., however, they frequently succeed. While some do not spontaneously use language for problem solving, those with nonverbal disorders may not detect the relevant features.

Adults with nonverbal disorders typically perform well on verbal tasks (e.g., What would you do if you saw a train approaching a broken track?) but in naturalistic settings might not detect the broken track nor even note the speed of the oncoming train. They may respond to verbal jokes and absurdities yet fail pictorial absurdities. Many do not scan and survey the environment to note the elements needed for problem detection and problem solving.

In summary, the assessment of nonverbal skills requires an investigation of performance at many levels in both structured settings and natural contexts. While certain problems can be detected with paper and pencil tasks, others will be more noticeable when the person is required to spontaneously solve real word problems.

Watching a highly verbal person struggling with the manipulation of basic utensils, using a ruler, or folding a paper provides more insight into the nature of the condition than most tests.

## PATTERNS OF PERFORMANCE AND TRENDS

Eighteen adults had primary nonverbal disorder problems related to nonverbal learning. In addition, they had difficulty with mathematics and some aspects of writing. Because of their problems, a few elected to live at home; one lived in a YMCA where daily needs were more easily managed. Others were functioning at home and at work, but were frustrated by their inability to perform seemingly simple routine tasks. The man who was described in the *handwriting* section (Fig. 10-1) of Chapter 10 wrote a list of several things he wanted to accomplish in remediation. These included tying shoe laces, unlocking doors, using a ruler, folding paper, using hooks, putting in a light bulb, using any machine, hammer, or copying machine, opening milk cartons, and putting on license plates. These were in addition to his goal of improving writing and mathematics. A brilliant woman with milder problems wanted to be able to set an alarm clock (getting all of the hands in the correct position), to develop better skills in measuring and estimating quantities, to find ways of "not getting lost," and in terms of academic goals, to complete a history paper that had interfered with her success in college. On the WAIS (Wechsler, 1955), all except 3 had at least 15 points discrepancy between Verbal and Performance intelligence (the latter lower). The lowest subtest mean for the group was Object Assembly (Mean = 7.42 S.D. 3.06), whereas the highest was comprehension (Mean = 13.4 S.D. 2.86). An analysis of their standard scores from the Wide Range Achievement Test (Jastak & Jastak, 1978) indicated that Reading was higher than spelling or arithmetic . In 14 cases their pattern of achievement was Reading > Spelling > Arithmetic and in 4 cases arithmetic was higher than reading. All except two people scored above the reading mean for the entire group.

The most significant deficit appeared to be in visual spatial analysis and synthesis, and in visual-motor integration. Tasks with recognition responses were generally easier than those requiring manipulation, construction, drawing, or writing. Thus, on the Spatial Relations Subtest of the Primary Mental Abilities Test (Thurstone, 1962), only five scored significantly below average. In contrast, their performance on Object Assembly and the test of Visual Motor Integration (Beery & Buktenica, 1982) was well below average. Errors included lack of closure, problems with angles, intersecting lines, and the ability to perceive relationships between figures. It should be noted, however, that the scores on the VMI were also low for a subgroup of dyslexics with perceptual-motor problems.

The Draw-a-Person subtest of the Goodenough-Harris Drawing Test (Goodenough & Harris, 1963) indicated that the nonverbal group, as a whole, performed very poorly. Only four scored above the 50th percentile. Several scored below the 30th percentile. Examples of their drawings are shown in Figure 12-2. Frequently the parts of the body were not connected but more often they were primitive and lacking in detail. Four subjects omitted fingers or drew the persons so the hands were not visible. In some instances this may have been related to finger agnosia. Spacing and proportions were noticeably deficient. A few could not get the drawing on a single page so asked for a second sheet to complete it rather than trying to reduce the figure.

Poor drawings were not unique to the Draw-A-Person test. The problems related to closure, detail, angle, and perception were observed in other figures as well (See drawing of objects in Fig. 12-3). One of the most difficult tasks for those who came for diagnostic teaching was the drawing of an object from three perspectives. When asked to draw a cup or a watch as it would appear from the side, bottom or top, three adults drew the identical figure for all perspectives.

Spatial visualization tasks used by Moyer (1978) were also difficult for those

**Figure 12-2.** Drawings of adults with learning disabilities.

in diagnostic teaching. Her procedures measured behaviors which Eliot (1970) suggested were the essence of spatial visualization. Subjects were required to identify the standard design after it had been rotated 90, 180, 270, and 360 degrees and to reconstruct the design after it had been rotated in the same way. She found the learning disabled children were more successful after having the opportunity to observe the rotation and concluded thay were less able to

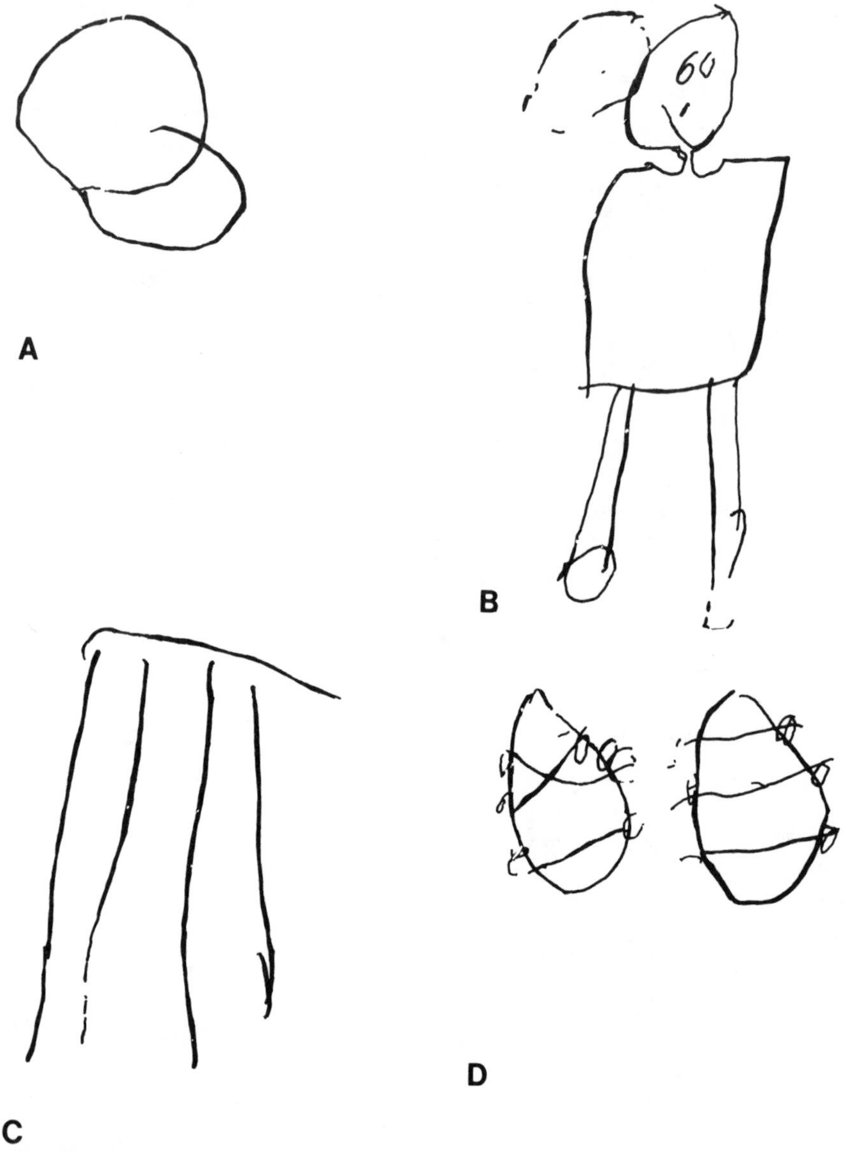


**Figure 12-3.** Drawings of a person with Nonverbal Disorder. (A) Hat, (B) Shirt, (C) Pants, and (D) Shoes.

mentally manipulate the design than their peers. Two adults were totally unable to mentally manipulate the figures.

Nonverbal conceptual problems were evident on many tasks requiring picture interpretation and reasoning. Five adults with nonverbal disorders had Picture Arrangement subtest scores below 5, and 5 below 6. This lead us to conclude they had difficulty abstracting ideas from observations. During diagnostic teaching verbal mediation was used to guide their looking and monitoring.

Several seemed to miss the point when asked to describe pictures. One woman, whose performance intelligence score was 24 points below her verbal could not interpret representational features in pictures. She did not know, for example, the lines around a person's head indicated "sneezing" nor that the lines on a tree represented bark. And, she often failed to scan an entire picture to note relationships. When given a picture of a mother pulling a boy's tooth with a string she said, "They are having a tug of war". As expected, she was having many problems at work because of her nonverbal social perception problems. In addition, she had difficulty making and keeping friends.

Another problem, more related to auditory learning, was their faulty prosody. Several adults talked too loudly, in some instances, too quickly. Their overall pragmatic, conversational skills were rather poor.

## Comparison of Performance with the Reading Disabled

An inspection of the WAIS subtest scores for the adults whose standard scores in reading were 85 or below indicated a different pattern from those with nonverbal disorders. The lowest mean subtest for nonverbal group was Object Assembly, whereas the lowest score for the severe dyslexics was Digit Span with a mean of 5.3 and a range of 4–9. Both groups scored relatively poorly on Picture Arrangement but the reasons for the failure may have been different. There were probably subjects in both groups who could not or did not use verbal mediation to solve the problem. However, picture interpretation and temporal organization also could have contributed to poor performance. In other instances, either nonverbal representation or temporal organization could have contributed to the poor performance.

Three people with both reading and severe nonverbal disorders had low scores on Digit Span and Object Assembly. They were deficient in both sequential and spatial learning.

Because time disorientation has been reported in dyslexics and those with nonverbal disabilities, a group of 44 adults was given the Buck Time Test (Buck 1946). They did not perform significantly below average (Mean 92.6; S.D. 16.6); however, several had difficulty providing answers to questions regarding the number of minutes in an hour, seasons, and the meaning of words such as decade and century.

In summary, adults with nonverbal disabilities present a major challenge for educators and for guidance personnel. They are different from those with primary academic handicaps in many ways because their problems are more obvious in daily life. Vogel highlights their difficulties in college in Chapter 13. Stress and anxiety also interfere with performance. Reitan (1966) said the interaction of stress and performance, which one observes in everyone, becomes more apparent in people with mild impairments due to brain damage. They are most readily subject to disorganization with any type of adverse influence. These factors need to be considered when counseling adults with learning disabilities.

## ACKNOWLEDGMENT

We wish to thank Dr. Blanche Podhajski for her assistance with data analysis for this chapter.

## REFERENCES

Allport, G., & Vernon, P. *Studies in expressive movement*. New York: Macmillan, 1933.

Badian, N. Arithmetic and nonverbal learning. In H. Myklebust (Ed.), *Progress in learning disabilities: Vol. 5* (pp. 235–264). New York: Grune & Stratton, 1983.

Badian, N., & Ghublikian, M. The personal-social characteristics of children with poor mathematical computation skills. *Journal of Learning Disabilities*, 1982, *16*, 154–157.

Beery, K., & Buketenica, N. *Developmental test of visual-motor integration* (Revised). Chicago: Follett, 1982.

Benton, A. Visual factors in dyslexia: An unresolved issue. In D. Duane & C. Leong, *Understanding learning disabilities: International and multidisciplinary views*. New York: Plenum, 1985.

Benton, A. Visuoperceptive, visuospatial, and visuoconstructive disorders. In K. Heilman & E. Valenstein (Eds.), *Clinical neuropsychology*. New York: Oxford University Press, 1979.

Birch, H., & Lefford, A. Two strategies for studying perception in "brain-damaged" children. In H. Birch (Ed.), *Brain damage in children: The biological and social aspects*. New York: Williams & Wilkins, 1964.

Birdwhistle, R. *Kinesics and context*. Philadelphia: University of Pennsylvania Press, 1970.

Blalock, J. *A study of conceptualization and related abilities in learning disabled and normal preschool children*. Unpublished doctoral dissertation, Northwestern University, 1977.

Bryan, T. Children's comprehension of nonverbal communication. *Journal of Learning Disabilities*, 1977, *10*, 501–506.

Buck, J. *The time appreciation test*. Los Angeles: Western Psychological Services, 1946.

Critchley, M. *The parietal lobes*. Baltimore: Williams & Wilkins, 1953.

Cruickshank, W. (Ed.), *The teacher of brain-injured children*. Syracuse: Syracuse U Press, 1966.

Crystal, D. Prosodic development. In P. Fletcher & M. Garman (Eds.), *Language acquisition: Studies in first language*. Cambridge, England: Cambridge University Press, 1979.

Duncan, S. Nonverbal communication. *Psychological Bulletin*, 1969, *72*, 118–137.

Eisenberg, A., & Smith, R., *Nonverbal communication*. Indianapolis: Bobbs-Merrill, 1971.

Ekman, P. *Facial expression, nonverbal behavior and communication*. New York: John Wiley, 1978.

Ekman, P., & Friesen, W. The repertoire of nonverbal behavior: Categories, origins, usage, and coding. *Semiotics*, 1969, *1*, 63–92.

Eliot, J. The spatial world of the child. In H. Myklebust (Ed.), *Progress in learning disabilities: Vol. 3*. New York: Grune & Stratton, 1975.

Frostig, M., & Horne, D. *The Frostig program for the development of visual perception. Teacher's guide*. Chicago: Follett Publishing Co., 1964.

Goodenough, F. & Harris, D. *Goodenough-Harris Drawing Test*. New York: Psychological Corporation, 1963.

Greenfield, P. *Mind and media*. Cambridge, MA: Harvard U Press, 1984.

Hall, E. *The silent language*. Garden City, NY: Doubleday, 1959.

Heilman, K., & Valenstein, E. (Eds.), *Clinical neuropsychology*. New York: Oxford U Press, 1979.

Jastak, J., & Jastak, S. *Wide range achievement test* (rev. ed). Wilmington, DE: Jastak, 1978.

Johnson, D., & Myklebust, H. *Learning disabilities: Educational principles and practices*. New York: Grune & Stratton, 1967.

Kephart, N. *The slow learner in the classroom*. Columbus, OH: C.E. Merrill, 1960.

Knott, G. *A study of gesture as nonverbal communication in preschool language disabled and preschool normal children*. Unpublished doctoral dissertation, Northwestern University, 1974.

Leiter, R. *International performance scale*. Santa Barbara, CA: State College Press, 1940.

McFie, J., Piercy, M., & Zangwill, O. Visual-spatial agnosia asociated with lesions of the right cerebral hemisphere. *Brain*, 1950, *73*, 167–190.

Moyer, M. *An investigation of spatial visualization abilities in normal and learning disabled children*. Unpublished doctoral dissertation, Northwestern University, Evanston, IL, 1978.

Myklebust, H. Nonverbal learning disabilities: Assessment and intervention. In H. Myklebust (Ed.), *Progress in learning disabilities: Vol. 3*. New York: Grune & Stratton, 1975.

Orton, S. *Reading, writing and speech problems in children*. New York: W.W. Norton, 1937.

Perecman, E. (Ed.), *Cognitive processing in the right hemisphere*. New York: Academic Press, 1983.

Podhajski, B. *Picture arrangement and selected narrative language skills in learning disabled and normal seven year old children*. Unpublished doctoral dissertation, Northwestern University, 1980.

Reitan, R. The needs of teachers for specialized information in the area of neuropsychology. In W. Cruickshank (Ed.), *The teacher of brain-injured children*. Syracuse: Syracuse U Press, 1966.

Siegel, I. The development of pictorial comprehension. In B. Randhawa & W. Coffman (Eds.), *Visual learning and communication*. New York: Academic Press, 1978.

Smith, F. *Comprehension and learning: A conceptual framework for teachers*. New York: Holt, Rinehart & Winston, 1975.

Strauss, A., & Lehtinen, L. *Psychopathology and education of the brain-injured child.* New York: Grune & Stratton, 1947.

Terris, S. *The interpretation of facial expressions by learning disabled and normal children: Can attentional deficits account for the differences?* Unpublished doctoral dissertation, Northwestern University, 1985.

Thurstone, T. *Primary Mental Abilities Test.* Chicago: Science Research Associates, 1962.

Wechsler, D. *Wechsler Adult Intelligence Scale.* New York: Psychological Corporation, 1955.

Wiig, H., & Harris, S. Perception and interpretation of nonverbally expressed emotions by adolescents with learning disabilities. Perceptual and Motor Skills, 1980, 50, 445–446.

# 13

## An Experiment in Group Therapy with Learning Disabled Adults

Louise Rosenblum

The discussions in the previous chapters have indicated that many of the adults were highly motivated to achieve, that they had good mental ability, and several areas of strength. However, their persistent problems often interfered with their feelings of self esteem. The staff became aware of heavily laden emotional issues among several who were in remediation and were asked if they would like to become a part of an on-going therapy group. The response was a combination of curiosity, enthusiasm, and skepticism—an impetus for beginning the group sessions. Some elected not to attend, either because they felt they did not need help or because they were receiving counseling elsewhere.

The group had eight or nine members, but not all came routinely. It is known that there is value in commonality of purpose when starting a group, and there was a strong need among these students to share a history of being misunderstood and confused about their capabilities. Frequently, they have a history of crushing setbacks in school. Often they have a history of social mishaps and uneasy family relationships. Establishing a purpose for the group came about as the depth of individual concerns were aired by students at the inception of the program. Many of the group had experienced failures that created a reluctance to communicate and, even more, a fear of projecting hopes about what they would like from the group. Active leadership was needed and clues had to be found for interaction. In those early stages, the leader needed to be inordinately sensitive that no one was overlooked and no one was pushed too quickly.

The group met in the evening after they had received an hour of individual remediation; the timing had both advantages and disadvantages. On one hand, they had already worked hard, but on the other hand, defenses were often down

ADULTS WITH LEARNING DISABILITIES
ISBN 0-8089-1795-1

at this late hour, so it became a time for release of tension and sharing with people they had passed only in the corridors or waiting room.

They were all at differing stages of occupational and professional development. The youngest was still trying to complete high school. A fine rapport developed between him and an older man who recalled his traumatic high school experience, which bore many similarities to the first young man's. Other members of the group offered their own accounts of "flunking" courses and what it was like to deal with the disappointment in oneself.

The group included a junior college student, a waitress, a supermarket clerk, a receptionist, a craftsman, a landscape gardener, a nurse's aide, a graduate student, and a custodian. There were widely diversified ages, occupations, and ethnic groups represented. They had been coming to the Learning Disabilities Center for varying lengths of time and their specific disabilities differed. Yet, it soon became apparent that the similarities between members, though subtle, were more numerous than their differences. They all felt misunderstood by friends, school, and family. They all recalled feeling "dumb" and being called stupid. They felt early education had been confusing and inadequate to help them. However, there was often one teacher they could recall who truly understood where they were in their thinking process.

They all felt highly motivated to learn and had come to the clinic to define their problem and work on it. This factor above all made this group "special." Often defeat is so discouraging that the learning disabled adult is lost to the learning process and does not seek help.

The trust factor was also slow to develop. No one initially felt free to be critical of someone else. Eventually, however, they were able to share their feelings of being misunderstood. They had experienced these feelings from early childhood. Often it was a result of being labelled in the school room. In other instances it was a parent's self-consciousness, or frustrated attempts to find help that added to the child's feeling of being misunderstood and "not okay." Parents often felt helpless because they did not see enough progress. They found it hard to know where and how to make demands of the school system. Usually the problem was recognized by the parent, but articulating the need for special training was difficult.

Evoking the past and discussing early family ties was a priority for the group. Yet the common task of introspection was often painful. Occasionally, it was necessary to use awareness exercises to accelerate the interaction and put people at ease with themselves. One exercise proved to be particularly successful in getting at their feelings and longings. It was suggested they "pretend" to tell their parents thoughts they had never had the courage to say. Gestalt games were effective after the group members had established an ongoing relationship.

One young man chose just to listen, saying he was sure he could say "anything" to his parents. Another told the group he would like his dad to do something special with him alone, go on a camping trip or to a ball game. At a later time he revealed that he had hesitatingly asked his father that night if he would take a photography class with him, and much to his surprise, his father said yes. He felt elated by the possibility of spending this extra time with him. The sharing of feelings of misunderstandings of their "difficulties" became an important part of growth and change.

There was increasing respect for each other and for the imaginative ways of circumventing problems and dealing with limitations. One member with very limited reading skills said he carried a briefcase with a calculator, a tape recorder, and other mechanical gadgets that he used to compensate for his deficits in writing and reading. His landscape business depended on extra help from family members.

The group members also empathized with an extremely attractive, tall brunette who was a receptionist to a drug executive, a position she had obtained with the help of an uncle. For the most part, her job involved oral communication. She described an incident after she had worked there for several weeks. A salesman phoned and said, "Would you tell the president I will be 30 minutes late and to substitute someone else for the 9 o'clock presentation?" The woman was stunned, knowing she could not interrupt her boss, nor write an intelligible note without revealing her horrendous spelling. She approached one of the secretaries near her desk and said, "I've got to leave for a moment—could you write a note to the president that Mr. L. is going to be late?" This young adult had learned how to come up with excuses at a moment's notice after years of these recurring crises.

The group knew her history. They were aware that she had ten jobs over the last eight years and was feeling discouraged. She had little trouble getting positions if she covered up the whole truth. In her heart she believed that if she told the truth, she would not get a job; she was not able to overcome the feeling that this would happen to her. The group encouraged her to risk the truth with some of her fellow workers in order to provide an internal support system. She retorted angrily at one point, saying that no one really knew what it was like to be fired. As time went on, however, she did find someone to share her secrets with at work.

One must examine the social and emotional needs of the learning disabled adult and why a group experience at this time filled an important gap in their lives. Some members had never left home; they were deeply enmeshed in family life, never having achieved their own identities. It seemed as though their parents could not extricate themselves from decision-making on behalf of their children; and the young adults in this particular group could not totally separate from their parents. The very nature of this conflict demands that the adults distance themselves and test their values before confronting the family. The group provides one vehicle for this separation.

It is known that the emotional problems we see in the older individual have been set in motion in subtle ways at an early age. The mutual resentment of parent and child has built up. As small children, these adults often did not bring gratification to their parents. Mothers had not always understood the behavior of the infant who quickly lost interest in an activity. Later, many a parent grew frustrated as the learning disabled child could not tie a shoe, learn how to set the knife and fork in place, or take instructions. Many anxious fathers, uncertain of how to cope with their disappointment, removed themselves to the family room to watch a ball game when their young son could not catch a ball. Documentation of early infant responses on a large scale, however, is thus far unattainable since the diagnosis of learning disabilities is traditionally not made until school age. Memory has a way of becoming unreliable or distorted. While there are numerous reasons for early breaches in the child-parent attachment, early manifestations of a learning disability may well be one of them.

The young adult with learning disabilities has gone through longer, more painful processes of growing up than his peers. Seeing friends who make it successfully through high school and move on to college while they bear the accumulated rebuffs and failures of school makes them truly vulnerable. The unresolved educational dilemmas also stir up anxiety and fear in parents. It may be that they see the children as inadequate extensions of themselves. It may be the fear that they did not set appropriate limits or were too permissive or too authoritarian.

Thus we face the dilemma of helping the learning disabled adult in the painful emotional struggle to achieve stability in his life with his family, while at the same time working through his ability to separate from and function, outside of the home. The group experience has some parallels to the family's experience; there will be new experiences of confronting and coping. Family roles and functions will have to be re-examined in the light of adulthood. The adults need peer feedback in determining how much freedom they want and how much dependency they need. Take the case of Sam, who, expressing despair, said, "You can't imagine what it was like when the boss called from out of town and asked what the receipts were so far this week. I had done all the work but I could not remember where I put the stuff. On top of it, when I told my wife about it, she said it was no wonder—I couldn't remember where I put the scissors she had just given me 10 minutes before—I just don't think I'm going to be offered that job advancement after this happened." Another member of the group who had been listening intently, responded, "I know what you mean. I've been unpacking crates at the supermarket for three years and I feel stuck. Every time the manager comes by I seem to be talking to some little kid. I'm sure he thinks I'm a goof-off."

In general, the basic ingredients of the group are tied to it being slow-moving, accepting, and supportive. Yet, change does occur over time in much the way learning has occurred. Considerable comfort and strength came from becoming well-accepted by the group. It was helpful in testing social norms and values in a protected setting. It helped develop trust for individuals who have experienced skepticism, disappointment, and frustration. The opportunities for developing this growth must be parallel to the opportunities for cognitive growth. While the 1960s and 70s shed more light on how to cope with the education of children and adults with learning disabilities, the 1980s and 90s must provide another dimension for building emotional strengths so they can develop and maintain self-esteem. As we continue to understand how to help the child and minimize failures, we will be hitting at the roots of the adults' social and emotional problems. The group therapy experience is one attempt at helping confront these problems while developing areas of strength.

## BIBLIOGRAPHY

Barneby, N., & Ruppert, E. Parents of chronically ill or physically handicapped children. In L. E. Arnold (Ed.), *Helping parents help their children* (174–182), New York: Brunner/Mazel, 1978.

Buscaglia, L. *The Disabled and their parents*, Thorofares, NJ: Charles B. Slack, 1975.

Chess, S., Fernandez, P., & Korn, S. The handicapped child and his family: Consonance and his dissonance. *Journal of American Academy of Child Psychiatry*, 1980, *19*, 56–67.

Dunlap, W., & Hollingworth, S. How does a handicapped child affect the family? Implications for practitioners. *The Family Coordinator*, 1977, *26*, #3, 286–293.

Featherston, H. *A difference in the family: Life with a disabled child.* New York: Basic Books, 1980.

Ross, A. *The exceptional child in the family*. New York: Grune & Stratton, 1964.

Siegel, E. *The exceptional child grows up*. New York: E. P. Dutton, 1975.

Stein, L., Mindel, E., & Jabaley, T. *Deafness and mental health*. New York: Grune & Stratton, 1981.

Suelzle, M. The impact of a developmentally disabled child on the family, American Medical Association 4th National Congress on the Quality of Life, April, 1978, Chicago.

Suelzle, M., & Keeman, V. The world of the developmentally disabled child. Center for Urban Affairs, Northwestern University, 1979, Evanston, IL.

Yalom, I. *Group Therapy*. New York: Basic Books, 1970.

# 14

# Issues and Concerns in LD College Programming

Susan A. Vogel

According to Margaret Rawson (1977) unused aptitudes make trouble for their owners and his or her world. Such may be the case for thousands of underemployed and unemployed learning disabled adults who, up until very recently, were excluded from postsecondary education because they did not meet the institution's entrance requirements. Others entered postsecondary institutions with open admission or were accepted to universities only to find that because of their learning disability and the increased academic demands of college courses, they required assistance and modifications that were unavailable. Presently, there is an insufficient but growing number of postsecondary settings that offer services to the learning disabled. Just as in the decade of the 70s, when secondary schools responded to the needs of LD adolescents, in the decade of the 80s, colleges, universities, graduate, and professional schools are responding to two powerful sources of pressure: (1) the community of concerned learning disabled adolescents, their parents, LD adults, and professionals, and (2) the passage of the regulations to enforce Section 504 of the Rehabilitation Act of 1973.

## SECTION 504 OF THE REHABILITATION ACT OF 1973

Sometimes referred to as the civil rights statute for disabled individuals, Section 504 of the Rehabilitation Act of 1973 provides that "No otherwise qualified handicapped individual shall, solely by reason of his handicap, be excluded from participation in, be denied the benefits of, or be subjected to discrimination under any program or activity receiving federal financial assist-

ADULTS WITH LEARNING DISABILITIES
ISBN 0-8089-1795-1

ance." Since most institutions are receiving federal assistance in the form of financial aid to students, they are, in fact, required to ensure the rights of qualified handicapped students to enter colleges and universities and to participate fully in all programs (Subpart E, Section 504).

## Identifying the Learning Disabled Applicant

In order for colleges and universities to be in compliance with Section 504 and, in particular, with Subpart E, college officials must know which applicants are handicapped. When the mobility, hearing, or visually impaired student comes to campus for an interview, the handicap is most often apparent. However, for the learning disabled, often referred to as those students with a "hidden" handicap, this is frequently not the case. According to Section 504, college officials are ". . . prohibited from furnishing or soliciting information about the handicaps of college applicants" (Guildroy, 1981, p. 17). Many learning disabled applicants are fearful that such information may, in fact, be used against them and, therefore, they withhold this information from admissions counselors. As a result, and depending on the stringency of the admissions requirements of the institution, there are some gifted learning disabled students who are presently enrolled or have completed degree programs in undergraduate, graduate, and professional schools. There are far more, however, who are average or above in ability and after a year in college are in serious academic difficulty, have dropped out, or have been asked to leave. Moreover, there are many, many more who were never given the opportunity to continue their education beyond high school.

Responsibility for the unaided LD student's failure in college is sometimes shared by institutions in other ways. Some institutions, motivated both by positive and worthy intentions and others, by fear of infringing on the rights of privacy and confidentiality of the handicapped, of becoming entangled in legal proceedings, or of losing federal funding, accept all learning disabled applicants who identify themselves in the admissions process. They do so, in some rare instances, with assurance of academic success, but in others, with the foreknowledge that the student will not be able to meet with success. At best, in these latter cases, the advisor and the counselor's assistance are enlisted to help the student accept her or his failing grades without losing perspective and to facilitate the student in the process of reevaluating his or her goals and formulating alternative plans.

## The Qualified Versus Unqualified Handicapped Student

As inadequate as this type of institutional response is, it should not be viewed as simplistic or uncaring. Rather, it is a reflection of the often ignored, ambiguous reference in Section 504 to "qualified" handicapped students, e.g., not unqualified handicapped students. Section 504 addresses itself only to the qualified handicapped students. This distinction raises several critical questions for postsecondary institutions: (1) How does one define the word, qualified, and (2) once defined, how can admissions counselors determine if a handicapped applicant is indeed a qualified handicapped student? These questions are even more complex in regard to learning disabilities as compared to other handicapping conditions because knowledge about learning disabilities is not universal. As a result, there are many highly educated individuals in postsecondary institutions who do not know very much about learning disabilities or, at worst, confuse the learning disabled with the retarded. Neither are higher education personnel entirely to be blamed. In the April, 1981 edition of the *Director of Personnel and Materials Dealing with Handicapped Students at the Postsecondary Level* (Elliot, 1981) the table of contents makes no mention of learning disabilities. Neither does the author list available slidetape presentations (Cordoni, 1980), informational booklets (Chesler, 1980; Makas, 1981; Sedita, 1980), and directories (Ridenour & Johnston, 1981) that provide specific information about learning disabled college students and programs.

Second, because the field is young, the "first generation" of children identified as learning disabled are only now reaching maturity, and there is very little research available to guide even well-intentioned college officials and LD specialists.

Lastly, there is still no universally accepted definition of learning disabilities among professionals, although progress is being made by the National Joint Committee for Learning Disabilities (Hammill, Leigh, McNutt, & Larsen, 1981). Even more difficult than defining learning disabilities is distinguishing between the *qualified* and *unqualified* learning disabled college applicants.

## Present Practices in Various Institutions

First, institutions with open admissions do not have to address themselves to either of these questions since all applicants who have earned a high school diploma are automatically accepted. Campuses with open admissions have other problems, however. College personnel must identify, evaluate, and serve a larger number of LD students who are already enrolled in degree programs. Other postsecondary institutions accept LD students unbeknownst to admissions counselors simply because they have met the entrance requirements. Once the students are enrolled on both these types of campuses, they often experience academic difficulty and according to Section 504, it is the responsibility of the institution to meet their needs. Still, other postsecondary institution officials evaluate all applicants in relation to the admissions criteria of the university. These institutions, therefore, have defined *qualified* to mean that the LD student meets the college's entrance requirements. The LD student's acceptance to the college is based on his or her ability to meet the same entrance requirements as the non-LD applicant. These requirements typically include high school class rank, grade point average, and the results of the college admissions testing (SATs and ACTs of the Educational Testing Service and American College Testing Program, respectively).

## Special Test Administration

If standardized tests are required, they must reflect what the students know, rather than the handicap. For this reason, modifications in administration procedures for the learning disabled are made available through ACT (1982) and ETS (1982), e.g., using a reader or scribe, and/or taking the tests untimed. Policies of test publishers differ regarding the reporting of special conditions under which tests are administered. ETS, for example, indicates on the report form that the reliability of these scores is not known since the tests were taken under special conditions. This practice raises several new questions. Since such a statement indicates to the admissions counselor that this student is handicapped, is ETS disclosing confidential information? Second, Dolan and Dolan (1980) believe that ETS is actually revealing that their tests may not be measuring achievement and aptitude (their intent), and they predict that as a result of Section 504, the SAT system will soon be challenged.

In spite of these paradoxes and possible drawbacks, Guildroy (1981), a former high school counselor, recommends that the learning disabled college applicant take advantage of the available test administration modifications if they allow for by-passing the area of disability and achieving higher scores. This recommendation is based on Guildroy's implied, over-riding recommendation for LD students to share voluntarily and openly with admissions counselors information about their learning disability, even when the institution may be in noncompliance with Section 504 by soliciting information directly about the possibility of a handicapping condition. As Guildroy points out, such information can be required ". . . when . . . taking remedial action . . . or when taking voluntary action to overcome the effects of conditions that resulted in limited participation" (U.S. Department of Health, Education, and Welfare, 1977).

Even though Section 504 and the LD pressure groups have not yet succeeded in making many postsecondary institutions accessible to the learning disabled, there is a growing awareness and many institutions are in the process of planning, initiating, or developing LD college programs. This chapter is therefore addressed to those individuals in postsecondary settings who are or will soon be engaged in such activities. The major purpose is to examine some of the critical issues in developing college programs to serve the LD adult.

# THE INSTITUTIONAL SETTING

## Location and Size

Programs have developed on campuses in a variety of settings. Not simply by chance did the earliest programs develop in small colleges, in suburban or rural communities, and in small towns. These settings offered the learning disabled a relatively safe environment. Getting lost on such a campus or making a wrong turn in the village did not endanger the LD student whose directionality and spatial orientation problems often persist into adulthood. More recently, comprehensive programs have also developed at larger universities, some located in rural areas and a few in metropolitan areas. However, for the LD adults with nonverbal, spatial, and directional problems there are obvious advantages to a small, rural, or suburban campus.

The size of the actual campus may also be an important consideration for students with nonverbal learning disabilities, especially those who have difficulties reading a map, who have a poor sense of direction, or cannot tell north, south, east, west, or even right and left when under pressure. Just as mobility orientation is offered for the visually impaired, spatial orientation could benefit the learning disabled. A big brother or sister, peer advocate, or a campus escort may also prove helpful for the LD adult with spatial orientation and directionality difficulties.

### The Student Body

The size and characteristics of the student body at a specific campus can play a substantial role in the LD adult's social acceptance (Ugland & Duane, 1981). Whether the student body is large or small is often not as important a factor as its heterogeneity. A diverse population of students, both ethnically, racially, and linguistically will often be more accepting of differences in behavior paterns, levels of social maturity, and social/interpersonal skills than a homogenous population. In a heterogenous environment, the likelihood of the LD student's finding a compatible roommate and a supportive group of friends will be enhanced.

### The Campus Climate

There is no secret among college students regarding the tone or climate of a particular campus. Some schools are known to be academically very competitive, others socially competitive, and still others, athletically. Of course, these are over-generalizations, but they help to highlight the importance of considering the campus climate when establishing a program. However, if the campus climate is not conducive to serious learning, that does not mean to say a program should not be established there. Just as within any student body, various subgroups, residence halls, or Greek houses have distinct personalities, LD programs can have a special learning and social climate conducive to the LD student's success. A nurturant atmosphere would be one in which scholarship and academic success achieved as the result of hard work (rather than brilliance) are valued and in which there is a sense of community, a mutual supportiveness, and good-humored cooperation.

## The Faculty

The size and characteristics of the faculty, the student-faculty ratio, and, more importantly, class size in typical freshman or required courses are important considerations. Although a large faculty can offer a broad spectrum of majors and subspecialties, an LD student with poor listening, notetaking, and study skills would be much more likely to flounder in a lecture hall with 400 students or in an adjacent room viewing the lecture on a TV screen without the opportunity to ask questions or interact in discussion than he or she would in a class of 10 or 15. Small classes, even in introductory courses, are more frequently found in the setting of a small college in which there is often a greater emphasis placed on teaching than on research and publication.

## The Mission

The relative importance of teaching excellence and faculty research is related to the broader question of an institution's mission. Many institutions have a clearly articulated mission and consciously seek out faculty and administrators who subscribe to it. The mission most compatible to the needs of LD adults is found in those institutions dedicated to developing each individual's fullest potential and fostering intellectual growth through tutorials, small class size, seminars, and independent studies, e.g., sustained one-to-one interaction between faculty and student, and to serving the under-served, whether they be the poorly prepared, the foreign student, the educationally deprived, the economically disadvantaged, or the handicapped. On such a campus, the 504 Coordinator and services of that office have a positive presence. The faculty are aware of Section 504 regulations, abide by them, and make use of the services of the 504 Coordinator. The most commonly used services and those that many faculty are already aware of are the provisions made for modified examination procedures.

## Institutional Resources

Many of the special services that LD students need, especially those that involve one-to-one instruction, are very costly. Estimates of the actual yearly costs of meeting the needs of one LD student enrolled in a comprehensive LD program range from \$3,000 to \$10,000 per year. Some, but very few, institutions have received private or federal grants. Even financially healthy institutions, especially in the private sector, have found it necessary to charge program participants additional fees to help defray expenses.

Federal funding is available at the postsecondary level for poorly prepared college-age students (e.g., Equal Opportunity, Basic Education, and Upward Bound Programs), for those who need to learn English as a second language, and for the economically needy. Why are the learning disabled, whose need for help is no more their own fault than the foreign student, no longer eligible for support once they receive their high school diploma (Vogel & Adelman, 1981)? Why should LD adults and their families have to pay additional fees as part of their financial responsibility in postsecondary education? Certainly, these questions are of high priority and will need to be resolved in the decade of the 80s so that postsecondary education will not be only for the fortunate minority of LD students who are economically advantaged or require of them a heavier financial burden.

## RECRUITMENT AND ELIGIBILITY

Services for the learning disabled have been designed to meet the needs of LD students who are (1) already accepted to the institution and having academic difficulties (internal applicants for service), and (2) LD students who apply to the institution because they know that there are appropriate services (external applicants). As was discussed earlier, internal candidates who are referred or refer themselves to the program director and are identified as learning disabled must be considered *qualified* handicapped students, assuming they were unconditionally accepted to the college having met the entrance requirements of the institution. In the case of external applicants, the institution must decide on the definition of *qualified* handicapped student and, once defined, how to determine which students are qualified and which are not. Programs that have been designed for internal applicants and those for external, differ mainly in the initial period of development since after a short time, colleges with service for internal applicants begin to receive applications from external applicants and vice versa. Programs that have been recruiting and accepting external applicants begin to receive requests for service from faculty-referred and self-referred students who learn about the services, want to be evaluated, and receive service. In fact, it is for this reason that it is essential for program directors to make the program known to their own constituents, even if the original design is to serve external applicants.

### The Admissions Process

In spite of this distinction between internal and external applicants, there are many similarities in the application process. First, the goal in both cases is to determine eligibility for service, i.e., to determine if the applicant is in fact learning disabled. Many programs require that extensive background information be submitted by the applicant (the psychological reports from previous evaluations, educational records including results of standardized tests, medical reports, and psychologist's reports). If an LD specialist had recently helped the LD applicant, he or she is sometimes asked to provide information. The applicant and his or her parents, if appropriate, are asked to fill out a case history form that will provide detailed information, for example, regarding family background, early developmental, medical, and educational history, current status, and future goals. External applicants are frequently asked to provide the results of a recently administered Wechsler Adult Intelligence Scale (WAIS) as an indication that they are college-able. Universities that require extensive background information and the results of the WAIS are typically institutions with stringent entrance requirements, not community colleges or vocational schools with open admission. Their rationale is that not all non-LD applicants are able to succeed in their academic environment and in order to predict which students are more likely to succeed in their academic environment, such colleges use the standard entrance examinations, high school grades, and class rank. Since these sources of information may reflect the LD applicant's disability rather than ability, the WAIS is substituted. Some institutions use the WAIS full scale, verbal, or performance intelligence quotient, while others use a cluster of specific subtest scores thought to correlate highly with academic success, e.g., Similarities and Block Design as an indication of abstract reasoning ability. In addition, current information may be requested as to the applicant's skill levels in reading, math, and spelling, such as can be provided by the Peabody Individual Achievement Test (Dunn & Markwardt, 1970).

## Assessment

Further additional psychoeducational (and sometimes medical) evaluation is frequently required. The extent of testing will vary depending on whether or not the services to be provided include individualized instruction and remediation in addition to the use of compensatory strategies (e.g., books on tape) and course support. The scarcity of standardized, reliable, and valid diagnostic instruments for the assessment of LD adults requires the diagnostician to be very skillful in eliciting important qualitative information during the testing. The readiness of the LD adults to reveal problem areas that they have spent a great deal of time and psychic energy hiding is often strongly influenced by the student's motivation for college and the rapport that is established between the diagnostician and the student. Both of these factors play a critical role in the assessment of learning disabilities in adults.

Though programs may vary as to whether the diagnostic testing is done prior to the student's formal acceptance or just after, the more extensive testing includes assessment of receptive and expressive oral language in the area of semantics, syntax, and morphology, reading skills, including word attack and comprehension of single words and passages (read orally and silently), and reading rate, written language, and math reasoning and computation (Vogel, 1985b). Assessment of oral language is a critical and often neglected area in adult assessment for several reasons: (1) Deficits in oral language among LD adults are widespread. Blalock (1982) reported that 63 out of 80 LD young adults evaluated at the Learning Disabilities Center at Northwestern University had deficits in oral language and auditory processing. They reported that these deficits interfered with academic performance; (2) much of traditional college teaching uses a lecture or discussion format; (3) although reading disabilities can be circumvented by listening to books on tape, this again places a heavy demand on oral receptive language abilities; (4) the demands for written language proficiency increase dramatically in college and also vary, according to the student's major. Although many instructors are willing to accept taped exams or oral presentations in place of written exams and papers, these accommodations force the students to rely heavily on their oral expressive abilities; (5) lastly, written expression begins with the oral (in adults at the subvocal level) expression of the idea. If LD students cannot recognize incorrect usage that they hear (e.g., She gave the books to Jon and I), why should they use the correct pronoun when they write or be able to identify and correct this error when they proofread? The writing process is the "translation" of the idea into the visual counterpart (handwriting and spelling), with correct sentence structure, usage, punctuation, and capitalization (mechanics), in an organized, logical progression of ideas (development), and in an appealing, sophisticated, and varied choice of sentence structure and vocabulary (style and diction). All of these areas in written language have to be assessed in order for appropriate intervention to be designed that meets the needs of the LD college writer.

Other areas of auditory functioning that have to be assessed, because so much of the college student's information comes in through the auditory channel, are auditory perception and memory. Assessment of auditory as well as visual perception, memory, analysis, and synthesis, (some of the underlying processes involved in spelling and reading), provides important diagnostic teaching information for remediation of the widespread and severe spelling disabilities that plague many LD adults. Medical evaluations often include auditory and visual acuity and in some cases, neurological examination, EEG studies, and dichotic listening.

## Decision-making

Whether or not extensive testing is done prior to admission or after, an interview is usually required by the program director and a representative from the admissions office prior to acceptance. At this time, the college staff has an opportunity to assess the student's level of maturity, social appropriateness, and motivation for college. In addition, a great deal of information can be acquired during the interview to supplement and/or clarify the information provided on the Case History form and in the specialists' reports. Appropriate topics include the student's educational background, including history of special education experiences, family background, especially as it pertains to other members of the family with learning problems, self-evaluation and self-knowledge, special interests and talents, and future goals.

Appropriate questions could include:

1. When did you first become aware of or learn that you have a learning disability?
2. What things were hard for you to learn in school, at home, in sports, or with friends?
3. In what subjects do you get the best grades? The poorest grades?
4. How much time do you spend on homework each day?
5. Is there anyone else in your family with learning problems? Other problems?
6. How do you spend your free time?
7. What do you do well? What are your special talents?
8. What work experience have you had?
9. What traveling have you done with your family? With a group? Alone?
10. Why are you interested in going to college?
11. What do you plan to study?
12. What do you think you will need help with in college?
13. What career options are you considering?

The student also has a chance to ask questions about the institution and the services provided that were not answered in the college's literature. Appropriate questions might be the following:

1. What are the requirements for admission?
2. How many LD students are on campus? What year are they in? Are they part-time, full-time, residents, commuters, traditional age, or older?
3. What are the goals and objectives of the program?
4. What services are provided?
5. Who provides these services?
6. What specialized training in learning disabilities do these individuals have?
7. Is remediation and/or support provided on a one-to-one basis or in a group? If in a group, how large is it?
8. What supervision is provided for non-certified instructors or tutors?
9. How long is service provided? One year only, or longer?
10. How is the duration of service determined?
11. Who will be my academic advisor and what training does this individual have in learning disabilities?
12. Do LD students take the regular college courses?
13. Are there any courses or programs unavailable to LD students?
14. What modifications have faculty or administrators been willing to make for LD students on this campus?
15. Are there additional courses required of LD students? If so, do they carry college credit and does the credit count toward graduation?
16. Has the program or services been evaluated? If so, are the goals and objectives being accomplished, and how well?

## Acceptance Criteria

We have already discussed some of the pitfalls in using the traditional criteria of high school grade point average, rank in class, and college entrance examination scores for determining the LD applicant's potential for success in the postsecondary setting. The question therefore before us is: What variables should be considered in order to identify potentially successful LD college students?

First, just as faculty vary widely in the demands they place on students, their level of expectations, and their method of evaluation, institutions vary in many of these same ways. In order to make a judgment about a student's chances of success, the demands of the environment must be assessed. Generally, the more demanding and the higher the expectations are in the institution, the more capable and the less deficient the LD student must be, and/or the more extensive the remediation of basic skills deficiencies and support services must be.

Second, the nature of the student's learning disability is an important variable. In liberal arts colleges, in contrast to vocational, technical, fine, or performing arts postsecondary institutions, there is a heavy reliance on verbal skills, both oral and written, higher level abstract thinking, and integrative abilities. For this reason, Curry College, for example, requires evidence of better-than-average abstract reasoning skills as is thought to be indicated by a scaled score of 13 or above on the Comprehension, Similarities, and Block Design subtests on the Wechsler Adult Intelligence Scale (WAIS) (Webb, 1980). The severely language-learning disabled student whose Verbal IQ as measured by the WAIS is in the low average range (with significantly lower scaled scores on the Information, Similarities, and Vocabulary subtests) may be able to succeed in only a very limited number of first-year courses, and even then only with much difficulty and a great deal of assistance. On the other hand, the LD adult whose verbal IQ is in the bright average or above range, but who has difficulty in social/interpersonal skills, as indicated often by a scaled score of seven or below on the Picture Arrangement and Comprehension subtests on the WAIS, may have considerably more difficulty blending in with peers, behaving in a socially appropriate manner, establishing and maintaining friendships, and especially in getting along with his or her roommate.

Some institutions do not make a distinction regarding the nature of the learning disability in their acceptance criteria, but rather consider the Full Scale IQ on the WAIS as a global predictor of college success. For example, one of Wright State University's criteria for admission to the LD program is high average ability as indicated by the Full Scale IQ on the WAIS of 115 or above (Bireley & Manley, 1980).

Lastly is the question of the severity of the learning disability. There is no widespread consensus as to the definition nor identification of severely learning disabled individuals. In fact, with the threat of significant cutbacks in federal and state aid to the handicapped, the Illinois State Board of Education sought the expertise of members of the Higher Education Advisory Committee on Special Education in addressing precisely these questions. However difficult this task, postsecondary institutions must determine whether they are going to accept only those few learning disabled students who have overcome their major deficiencies, e.g., those whose residual problems may be limited to slightly below average reading rate and written language abilities. On the opposite end of the continuum, an institution may decide that it is able to accept LD students with average ability and severe basic skills deficiencies, e.g., students with reading comprehension, math, or spelling skills at the fourth grade level, because it provides extensive remediation and support.

To summarize, some of the important variables that should be considered include the degree, program options, academic demands of the institution, the nature and severity of the student's learning disability, the pattern of strengths and deficits as well as the overall potential of the student, and the type and extensiveness of services provided by the LD program. In the last analysis, for many institutions, the basic question is, does the LD program at this specific institution provide the services necessary to ensure a reasonable chance of success given this individual's learning strengths and needs.

## SPECIAL NEEDS OF LD COLLEGE STUDENTS

Postsecondary institutions are both similar and different from high school settings. They are similar in the nature of some of the demands they place on the student, for example, textbook reading, but because college courses require so much more reading, the student must develop new skills and compensatory strategies. On the other hand, resident college life requires qualitatively different patterns of behavior in the areas of independent living skills, group living, and time management. The LD college specialists can facilitate the LD adults' successful adjustment to these new and increased demands by understanding the demands of their specific postsecondary setting, assessing the LD students' coping strategies and skills in these and other areas, and then providing the appropriate support services. Following is a discussion of some of these special needs and strategies for meeting them in postsecondary institutions. They were selected because they were thought to typify situations in which the usual college procedures or readily accessible solutions can be easily modified to meet the needs of the LD college student.

### Academic Advising

Careful academic planning should be based first on the advisor's knowledge and understanding of learning disabilities and of the specific LD student's learning disability, i.e., the student's academic strengths and weaknesses, processing deficits, and learning style. Typically, faculty in the special education department have taken on the role of academic advisor, although often unofficially, after the LD student is in serious academic difficulty. For example, the student whose major difficulty is in reading comprehension and rate should be advised to take only one heavy reading course per semester. The student with fine motor coordination difficulties would be well advised not to take ceramics. Art history may not be recommended for the student with a severe nonverbal visual memory deficit.

Second, course selection should be based on complete and accurate information not only about the student's strengths and weaknesses, goals, and interests, but about the course itself, i.e., how it fits into the departmental sequence of courses, the level of difficulty, the prerequisites or assumed background knowledge and skills, and the method of instruction. It is very helpful for the LD student to read the course description and syllabus in advance, and, whenever feasible, to speak to the instructor personally about the questions raised above, as well as the reading load, course requirements, and frequency and method of evaluation (Weiner, 1975). Possible modifications as to method of instruction and/or evaluation can be discussed at that time, as well as tutorial assistance and reading assignment so that the student can begin studying course material during intersession or summer vacation. Reassurance can be given to the instructor as to the extent of additional demands or modifications that he or she may be asked to make. The faculty member also gets a first-hand impression of the seriousness, motivational level, and commitment to learning that the LD student has made, which are very often greater than, rather than less than, the average college student.

Third, the time frame of a course often determines the difference between success and failure for some LD students. For those with long term memory deficits, the shorter the grading period, and the more frequent the instructor evaluates the students, the better. Classes that meet three or four times per week are often preferred over those classes that meet for an extended class period once a week.

Lastly, the number of courses that a student enrolls in as well as the balance among the courses is an important key to success. In many colleges with LD programs, students are advised to carry a minimum full-time load (usually 12 semester hours). Whereas non-LD students estimate that they should spend two to three hours in preparation for every hour in class, the LD student should expect to spend four or five. A 12 hour load could require a minimum of 48 hours of preparation per week for the LD student. Some students, in fact, may do even better if enrolled part-time, especially at the beginning of their college careers when they are working on improving their basic skills, acquiring new or more effective study habits, and/or learning new group living skills, time management, and organizational skills.

## Faculty Advocate

The academic advisor who is, ideally, a learning disabilities specialist and also member of the faculty, can provide another very important service to the LD adult as a faculty advocate, especially in the developmental phase of the college program and in the program participant's freshman year (Miller, McKinley, & Ryan, 1979). Ideally, this person should be viewed as sharing in the mission and values of the institution and be fully identified with the faculty (rather than with a corps of professional advisors, 504 coordinator's staff, or administration). To be an effective advocate this individual should be highly skilled in interpersonal relationships and in addition, be open, honest, and straightforward. One of the most important functions of the faculty advocate is in the education of the faculty, administration, and staff regarding learning disabled adults through a case-by-case approach. At Barat College, students who enter the College through the Learning Opportunities Program give their academic advisor and LD specialist permission to discuss the nature of their learning disability and strategies to enhance their chances for success with faculty and staff who have a need to know. Faculty members have been asked if they want such information about an LD student enrolled in their class at the beginning of the semester or only if or when a problem arises. This system provides the opportunity to meet with the faculty on a one-to-one basis and describe the student's strengths and weaknesses, explain how the learning disabled student is able to learn most effectively, how the learning disability may affect the student in this particular course, learn more about the course requirements, method of instruction and evaluation, discuss appropriate instructional modifications that may be needed to enhance the student's learning and accomplish the course objectives, and discuss modifications for evaluation that will allow the instructor to measure the degree to which the student has achieved the course objectives. Most faculty welcome the opportunity to acquire this new information and find these students' unique patterns of strengths and weaknesses, the problems they face, and their determination to persevere, a teaching challenge. When the faculty discover that the LD student will receive tutorial support if needed and not demand a heavy commitment of their time, they become even more interested and receptive. The response of one faculty member perhaps typifies the reaction of many when he said that if these students are able to expend so much energy to overcome their problems, certainly we, as faculty, can be responsive to their needs. As the student acquires greater self-understanding, the faculty advocate can aid the student to improve self-advocacy skills. While at first, the faculty advocate may meet with colleagues individually, gradually the LD student becomes involved in these meetings and eventually the student takes on full responsibility and meets with instructors without the advocate. However, when the nature of the demand changes, for example when a student has completed a course requirement and is ready to write the thesis, do an internship, or take qualifying examinations, the faculty advocate may again have to assume temporarily the role of advocate.

## Effective Study Habits

### *Note-taking*

For many LD adults the task of taking notes in lectures is overwhelming. This is not surprising since note-taking requires simultaneously listening, comprehending, synthesizing and/or extracting main ideas, while retaining them long enough to formulate and write a synopsis. The writing act, in turn, requires automaticity and speed in letter formation, sufficient legibility and spelling ability to decipher what has been written at a later time. It is not surprising that LD college students' notes are often sparse, incomplete, and/or inaccurate. Frequently, they have written an over-abundance of details without the main ideas, misperceived unfamiliar words, or misunderstood the major concepts. Many of these problems reflect their auditory language deficits that often persist into adulthood. Johnson (1980) described the most persistent auditory disorders that follow the learning disabled into adulthood. Several of them interfere significantly with note-taking in lectures. The first she described was difficulty in phonemic discrimination, especially when the words were lexically unfamiliar or multi-syllabic. The LD specialist must be careful to distinguish among difficulty hearing differences in words, retaining specific words, and reproducing them, i.e., discrimination, memory, and expressive language difficulties. The less familiar the student is with the vocabulary of the subject matter, (as in medicine, for example, where much of the terminology retained its Latin or Greek root and is multisyllabic), the greater the difficulty at the level of phonemic discrimination.

A second deficit described by Cordoni (1980) and Johnson (1980) and one directly related to note-taking difficulties is in listening comprehension. Again, at the semantic level, the LD student may have a generalized deficit in vocabulary, in the vocabulary of a specific course, or have difficulty understanding multiple meanings of words used in a new context. Problems of abstraction may also be manifested when familiar words are used in metaphors, idioms, or figures of speech.

A third problem that can cause difficulties for LD students is slow rate of comprehension. Just as the foreigner can often comprehend better when the native speaker slows down his or her rate of speech, some LD adults also benefit when the instructor speaks at a comfortable rate. One of our students reported that she was in danger of failing an undergraduate course in accounting because of the instructor's rate. She was unsuccessful in explaining her difficulty to the instructor who misinterpreted her request to speak more slowly as an attempt to do less work, and she decided to drop the course when she realized she was in danger of failing. The next semester she registered for the same course with a different instructor who spoke more slowly and coincidentally had the well-deserved reputation of being more demanding. Much to the bewilderment and consternation of the first instructor, she received an honor grade.

Lastly, and perhaps most essential to the note-taking process, is the learning disabled student's deficit in short term auditory memory. For some, the difficulty is specific to a series of numbers; for others it may be unfamiliar proper names, or isolated facts. Much more debilitating is the problem some LD adults have in remembering sentences that may reflect an underlying problem in acquiring the syntax of their native language (Johnson, 1980; Vogel, 1975).

To help the LD student with poor note-taking skills, many institutions have made provisions for non-LD students enrolled in the classes to make a duplicate set of their lecture notes, or they have provided salaried notetakers (as is done for the hearing impaired students). Another less costly solution routinely recommended is to tape-record lectures after receiving permission of the instructor. However, given the nature of their underlying auditory deficits and the complexity of the task, we have found that this compensatory strategy helps the LD student overcome only some of the problematic aspects of this task, primarily the necessity to rely on auditory memory. We have found that tape-recording lectures is an important first step and provides the LD specialist with relevant content for teaching note-taking skills. Listening to the taped lecture with the LD specialist, the student learns what to listen for, to recognize frequently used cues that lecturers provide that signal a preview, the main ideas, new terminology, summary statements, or the introduction of a new topic. The taped lectures are also the vehicle for the LD specialist to teach outlining techniques, organizational skills, and summarizing strategies necessary for integration and later review of large bodies of information, such as would be presented during the semester and included in final evaluations. In other words, tape-recording lectures is not used as a substitute for note-taking, but rather a device that allows for unhurried listening, integration, organization, and writing of complex ideas so as to comprehend, organize, and retrieve them.

### *Organizational skills*

Many LD young adults in their freshman year need a great deal of assistance keeping track, not only of their personal belongings, but also of the reams of important information that have to be read, categorized, and stored in an easily retrievable fashion. At the beginning of every semester, at least one frantic upperclassman comes racing into the advisor's office to find out what he or she registered for at the end of last semester. Not only do they have trouble keeping track of their preregistration form, but also registration bulletins, course descriptions, general distribution requirements, and major requirements. Later, course syllabi, hand-outs, study guides, reading lists, assignments, lecture and reading notes, etc. only add to the confusion. Several of our students began carrying around all of these papers, their textbooks, tapes, and tape recorder in a suitcase-size canvas bag because they could not sort out and retrieve the essential from the nonessential for the day's activities. Such tools as color-coded three-ring binders, sectional dividers, hole punchers, folders with side pockets, spring binders, spiral notebooks with dividers, and notebooks and file boxes with alphabetical tabs (again color-coded) should be introduced as needed.

A second category of organizational tools that the LD adult may never have used is a variety of calendars. While their class schedule in high school may have been hard to keep track of, they had consecutive blocks of time between approximately 8:30 and 3:00. In college they must remember a variable schedule each day with classes spread over a longer school day. Assignments are no longer made on a daily or weekly basis, but for a quarter or semester. Appointments with advisors, LD specialists, counselors, tutors, lab partners, and study groups must be arranged and kept. The LD young adult must learn to keep track of appointments and personal commitments in a pocket calendar, assignments in an academic calendar, and a weekly calendar for special appointments.

### *Time Management Skills*

There is still a need for one other calendar-type device that addresses another of the LD adult's needs. Knowing when to go where and when assignments are due does not necessarily guarantee that the student will complete assignments by the deadline. Certainly, many beginning college students have crammed for exams and lived through some all-nighters, but many LD adults do not even get that close to finishing and therefore, they accumulate incompletes or failing grades based on lack of evidence rather than level of mastery as they transfer from one institution to another. One student, who was identified as a gifted photographer, had completed only 7 of the 20 required prints by the end of the semester. Time management strategies and expert help in breaking down a task and estimating realistically how long each step in the task will take are needed. Working on a monthly calendar, or even quarter or semester calendar, the student and LD specialist can work backwards from the due-date, building in margins of safety for the unexpected at regular intervals along the way, and planning for each step of the assignment. Without this assistance, it is very easy for first-year college students to become "drunk" with their new-found freedom, lack of curfew, enforced study hours, etc., and to respond to the large variety of enticements on a college campus and neglect their course work. Developing a daily, weekly, and long-range plan, also allows the student to plan for relaxation and recreation on a regular basis as well.

### *Test-taking Strategies*

In high school weekly quizzes are often given in addition to midterm and final examinations, providing the student with feedback, an early warning signal to seek additional help, or the assurance that he or she is successfully meeting the course objectives. Many teachers rely heavily on objective examinations rather than read 150 essay exams (a typical high school faculty-student ratio). High school teachers may also be flexible as to the method of evaluation, e.g., allowing for demonstration of learning through projects, creative endeavors, oral presentations, instead of objective or essay examinations, thus the LD college student may have had only limited experience in test preparation and test-taking strategies and successfully avoided writing essay exams and extensive research papers. One learning disabled high school student was accepted at a very competitive university based on the results of the American College Testing (ACT) entrance examinations (approximately in the 95th percentile) and his respectable high school grades, only to fail in the first year because he could not demonstrate his knowledge on essay examinations.

In addition to written language abilities (discussed below), there are other prerequisite skills that LD adults should master before they can benefit fully from the typical college course that deals with test preparation and test-taking strategies. One, for example, is the ability to abstract the essential information, principles, and unifying themes in lectures and in readings. One LD adult, who was highly successful in high school, reported that her lecture notes are useless and she rarely refers to them because she has written down the unimportant information and missed the main point. Rudel (1981) describes a different manifestation of this same problem in LD college students' responses to essay questions. She reports that in their responses, LD students often have difficulty coming to the point, focusing on the essential information that is asked for, and resisting the tendency to ramble and write down everything they know about the subject. For these students it is helpful to focus on key principles in preparation and later on key verbs used in essay questions (e.g., describe, compare and contrast, analyze and apply), discuss their meaning, and practice writing answers that use appropriate paragraph and essay organizational patterns.

Other necessary subskills are the ability to outline and summarize large bodies of information and to retain this information. Deficits in auditory and visual memory are two of the frequently reported residual processing deficits in LD adults. None of the LD students in the Learning Opportunities Program at Barat College and in Project Achieve at Southern Illinois University has completely memorized the multiplication tables (Cordoni, 1979). Most of the students in Barat's program missed early items on the Information subtest of the WAIS that would be assumed to be common knowledge, (e.g., How many weeks are there in a year?). While non-LD students seem spontaneously to devise memory strategies, the LD students do not (Torgesen, 1977). The LD specialist needs to introduce the student to a variety of memory improvement devices, such as mnemonics, acronyms, association, rhymes and limericks, and numerical relationships, and show the student how to apply them in test preparation using their course material. Because of the severity of the memory deficits, the LD student has to be not just well-prepared, but over-prepared for examinations.

Being over-prepared is necessary for another reason as well, namely, the extreme test anxiety experienced by many LD college students. Awareness of the test anxiety among many LD college students can lead to appropriate individual and group counseling in which effective coping strategies can be taught for dealing with test pressures, while simultaneously improving their test-taking strategies. Teaching the use of biofeedback, breathing exercises, and relaxation techniques, as well as the more traditional psychotherapeutic approaches, may be needed.

## Written Language Skills

The number of LD adults with written language disorders has been estimated to be between 80 and 90 percent by Blalock (1981) and even higher by Cordoni (1980) who describes significant written language deficits among all of the LD students in Project Achieve. The ability to express oneself in writing clearly and precisely is considered by some faculty to be synonymous with the Bachelor's degree. Others feel very strongly that it is essential to master the art of writing because the writing process is a catalyst for the thinking process itself, as Forster said, "How can I know what I think until I see what I say?" (Murray, 1968). Therefore, the area of greatest concern to faculty and LD adults themselves in postsecondary settings is written expression.

Several clinical observations have highlighted some of the written language deficits that seem to persist into adulthood. In the area of mechanics, punctuation is particularly problematic (Herbert & Czerniejewski, 1976). According to Blalock (1981), knowledge of the rules for punctuation and capitalization was severely limited for some LD adults, while others experienced problems only at the level of monitoring. Cordoni (1979) reported that the lowest subscore on the Peabody Individual Achievement Test (Dunn & Markwardt, 1970) was on the Spelling subtest. Critchley (1973) also observed that the exdyslexic is an inaccurate speller in spontaneous writing as well as on standardized spelling tests. LD adults themselves list spelling difficulties more frequently than any other deficit (Blalock, 1981).

In addition to deficits in mechanics and spelling, Blalock (1981), Critchley (1973), and Herbert and Czerniejewski (1976) noted that LD adults also have difficulty writing complete sentences and varying sentence structure. Critchley (1973) observed that exdyslexics wrote sentences of approximately the same length, and their writing was stylistically unsatisfying and monotonous. Problems between sentences as well as within sentences were also observed. Herbert and Czerniejewski (1976) described problems of coherence between sentences and attributed this problem to insufficient use of transitional words and phrases. Cohesion between paragraphs and the lack of an overall organization structure characterized their larger pieces of writing (Herbert & Czerniejewski, 1976).

Lastly, Critchley (1973) observed that exdyslexics used fewer multisyllabic words than their nondyslexic peers. Related to this aspect of word choice is his hypothesis that the ratio of adjectives to verbs will differ in the writing of the exdyslexic as compared to the nondyslexic. Herbert and Czerniejewski (1976) also found limitations in variety and agreement of adjectives and adverbs in the written language of the LD college students who comprised their sample.

A pilot study, done by Vogel and Moran (1982) provided preliminary empirical data regarding the above observations. In this study, both holistic and analytic scoring were applied to elicited writing samples. Holistic scoring is a method of rating a piece of writing impressionistically, quickly, and reliably. An essential ingredient of holistic scoring is that each essay is read and scored by at least two trained readers. In addition, selected analytic scoring procedures from an experimental version of the Diagnostic Evaluation of Expository Paragraphs (DEEP), developed by Moran (1981) were employed. This scoring procedure provides an in-depth analysis of writing skills by assessing mechanics, spelling, conventions, complexity and variety of sentence structure, complexity of t-units, and word selection. The major question addressed and the primary concern was: Do LD students differ significantly from their nondisabled peers in number and correctness of punctuation marks and capitalization, in correctness of spelling, sentence structure and usage, in syntactic complexity, and in word selection?

The eight LD subjects who participated in the pilot study were enrolled in the LD college program at Barat College. Most had been identified as LD prior to their entering this special program. Their Verbal or Performance IQ based on the Wechsler Adult Intelligence Scale fell within the average of above-average range. Their essays were compared holistically with essays written by 226 students.

Using holistic scoring, Vogel and Moran (1982) found that the LD students' essays were significantly poorer in overall quality than the essays written by entering students. When the essays were scored analytically, the LD students scored significantly lower than the randomly selected students on mechanics, spelling, subject/predicate/number agreement, total sentence points, percentage of complex sentences, and percentage of compound and compound/complex sentences. Although the LD group means were lower on word selection, total t-unit points, and the percent of complex t-units the differences were not significant.

The results confirmed Critchley's (1973) observation that LD adults used significantly fewer punctuation marks and those they used were more frequently incorrect. Also confirmed was the observation that spelling ability remains a serious deficiency in LD adults, even in spontaneous writing in which they are free to avoid words they cannot spell.

Significantly greater syntactic complexity was used by the contrast group in three out of the five subscores. However, an important finding of the study was that when sentence-boundary markers of capitalization and punctuation were not considered (by using t-unit analysis), the discrepancy between the two groups in syntactic complexity diminished considerably. Though the differences still favored the random sample, they were not significant. The authors also noted an increased use of infinitives and gerunds by the LD writers and, with cautious optimism, reported that these findings reflect hidden strengths as well as writing problems in the LD college students (Vogel and Moran 1982).

Gregg (1982) also explored the nature of the written language deficits of LD college writers as compared to average and basic writers. She analyzed an expository essay, a controlled stimulus passage, and responses to an experimental sentence combining test. She first analyzed the expository essays using the same holistic scoring procedures and t-unit analysis procedures employed by Vogel and Moran (1982) and confirmed their results. Second, Gregg analyzed the essays for accuracy of spelling and mechanics. Here, too, Gregg's findings confirmed Vogel and Moran's, in fact, the LD writers' performance was significantly below not only the average writers but the basic writers as well.

Gregg then categorized the various types of mechanical errors in each essay and examined the data for each of the three groups to determine the pattern of errors. Her findings revealed that LD writers made the highest percentage of comma errors and errors of omission of articles, demonstratives, and prepositions. They were also the only group to omit verb and other word endings. In the error analysis of the controlled stimulus passage, dropped endings and spelling errors also differentiated the LD group from the other two.

Because t-unit analysis can transcend the punctuation and capitalization constraints imposed by sentence scoring, Vogel and Moran (1982) suggested it may be a sensitive tool in future studies. There is no doubt a need for careful and complete assessment of writing ability, including t-unit analysis and accuracy, in order to determine each student's strengths as well as deficits. Based on this study we can assume that some, if not many, LD college students know how to write complete and complex t-units, but they do not know how to punctuate them. Intervention strategies for many LD adults may have to begin at the level of the simple t-unit. Sentence combining strategies utilize this approach and may prove to be a very effective method for remediation.

The LD adult also needs an individualized, structured approach to improved spelling, as well as an abundance of compensatory devices to serve as convenient references (Norback & Norback, 1974; Venolia, 1980; Webster, 1978; Wittels & Greisman, 1978). Review of the rules of punctuation and capitalization with ample opportunity for reinforcement and generalization to occur in spontaneous writing and proofreading should be planned by writing instructors and/or LD specialists.

Lastly, organization of longer pieces of writing will not just "happen." Formal instruction and practice in paragraph writing in a variety of modes and organizational models should be provided. Attention to the prewriting stage with emphasis on thinking, planning, discussing, and outlining is a prerequisite to improving organization and development of written language. Through an intensive, one-to-one, individually designed program of instruction based on in-depth assessment, it is hoped that the LD college student can accomplish this last hurdle in the hierarchy of language learning.

## Social/Interpersonal Skills

The need for assistance in improving social/interpersonal skills has been identified by learning disabled adults themselves (Brown, 1980a; 1980b; 1982; Johnson, 1981) and by those experts who have worked extensively with LD adults (Cordoni, 1979, 1980, 1981; Cox 1977). The difficulties they describe include making and keeping friends, knowing what to say and how to interact appropriately with a variety of individuals, (e.g., professors, supervisors, peers, coworkers), understanding social cues such as facial expressions and body language, and knowing how to join a group of people in conversation and enter into the discussion without interrupting the flow. Brown (1980a) feels that the LD adult's social behavior and/or appeaance is often unacceptable because of the nature of the learning disability itself. For example, the individual with fine motor and visual perceptual problems may experience difficulty with grooming and therefore look conspicuous. We have observed that these problems are particularly evident in some LD women who have difficulty following their lip line or eyebrow; they may also apply make-up too heavily. Or, on the other hand, the adults with auditory perceptual deficits may misperceive sounds in words resulting in incomplete comprehension and be thought of as "queer" or "dumb" by those who do not understand the nature of their learning disability.

Brown (1980b; 1982) and Cordoni (1982) make specific recommendations for improving social skills beginning with assisting the LD adults in understanding the nature of their learning disability. All of the LD adults who entered Barat's LD program and had been identified previously, had only a vague notion as to their academic strengths and weaknesses, potential for success in college, or performance levels in the areas of academic achievement. LD adults frequently have underestimated their potential because of the constant frustration and all-too-frequent failure experiences they encountered. This information can serve as a first step in improving self-image and self-esteem. Knowing performance levels in areas of academic achievement can also provide objectivity, a perspective for goal-setting, motivation for improvement, decision-making, and career choices. Lastly, this information provides a firm foundation for understanding their behavior.

After in-depth discussion of the diagnostic test results, Brown (1980b) recommends that the LD adult be given a report or tape-recording of this information for future reference and review. We have found that the students at Barat frequently refer back to a summary statement in outline form which we provide following oral discussion of test results.

Based on the students' understanding of their learning disability, those with a weakness in social/interpersonal skills need specific feedback about the way their behavior influences others (Brown, 1980b; Cordoni, 1982). The most helpful feedback specifies the students' behavior and feelings of the observer/listener. For example, the student who frequently interrupts could be told, "When you interrupt me before I finish what I want to say, I feel that you are not interested in me and what I am saying." Cordoni (1982) suggests the use of peer advocates who not only can accompany the student to various activities and familiarize the student with the campus and nearby town, but also can provide a role model of appropriate behavior and verbal responses.

Another forum for receiving feedback and for improving social skills, originally established and now widely advocated by LD adults themselves, is the self-help group (Johnson, 1981). At these informal meetings LD adults spontaneously share experiences, effective ways of dealing with difficult situations, organization difficulties, tension, or test anxiety. Such informal support groups are a regular feature of many well-established LD college programs. At one of the first fall meetings of such a group on Barat's campus, it was a pleasure to observe how confidently one of the upperclassmen reassured a freshman who was feeling defeated and guilty because she was having roommate problems, shared her own experiences, and recommended alternative plans of action.

In some instances, constant frustration and frequent failure result in associated disorders of personality requiring counseling or therapy (Cox, 1977; Geib, Buzzardi, & Genova, 1981; Miller et al, 1979). Some LD adults react by withdrawing socially; others, by becoming excessively dependent on their parents, friends, teachers, or counselors for emotional support (Cox, 1977). To be most effective, Cox recommends that the psychotherapist work closely with the LD specialist in an interdisciplinary team approach to assist the LD student in acquiring greater ego strength and building self-confident, necessary prerequisites to involvement in remediation.

## GENERAL PROGRAMMING CONSIDERATIONS

To maximize learning, educators would no doubt agree that individualized, one-to-one instruction is the ideal. Such instruction allows for the maximum opportunity for active learner involvement, matching the method of instruction to the student's modality strengths and cognitive style, adjusting the pacing to the student's rate of learning, etc., i.e., controlling all of the variables that effective LD specialists are trained to do. However, one-to-one instruction (like the Oxonian tutorial method) is the most costly to provide and reality dictates that universities, especially at the undergraduate level, must educate students in groups of various sizes. There are, however, a variety of alternative models that have been developed that attempt to adapt presently available course offerings to include some of the characteristics of individualized, diagnostic teaching and thus be better suited to meet the individual needs of LD students. In developing LD college programs, there are four basic questions that have to be addressed and for each, a myriad of alternative solutions. These four questions relate to the major question: How can LD specialists and college teaching faculty help LD college students to succeed in postsecondary institutions? More specifically,

1. Is the LD college program designed to help LD students improve in the area of basic skills, to compensate for deficits by using by-pass strategies, or both?
2. If the program is committed to improvement of basic skills deficiencies, how can that be accomplished?
3. What by-pass strategies are effective in working with LD college students?
4. Are LD college programs achieving their objectives? How can LD college programs be evaluated?

The discussions that follow are based on the premise that most LD college students by the fact of their involvement in continuing their education, may find themselves in a situation where they are forced, whether from internal or external pressure, to improve their basic skills and to use compensatory strategies. We, therefore, will address both of these aspects of college programming.

### Developmental versus Special Remedial Courses

Higher education in the 70s began to be aware of the large number of non-LD freshmen who were deficient in written language skills. At the University of California—Berkeley, the campus with the most stringent entrance requirements, more than 50 percent of first-year students were required to take remedial English. Berkeley was not alone. In response to the "national writing crisis," many colleges and universities developed remedial courses for these underprepared students. Attention was not only directed to English deficits, but to reading and math skills as well. Thus, in the late 70s a number of developmental courses in writing, reading, and math, accompanied by appropriate labs and centers, became staple offerings, even at prestigious universities. Many LD adults have enrolled in these courses with varying degrees of success. There are several questions that program developers and LD adults themselves must address. Are developmental courses appropriate for LD college students? Can LD students accomplish the course objectives? Do they, in fact, make significant progress in the specific area of basic skills being addressed? In order to answer these questions, many more must be raised and answered. The following questions are thought to address significant factors that contribute to the LD student's success or failure in postsecondary settings.

Research in education has shown that one of the most critical factors, if not the most critical factor, in a student's learning is the individual teacher. In the case of the battle-scarred and insecure LD adult, this is even a more critical factor. Therefore, the first set of questions focuses on the specific instructor.

1. Is the teacher sympathetic to LD adults and their problems?
2. Is the teacher patient with and tolerant of individuals with unique learning styles?
3. Is the instructor easy to talk with?
4. Does the instructor have formal training in learning disabilities or have an interest in acquiring some expertise?
5. Is the teacher flexible and willing to try out new ideas?

This last question leads to the second area of concern, namely, the course itself and method of instruction.

1. Are the course objectives appropriate to the LD student's skill levels, needs, and goals?
2. Can the course objectives be accomplished by the LD adult within the time frame of the course? If not, is the instructor willing to give extensions?
3. What is the institution's policy regarding incomplete grades?
4. What is the rate of presentation of material?
5. How much opportunity is provided for questions, discussion, reinforcement, and review?
6. What is the method of input—mainly lecture, overheads and transparencies, slides and films, or demonstration followed by actual hands-on experiences?
7. Is the method of input appropriate to the learning style of the specific LD student?
8. If not, can the student develop compensatory strategies in order to benefit from the course?
9. What is the class size?
10. Is the instructor available for occasional assistance if a student is having trouble?
11. Is the faculty or teaching assistant available for one-to-one help on a regular basis?
12. Is there an instructor available in a supplementary lab or center for assistance, should the need arise?
13. Is the teacher "wedded" to a program, prepackaged system of instruction, or his or her own publications?
14. Are the materials used appropriate in content, level of difficulty, visual and organizational lay-out, and reading ability?

Since most students that are in college settings have "bought into the system," they are anxious to know how well they are doing and how to improve. This last set of questions relates to the teacher's method of evaluation.

1. Are the exams timed or untimed?
2. Will the instructor allow a student to tape-record an essay exam (perhaps later to be transcribed), or to type an exam rather than use long-hand?

3. How frequently does the instructor evaluate the students? Is the final grade based on one examination, the mid-term and final, or a series of quizzes, assignments, class participation, and perhaps an oral presentation?
4. Are the quizzes and examinations essay or objective tests?
5. If essay, are there questions embedded within questions?
6. What is the level of cognitive complexity demanded by the examinations, e.g., recall, integration, application, problem-solving?
9. Is the course competency-based, i.e., students are given an opportunity to work at their own pace in order to accomplish the course objectives usually at a specified level of mastery, e.g., 80 percent mastery. In such courses, the objectives, method of instruction, and evaluation are uniform for all students, but the rate of meeting the objectives can vary.
10. Are parallel forms of quizzes available for students who want to retake an exam at a later time?
11. Are alternative methods of evaluation acceptable, e.g., an objective instead of an essay exam, or vice versa, or a research paper instead of a final examination?

## Credit versus Non-credit Remedial/Developmental Courses

Another one of the decisions that has to be made is whether to grant college credit for remedial courses, and if so, how much credit should be granted? Depending on the severity of the LD student's deficiencies and the variety of developmental courses offered, should there be an upper limit on the number of 100-level courses of student is allowed to take? Some faculty argue that developmental courses are not college-level work and prefer that no credit be given for these courses. At Harvard University, for example, non-credit reading courses are offered through the Bureau of Studies Counsel.

However, there are some serious problems with non-credit courses. First, human nature being what it is, student motivation for such courses may be very low, and even when students do enroll, irregular attendance, lack of involvement, and expenditure of effort often result in minimal gains. In order to increase motivation, some institutions make the non-credit course a prerequisite for a higher level course. A third solution is to provide a form of quasi credit that counts toward a certificate of completion or competence, but not toward the degree.

Second, the institution that offers non-credit, developmental courses has to fund these courses without generating any income. Indirectly, one might argue that these courses are actually cost effective because they prepare students to succeed in future courses, but that income still does not begin to pay the salary of the remedial English, math, and reading instructor because typically these courses are expensive due to the faculty-student ratio. To generate income, some institutions charge extra fees for the developmental courses. However, in order to encourage the student who needs this course, fees have been nominal and only partially cover expenses.

Third, students are awarded financial aid on the basis of the credits they carry. Whether or not they get credit for the developmental course, they are attending classes and preparing for it, which means that they can neither get financial aid, nor can they be employed during that time to make up for the loss of aid, making the course a double hardship.

All of these alternatives, including giving full credit, must be considered along with their pros and cons within the context of the specific institution, its entrance requirements, student body characteristics, institutional mission, curriculum, and the institution's fiscal stability.

### Remediation and Course Support/Tutoring

Remediation at the college level refers to one-to-one or small group instruction provided by an LD specialist in language, processing, and basic skills deficits, especially in the areas of reading (word attack, comprehension, and rate), written language (mechanics, spelling, sentence structure, organization, and penmanship) and mathematics (computation and problem solving). Course support or tutoring is one-to-one or small group instruction provided by a subject matter specialist who may or may not be trained also in learning disabilities, who ideally would be supervised by the LD specialist. The tutor may be an undergraduate or graduate student (peer tutor), retired teacher, or paraprofessional, salaried or unsalaried. We assume that most LD college programs will provide both types of service. Each has its strengths and drawbacks.

First, remediation is an expensive service to provide. The full-time college LD specialist who provides one-to-one remediation can provide support two hours per week for between 12 to 14 LD students. Not all programs, nor all students (when extra fees are charged), can afford this service. In order to economize, some college programs utilize graduate students in the LD teacher training program instead of certified LD teachers and/or meet with the LD students in small groups of three or four, thus being able to increase the case load from 12 to perhaps 16 students per LD teacher.

It must also be kept in mind that the need for remediation will vary from one LD student to another depending on the severity of the deficits, the level of proficiency needed in the student's anticipated career (e.g., teaching versus photography), and the individual's personal goals.

Motivational level will also vary by individual and within the same individual depending on the student's age, life experiences, employment experiences, and the stage he/she is at in the process of coming to terms with the fact of being learning disabled and what to do about it.

It has been our experience, that when the student's motivational level is high, energy level is consistent and high, and the LD specialist provides intensive one-to-one remediation for a minimum of 2 hours per week, gains can be dramatic (e.g., 5 years growth in reading ability in 1 year). For these students, the need for both kinds of support diminishes and self-concept improves, sometimes dramatically reflected in penmanship even though no direct instruction had been provided. As basic skills improve and the need for course support diminishes, the student's self-confidence increases with commensurate decreases in level of dependency and increases in degree of acceptance of responsibility for his/her own learning.

On the other side, all students are highly motivated when the support service has a direct, one-to-one correspondence with coursework. Depending on the tutor's familiarity with the course, i.e., reading material, teaching techniques, and method of evaluation, the results are usually positive. The use of tutors is also cost effective since they are paid much less than LD specialists. However, in our experience, the need for tutoring, when used exclusively, does not diminish. On the contrary, it usually grows as the courses get more demanding, and as a result, as the student's needs continue, their feelings of inadequacy and dependency are reinforced and increase. Initially, there is also the expense involved in developing tutor training materials and the on-going expense of training and supervising the corps of tutors. One other drawback in using peer tutors and graduate students is the added problem of availabilty. When the LD students need their help the most (before exams), they are the least accessible since they too are often preparing for finals. Nonetheless, tutors are a necessary and invaluable addition to the LD college program staff because LD specialists can not be knowledgeable in every subject area at the college level or be familiar with all of the assigned readings for every course.

## Compensatory Strategies

The use of compensatory strategies refers to devising and using coping strategies which allow the learning disabled to bypass the area of disability. Many compensatory strategies have been described by learning disabled adults themselves who have addressed problems in the areas of independent living, social skills, employment, organizational skills, time management, specific processing deficits (auditory and visual perception and memory deficits), as well as specific areas of academic achievement (Brown, 1980; Terry, Grigar, & Ridenour, 1982). For example, reading material is typically made available on tape with supplementary input of information from visuals such as films, slide-tape presentations, and field experiences. Because taped materials are so commonly used as a bypass strategy in college settings, we will focus on ways to improve the effectiveness of taped materials and some of the pro's and con's regarding their use.

Many LD adults discovered that although they thought they would be able to "read" unhampered by hearing the text, they had trouble knowing what to listen for, understanding the critical points, taking reading notes, and retaining what they had "read." Mosby (1981) made several concrete suggestions as to ways that learning can be enhanced when using materials that have been taped. He recommended that listening periods be alternated with activities related to the text, for instance, keeping a list of key phrases, paraphrasing the critical points, and writing summary paragraphs as dictated by the teacher for use in later reviews.

In most instances, dyslexic college students order their textbooks on tape from Recordings for the Blind. However, when prerecorded textbooks are unavailable, or reprints and other handouts have to be made in-house, the LD specialist has the opportunity to implement some, if not all, of the six recommendations made by Deshler and Graham (1979) to improve the effectiveness of taped material. In contrast to verbatim tapes, they suggest that the teacher first decide what should be taped. They warn against taping entire chapters and books because of the length of time it takes to tape and the time involved in listening, which may extend beyond the time a student has available. The student may also have difficulty maintaining attention to lengthy recordings. Deshler and Graham (1980) recommended that the LD specialist identify, with assistance from the subject matter expert if needed, the critical content as it relates to the course objectives. These shorter sections can then be recorded and listened to more than once, which also aids the student in mastering the material.

The second recommendation relates to the use of taped materials to teach study skills. For example, before beginning a new chapter, the reader could teach preview techniques, e.g., instructing the student to follow along as the reader previews the chapter subheadings, reads the introductory paragraph, summaries, and study questions at the end of the chapter. In the reading itself, the LD teacher can help the student by pointing out the main ideas and supportive data. When describing a graph or chart, the reader can teach the listener to interpret the information presented. One of our students with good reading ability and severe math deficits was working with the LD specialist on basic math in preparation for enrolling in a statistics course. We later discovered that not only did she have to review basic arithmetic to succeed in statistics, but she also had to learn how to "read" tables, graphs, and charts. By listening to tape-recordings of the explanations, this student was better able to "crack the code" and interpret the highly condensed information summarized in tables and graphs. When preparing tapes, Deshler and Graham (1980) recommend highlighting important points, interspersing paraphrased paragraphs with verbatim reading, explanations of abstract terms, and repetition of key concepts.

Because the written material is not taped from beginning to end, the reader will need to include careful verbal instructions as well as visual markings in the text in order for the listener to follow the tape. A visual marking system recommended by the authors makes use of a wavy line ( ≀ ) in the left-hand margin for material that is paraphrased, a dotted line ( ⋮ ) for material deleted, and a solid line ( | ) for material read verbatim.

There is no doubt that taped texts can be an effective tool in helping some, though not all, LD college students to acquire and retain new bodies of knowledge, as well as more effective study habits. Whether or not using taped materials has aided a specific student must be evaulated periodically. Only those students who have benefitted from using taped materials should be encouraged to use them. Just as no one teaching method works for all LD students, no one compenstory strategy should be prescribed for all students. It is important to keep in mind, however, the necessity of teaching the effective use of taped materials and ways of enhancing comprehension and retention of books on tape when recording written materials.

## Section 504 Requirements Regarding Reasonable Accommodation

There is very limited information regarding the implementation of Section 504 of the Rehabilitation Act of 1973 for the learning disabled college student. However, Section 504 has implications not only for recruitment and admission of qualified handicapped students to post-secondary institutions that receive Federal financial assistance (see above), but for programs and activity accessibility. Furthermore, modifications of academic requirements and auxiliary aids must be provided by universities according to Section 504 (Dolan & Dolan, 1978; Sedita, 1980). It should be kept in mind that the rationale behind Section 504 requirements is to ensure that colleges and universities do not discriminate against qualified handicapped persons.

## Reasonable Modifications of Academic Requirements

Operationalizing this concept is in the infancy stage. There has been no official Federal interpretation of the word "reasonable" or what constitutes the modifications of academic requirements that must be made. However, Dolan Dolan (1978) have done so for the state of New Jersey, and MacGugan (1978), for Leeward Community College in the state of Hawaii. They suggest that reasonable modifications of academic requirements might include:

1. Extending time allowed to complete a program.
2. Adapting the method of instruction.
3. Substituting one course for another required course.
4. Modifying or waiving foreign language requirement.
5. Allowing for part-time rather than full-time study.
6. Providing modifications in examination procedures so as to measure achievement without contamination from the areas of deficit.

Kahn (1980) and Vogel and Sattler (1981) described a variety of other modifications that both teachers and students can make that are appropriate to classrooms in higher education settings. In addition, Vogel and Sattler (1981) suggested the following 12 methods of modifying evaluation procedures for the learning disabled:

1. Allowing for untimed tests.
2. Allowing a reader for students in objective exams.
3. Providing essay instead of objective exam, or vice versa.
4. Allowing students to take exam in a separate room with a proctor.
5. Allowing for oral, taped, or typed instead of written exam.
6. Allowing students to clarify questions and rephrase them in their own words as a comprehension check before answering exam questions.
7. Analyzing process as well as final solution (as in math problems).
8. Allowing alternative methods of demonstrating mastery of course objectives.
9. Allowing students to use a multiplication table, simple calculator, and/or secretary's desk reference in examinations.
10. Avoiding double negatives, unduly complex sentece structure, and embedding questions within a question when composing examination questions.
11. Providing adequate scratch paper and lined paper to aid those students with overly-large handwriting and/or poor handwriting.
12. Providing alternative to computer-scored answer sheets.

### Auxiliary Aids

Just as visually impaired college students make use of taped materials and readers, some learning disabled students with severe reading disabilities rely heavily on books or tape. These same students often have auditory processing and written language deficits. In such cases, the student is encouraged to tape-record lectures once permission has been obtained from the instructor. Taping lectures and using taped materials are considered the first step in the sequence of instruction, rather than a satisfactory solution (see above). The importance of Section 504 is that it insures the student the right to take the first step in using auxiliary aids, to request that reasonable modifications of academic requirements be made, and hopefully to enforce that they be made.

## PROGRAM EVALUATION

It is the responsibility of the service provider to incorporate formative and summative evaluation as an integral aspect of program development. Formative evaluation refers to a process that begins in the program planning phase, is on-going and periodic, and provides information that affects the future direction of the program. In contrast, summative evaluation is a one-time occurrence and

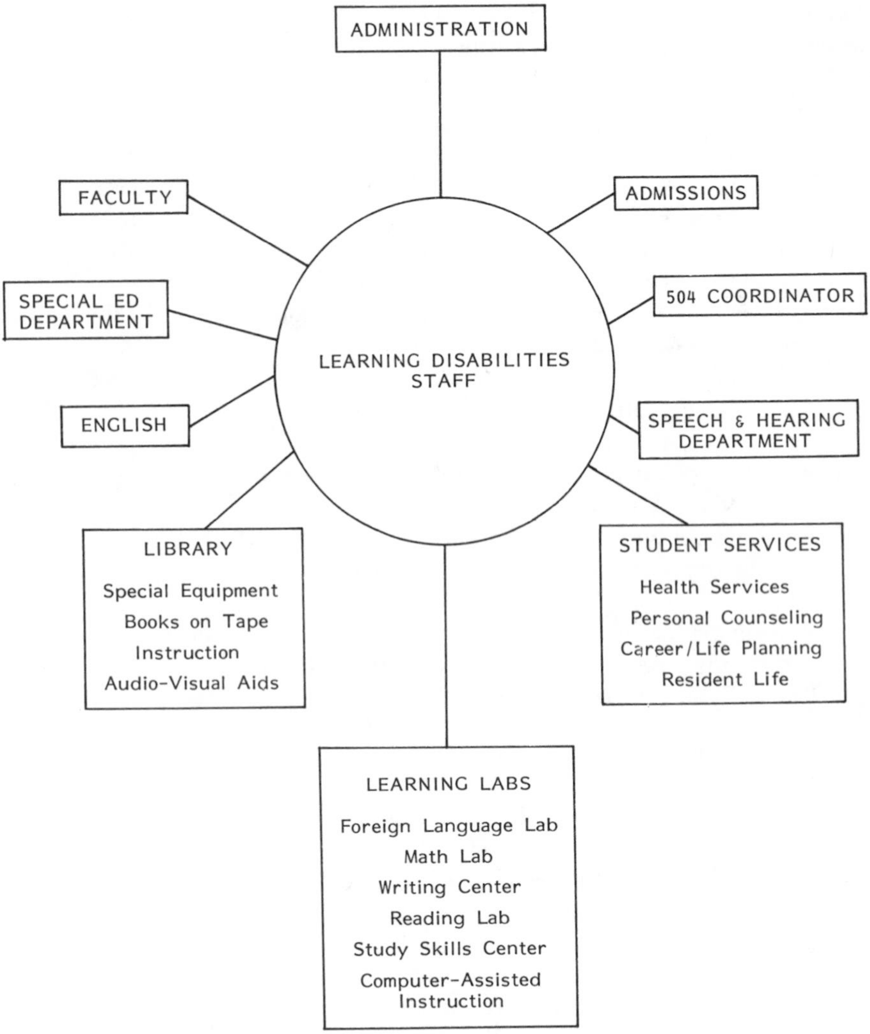


**Figure 14-1.** Learning Opportunities Program Components.

takes place at the end of a prescribed period. The purpose of summative evaluation is to determine if and how well the goals and objectives have been met at the termination of a project or program, or end of one phase of a program.

Each college LD program's evaluation study and instruments will differ because they will address the goals and objectives of that specific program. However, the major question of all program evaluations will be the same: How well is the program accomplishing its goals and objectives? Program evaluation should be designed to address not only the specific program's objectives, but all service providers and program components (see Fig. 14-1).

There are at least three major types of information that can help answer this basic question (1) statistical data, (2) hard data, and (3) soft data.

Statistical data refer to the types of information that can be quantified, such as, a tally of the numbers of contact hours of each student with an LD specialist, counselor, or tutor; semester and cumulative grade point averages, number of or percent of withdrawals, incompletes, honor grades, and failing grades, number of scholastic awards, number of scholastic warnings; number of graduates, transfers, withdrawals; and employment patterns of graduates.

The hard data are results that can be analyzed statistically, e.g., pre- and post-testing results from formal and informal measures that can be used as an indication of improvement and/or retention. The importance of hard data cannot be underestimated in terms of program evaluation because they provide direct evidence regarding basic skills deficiencies.

However, the least quantifiable, but most valuable information in program development is that provided in the form of soft data, i.e., questionnaires and rating scales. There are at least five knowledgeable and appropriate groups of evaluators that can provide this type of input; the program participants, program staff (including tutors), faculty, student development staff, and administrators. Each of these groups, either consciously or unconsciously, rank-orders the program's goals and objectives differently, or has its own set of goals, and, therefore, evaluates the program from a slightly different perspective. For the students, success in their college courses is the central goal and they may, therefore, see less of a need to improve in understanding their learning disability, in social skills, or in oral communication, while for the LD specialist, these latter three goals are viewed as more central to lifelong success.

On the other hand, administrators' perspectives are college-wide and they will be able to assess the responsiveness of the college environment to the LD program, faculty receptivity, and general student body sensitivity. Administrators also are responsive to boards of trustees whose major responsibility is fiscal, and therefore, they focus on direct and indirect costs incurred. However, the most persuasive arguments that can be made for funding such programs are first and foremost, to be in compliance with Section 504, and secondly, to attract good students to the college who, when they receive the necessary help, are successful students. By tailoring the evaluation instruments to each of these groups of evaluators and their specific concerns and first-hand experiences, valuable information can be elicited and then used to strengthen the program.

## COMMUNICATION AND COORDINATION

There are many well-endowed and well-equipped universities that have facilities that have been adapted to serve the learning disabled. It is hoped that many more postsecondary institutions will do so in the future. What is required in addition to selectively adapting and supplementing presently offered services in order to enhance the LD college students chances of success is the

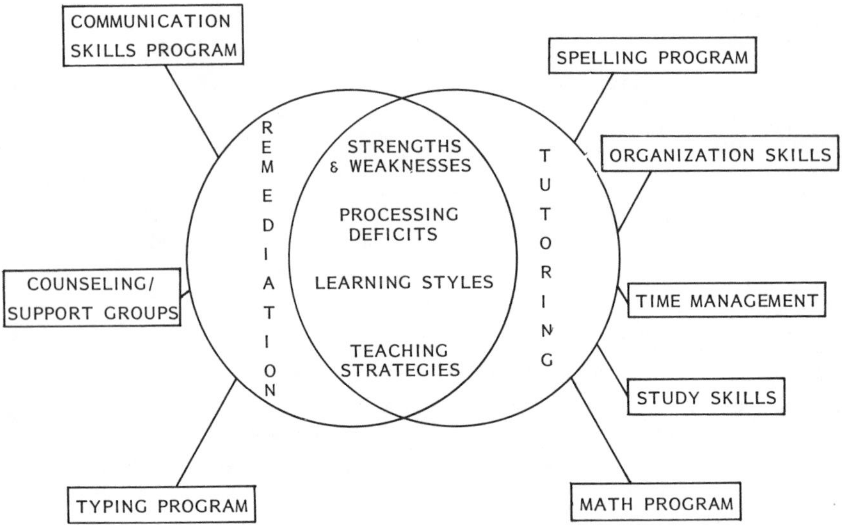


**Figure 14-2.** Communication Network.

coordination of effort among all of the departments and services beginning with the initial application to the institution (see Fig. 14-2). The larger the institution, the greater the need for the establishment of effective procedures for communication and coordination of effort. When the LD program staff are also teaching faculty in departments like special education, English, and math and also service providers in the student services area (e.g., counselors), channels of communication are more easily or better established. Another model well-established on Barat's campus is the Internal Advisory Board (see above) and soon to be established is the selection and training of departmental liaisons who will help the LOP advisors in program planning. Through the communication and coordination of effort, a pro-active approach to problems can be initiated and hopefully problems minimized, so that the LD student on college campuses can succeed in acquiring the higher education that will enable them to be productive, self-fulfilled, and contributing members of society.

## REFERENCES

Birely, M., & Manley, E. The learning disabled student in a college environment: A report of Wright State University's program. *Journal of Learning Disabilities*, 1980, *13*, 12–15.

Blalock, J. Persistent problems and concerns of young adults with learning disabilities. In W. Cruickshank & A. Silvers (Eds.), *Bridges to tomorrow, Vol. 2: The best of ACLD.* Syracuse: Syracuse University Press, 1981.

Blalock, J. Persistent auditory language deficits in adults with learning disabilities. *Journal of Learning Disabilities*, 1982, *15*, 604–609.

Boyan, C., & Kaplan, P. Preparing teachers to work with exceptional adults. *Exceptional Children*, 1980, *46*(7), 557–559.

Brown, D. *Steps to independence for people with learning disabilities*. Washington, DC: Closer Look, Parents' Campaign for Handicapped Children and Youth, 1980a.

Brown, D. Counselling and accommodating the student with learning disabilities. In *Proceedings of the third national conference on the handicapped student on college campuses—advocacy, responsibility, and education*. Denver, May 18–21, 1980b.

Brown, D. Rehabilitating the learning disabled adult. *American Rehabilitation*, 1982, *7*, 3–11.

Chesler, B. *A talking mouth speaks about learning disabled college students*. P. O. Box 22206, Sacramento, CA 95822, 1980.

Cordoni, B. A directory of college LD services. *Journal of Learning Disabilities*, 1982, *15*, 529–534.

Cordoni, B. Assisting dyslexic college students: An experimental program designed at a university. *Bulletin of the Orton Society*, 1979, *29*, 263–268.

Cordoni, B. Learning disabilities: An audio journal for continuing education. In Gottlieb, Marvin, & Bradford (Eds.), *College options for the learning disabled*. New York: Grune & Stratton, 1980.

Cordoni, B. Services for college dyslexics. In R. Malatesha & P. Aaron (Eds.), *Neuropsychological and neurolinguistic aspects of reading disorders* (Vol. 1). New York: Academic Press, 1981.

Cordoni, B., O'Donnell, J., Ramaniah, N., Kurtz, J., & Rosenshein, K. Wechsler Adult Intelligence score patterns for learning disabled young adults. *Journal of Learning Disabilities*, 1981, *14* (7), 404–407.

Cox, S. The learning-disabled adult. *Academic Therapy*, 1977, *13* (1), 70–86.

Critchley, M. Some problems of the ex-dyslexic. *Bulletin of the Orton Society*, 1973, *23*, 7–14.

Deshler, D., & Graham, S. Tape recording educational materials for secondary handicapped students. *Teaching Exceptional Children*, 1980, *winter*, 52–54.

Dolan, F., & Dolan, E. *The implications of Section 504 of the Rehabilitation Act of 1973 on health, education, and social service providers in New Jersey*. Governor's Committee on Employment of the handicapped, Trenton, NJ: 1978. (ERIC Document Reproductions Service No. ED 165-360).

Dunn, L., & Markwardt, F. *Peabody individual achievement test*. Circle Pines, MN: American Guidance Service, 1970.

Elliot, R. *Directory of personnel and materials dealing with handicapped students at the post-secondary level*. Terre Haute: Cooperative Education Association and Handicapped Affairs Committee, April, 1981.

Garnett, K. and S. Laporta. *College Students with Learning Disabilities*. New York: Hunter College, 1984.

Geib, G., Buzzardi, L, & Genova, P. Intervention for adults with learning disabilities. *Academic Therapy*, 1981, *16*, 317–325.

Gregg, N. *An investigation of the breakdown in certain aspects of the writing process with college age learning disabled, normal and basic writers*. Unpublished doctoral dissertation, Northwestern University, 1982.

Guildroy, J. The learning-disabled college applicant. *The College Board Review*, 1981, *120*, 17–30.

Hammill, D., Leigh, J., McNutt, G., & Larsen, S. A new definition of learning disabilities. *Learning Disabilities Quarterly*, 1981, *4*, 336–342.

Herbert, M. & Czerniejewski, C. Language and learning therapy in a community college. *Bulletin of the Orton Society*, 1976, *26*, 96–106.

Johnson, C. LD adults: The inside story. *Academic Therapy*, 1981, *16*, 435–442.

Johnson, D. Persistent auditory disorders in young dyslexic adults. *Bulletin of the Orton Society*, 1980, *30*, 268–276.

Kahn, M. Learning problems of the secondary and junior college learning disabled student: Suggested remedies. *Journal of Learning Disabilities*, 1980, *13* (8), 445–449.

MacGugan, K. *An analysis of the implications of Section 504 of the 1973 Rehabilitation Act related to Leeward Community College*. Hawaii: Nora University, 1978. (ERIC Document Reproduction Service No. 164-032).

Mangrum, C. and S. Strichart. *College and the learning disabled student*. New York: Grune & Stratton, 1984.

Mangrum, C. and S. Strichart (Eds.). *Guide to colleges with programs for learning disabled students*. Princeton, N.J. Peterson's Guides, Inc., 1985.

Miller, C., McKinley, D., & Ryan, M. College students: Learning disabilities and services. *The Personnel and Guidance Journal*, 1979, *58*, 154–158.

Moran, M. *A comparison of formal features of written language of learning disabled, low-achieving and achieving secondary students*. Research Report No. 34. Lawrence, KS: The Kansas Institute for Research in Learning Disabilities, 1981.

Mosby, R. Secondary and college LD bypass strategies. *Academic Therapy*, 1981, *16*, 597–610.

Murray, D. *A writer teaches writing: A practical method of teaching composition*. Boston: Houghton Mifflin, 1968.

*Nondiscrimination on basis of handicap*. Washington, DC: U.S. Department of Health, Education, and Welfare, p. 22683, 1977.

Norback, P., & Norback, C. *The misspeller's dictionary*. New York: New York Times Books, 1974.

Rawson, M. Dyslexics as adults: The possibilities and the challenge. *Bulletin of the Orton Society*, 1977, *27*, 193–197.

Ridenour, D., & Johnston, J. *A guide to post-secondary educational opportunities for the learning disabled*. Oak Park, IL: Time Out to Enjoy, 1981.

Rudel, R. Residual effects of childhood reading disabilities. *Bulletin of the Orton Society*, 1981, *31*, 89–102.

Sedita, J. *Section 504: Help for the learning disabled college student*. Prides Crossing, MA: Landmark School, 1980.

Skyer, R. and G. Skyer. *What do you do after high school?* Rockaway Park, New York: Skyer Consultation, Inc., 1982.

Terry, C., Grigar, M., & Ridenour, D. *Daily living skills for LD adolescents: ADCLD fastback series*. Chicago: 1982.

Torgesen, J. Memorization processes in reading disabled children. *Journal of Educational Psychology*, 1977, *69*, 571–578.

Torrance, E. Growing up creatively gifted with learning disabilities. In W. Cruickshank, & J. Lerner (Eds.), *Coming of age, Vol. 3: The best of ACLD 1982*. Syracuse: Syracuse University Press, 1982.

Ugland, R. & Duane, G. *Serving students with specific learning disabilities in higher education—A demonstration project at three Minnesota community colleges*, A Project Evaluation Report, November 1976.

Venolia, J. *Write right! A desk drawer digest of punctuation, grammar, and style*. Woodland Hills, CA: Periwinkle Press, 1980.

Vogel, S. On developing LD college programs. *Journal of Learning Disabilities*, 1982, *15*, 518–528.

Vogel, S. *Syntactic abilities in normal and dyslexic children*. Baltimore: University Park Press, 1975.

Vogel, S. A. Syntactic complexity in written expressions of LD college writers. *Annals of Dyslexia*, 35, 137–157, 1985c.

Vogel, S.A. The college student with a learning disability: A handbook for college LD Students, admissions officers, faculty, and administrators. *ACLD*, 4156 Library Road, Pittsburgh, PA , 1985a.

Vogel, S. A. Learning disabled college students: Identification assessment, and outcomes. In *Understanding learning disabilities: International and multidisciplinary views*. Duane, D. and C. K. Leong (Eds.), New York: Plenum Press, 1985b.

Vogel, S., & Adleman, P. Personnel development: College and university programs designed for learning disabled adults. *ICEC Quarterly*, 1981, *1*, 12–18.

Vogel, S., & Moran, M. Written language disorders in learning disabled college students: A preliminary report. In W. Cruickshank, & J. Lerner (Eds.), *Coming of Age, Vol. 3: The best of ACLD 1982*. Syracuse: Syracuse University Press, 1982.

Vogel, S., & Sattler, J. *The college student with a learning disability: A handbook for college and university admissions officers, faculty, and administration*. Illinois Council for Learning Disabilities. 1981.

Webb, G. Personal communication, October, 1980.

*Webster's spelling dictionary*. New York: Galahad Books, 1978.

Weiner, E. Transition to college for LD students. *Academic Therapy*, 1974, *11* (2), 199–213.

Wittels, H., & Greisman, J. *The perfect speller*. New York: Grosset & Dunlap, 1978.

Wren, C. and L. Segal. *College students with learning disabilities*. De Paul University, Chicago, IL: 1985.

# 15

## Summary of Problems and Needs

Doris J. Johnson
Jane W. Blalock

The descriptions of problems observed among the adults in these clinical studies indicate both the heterogeneity and homogeneity of the group. All had basic integrities for learning including sensory acuity, mental ability, and motivation. Nearly all had been aware of their learning difficulties from early childhood, some even before entering school. All were troubled by their problems, the unevenness of their abilities and performance, and were attempting to gain more insight into their difficulties. However, their specific problems and objectives for the diagnostic study varied. Some only wanted a better understanding of their strengths and weaknesses whereas others were seeking recommendations for occupations, education, and long term plans.

The analyses of their test data indicated that a problem rarely, if ever, occurred in isolation. That is, none had isolated difficulties in reading, spelling, written language, or mathematics. Rather, certain problems tended to co-occur in patterns similar to those we observed among learning disabled children (Johnson & Myklebust, 1967). Although more research is needed to further clarify and validate these patterns, the following were observed clinically. Analyses of histories, test performance, and observations were used in designating these groups.

### PATTERNS OF PROBLEMS

#### Generalized Meaning Problems

One small group of adults had general problems with the acquisition of meaning and concepts. They generally scored within the average range of ability on tasks requiring perception, perceptual-motor functions, and short term memory, but below average on tasks of conceptualization, reasoning,

ADULTS WITH LEARNING DISABILITIES
ISBN 0-8089-1795-1

comprehension, and transfer of knowledge. They could memorize facts, decode words, and spell, but their language and information was context specific. At times they had rather superficially high social skills, and, as a result, were accepted for schools or jobs that were too difficult. They failed to detect problems or use previously acquired knowledge for solving new problems. Some overestimated their abilities. Because of difficulties with problem detection, they did not fully understand the complexity of tasks nor the decision-making and planning that was required to complete them. Their problems interfered with both verbal and nonverbal learning. One of the men in this group wrote the following:

> The problem is if I have been told something by a written or oral media I understand what I'm told but an hour, day or week later, I remember some of the concepts but forget others; Also, there is a problem with integrating a portion of a concept into the larger concept which prevents me from understanding the whole concept: and, if I'm under a pressure situation my thinking and writing is not the sharpest. I think best after doing it over and over again.

Not everyone had this much insight into their own problems. Consequently, many did not understand why they failed in school, lost a job, or had trouble keeping friends. In general, they performed best when they had an opportunity to use their perceptual-motor skills and when problems were clearly defined for them. They were quite successful in jobs that had set routines and a reasonable amount of supervision.

### General Language Comprehension Disorders

In contrast to the previous group, people with generalized language comprehension difficulties had good nonverbal skills. They could abstract concepts from observation, reason nonverbally, detect and solve many nonverbal problems. Their primary deficits were in oral language comprehension, which, in turn, interfered with verbal expression, reading comprehension, written expression, and mathematical reasoning. They had higher performance intelligence than verbal. Often they were sensitive and adept in processing nonverbal communication, but they had difficulty with idiomatic or figurative language used in social situations.

Their strengths tended to be in the arts, graphic design, and mechanics. Some were frustrated because they were unable to actualize their relatively high nonverbal ability. Some tried college but all reported difficulty. Typically they failed foreign language courses (if they were not waived).

The impact of their verbal deficits was evident in some nonverbal reasoning because higher level concepts usually require verbal labels or verbal mediation.

Most were good workers but wanted to advance or change positions. Many needed extra training to understand job requirements. Occasionally they had difficulty with supervisors or coworkers when they did not understand the tasks.

## Expressive Language, Reading, and Writing Disorders

The adults in this group came primarily for assistance in reading, but all had noticeable expressive language disorders. Comprehension was generally good but they had minor problems perceiving and pronouncing multisyllabic words. Many also had difficulty with word retrieval and syntax. Typically they scored low on digit span, sentence repetition, and sentence building. In reading they could use some whole word strategies and context but were deficient in decoding, linguistic awareness, and auditory analysis. Although they tried to use context when reading they often distorted the syntax. Some read better silently than orally. Their spelling errors reflected problems in morphosyntax and linguistic awareness. Written sentence building was particularly difficult. Mathematics was often good.

Most had finished high school and had tried college but were frustrated by their lack of reading skills. They were generally intellectually curious, and obtained information from listening and observation. While their chief concerns were related to reading, their language deficits were observable to the casual listener.

## Reading (Decoding) and Spelling Disorders

Another group had primary problems with visual verbal codes. In some respects, they were "classic dyslexics." If they could decode a word, they usually understood it. Many, however, had sequencing and auditory analysis problems. In addition, some had difficulty synchronizing the order of auditory, visual, and motor information. Thus, they missequenced telephone numbers, letters, and words. Their spelling errors tended to be nonphonetic because of transpositions and omissions of syllables or letters. Many could not say the alphabet or months of the year. Most also had difficulty rhyming and manipulating sounds in words. They usually understood quantitative concepts but often had difficulty with arithmetic.

Many found ways to compensate for their problems and held rather responsible jobs. Several had helpful supervisors and secretaries. In contrast, a few were working in positions far below their intellectual potential. Overall, their problems were related to the transmission of messages rather than to comprehension.

## Primary Spelling and Written Language Disorders

The people in this group had relatively good oral language but did not have the language flexibility to vary sentence structure, to summarize, outline, re-organize and write for various audiences. While many had residual reading disorders, they tended to have more difficulty with the *accessing* of visual forms, rules, and words. They reversed letters, or portions of letters, and used mixed manuscript and cursive codes. They spelled more phonetically than the preceding group, perhaps because their reading levels were higher and they had better auditory analysis skills. Many complained that they could not generate ideas for writing. Monitoring problems were noted in both writing and arithmetic.

In general, these people were among the most successful and well educated. Since their problems were related primarily to output, they could perform well on many jobs. Yet several experienced failure and disappointment when they were promoted, especially if the new position required writing.

### Nonverbal, Visual-Spatial, Quantitative Disorders

Most adults in this group requested help for handwriting and arithmetic; however, as stated in previous chapters, they also had difficulty with many everyday living skills. They selected occupations that required minimal mechanical skill, however, since many jobs require writing and computation, they requested help. They tended to be good *verbal* problem solvers, but had difficulty with tasks requiring visual analysis, synthesis, or manipulation. They often had a poor sense of direction and were poorly organized. They could not properly align buttons and button holes, pack boxes, organize themselves to prepare a meal, or fold papers appropriately to fit in various size envelopes. A few had reading disorders.

### Nonverbal Conceptual Disorders

A relatively small number of adults had major difficulty with nonverbal conceptualization and reasoning. Their problems were most obvious on tasks requiring the abstraction of meaning from observation. Usually they had low Picture Arrangement scores but performed well on verbal subtests. Mathematical reasoning and reading comprehension were lower than arithmetic and decoding.

Social skills were frequently deficient, in part because they had difficulty processing nonverbal cues. Their manners had a "trained" quality, as though they had been told what to say or do. Many were concerned about their lack of friends but did not know how to establish relationships. Eye contact and conversational skills were often poor. Yet, overall, they were sensitive, caring people.

### Disorders of Organization, Planning, and Attention

A final group had poor organization and problem solving skills. Frequently, they were among the brightest and tended to be good readers. However, they did not actualize their potential because of poor planning, an inability to prioritize activities and complete assignments. Many had poor self monitoring skills and were unable to detect their mistakes.

Several reported difficulties with attention and "overload." They seemed unable to process multiple stimuli for any length of time. As a result they had low frustration tolerance and occasionally burst into tears, anger, or rage. A few were similar to the adult aphasics who had periodic "catastrophic reactions" (Goldstein, 1948).

The woman who wrote the letter at the beginning of chapter 3 had many of these tendencies. While she made spelling and writing errors in spontaneous writing, she performed well on highly structured tasks that did not require multiple processes and subskills. The problems were also described by a 26-year-old man as follows:

> I have a college degree. I had learning problems while in school, and a lot of trouble concentrating. I tried very hard but still had trouble. But I couldn't concentrate on studying for more than about 15 minutes at a time. I was flunking out, grade-wise.
>
> In school if I took one science course at a time thinks were fine—but two science classes and I invariably failed several coures. I feel overloaded a lot, and get easily distracted from a task. I lose my train of thought. I guess I just need a lot of structure and consistency.
>
> I have trouble hearing what pepple say to me—sometimes I hear them talking but it sounds too fast—like a speeded-up record, or just muffled. I can't tell what they're saying and have to ask them to repeat it several times, until I can understand.
>
> A lot of things that are obvious to other people, as far as seeing a situation or solving a problem, are not obvious to me. If someone explains it to me I can often understand it, of if it is a situation I've had a lot of experience with.
>
> A lot of times I say things out of order. People sometimes don't understand what I'm saying and have to go back over it with me until I re-explain in detail. I've worked on this problem for 10 years but to no avail.
>
> I have been a _____, _____ [he listed several jobs], I have had a lot of trouble with all the jobs that have not been highly-structured. If it's undefined I fail. And as soon as I begin feeling overloaded by my environment and tasks, I fail.
>
> I have many problems on the job so my supervisor has to explain directions over and over. But I still make mistakes. They have often been disappointed and surprised about my performance because they say I am not performing nearly up to my potential.

From this letter and others it is evident that the people tried to modify their behavior but often felt guilty because they never improved even if they exerted maximum effort. Many had tried various forms of therapy including counseling, psychotherapy, biofeedback, and medication. The results varied. Some indicated that medication was helpful, and that counselling helped them feel less guilty, but they felt their primary needs were in the areas of immediate problem solving rather than a resolution of personal conflicts.

While these subgroups need further study for clarification and validation, these general descriptions are included to emphasize the need for studying co-occurring disorders among all learning disabilities. Mean standard scores for these eight groups are shown in Table 15-1.While interesting research has been done to highlight *reading* subgroups, other populations need investigation. The characteristics of adults with learning disabilities in various settings need to be

**Table 15-1**
Profile of Mean Standard Scores For Eight Subgroups*

| Test | I | II | III | IV | V | VI | VII | VIII |
|---|---|---|---|---|---|---|---|---|
| WAIS | | | | | | | | |
| FSIQ | 88 | 87 | 105 | 108 | 122 | 108 | 96 | 114 |
| VIQ | 96 | 83 | 105 | 108 | 120 | 118 | 109 | 117 |
| PIQ | 83 | 94 | 103 | 108 | 117 | 94 | 86 | 109 |
| PPVT | 94 | 87 | 109 | 111 | 119 | 117 | 118 | 123 |

* Groups: I Generalized Meaning; II General Language Comprehension; III Expressive language, reading and writing; IV Primary Reading (Decoding) and Spelling; V Spelling and Written Language; VI Nonverbal-Visual-Spatial Quantitative; VII Nonverbal Conceptual; VIII Organization, planning, and Attention.

studied in more depth. Those in mental health agencies, vocational programs, or correctional institutions may yield different patterns. Similarly, those seen by psychologists, neurologists, and remedial tutors may be different. We have been impressed with the high level of social responsibility exhibited by this particular population. Even though most had difficulty at work or in school, they had a relatively strong work ethic and tried to find employment that was in keeping with their abilities.

## PATTERNS OF ACHIEVEMENT

In order to investigate other patterns of performance we used standard scores from the WRAT and tabulated the number of people who had a discrepancy of at least five points between their reading, spelling, and arithmetic and rank ordered them. As expected, not all adults had discrepancies; however, the patterns shown in Table 15-2 emerged. The findings indicate that a relatively large percentage of the group performed better in reading than spelling, and better in spelling than arithmetic. There were, however, 25 adults

**Table 15-2**
Patterns of Achievement

| Pattern of Performance | # of Subjects |
|---|---|
| R > S > A | 18 |
| R > S = A | 16 |
| R = S > A | 6 |
| R = A > S | 6 |
| A > R > S | 13 |
| A > R = S | 9 |
| S > R = A | 9 |
| S = A > R | 3 |

who performed better in arithmetic than in reading. And, as indicated in the chapter on written language, a small percentage of the group scored higher on spelling than reading tests.

These patterns probably reflect several factors. First, with regard to reading and spelling, the scores suggest that reception typically precedes expression. However, the patterns also may reflect processing differences. That is, more auditorization is needed for oral reading, whereas more visualization is needed for spelling from dictation. Thus, adults with retrieval problems might do better in spelling than in reading because the auditory input is provided by the examiner.

The patterns also may reflect the amount and type of instruction provided in schools and remedial programs. It is hypothesized that more services were provided for reading than either spelling or arithmetic. In addition, perhaps adults can survive more easily in society with fewer computational skills than with minimal reading ability.

## PATTERNS OF PERFORMANCE BY SEX

The ratio of males to females in our clinical population was approximately 3:1 (70% male, 30% female). This is generally in keeping with the ratios reported by other investigators although some studies suggest even higher proportions of males.

Myklebust and Boshes (1969) found the ratios varied according to the severity of the learning disability. For example, their borderline group had a 2:1 male to female ratio, whereas the more severe group had a ratio of 4:1. Our clinical observations of adults indicated there were more men in the severe reading disabled group, but there were a few women reading below the fourth grade level. Similarly, some of the most severe visual-nonverbal cases were women, but there were males in the group as illustrated in the previous chapter.

An inspection of case records, chief concerns, and histories indicated no differences between males and females with regard to age, educational level, overall intelligence, or marital status. A higher percentage of females, however, reported a history of learning disabilities in the family (57% to 29%), but these figures should be interpreted cautiously. It may be that the females had asked more questions about familial difficulties.

An analysis of their chief concerns also revealed no differences. Reading and writing, for example, were of no greater concern to males than females. Similarly, mathematics was of no greater concern to females than to males.

A comparison of mean scores on the WAIS indicated minimal differences between males and females (See Table 15-3). It is interesting, however, that the women scored slightly higher on Performance Intelligence than the men. It is also interesting that the men performed slightly above the women on digit span. Often, it is assumed from previous studies that girls perform better than boys

**Table 15-3**
Comparison of Male's and Female's WAIS Scores

| | Male (N = 64) | | Female (N = 28) | |
|---|---|---|---|---|
| Verbal IQ | 106.4 | 12.4 | 105.1 | 15.3 |
| Performance IQ | 102.4 | 15.0 | 106.5 | 10.5 |
| Full Scale IQ | 104.9 | 12.5 | 106.0 | 12.8 |
| Information | 10.9 | 2.5 | 10.9 | 3.3 |
| Comprehension | 12.0 | 3.3 | 12.1 | 3.9 |
| Arithmetic | 9.7 | 3.0 | 9.6 | 3.5 |
| Similarities | 12.0 | 2.7 | 12.3 | 2.3 |
| Digit Span | 9.9 | 3.3 | 8.7 | 2.9 |
| Vocabulary | 11.3 | 2.6 | 11.3 | 3.4 |
| Digit Symbol | 9.3 | 2.6 | 11.1 | 3.1 |
| Picture Completion | 10.7 | 2.3 | 10.9 | 2.3 |
| Block Design | 10.6 | 3.3 | 10.7 | 2.5 |
| Picture Arrangement | 9.9 | 2.9 | 10.1 | 2.6 |
| Object Assembly | 10.6 | 4.0 | 11.4 | 2.9 |

on verbal tasks. Such was not the case in this population. The mean standard scores on the *Peabody Picture Vocabulary Test* (Dunn, 1965) were virtually identical. The mean Peabody IQ for the males was 107.4 (SD 14.9) and 107 (SD 18.0) for the females. A further examination of adults with discrepancies of 15 points or more between Verbal and Performance IQ revealed a disproportionate number of males in the Low Performance group (90%) and a disproportionate number of females in the Low Verbal group (50%).

The women in this population scored slightly above the males on the subtests of the WRAT. In general, these findings suggest the need for further study of achievement among males and females with learning disabilities across age levels and in various settings such as college, mental health institutions, vocational guidance programs, correctional institutions, and unemployment agencies.

## NEEDS FOR THE FUTURE

### Comprehensive Assessments and Integration of Findings

During discussions with the adults it became evident that professionals working with this population need to define terminology and explain the results simply. Nomenclature varies both within and between fields, and as a result, the adults are frequently confused. We are not necessarily advocating any particular terminology, but professionals should use language the adults comprehend. It may be helpful for agencies to prepare a glossary of terms (even on tape recorders if necessary) so the adults have an opportunity to review and assimilate the findings.

For example, "perception" may refer to relatively simple discrimination tasks or to broader functions including sequencing, analysis, or synthesis of sounds. If unfamiliar or ambiguous terms are used, clinicians should describe the kinds of tasks used and then discuss the possible significance of the problems for education, occupation, and social interactions.

Finally, efforts should be made to help the adult understand how various disabilities may be related. That is, the same disturbance of visual-spatial-motor integration may interfere with handwriting, some aspects of arithmetic, and many independent living skills. Or, the same language comprehension disorder may interfere with reading comprehension and some aspects of mathematics.

One overall objective is to help the adults gain a better understanding of themselves, and their patterns of strengths and weaknesses in relation to the world of work, education, and social life.

## VOCATIONAL NEEDS

Successful vocational adjustment is a problem for many adults with learning disabilities. A survey conducted by a committee of the Association for Citizens with Learning Disabilities (ACLD) indicated that approximately 50 percent of the adults who responded felt they needed vocational services (Chesler, 1982). Those surveyed were concerned about unemployment, their performance at work, and job dissatisfaction. White, Schumaker, Warner, Alley, and Deshler (1980) found that learning disabled adults, as a group, were less satisfied with their jobs than their nondisabled peers. Similarly, Fafard and Haubrich (1981) identified many who were employed but who hoped to obtain "good jobs" in the future.

Follow-up studies of learning disabled children also revealed the majority maintained jobs and supported themselves and their families, but a significant number had difficulty obtaining and/or maintaining positions (Cruickshank, Morse, & Johns, 1980; Lewis, 1977 Rogan & Hartman, 1976). In a review of longitudinal studies, Horn, O'Donnell, and Vitulano (1983) report that the actual *vocational attainment* levels of learning disabled adults is often commensurate with that of the general population. While these figures are encouraging, level of attainment may not reflect vocational struggles and adjustment problems. Stated differently, the presence of a learning disability does not necessarily preclude the achievement of certain vocational goals. Reports indicate learning disabled adults have succeeded in a variety of fields (Chesler, 1982; Johnson, 1980 Lewis, 1977; Rawson, 1968; Thompson, 1969), but attainment of these goals often required extraordinary effort, persistence, and resilience.

Success depends upon overall ability, a clear understanding of the problem, good support systems, including special adjustments made by the employer, use of effective strategies, and remediation.

Among the factors that impede performance are low reading levels, poor written language, feelings of inadequacy, fear of failure, attention disorders, and organizational difficulties (Alley & Deshler, 1979; Gordon, 1970; Lenkowsky & Saposnek, 1978; Mann & Greenspan, 1976; Siegal, 1974). There are also reports of high incidence of social learning problems that interfere with communication and occupations (Bryan, 1974, 1977; Kronick, 1981; Osman, 1982; Schumaker, Hazel, Sherman & Sheldon, 1982). In a study of normal and learning disabled adolescents Mathews, Whang, and Fawcett (1982) found the latter group had difficulty participating in an interview, providing and accepting constructive criticism, explaining a problem, and writing applications and follow-up letters.

Although, the adults from our clinical population were employed in a wide range of occupations (See Chapter 3), most reported job related problems. Several did not understand the general skills needed for various occupations, and failed to understand their deficits in relation to potential jobs. They could not "previsualize" the demands for attention, language, memory, writing, mathematics, perceptual-motor skills and organization needed in a work environment. Therefore, some set unrealistic goals. Many need to literally walk through a day at work in order to understand the requirements.

Others fully understood the job requirements but experienced excessive fatigue because of the effort needed to compensate for their problems. Still others were successfully employed but anxious about trying new positions because of fear (often realistic) of failure.

## Prevocational Planning/Vocational Selection

People with learning disabilities may or may not need specific vocational training, but their deficient occupational, social, and academic skills indicate a need for early *career awareness* to help them develop options and realistic employment goals (Gerber, 1982; Kendall, 1981; Phelps & Lutz, 1977). Those who have difficulty with decision making and problem solving may prolong this process of vocational goal setting. A comprehensive, well-integrated assessment can often aid the adult as well as the adolescent in making a more mature career choice.

## Vocational Services

Prior to 1981, options for vocational services were limited by the ineligibility of learning disabled individuals for Rehabilitation Services Administration (RSA) programs. Services offered by private and community agencies were limited and fragmented, often leaving the interpretation and integration of findings to the individuals who themselves had difficulty with comprehension and interpretation. Information obtained from testing needs careful interpretation by several types of professionals to properly assist the learning disabled. Guidelines may be found in the Report of the Ninth Institute of Rehabilitation Issues (1982) and in Specific Learning Disabilities: A Resource Manual for Vocational Rehabilitation (Vocational Rehabilitation Center of Allegheny County, 1983).

## Acquiring Knowledge and Skills for Specific Vocations

Once a potential occupation is chosen, many learning disabled young people are motivated to attain the academic levels and/or social skills necessary to succeed in the training program and the particular vocation. At times, compensatory techniques must be developed to help circumvent specific problems. Problems of adaptability and/or flexibility should be addressed (Blalock, 1982; Pihl & McLarnon, 1984). Adaptations may include waiving or modifying certain requirements. It is probably unwise to apply for and accept jobs that require excessive adjustments without first discussing them with the employer. Sometimes the adults need to learn how to describe their problems and how to *request* adjustments in a manner that is not offensive or demanding. Employees should be honest if they feel they will need special considerations.

## Maintaining a Job

After securing employment, some adults need assistance in maintaining jobs. Occasionally, those with social perception deficits do not "wear well" over time and may have difficulty working with others. Unexpected tasks also create new problems. The development of a "routine" may be difficult and disruptions in the established pattern may result in over-reaction, defensiveness, and/or apparent inflexibility.

In summary, to ensure success on the job, both the employee and employer need to understand the nature of the learning disability and the significance of the problems. During the initial interview, the employer may raise questions regarding various areas of learning (See Appendix). In addition, it may be necessary to discuss types of accommodations that can be made at work. If possible adaptations are discussed prior to employment, greater satisfaction can be achieved for both the employer and the employee. Suggestions and types of questions are included in the Appendix.

One of the important factors when working with learning disabled adults is that the condition will probably always be present, but the *level* of performance may change or improve. Thus, unlike the person with a physical handicap who will always need to work from a wheelchair, or the blind individual who will always need specific modifications, the person with a learning disability may, even in adulthood, improve in deficit areas. Thus, certain accommodations may be needed only on a temporary basis. For example, the person may need a longer training period or more supervision to achieve certain skills, but eventually he or she may be able to perform without additional support. Many adults need explicit feedback in order to improve their performance.

## MENTAL HEALTH NEEDS

When planning for the needs of people with learning disabilities it is important to remember their problems may cause stress in all aspects of life, not just academic work. Silver (1974) says they are "total life disabilities." Because of stress, many adults are in need of support systems and mental health services. An ACLD survey of learning disabled adults revealed that at least one-half of the respondents wanted services related to social-emotional issues (Chesler, 1982). In a follow-up study of students who had attended the Cove School, Rogan and Hartman (1976) found that 75 percent of the adults sought counseling services.

Social adjustment problems may be directly related to certain processing difficulties or a result of failure and frustration. Rourke and Fisk (1981), for example, suggest the emotional problem and the learning disability may stem from the same underlying deficit. Coexisting emotional problems may lessen the effectiveness of remediation and may even make the learning disabled individual unavailable for learning.

Silver (1984) believes the majority of emotional problems are the result of the learning deficit. Other researchers and clinicians feel learning disabled children are "at risk" for secondary emotional problems that can become significant (Connolly, 1971; Gardner, 1968; Kuhn, 1969; Rourke & Fisk, 1981). The secondary emotional problems reported most frequently include low self-esteem, poor self concepts, social isolation, withdrawal, anxiety, depression, and frustration (Colemen & Sandhu, 1967; Rosenberg & Gaier, 1977; Silver, 1984).

In a study done by Pihl and McLarnon (1984), a group of parents said their learning disabled children had less satisfactory social and emotional adjustment as teenagers than their nondisabled children. The researchers also noted that the learning disabled were less satisfied with themselves and less flexible than their nondisabled peers.

While many clinicians and investigators report social-emotional problems among learning disabled adults, they are not apparent in all instances. Therefore, one should not assume that a poor self concept is an inevitable consequence of learning disablilities. Porter and Rourke (Rourke, 1981) support this notion. They found that 46 percent of the learning disabled children exhibited no more personality problems than their normal peers. While one cannot predict which people might be at risk for emotional problems both Connolly (1971) and Silver (1984) indicate early recognition, understanding, and treatment for the learning disability may prevent confusion, frustration, and failure, and therefore, reduce the risk of emotional problems.

Thirty-six percent of the 93 adults in our clinical study had received counseling or psychotherapy. Several were in therapy at the time of the evaluation and four were on medication for depression. Some not in therapy said they needed counseling or a support group. Their concerns included feelings of loneliness, embarrassment, inadequacy in interpersonal relationships, confusion about goals, and general frustration or depression. During the time of the evaluation we also observed a few with relatively flat affect, over-aggressiveness, sadness, and in certain instances, hostility toward employers and others. Others showed obvious signs of "overload."

When the adults were asked to describe the type of support that was most helpful, they universally responded with "someone who understands learning disabilities." They were negative toward people who had told them to "try harder" or "don't worry." They also preferred therapists who assisted them with short term problem solving rather than those who searched for causes of the difficulties. Several said they needed people who were somewhat direct so they could decide what behaviors to try to change. Others, however, did not want to be pushed. Those with social perception problems said they needed to learn how to "read" people. In sum, various support systems may be needed to foster the greatest sense of well being.

## ADULT ORGANIZATIONS

Adult self-help organizations can provide a means of effecting change in society's attitudes and heighten awareness of the needs of the learning disabled. Most groups have four primary functions including (1) self-help, (2) resource dissemination, (3) interagency cooperation and communication, and (4) self-advocacy. A key element of the self-help groups is that they are developed by and for the learning disabled adult. No single group leader, educator, or medical professional directs the activities. Therefore, there is no single figure who "knows all" and attempts to transmit this knowledge to passive participants. The questions posed by group members often have no single or simple answers. Together as a group the members seek alternative methods to unsolved problems. The strength of the self-help groups rests in the coming together with different perspectives in search of answers still unformulated. "It is a dialogical process which brings individuals together to solve common existential problems." (Smith, 1983, p.3).

Self-help groups begin on the local level when two or more individuals meet to discuss their learning disabilities. Such groups serve to provide a community within which the learning disabled adult can seek friendships, develop an understanding of his or her problems, and express the frustrations and problems too personal to discuss with nonlearning disabled adults. It is helpful for the adult to find he or she is not the "only one." Self-help groups can provide a network to facilitate a more positive view of *self*. They also help individuals develop independence and reduce dependence on their families.

A major goal of adult organizations is to educate others about the needs and problems of learning disabled adults. Resource dissemination may take the form of public speaking at schools, organizations and churches, newsletters, and articles. Through such dissemination, the public should be aware of both academic and nonacademic problems facing the learning disabled adult. Personal descriptions of their struggles reinforce the fact that a learning disability affects areas of life outside of school.

Adults in these organizations have recognized that only through a joint effort with other advocacy groups will changes in educational, economic, and political policies begin to occur. Therefore, many have established a cooperative relationship with educational, vocational, and social agencies.

The increasing competition for jobs and rapidly changing job requirements necessitate sophisticated and flexible work skills (Bellamy, 1980). Hence the adult organization should continue to provide input to vocational training programs, the labor market, and institutions of higher learning to highlight the contributions of learning disabled adults in society.

One of the ways to meet the needs is to encourage self-advocacy. The learning disabled adult should be well-informed of the legislation and litigation affecting his or her life. To teach and encourage self-advocacy the Association for Citizens with Learning Disabilities—Youth and Adult Section—has sponsored short courses on self-assertiveness and self-advocacy. Similar workshops are conducted at the local level. Training in leadership has also been discussed as an important part of the program to develop self-advocacy. Along with an understanding of the learning disabled adult's rights and privileges in society, there is a need to emphasize the responsibilities that come with the rights and privileges.

## REMEDIATION

Approximately one-third of the adults in this group wanted remediation for specific learning problems. The others were interested primarily in obtaining a better understanding of their strengths and weaknesses. Those who wanted remediation generally had rather specific objectives for going back to school or changing jobs. However, a few wanted to read to their children, take care of their own accounts, or to communicate more effectively. Most wanted help with some facet of oral language, reading, written language, or mathematics. Since our remediation program was relatively small with individualized sessions one evening each week, those unable to attend were referred to other agencies or private tutors.

Before beginning remediation the objectives are discussed to determine whether they are compatible with those of the adult. No guarantees regarding amount or rate of progress are made. Once they began, some found it overwhelming to repeatedly expose their weaknesses and even felt guilty if they made mistakes. Others were pleased with even minimal gains.

Our general philosophy is a clinical teaching approach designed to raise deficits by using strengths. It is not just compensatory since many adults have found ways of circumventing problems. However, we may help them with certain strategies for work, independent living, and social skills.

Instruction is provided in specific areas of learning such as language comprehension, oral expression, decoding, spelling, and other verbal or nonverbal skills. While techniques for each area are not included here, we use several basic principles in remediation.

First, we heighten the person's awareness to specific patterns of errors. By making them conscious of these patterns they understand the rationale for working on certain types of words in reading, spelling, language, etc. or for emphasizing certain procedures in mathematics or in nonverbal skills.

Secondly, we are as explicit as possible in defining goals, procedures, and expectancies. Since many adults have not learned from experience or traditional education, our goal is to identify specific needs. During diagnostic teaching we explore forms of input, probes, and cues that facilitate learning.

In general, every effort is made to help the adult become a more independent learner, a better problem detector and solver, and a better communicator. We hope they will be able to acquire the symbol systems of the culture and actualize their potential.

One cannot predict the amount of progress adults can make. In our program the degree of progress varied widely. Occasionally, adults made as much as four years gain in reading, whereas others improved only minimally. Even the latter group, however, said that limited progress made a positive difference in their work and choice of occupation.

Because of the heterogeneity of the group, the severity and nature of the conditions, as well as variation in motivation, it is difficult to predict exactly how far an individual can progress. Therefore, it is difficult to define specific outcomes. Rather, individual goals are adjusted according to the patterns of performance. In general, we feel it is important for the adults to begin with work they can handle successfully, since success breeds more motivation and yields a better employment record. Satisfactory vocational adjustment is a major factor for a sense of well being in adulthood. Occupations affect both physical and mental health and influence self-perception and judgments of other people.

## SUMMARY

Adults with learning disabilities have many needs. Professionals from many fields have both the opportunity and obligation to find more effective ways of responding to those needs. As a group, they offer a major challenge to theorists, researchers, clinicians, and educators. Daily they encouraged us to think about relationships between language and thought, brain and learning, cognition and affect, and many other issues. Above all, they taught us about persistence, resilience, and the tenacity of the human spirit.

## ACKNOWLEDGMENT

We wish to acknowledge the helpful comments regarding adult organization from Dr. Noel Gregg.

## REFERENCES

Alley G, & Deshler D. *Teaching the learning disabled adolescent: Strategies and methods.* Denver: Love Publishing, 1979.

Blalock J. Residual learning disabilities in young adults: Implications for rehabilitation. *Journal of Applied Rehabilitation Counseling.* Summer, 1982.

Bryan T. Peer popularity of learning disabled children. *Journal of Learning Disabilities*, 1974, *7*, 621–625.

Bryan T. Learning disabled children's comprehension of nonverbal communication. *Journal of Learning Disabilities*, 1977, *10*, 501–506.

Chesler B. ACLD vocational committee survey on LD adults. *ACLD Newsbrief*, No. *145*, 1982, July/August & September/October.

Coleman J, & Sandhu M. A descriptive relationship study of 364 children referred to a university clinic for learning disorders. Psychological Reports, 1967, *20*, 1091–1105.

Connolly C. Social and emotional factors in learning disabilities. In H. Myklebust (Ed.), *Progress in learning disabilities (Vol. 2).* New York: Grune & Stratton, 1971.

Cruickshank W, Morse W, & Johns J. *Learning disabilities—The struggle from adolescence toward adulthood.* Syracuse: Syracuse University Press, 1980.

Fafard MB, & Haubrich P. Vocational and social adjustment of learning disabled young adults: A follow-up study. *Learning Disability Quarterly*, 1981, *4*, 122–130.

Gardner R. Psychological problems of brain-injured children and their parents. Journal of the American Academy of Psychiatry, 1968, *7*, 471–491.

Gerber P. Learning disabilities and vocational education: Challenges and realities. In J Stark, K Lynch, & W Kiernan (Eds.), *Prevocational and vocational education for special needs youth: A blueprint for the 80s.* Baltimore: Paul Brooks, 1982.

Gordon S. Reserving a negative self-image. In L Anderson (Ed.), *Helping the adolescent with the hidden handicap.* Los Angeles: California Association for Neurologically Handicapped Children, 1970.

Horn W, O'Donnell J, & Vitulano L. Long-term follow-up studies of learning disabled persons. *Journal of Learning Disabilities*, 1983, *16*, 542–555.

Johnson D. Persistent auditory disorders in young dyslexic adults. *Bulletin of the Orton Society*, 1980, *30*, 269–276.

Johnson D, & Myklebust H. *Learning disabilities: Educational principles and practices*, New York: Grune & Stratton, 1967.

Kahn J. The emotional concomitants of the brain-damaged child. *Journal of Learning Disabilities*, 1969, *2*, 644–651.

Kendall W. Affective and career education for the learning disabled adolescent. *Learning Disability Quarterly*, 1981, *4*, 69–75.

Kronick D. *Social development of learning disabled persons*. San Francisco: Jossey-Bass, Inc., 1981.

Lenkowsky L, & Saposnek D. Family consequences of parental dyslexia. *Journal of Learning Disabilities*, *11* 1978.

Lewis R. *The other child grows up*. New York: Times Books, 1977.

Mann H, & Greenspan S. The identification and treatment of adult brain dysfunction. *American Journal of Psychiatry*, *133*, 1976.

Mathews R, Whang P, & Fawcett S. Behavioral assessment of occupational skills of learning disabled adolescents. *Journal of Learning Disabilities*, 1982, *15*, 38–41.

Myklebust H, & Boshes, B. *Minimal brain damage in children*, Washington, D.C.: Department of Health, Education and Welfare, U.S.P.H.S., 1969.

Ninth Institute on Rehabilitation Issues. Rehabilitation of clients with specific learning disabilities. Arkansas Rehabilitation Research and Training Center, 1982.

Osman B. *No one to play with—The social side of learning disabilities*. New York: Random House, 1982.

Phelps L, & Lutz R. *Career exploration and preparation for the special needs learner*. Boston: Allyn & Bacon, 1977.

Pihl R, & McLarnon L. Learning disabled children as adolescents. *Journal of Learning Disabilities*, 1984, *17*, 96–100.

Rawson M. *Developmental language disability: Adult accomplishments of dyslexic boys*. Baltimore: Johns Hopkins Press, 1968.

Rogan L, & Hartman L. *A follow-up study of learning disabled children as adults. Final report*. Evanston, IL: Cove School Research Office, 1976.

Rosenberg B, & Gaier, E. The self-concept of the adolescent with learning disabilities. Adolescence, 1977, *12*, 490–497.

Rourke B, & Fisk J. Social-emotional disturbances of learning disabled children: The role of central processing deficits. Bulletin of the Orton Society, 1981, *21*, 77–87.

Schumaker J, Hazel S, Sherman J, & Sheldon J. Social skill performances of learning disabled, non-learning disabled, and delinquent adolescents. *Learning Disability Quarterly*, 1982, *5*, 388–397.

Siegel E. *The exceptional child grows up*. New York: Dutton, 1974.

Silver L. Emotional and social problems of children with developmental disabilities. In R. Weber (Ed.), *Handbook on learning disabilities*. Englewood Cliffs, NJ: Prentice-Hall, 1974.

Silver L. The joy of learning should not be a nightmare: The emotional problems faced by individuals with learning disabilities. Evanston, IL: Dian Ridenour Memorial lecture Series, Learning Disabilities Center, Northwestern University, 1984.

Smith D. *Learning disabilities: The interaction of learning, task, and setting*. Boston: Little Brown, 1983.

Thompson L. Language disabilities in men of eminence. *Bulletin of the Orton Society*, 1969, *19*, 113–120.

White W, Schumaker J, Warner M, Alley G, & Deshler D. The current status of young adults identified as learning disabled during their school career. University of Kansas Institute for Research in Learning Disabilities, Research Report #21, 1980.

# Appendix A

## Definitions of Learning Disability

***Review of Educational Research, February, 1969, Vol. XXXIX, No. 1.***

"In an effort to clarify the concept of learning disabilities for the special educator, an institute for advanced study was funded by the Bureau of Education for the Handicapped, U. S. Office of Education, and held at Northwestern University. The resulting definition was written by the fifteen invited participants."

Learning disability refers to one or more significant deficits in essential learning processes requiring special education techniques for remediation.

Children with learning disability generally demonstrate a discrepancy between expected and actual achievement in one or more areas, such as spoken, read, or written language, mathematics, and spatial orientation.

The learning disability referred to is not primarily the result of sensory, motor, intellectural, or emotional handicap or lack of opportunity to learn.

Significant deficits are defined in terms of accepted diagnostic procedures in education and psychology.

Essential learning processes are those currently referred to in behavioral science as involving perception, integration, and expression, either verbal or nonverbal.

Special education techniques for remediation refers to educational planning based on the diagnostic procedures and results.

***Definition adopted by the National Advisory Committee on Handicapped Children 1968.***

Children with special learning disabilities exhibit a disorder in one or more of the basic psychological processes involved in understanding or in using spoken or written language. These may be manifested in disorders of listening, thinking, talking, reading, writing, spelling or arithmetic. They include conditions which have been referred to as perceptual handicaps, brain injury,

ADULTS WITH LEARNING DISABILITIES
ISBN 0-8089-1795-1

minimal brain dysfunction, dyslexia, developmental aphasia, etc. They do not include learning problems which are due primarily to visual, hearing, or motor handicaps, to mental retardation, emotional disturbance, or to environmental disadvantage.

***Definition from Federal Register, Vol. 42, No. 163, August 1977.***

. . . a disorder in one or more of the basic psychological processes involved in understanding or in using language, spoken or written, which may manifest itself in an imperfect ability to listen, think, speak, read, write, spell, or to do math calculations. Term includes such conditions as perceptual handicaps, brain injury, minimal brain dysfunction, dyslexia, and developmental aphasia. The term does not include children who have learning problems which are primarily the result of visual, hearing or motor handicaps, of mental retardation, of emotional disturbance, or of environmental, cultural or economic disadvantage.

***Proposed definition of NJCLD:***

Learning disabilities is a generic term that refers to a heterogeneous group of disorders manifested by significant difficulties in the acquisition and use of listening, speaking, reading, writing, reasoning or mathematical abilities. These disorders are intrinsic to the individual and presumed to be due to central nervous system dysfunction.

Even though a learning disability may occur concomitantly with other handicapping conditions (e.g., sensory impairment, mental retardation, social and emotional disturbance) or environmental influences (e.g., cultural differences, insufficient/inappropriate instruction, psychogenic factors), it is not the direct result of those conditions and influences.

The National Joint Committee for Learning Disabilities is a committee of cooperating organizations concerned with individuals with learning disabilities. Organizations represented include: Association for Children and Adults with Learning Disabilities; American Speech-Language-Hearing Association; Division for Children with Communication Disorders, Council for Exceptional Children; Division for Children with Learning Disabilities, Council for Exceptional Children; International Reading Association; and The Orton Society.

# APPENDIX B

## Adult Case History
## Northwestern University
## Learning Disabilities Center

Name: Birthdate:
Address:
Home Phone: Business Phone:
Marital Status: Name of Spouse:
Parents' Names:
Parents' Address:
Emergency Name: Phone:

What are your chief concerns at this time?
Describe your learning problem and indicate the ways it interferes with educational performance, social interactions, and/or employment.
What do you hope to accomplish here?

Educational Background and Current Educational Status

Are you currently enrolled in school?
If not, when were you last in school?
How far did you go in school? What was the highest grade completed?
Where:
Level:
Courses and major area of study:
What kinds of grades and feedback do you get?
Are you getting special help? Type:
Goals:
If not in school, would you like to return?
Summarize your educational background. Indicate the type of schools you attended, when you first recall having a problem and what was done about it. Who first noted it?
Kindergarten:

Elementary School:
Junior High and Secondary School:
College:
Technical or Vocational Schools:
Graduate School:

What kinds of grades did you get?
What was the most difficult subject? Least difficult?
Did you repeat any grades? Which one(s)?
When was your problem first noted? What type of problem?
Did you have an evaluation? When? Where? What were you told?
Have you ever been told you have a learning disability?
By whom? When? What were your reactions?
Did you receive special help? If so, what kind?

Tutoring (type):
Learning Disabilities Instruction (type):
Remedial Reading:
Speed Reading:
Speech Therapy:
Counseling:
Group Therapy:
Special Classes:
Visual Training:
Occupational Therapy:
Other:

Was the special help beneficial? Which?
Did you go to any special schools? Which? When? Reactions.
What kinds of help were most beneficial? Least?
Did you have any other problems in early childhood?

Specific Learning Problems

Do you have difficulty comprehending oral language in any situation (home, school, particular courses, TV, films, radio, etc.)?
Do you have difficulty taking directions?
Do you think you have any memory problems? Describe.
Do you have difficulty with any aspect of writing? Describe.
Which hand do you prefer?
Do you have difficulty with arithmetic or mathematics?

Academically or practically?
Problems making change?
Checkbook?
Figuring cost of items, doubling recipes, estimating quantities of supplies, etc.?

Do you have problems with time orientation? Being on time, estimating time, etc.?
Do you have difficulty with spatial orientation? Reading maps? Getting lost?

Do you feel you have any problems with attention: Distractability, span, etc.?
Do you have problems with organization in school, at work, at home?
Other:
Have you discussed your problems with anyone? With whom? What explanations do you give?
What types of strategies have you used to cope with your problems? Which have been most or least effective?
What types of situations are most difficult? Which cause "overload" or frustration?
What does your family/spouse say about your problems?
What do your friends say?
What have your employers said?
If you are married, have the problems interfered with your marriage in any way?

## Occupational Goals and History

Summarize your work history: Begin with your first job and review each with regard to the degree of success and satisfaction. Indicate the length of time on each job. Include both full-time and part-time work. Describe the ways in which learning problems interfered with any aspect of employment.
Have you ever gone to a vocational counselor? What was done? What type of recommendations were made? Did you follow them? Which were most successful? Least? Have you ever participated in special vocational workshops or vocational training? Describe:

## Family History

List educational level, occupation, and handedness of each parent.
List educational level, occupation, age, sex, and handedness of each sibling.
Your position in the family:
Do any members of your family have learning problems? Indicate who, what type.
Are you currently living with your family? What are the living arrangements?
If you are not living with your family and are not married, what are your living arrangements? Do you support yourself? Do you manage your own finances?
Do you have children? If so, list age, sex, handedness, learning and achievement.

## Social History and Recreation

How do you spend your leisure time? Do you prefer to spend time alone, with friends, and/or family? Age and sex of friends?
Have you had any problems making and keeping friends?
List hobbies.
Do you enjoy sports? Observer or particpant? Have you taken lessons?

Do you feel you have any coordination problems that have interfered with work or recreation?

Do you enjoy music? Have you played a musical instrument? Do you/can you dance?

Do you enjoy the visual arts? Painting, ceramics, etc.

Do you read for pleasure? What do you read?

Do you travel? By yourself? With family? With others? Do you plan the trips?

Do you drive a car? Describe any problems.

Do you enjoy movies? TV? Which types of films or programs? Do you understand them?

What problems, if any, do you have with any of these leisure time activities?

Are there any situations that are difficult to deal with (distractions, noise)?

What did you enjoy as a child?

## Medical History

Do you see physicians routinely? What types? (Internist, neurologist, dentist, etc.)

Are you on any type of medication? Have you taken medication previously? For what? Which were beneficial? Not?

Have you had any evaluations related to learning problems (EEG, etc.)?

Other:

Do you have any allergies? Have you ever had allergic reactions to medications.

Repeated ear infections?

Illnesses that caused repeated absence from school or work?

Serious accidents or extended illnesses?

Weight problems?

Any chronic conditions (diabetes, thyroid, etc.)?

Has your hearing been checked recently? Have you ever had a hearing aid?

Have you had a recent visual examination? Findings? Do you wear glasses? Reasons:

Have you have been given medication for depression?

Have you ever been hospitalized? Reason(s):

## Special Problems

Do any of the following pertain to you:

Did you have a history of truancy in school?

Have you been known to have a behavior problems? Special class? Correctional institution?

Have you ever been involved in drugs? Alcohol? Have you ever been arrested? Reason(s):

## Mental Health

In general, how do you feel about yourself?
Have you felt the need for counseling, support groups, therapy? Has this type of help been recommended?
Have you ever been hospitalized for mental illness?

## Summary

Do you have additional questions or concerns?

# Appendix C

## Diagnostic Questions

Auditory Receptive Language

1. Does the person have difficulty discriminating sounds in words?
   A. In quiet surroundings
   B. In noise
   C. By phone
   D. Face to face
2. Does the person have difficulty comprehending new words?
   A. From verbal context only
   B. In natural context
3. Does the person have difficulty comprehending and following instructions?
   A. With or without demonstration
   B. With or without repetition
4. Does the person have difficulty understanding verbal discourse?
   A. Adult conversation
   B. Technical and inferential language
   C. Ambiguous and metaphorical language
5. Does the person have difficulty remembering auditory verbal information?
   A. Short term memory span
   B. Long term memory

Auditory Expressive Language

1. Does the person have difficulty recalling words?
   A. In conversation
   B. Under pressure
2. Does the person have difficulty pronouncing words?
   A. Multisyllabic words
   B. Specific sound substitutions, omissions, distortions
3. Does the person make grammatical mistakes when speaking?
   A. Informal situations
   B. Formal situations

4. Does the person organize thoughts to convey a series of ideas?
   A. With or without rehearsal
   B. For individuals or groups
5. Can the person give clear explanations of procedures?
6. Does the person use appropriate language for the environment and situation?
7. Does the person have any difficulty conveying ideas to others?
8. Is the person aware of communication errors or problems?
9. Is the person willing to request assistance or repetition of instructions?
10. Does the person care about improving performance?

Visual Receptive Language (Reading)

1. Does the person have any problems reading basic sight vocabulary for personal protection or mobility?
2. Does the person have difficulty sounding out words or reading aloud?
3. Does the person have reading comprehension problems?
   A. Vocabulary
   B. Factual information
   C. Technical terminology
   D. Complex texts requiring inference
4. Can the person use a dictionary?
   A. To obtain pronunciation of words
   B. To obtain meaning
5. What is the reading level?
   A. Familiar material
   B. Unfamiliar material
6. Does the person have difficulty remembering what was read?
   A. Short term
   B. Long term
7. Does the person have the capacity to utilize what has been read?
8. Does the person have problems related to speed of reading?
9. Does the person report difficulty reading?
10. Is the person interested in improving reading performance?
11. Does the person read for pleasure or information?

Visual Expressive Language (Writing)

1. Does the person have legible handwriting?
2. Does the person have difficulty copying letters or words?
3. Does the person have adequate spelling ability?
4. Does the person write grammatically correct sentences?
5. Can the person complete basic forms and documents?
6. Can the person write letters with appropriate form?
   A. Personal notes or memos

B. Invitations, responses, and thank-you letters
C. Business letters to familiar and unfamiliar people

7. Can the person summarize ideas in writing
   A. With appropriate organization
   B. With relevant information
   C. Business letters to familiar and unfamiliar people
8. Does the person attempt creative writing?

Mathematics and Related Skills

1. Does the person have difficulty with quantitative thinking?
2. Can the person perform basic arithmetic operations?
3. Can the person use the number system for life skills?
   A. Making change (with speed and accuracy)
   B. Budgeting own accounts
   C. Estimating time, speed, distance, quantity
4. Can the person perform higher mathematical functions?

Orientation

1. Does the person have difficulty with spatial orientation?
   A. Body image
   B. Left-right
   C. Direction
   D. Getting lost in environment
2. Does the person have difficulty with time orientation?
   A. Telling time
   B. Estimating time
   C. Budgeting time
   D. Sequencing days, months, seasons

Perceptual Motor Functions

1. Does the person have difficulty with fine motor coordination?
2. Does the person have any gross motor coordination problems?
3. Does the person have difficulty learning new motor patterns?
4. Does the person have difficulty with balance?
5. Is the person appropriately cautious with equipment?

General Problem Solving and Reasoning

1. Can the person detect problems that need to be solved?
2. Does the person have good problem solving skills?
   A. Verbal
   B. Nonverbal
3. Does the person have difficulty with reasoning?
   A. Understanding cause and effect
   B. Conceptualization

Nonverbal Communication

1. Does the person have difficulty understanding body language?
    - A. Facial expression
    - B. Gesture
    - C. Proxemics
2. Is the person aware of his or her own body language?
3. Can the person interpret multiple communication messages?
    - A. Language
    - B. Tone of voice
    - C. Body language

Social Skills

1. Does the person have adequate social skills?
2. Does the person appear to be tactful?
3. Does the person have the ability to see another point of view?
4. Can the person relate well to others?
5. Can the person utilize feedback from others?

Self Concept

1. Does the person have a good sense of self?
2. Is the person able to accept constructive criticism?
3. Does the person display appropriate affect in various situations?
4. Can the person cope with frustrations?

Attention

1. Does the person have an attention disorder?
2. Can the person maintain attention in quiet and noise?
3. Does the person have difficulty working at the same task for lengthy time periods?

## Questions Regarding Occupations

1. Listening Skills: General
    - a. Requirements

      To what extent are accurate listening and language comprehension skills required?

      e.g.,—taking instructions or messages in either quiet or noisy environments

      —taking orders in a specified sequence

      —taking lengthy instructions
    - b. Modifications

      Can modifications be made temporarily or permanently?

      Can person be placed in another location?

      Can instructions be repeated, typed out or tape recorded?

2. Listening: Verbal Comprehension
   a. Requirements
      To what extent must the person acquire new and/or technical vocabulary?
      e.g.,—Is the person expected to comprehend more than casual, adult conversational language?
   b. Modifications
      Can modifications be made?
      Can instructions or vocabulary be simplified, explained, or demonstrated? Are there supervisors who can assist temporarily (i.e., while the employee is learning? and/or permanently?)
3. Oral Expression
   a. Requirements
      To what extent are precise and accurate pronunciations of words (both familiar and unfamiliar) required?
      e.g.,—pronouncing multisyllabic names, technical terms, etc.
      To what extent is accurate, quick recall of specific vocabulary required?
      To what extent is accurate grammar required?
      To what extent is the prospective employee expected to give clear, concise explanations or summaries?
      To what extent are good conversational skills required?
      To what extent are auditory sequencing skills required (i.e., numbers or words in a specified order)?
   b. Modifications
      Can any of the requirements be changed?
      e.g.,—Can supervisors provide additional training or support on either a temporary or permanent basis?
      Would the employer allow time off for remediation or special instruction?
4. Reading
   a. Requirements
      What level of reading is required for the position?
      e.g.,—accurate reading of warning signs?
      instructions and manuals?
      reading names, addresses, street signs?
      To what extent is the person expected to acquire *new* information and vocabulary from reading?
      To what extent is reading speed or quick scanning of material expected?
      Is the person expected to demonstrate comprehension by:
      1) following instructions,
      2) manipulating or operating equipment,
      3) summarizing content orally,

4) writing,

5) calculating or performing some mathematical operation

What quantity of reading is expected daily or weekly?

Is the person expected to read graphs, charts, maps, or other graphic representations?

b. Modifications

Could any of the printed information be transmitted in another form? e.g.,—by tape recorder or other graphic presentations such as drawings or diagrams?

Could someone else read the material to the employee?

Can more time be allowed for scanning and review?

Could the mode of response be altered? (i.e., could the person provide a summary in another way—oral rather than written?)

To what extent will errors jeopardize the safety of anyone?

To what extent could errors create an embarrassment for the employee or the employer?

5. Written Language

a. Requirements

To what extent is clear and accurate copying of letters, words, or numerals needed?

To what extent is accurate spelling required? At what level?

To what extent must the employee write accurate sequential messages for others (i.e., telephone orders)?

Is speed an important factor?

Is sequence relevant? an important factor?

To what extent are written explanations, summaries, reports, letters, and other narratives required?

Must the material be hand written or typed?

To what extent are word processors and other equipment available—needed?

b. Modifications

Could oral responses be substituted for written ones? How often? All or some?

Could the quantity of written work be reduced? If so, how?

Could a supervisor proof and/or correct the written work for accuracy, spelling, etc. (temporarily, permanently)?

If typewriters and/or word processors are available, can the person with poor handwriting use them or be taught to use them?

If quantity of work cannot be modified, could the person be permitted to work longer hours or take work home in order to successfully complete an assignment (without additional pay)?

Could the employer provide special instruction in any aspect of writing?

Would the employer allow a period of trial learning while the employee received special remediation?

6. Mathematics
   a. Requirements
      To what extent are quantitative concepts needed for the position?
      To what extent is accurate writing of numbers essential?
      To what extent does the job require accurate use of tools and measurement devices such as rulers and gauges?
      To what extent is ability to rapidly calculate and/or make change required?
   b. Modifications
      Can calculators be used or made available?
      Can supervisors assist the employee?
      Can the quantity and/or speed of work be reduced?
7. Time and Spatial Orientation
   a. Requirements
      To what extent is a sense of direction and knowledge of directionality and left-right required?
      To what extent is timing, estimation of time, and speed a factor?
   b. Modifications
      Can a compass or verbal guides be provided to aid directionality?
      Can the employee be given more structure or time to complete the work?
8. General Problem Solving and Organization
   a. Requirements
      To what extent must the employee identify problems that must be detected? Is the person required to watch for hazards and potential problems?
      To what extent is independent problem solving required?
      To what extent is the employee expected to prioritize, organize, and execute a series of activities each day or week? Verbal and/or nonverbal?
      To what extent is speed of problem solving required?
   b. Modifications
      Are supervisors available to help with prioritizing and making suggestions for organization?
      Can supervisors assist in monitoring the employee's performance?
9. Social Skills and Interpersonal Communication
   a. Requirements
      To what extent does the job require both verbal and nonverbal communication competence?
      To what extent does the employee need good telephone skills?
      To what extent must the employee be able to respond to nonverbal signals including gesture, facial expression or body language?

To what extent is team work and group problem solving required?
To what extent would the employee be interacting with new, unfamiliar people on the job?

b. Modifications

Could supervisors help the employee develop some of the interaction skills required?
Are there films or demonstrations which can be used during an initial training period?
Could the employee be given additional breaks or time out periods for attention problems or "overload"?

10. Evaluation

a. Requirements

How are employees evaluated?
Are the expectations for performance stated explicitly?
How is the feedback provided? e.g., in writing, face to face, orally?
How frequently is feedback provided?
Are there probationary periods?
Does the employer have any provisions for remedial work?
How are dismissals and terminations handled?
Are criteria for promotions and advancements stated explicitly?
What are the consequences of tardiness/absenteeism?

b. Modifications

Can criteria be provided more explicitly and in a form that is easily understood by the employee?
Can a probationary period be extended if the employee seeks outside help?

# APPENDIX D

## Tests Used for Assessment

*Bender Visual Motor Gestalt Test*. Bender L. American Guidance Services, 1946. Design copying test for perceptual motor integration widely used in clinical assessment.

*Berry-Talbott Language Test: Comprehension of Grammar*. Berry M. 1966 (revised edition available). Tests the application of morphological rules to nonsense words.

*Clinical Evaluation of Language Functions*. Semel E. & Wiig E. Charles E. Merrill, 1980. Thirteen subtests assessing oral language (grades K–12).

*Cognitive Abilities Test*. Thorndike R & Hagen E Houghton Mifflin, 1971. Yields verbal, quantitative and nonverbal scores (grades 3–12).

*Detroit Tests of Learning Aptitude-2*. Hammill D. Pro-Ed, 1984. Revision of Baker & Leland edition. Eleven subtests (ages 6–17).

*Developmental Test of Visual-Motor Integration (Rev'd.)*. Beery K. & Buktenica N. Follett, 1982. Design copying (ages 5–15).

*Four Factor Tests of Social Intelligence* (Behavioral Cognition). O'Sullivan M & Guilford J. Sheridan. Psychological Services, 1976. Measures of understanding thoughts, feelings, and intentions of other people through behavior. Assessed with drawings, cartoons, etc. (norms for 10th graders & college students).

*Goldman-Fristoe-Woodcock Auditory Skills Battery*. Goldman R, Fristoe M, & Woodcock R. American Guidance Services, 1976. Twelve tests of auditory skills including selective attention, discrimination and memory (ages 3–adult).

*Goldman-Fristoe-Woodcock Test of Auditory Discrimination*. Goldman, R, Fristoe M, & Woodcock R. American Guidance Services, 1970. Speech sound discrimination in quiet and in noise (ages 4–adult).

*Goodenough-Harris Drawing Test*. Goodenough F & Harris D. The Psychological Corp., 1963. Human figure drawing test (ages 3–15).

*Gray Oral Reading Tests*. Gray W & Robinson H. Pro-Ed., 1967. Assesses fluency and accuracy of oral reading (grades 1–12).

*Gray Oral Reading Tests-Revised*. Wiederholt J & Bryant B. Pro-Ed., 1986. Assesses rate, accuracy, and comprehension of oral reading (ages 7–17 years).

*Leiter International Performance Scale*. Leiter R. Stoelting, 1969. Nonverbal intelligence test (ages 2–adult).

*Memory-for-Designs Test*. Graham F & Kendall B. Psychological Test Specialists, 1973. Drawing 15 designs after 5 seconds' exposure each (ages 8½–adult).

*Peabody Individual Achievement Test*. (PIAT) Dunn L & Markwardt F. American Guidance Services, 1970. Test of five areas: mathematics, reading recognition, reading comprehension, spelling, and general information (kindergarten–adult).

*Peabody Picture Vocabulary Test-Revised*. Dunn L & Dunn L. American Guidance Services, 1981. Receptive vocabulary test (ages 2 through adult).

*Picture Story Language Test*. Myklebust H. Grune & Stratton, 1965. Written language test which evaluates productivity, syntax, and level of abstraction (7–17 years).

*Primary Mental Abilities Tests*. Thurstone T. Science Research Associates, 1962. Group intelligence test yielding MA and IQ scores for verbal meaning, reasoning, number facility, and spatial relations (K–adult).

*Raven Progressive Matrices*. Western Psychological Services, 1938. Nonverbal test of intelligence, standardized in England (ages 8–65 years).

*Road-Map Test of Direction Sense*. Money J. Johns Hopkins Press, 1965. Tests ability to orient oneself in space and translate this to two-dimensional space (ages 7–18).

*Stanford-Binet Intelligence Scale-Third Rev*. Terman L & Merrill M. Houghton Mifflin, 1960. Intelligence test individually administered by qualified psychological examiner (ages 2–adult).

*Stanford-Binet Intelligence Scale: Fourth Edition*. Thorndike R, Hagen E, & Scattler J, Riverside Publishing Co., 1986. Intelligence test yielding a composite score, 15 subtest scores and area scores. Individually administered by qualified psychological examiner (ages 2–adult).

*Stanford Diagnostic Mathematics Test, Third Ed*. Beatty L, Madden R, Gardner E, & Karlsen B. The Psychological Corp., 1984. Assesses basic mathematics concepts and skills. Has 3 sections: number system and numeration, computation, applications (grades 1.5–12).

*Stanford Diagnostic Reading Test-Third Ed*. Karlsen B, Madden R, & Gardner E. The Psychological Corp., 1983, 1984. Test to diagnose reading problems. Assesses rapid reading, vocabulary, comprehension, phonetic analysis (grades 1.5–12).

*Stanford Diagnostic Reading Test-2nd Ed*. Karlsen B, Madden R, & Gardner E. The Psychological Corp., 1978. Assesses comprehension, decoding, vocabulary, rate (grades K–13).

*Stanford Test of Academic Skills (TASK): 2nd Ed*. Gardner E, Callis R, Merwin J, & Rudman H. The Psychological Corp., 1982, 1983. Achievement test for high school and junior college students. Areas: reading, English, mathematics.

*Test of Adolescent Language–2*. Hammill D, Brown V, Larsen S, & Wiederholt J.

Pro-Ed., 1982. Test of spoken and written language. Eight subtests (ages 12–18-5).

*Test of Concept Utilization.* Crager R. Western Psychological Services, 1972. Assessment of identification of relations between pictured objects (ages 5–18).

*Test of Language Competence.* Wiig E & Secord R. The Psychological Corp., 1985.

*Test of Mathematical Abilities* (TOMA). Brown V & McEntire E. Pro-Ed., 1984. Assesses computation, story problems, attitude, vocabulary and information (ages 8-6–18-11).

*Test of Nonverbal Intelligence.* Brown L, Sherbenou R, & Dollar S. Pro-Ed., 1982. Language-free measure of intelligence similar to the Raven Progressive Matrices (ages 5–85).

*Test of Reading Comprehension* (TORC). Brown V, Hammill D, Wiederholt J. Pro-Ed., 1986. Seven subtests assessing reading comprehension: vocabulary, syntax, sentences, paragraphs (ages 7–17).

*Test of Written Language* (TOWL). Hammill D & Larsen S. Pro-Ed., 1983. Written expression (ages 7–18).

*Test of Written Spelling* (TWS-2). Larsen S & Hammill D. Pro-Ed., 1986. Assesses spelling of predictable and unpredictable words. Appropriate for individuals with significant spelling problems (grades 1–12).

*Time Appreciation Test.* Buck J. Western Psychological Services, 1946. Test of time concepts consisting of 30 questions relating to various aspects of time (10 years–adult).

*Wechsler Adult Intelligence Scale-Revised (WAIS-R).* Wechsler D. The Psychological Corp., 1981. Individual intelligence test yielding verbal, performance and full scale IQ administered by qualified psychological examiner (ages 16–adult).

*Wide Range Achievement Test-Revised (WRAT-R).* Jastak S & Wilkinson G. Jastak Associates, Inc., 1984. Screening test of oral reading of single words, dictated spelling, and arithmetic computation (ages 5–adult).

*Woodcock-Johnson Psycho-Educational Battery.* Woodcock R & Johnson D. DLM-Teaching Resources, 1978. Tests of cognitive ability, learning aptitude, scholastic achievement, interest level in three parts: cognitive ability, achievement, interest level (ages preschool–adult).

*Woodcock Reading Mastery Tests.* Woodcock R. American Guidance Services, 1973. Individual tests of oral reading (single words), word attack, word comprehension, and passage comprehension (grades K–12).

# APPENDIX E

## Addresses of Test Publishers

Academic Therapy Publications, P.O. Box 899, San Rafael, CA 94901
American Guidance Services, Inc. Publishers' Bldg., Circle Pines, MN 55014
Mildred Berry, 4332 Pinecrest Road, Rockford, IL 61107
Bobbs-Merrill Co., 4300 W. 62nd St., Indianapolis, IN 46206
Charles Merrill Publishing Co., Columbus, OH 43216
Follett Publishing Co., 1010 W. Washington Blvd., Chicago, IL 60607
Grune & Stratton, Inc., Orlando, FL 32887
The Psychological Corp., 7555 Caldwell Ave., Chicago, IL 60648
Houghton-Mifflin Co., Wayside Road., Burlington, MA 01803
Jastak Associates, Inc., 1526 Gilpin Ave., Wilmington, DE 19806
Johns Hopkins Press, Baltimore, MD 21218
Pro-Ed, 5341 Industrial Oaks Blvd., Austin, TX 78735
Psychological Tests Specialists, Box 1441, Missoula, MT 59801
Science Research Associates, 155 North Wacker, Chicago, IL 60611
Stoelting Co., 1350 Kostner Ave., Chicago IL 60623
DLM-Teaching Resources Corp., P.O. Box 4000, One DLM Park, Allen, TX 75002
Western Psychological Services, 12031 Wilshire Blvd., Los Angeles, CA 90025

# Author Index


Abel, E., 91
Ackerman, P., 48, 152
Adelman, H., 16
Adelman, P., 245
Aiken, L., 206
Al-Issa, I., 141
Alley, G., 4, 215, 285, 286
Allington, R., 152
Allport, G., 224
Amatruda, C., 2
Anderson, R., 132
Anglin, J., 132
Ansara, A., 4
Applebee, A., 196
Armstrong, S., 210, 211
Asch, S., 81
Atchison, M., 84
Aten, J., 84
Atterbury, B., 224
Atwell, C., 163

Baddelly, A., 199
Badian, N., 205, 206, 211, 214, 222
Bailet, L., 190, 192
Baker, H., 94
Bakker, D., 145, 156
Bannatyne, A., 48, 52, 53, 63
Bannochie, M., 48, 57, 59, 64
Bates, H., 209
Beadle, K., 175
Beaty, L., 207
Beers, J., 186
Beery, K., 181, 226
Behrens, T., 4, 51
Belmont, L., 22
Bender, L., 145
Bent, D., 55
Benton, A., 145, 220, 222
Bereiter, C., 173
Berko, J., 98
Berlow, J., 91
Berman, A., 5
Berry, M., 97, 98, 156
Bever, T., 86
Bijou, S., 177, 186
Birch, H., 22, 223
Birdwhistle, R., 224
Bireley, M., 249
Blake, H., 174
Blalock, J., 4, 37, 81, 84, 88, 93, 189, 206, 208, 220, 246, 257, 287
Blank, M., 162
Blankenship, C., 209
Bloom, L., 88
Boder, E., 145, 146, 187
Borden, G. J., 112
Bos, C., 160
Boshes, B., 283
Bradley, L., 187
Bransford, J., 87
Britton, J., 173, 175
Broder, P., 5
Broen, P. A., 107
Bronfenbrenner, U., 28
Brown, A. L., 69, 162
Brown, D., 4, 260, 261, 266
Brown, V., 90
Bruce, D., 85
Bruskin, C., 162
Bryan, J., 81
Bryan, T., 81, 97, 220, 286
Bryant, N. R., 69
Bryant, P., 186
Bryant, T., 4
Buck, J., 230
Buktenica, N., 181, 226
Burgess, T., 173
Burke, C., 152, 161
Burns, W., 93
Burris, N., 188
Busse, L. A., 84, 85
Buzzardi, L., 261

Cable, B., 27
Calfee, R., 162
Cambon, J., 89
Campbell, R., 84
Campione, J. C., 69
Canter, G., 84
Capelli, C., 14, 162

Carroll, J., 161
Carter, B., 85
Case, R., 67
Cattell, R., 56
Cawley, J., 209
Cazden, C., 85
Chalfant, J., 22, 205, 206
Chall, J., 152, 153, 158
Chapman, R., 87
Chesler, B., 241, 285, 286, 289
Chomsky, C., 81, 89
Cicci, R., 187, 191
Clark, E., 88, 136
Clark, H., 88
Clay, M., 152
Clifton, L., 111
Coburn, L., 156
Cohen, C., 195
Cohen, J., 55, 56, 57, 64
Cohn, R., 206
Coleman, J., 48, 289
Connolly, A., 207
Connolly, C., 289
Cooper, C., 173, 199
Cooper, J., 4, 27
Copeland, R., 205
Cordoni, B., 4, 48, 50, 52, 53, 241, 253, 256, 257, 260, 261
Cox, S., 260, 261
Critchley, M., 4, 145, 174, 222, 257, 258
Cromer, R., 89, 190
Cruickshank, W., 4, 219, 285
Crystal, D., 91, 225
Czerniejewski, C., 257, 258

Dagenais, D., 175
Danner, F., 92
Das, J., 146
Davis, E., 48
Davis, J., 84
Day, M. C., 67
deHirsch, K., 94
Denckla, M., 94, 146
Deno, S., 152
Deshler, D., 4, 215, 267, 285, 286
deVilliers, J., 88, 90, 92
deVilliers, P., 88, 90, 92
Doehring, D., 146
Dolan, E., 242, 268
Dolan, F., 242, 268
Dokecki, P., 48
Doll, E., 43
Dominic, J., 173
Donahue, M., 81, 97
Donalson, M., 87
Dorfmueller, D., 91
Downing, J., 161, 166, 191
Duane, D., 4, 152
Duane, G., 243
Duchan, J., 87, 92, 99
Duffy, F., 152
Duncan, S., 224
Dunn, L., 88
Dunn, L., 88, 246, 257
Dykman, R., 48, 152

Eisenberg, A., 221, 225
Eisenson, J., 81, 107
Ekman, P., 224
Eliot, J., 229
Elliott, L., 84, 85, 109, 110, 111, 112, 116, 118, 121, 124, 126
Elliott, R., 241
Emig, J., 173
Evens, M., 132
Ewing, A., 1, 2

Fafard, M. B., 285
Fawcett, S., 286
Fernald, G., 2
Ferrara, R. A., 69
Fey, S., 91
Filip, D., 14
Fine, H., 91
Fisher, F., 85
Fisk, J., 289
Fitzmaurice, A., 209
Fleischer, J., 214
Flood, J., 85, 166
Flowers, L., 173
Foth, D., 93
Frederiksen, C., 173
French, J., 145, 146, 185
Friesen, W., 224
Fristoe, M., 84, 94
Frith, U., 173, 186, 188, 190
Frostig, M., 219

Gaier, E., 289
Galaburda, A., 166
Gallagher, T., 98
Gardner, E., 207
Gardner, R., 289

Garner, R., 153
Garnett, K., 214
Geib, G., 261
Genova, P., 261
Gerber, P., 286
German, D., 94
Gesell, A., 2
Gibson, E., 85, 153, 160, 161
Gillingham, A., 2
Gilmore, E., 152
Gilmore, J., 152
Ginsburg, J., 67
Glenn, C., 92, 161, 196
Glenn, J., 215
Goldman, R., 84, 94
Goldman, T., 158
Goodman, L., 4
Goodman, Y., 152, 161
Goodstein, H., 209
Gordon, S., 286
Graham, S., 267
Graves, D., 175
Gray, W., 151, 152
Greenfield, P., 23, 199, 224
Greenspan, S., 286
Gregg, K., 197, 198
Gregg, L., 173
Gregg, N., 259
Greisman, J., 259
Griffith, P., 4
Grigar, M., 266
Groshong, C., 91, 177
Guildroy, J., 240, 242
Guthrie, J., 160
Guttmann, E., 206

Hagin, R., 4
Hall, E., 225
Hallgren, B., 145
Halliday, M., 173
Hammill, D., 3, 90, 173, 177, 179, 187, 241
Hanna, J., 173, 186
Hanna, R., 173, 186
Harris, K. S., 112, 220
Hartman, L., 4, 285, 289
Hasan, R., 173
Hasbrouck, J., 84
Haubrich, P., 285
Hayes, J., 173
Hazel, S., 286
Hebb, D., 22
Heidenheimer, P., 132
Heilman, K., 222
Henderson, A., 159
Henderson, E., 186
Hendrickson, A., 205
Herbert, M., 257, 258
Herman, L., 145, 168
Hinshelwood, J., 1, 145
Hodges, R., 173, 186
Hoff, L., 192
Hoffman, R., 87, 91
Honeck, R., 87, 91
Hook, P., 81, 84, 86
Horn, W., 4, 285
Hoshko, J., 146
Hoskins, B., 39, 177
Hoy, C., 211
Hull, C., 55
Humes, A., 173
Hunt, K., 173
Huntington, D. A., 107
Huttenlocher, J., 87

Ilmer, R., 84
Inhelder, B., 67
Isard, S., 84
Ivey, C., 93

Jacobson, F., 5
James, J., 161
James, K., 206
Jansky, J., 94
Jarman, R., 146
Jastak, J., 60, 87, 151, 154, 177, 186, 207, 210, 226
Jastak, S., 60, 87, 151, 154, 177, 186, 207, 210, 226
Jenkins, J., 55
Johns, J., 4, 285
Johnson, C., 260, 261
Johnson, D., 3, 4, 7, 43, 81, 84, 85, 87, 88, 90, 92, 93, 94, 95, 96, 145, 147, 166, 175, 179, 184, 186, 206, 207, 208, 219, 223, 230, 253, 254, 277, 286
Johnson, M., 87, 94, 95, 207
Johnston, J., 241
Jones, J., 91

Kahn, M., 268
Kail, R., 93
Kalikow, D. N., 121
Kaliski, L., 206

Kallman, C., 107
Karlsen, B., 207
Karmiloff-Smith, A., 81, 89
Karn, H., 209
Katz, D. R., 108, 109, 110, 111
Katz, J., 84
Kaufman, A., 23, 48, 52, 54, 55, 64, 146
Kaufman, N., 23, 146
Keating, D. P., 67
Keilitz, I., 5
Kemper, T., 166
Kendall, W., 286
Kephart, N., 219
Kessel, F., 89
Killen, J., 48, 57, 59, 64
Kintsch, W., 92
Kirby, J., 146
Kirk, S., 2
Klees, M., 90
Kline, C., 4
Kline, C., 4
Knott, G., 220
Koenigsknecht, R. A., 107
Kosc, L., 206, 211, 212
Krieger, V., 155
Kronick, D., 3, 4, 286
Kuhl, P., 83, 84
Kuhn, D., 77, 289
Kulick, M., 84
Kurtz, J., 48

LaBerge, D., 165
Lahey, M., 88
Larsen, S., 3, 90, 173, 177, 179, 187, 209, 241
Larson, R., 173, 174
Lebrun, L., 91
Lefford, A., 223
Lehtinen, L., 2, 15, 178, 206, 219, 223
Leigh, J., 3, 241
Leland, B., 94
Lenkowsky, L., 286
Leong, C., 146, 4
Lesgold, A., 146, 160
Levin, H., 85, 86, 153, 160, 161
Levitt, H., 111
Levy, W., 209, 213
Lewis, R., 285, 286
Liberman, I., 85, 86, 154, 155
Lindquist, M., 205
Litowitz, B., 15, 89, 132, 133, 134, 175, 200
Loban, W., 81, 196
Longinotti, C., 111
Looney, P., 88
Lopate, P., 173
Lorge, I., 134
Lovett, M., 166
Lovitt, T., 209
Lowe, A., 84
Lubert, N., 84, 107
Lund, N., 87, 92, 99
Luria, A., 23, 192
Lutey, C., 48, 50, 51, 52, 59
Lutz, R., 286
Lyon, G. R., 146
Lyon, R., 5
Lyons, J., 131

MacGinitie, W., 165
MacGugan, K., 268
Madden, R., 207
Manley, E., 249
Mann, H., 286
Mann, L., 4
Manzo, A., 162
Mardell, C., 206
Maria, K., 165
Markman, E., 14, 87, 90, 153, 162
Markowitz, J., 132
Markwardt, F., 246, 257
Marston, D., 152
Martin, N., 173
Masland, R., 23, 166
Masson, M., 153, 162
Matarazzo, J., 51, 57, 209
Mathews, R., 286
Mattingly, I., 85
Mattis, S., 145, 146, 185
McFie, J., 222
McGinnis, M., 2
McKinley, D., 252
McLarnon, L., 287, 289
McLeod, A., 173
McLeod, T., 210, 211
McNemar, Q., 57
McNutt, G., 3, 241
McReynolds, L., 84
Mellits, D., 107
Menn, L., 84
Menyuk, P., 84, 85, 88, 166
Mercer, C., 179
Meyen, E., 4
Meyer, D., 111
Michals, D., 225
Miles, T., 145, 147, 188, 189

Miller, C., 252, 261
Miller, G., 84, 136
Monnin, L. M., 107
Moran, M., 258, 259
Morgan, W. P., 1, 145
Morris, R., 146
Morrison, B., 165
Morse, W., 4, 285
Mosby, R., 266
Moyer, M., 181, 207, 229
Mulligan, W., 5
Murphy, H., 93
Murray, D., 199, 257
Myklebust, H., 2, 3, 9, 12, 17, 19, 20, 22, 43, 47, 48, 50, 57, 59, 64, 81, 84, 85, 88, 90, 92, 93, 95, 96, 145, 146, 147, 173, 174, 177, 179, 184, 186, 191, 196, 197, 206, 207, 219, 220, 223, 230, 277, 283

Nachtman, W., 207
Nahmias, M., 92, 161
Nathan, R., 188
Neimark, E. D., 67, 68
Nelson, K., 87, 132
Nerlove, H., 81
Nesbitt, J., 37, 208
Nettleship, E., 1
Newman, D., 17, 93
Newman, M., 93
Nie, N., 55
Nippold, M., 91
Noell, E., 156
Norback, C., 259
Norback, P., 259
Nunnally, J., 56
Nystrand, M., 173, 175

Ochs, E., 81
Odell, L., 27, 173, 199
O'Donnell, J., 4, 48, 285
Oliver, P., 191
Olson, D., 142, 175
Opper, S., 67
Orton, S., 1, 2, 156, 220
Osman, B., 286

Parker, R., 209
Pasternack, R., 5
Patten, B., 2
Pavlidis, G., 145, 156
Pearl, R., 81, 97
Pennock, C., 162
Perecman, E., 222
Perfetti, C., 87, 146, 160
Peters, J., 48, 152
Petrauskas, R., 146
Phelps, L., 286
Phelps-Gunn, T., 173, 193
Phelps-Terasaki, D., 173, 193
Piaget, J., 67, 205
Picket, J. M., 112
Piercy, M., 84, 222
Pihl, R., 287, 289
Piontowski, D., 162
Podhajski, B., 195, 224
Pollio, H., 91
Pritchett, E., 207
Prutting, C., 99
Pysh, M., 28

Ramaniah, V., 48
Rapin, I., 145, 146, 185
Rawson, M., 4, 174, 239, 286
Raz, I., 118
Read, C., 85
Rees, N. S., 127
Reitan, R., 230
Reynolds, C., 54
Reys, R., 205, 208, 210, 215
Ridenour, D., 241, 266
Riegel, K., 132
Rintleman, W. F., 108
Roach, M., 88, 93
Robinson, H., 151
Rogan, L., 4, 285, 289
Rosen, H., 173
Rosenberg, B., 289
Rosenshein, K., 48
Rourke, B., 146, 187, 188, 206, 211, 289
Rudel, R., 94, 256
Rugel, R., 48
Rumelhart, D., 146
Rutherford, D., 95
Ryan, M., 252

Sammarco, J., 28
Samuels, S. J., 151, 160, 165
Sandhu, M., 289
Saposnek, D., 286
Sattler, J., 268
Satz, P., 145, 146
Savin, H., 85, 86, 87
Scheffelin, M., 22, 205, 206

Schieffelin, B., 81
Schiffman, G., 57
Schmid-Kitsikis, E., 76
Schreiner, R., 151
Schumaker, J., 285, 286
Sedita, J., 241, 268
Seifert, M., 160
Semel, E., 4, 81, 84, 88, 89, 90, 91, 92, 93, 95, 99
Shankweiler, D., 85, 154, 155
Sharma, M., 208, 209
Shaugnessy, M., 178, 184
Shaw, R., 209
Sheils, M., 173
Sheldon, J., 286
Sherlock, D., 206
Sherman, J., 286
Shinn, M., 152
Shores, R., 159
Siegel, I., 224, 286
Silver, A., 4
Silver, D., 288, 289
Silvius, J., 206
Simpson, E., 1
Sinclair, H., 89
Slingerland, B., 95
Smith, D., 290
Smith, F., 152, 160, 222
Smith, M., 48
Smith, R., 221, 225
Sordon, S., 132, 134, 165
Spache, G., 152, 166, 188
Spector, J., 162
Spekman, N., 81, 99
Stahl, S., 162
Stanovich, K., 152, 158, 165
Stark, J., 87
Stark, R., 107
Stein, N., 92, 161, 196
Steinberg, E., 132, 173
Steinbrenner, E., 55
Stevens, K. N., 121
Stillman, G., 2
Stone, C. A., 67, 68, 70, 72, 73, 77, 150, 165, 225
Strange, W., 107
Strauss, A., 2, 15, 178, 206, 219, 223
Stricht, T., 161
Strohner, H., 87
Strong, L., 4
Stubbs, M., 176
Suydam, M., 205
Svien, K., 206

Tabachnick, R., 55
Tallal, P., 84, 107
Tarnopol, M., 4
Taylor, L., 16
Telser, E., 95
Temple, C., 188
Terris, S., 220
Terry, C., 266
Thomas, C., 1
Thompson, L., 1, 286
Thorndike, E. L., 134
Thorndike, R., 56
Tindal, G., 152
Tobias, S., 214
Torgesen, J., 27, 93, 94, 158, 256
Trabasso, T., 161
Trenholme, B., 209
Trout, S., 192

Ugland, R., 243

Valenstein, E., 222
Van Dijk, T., 92
Vellutino, F., 145, 155
Venezky, R., 173, 186
Venolia, J., 259
Vernon, P., 224
Vitulano, L., 4, 285
Voegtle, E., 91
Vogel, S., 50, 81, 92, 98, 156, 245, 254, 258, 259, 268
Vygotsky, L., 176

Wallach, G., 87
Wallin, J., 1
Warner, M., 285
Webb, G., 249
Wechsler, D., 16, 47, 51, 57, 60, 64, 88, 94, 207, 209
Weiner, E., 177, 197, 251
Weismer, S., 92
Weiss, M., 199
Wells, F., 152, 163
Wepman, J., 81, 84, 96
Werner, O., 132
Whang, P., 286
White, S., 28
White, W., 285
Wiederholt, J. L., 4, 90
Wiedmier, B., 84
Wightman, F. L., 118
Wiig, E., 4, 81, 84, 88, 89, 90, 91, 92, 93, 95, 99, 220

Wing, S., 199
Wittels, H., 259
Wolf, M., 145
Wong, B., 93, 153
Wong, R., 93
Woo-Sam, J., 47, 51, 52, 59
Woodcock, R., 84, 94, 95, 207
Woolf, C., 177
Wren, C., 19, 81

Yongeshige, Y., 111

Zangwill, O., 222
Zaremba, B., 5
Zhurova, L. Y., 85
Zigmond, N., 4
Zimmerman, I., 47, 51, 52, 59
Zlatin, M. A., 107

# Subject Index


Abstraction and story organization, 196
Abstract language, 90–91
Abstract reasoning, assessment of. *See* Rods task
Academic problems, 37–38
Achievement patterns, 282–283. *See also* Cognitive processes and achievement
Activity and learning, 27–28
Adaptive syllable learning in auditory processing, 118–119
Addition, 210. *See also* Mathematics disorders
Admissions process for LD college program, 245–246
Adult organizations, 290–291
Age ranges of adults studied, 34
Ambiguous language, 90–91
Arithmetic, 280. *See also* Mathematics disorders
  intelligence tests and, 59
  nonverbal disorders and, 222
Assessment
  of auditory language disorder, 82
  for college programming, 246–247
  of mathematics disorders, 207
  of nonverbal disorders, 222–223
  of reading disorder, 151–153
  tests for, *313–316*
  of written language disorder, 177
Attentional problems, 33
  auditory processing and, 127–128
  job performance and, 41
  summary of, 281–282
Audience and written discourse, 195–196
Auditory acuity, 16
Auditory analysis, 85–87. *See also* Linguistic awareness
Auditory comprehension. *See* Auditory language disorders, auditory comprehension and
Auditory disorders, 1
  job performance and, 40–41
Auditory expressive processes. *See* Auditory language disorders, auditory expressive processes and
Auditory language disorders
  assessment of, 82
  auditory comprehension and, 87–88
    ambiguity and abstraction, 90–91
    directions, 90
    discourse, 92–93
    grammar, 89–90
    prosody, 91–92
    vocabulary, 88–89
  auditory expressive processes and
    oral communication, 98–99
    pronunciation, 95–96
    syntax and morphology, 96–98
    word retrieval, 94–95
  auditory memory and, 93–94
  auditory perception and, 83–84
    auditory analysis, 85–87
    phoneme discrimination, 84–85
Auditory memory, 93–94
Auditory pathology, assessment of, 110
Auditory perception. *See* Auditory language disorders, auditory perception and
Auditory processing disorders in young adults
  conventional tests and, 108–110
  experimental tests and, 110
    adaptive syllable learning, 118–119
    open-set response, 112–113
    pure tone detection, 110–111
    sentence perception, 121–126
    summary of, 126–128
    syllable detection, 113
    syllable discrimination, 119–120
    syllable identification threshold, 114–118
    synthesized syllables, 111–112
Auditory-temporal disorders, 24
Auxiliary aids for college students, 269

Bending rods task. *See* Rods task

Case history
  in diagnostic process, 12–13
  from Northwestern University Learning Disabilities Center, 299–303

Chief complaints, 35, 40–41
Climate for testing and teaching, 13–14
Clinical procedures, 12–13
Clinician's attitude, 13–14
Cognitive processes and achievement
  active learners and, 27–28
  discussion of, 16–20
  rules and, 24–27
  simultaneous and successive processing and, 23–24
  systems analysis of, 20–24
College programming, LD, 4. *See also* College student, LD
  academic requirements for, 268–269
  acceptance criteria for, 249–250
  admissions process for, 245–246
  applicant selection for, 240, 247–248
  assessment for, 246–247
  coordination of services in, 272
  credit *v* noncredit for remedial courses in, 264–265
  development *v* special remedial courses for, 262–264
  evaluation of, 269–271
  general considerations for, 261–262
  present practices in, 241–242
  qualified *v* unqualified handicapped student for, 240–241
  remediation and course support/tutoring in, 265–266
  Section 504 of Rehabilitation Act of 1973 and, 239–240, 242, 244, 268
    reasonable accommodation, 268–269
  setting for, 242–245
  test administration for, 242
College student, LD. *See also* College programming, LD
  academic advising for, 250–251
  auxiliary aids for, 269
  compensatory strategies for, 266–268
  faculty advocate for, 252–253
  general considerations for, 250
  social/interpersonal skills and, 260–261
  study habits for
    note-taking, 253–254
    organizational skills, 254–255
    test-taking, 255–257
    time management, 255
  written language skills and, 257–260
Communication
  in college programming, 272
  oral, 98–99
  social problems and, 41–44
Compensatory strategies. *See* Coping strategies
Complex syntax, 26
Comprehension. *See also* Auditory comprehension, Reading comprehension
Comprehension problems, personal descriptions of, 149–150
Computational skills, mathematics and, 209–212. *See also* Mathematics disorders
Concepts
  language problems and, 131–142
  mathematical, 205
Control-of-variables strategy, 67–68, 70–73. *See also* Rods task
Conversation skills, 99
Co-occurring problems, 10
  nonverbal disorders and, 222
Coping strategies, 13, 45, 235
  for college student, 266–268
  personal description of, 150–151
Counseling, 37, 261
Current problems of adults studied. *See* Chief complaints

Daily living, 43–45
  mathematics and, 214–215
Decoding, 279–280
  oral reading and, 157–160
  spelling problems and, 149
Definitions of learning disability, 2–4, *297–298*
Detroit Tests of Learning Aptitude, 94
Developmental history, 12
Diagnostic questions, *305–312*
Differential diagnosis, 9
Digit Span subtest of WAIS, 15, 94, 213
Digit Symbol subtest of WAIS, 59, 60, 62, 63
Directions, comprehension of, 90
Discourse, comprehension of, 92–93
Dyscalculia, 206
Dyslexia, 279
  in children
    auditory analysis, 85, 86
    prosody, 92
  nonverbal disorders and, 220
  reading disorders and, 145–146. *See also* Reading disorders
    tapes, 267

Educational history
  of adults studied, 35–36

Educational history (*Cont.*):
  mathematics and, 207
Educational level, intelligence tests and, 60, 61(*t*), 63. *See also* Intelligence tests, patterns in
Eligibility for college programming, 245–250
Emotional needs, 235. *See also* Counseling; Group therapy
Emotional problems, 235–236
Emotional status, evaluation of, 16
Evaluation of LD college programming, 269–271
Exclusion clause, 2–3
Ex-dyslexic, written language disorders in, 257, 258
Expressive language disorders, summary of, 279

Factor analysis of intelligence tests, 55–57, 64. *See also* Intelligence tests, patterns in
Familial learning problems, 34
Family relationships, 234–236
*Federal Register, August 1977*, 298
Figurative language, 90–91
Financial aid for LD college students, 266
Formal operational thinking, control-of-variables strategy and, 67–68
Future needs
  for adult organizations, 290–291
  for integration of findings, 285
  for mental health, 288–290
  for remediation, 291–293
  for terminology, 284–285
  vocational. *See* Vocational needs, future

Generalized language problems, 147–148
Grammar comprehension, 89–90
Group therapy, 233–237

Handwriting
  discussion of, 179
  mixed forms and automaticity in, 184–185
  nonverbal disorders and, 222
  reading disorders and, 185–186
  visualization and related memory problems, 184
  visual-spatial-motor integration in, 179–183
Haptic perception, activity and, 27
Hierarchy of experience, 17, 18(*f*)

Imagery, 17
  nonverbal disorders and, 223–224
Independence, 43–44
Input-integration-output-feedback, 20–22
Instruction and learning, 27–28
Intellectual levels and patterns. *See* Intelligence tests, patterns in
Intelligence tests, patterns in
  ACID, 48–53, 63
  discussion of, 47–48, 52–54, 63–64
  educational levels and, 60, 61(*t*)
  factor analysis and, 55–57, 64
  interest correlations in, 57–60, 64
  IQ and, 48–49, 50(*t*)
  mathematics and, 212–213
  scatter in, 54–55
  verbal-performance discrepancies in, 47, 48, 50–52
    description of groups, 61–64
Interpersonal problems, 41–43
Intersensory learning, 22
Interest correlations in intelligence tests, 57–60, 64. *See also* Intelligence tests, patterns in
Intrasensory learning, 22
IQ levels, 48–49, 50(*t*). *See also* Intelligence tests, patterns in
  sex differences in, 283

Job keeping behaviors, 39
Job performance, 40

Language comprehension disorders, generalized, 278–279
Language disorders, 3
  conceptualization and, 131–142
    mathematics and, 206, 212
  social problems and, 41–42
Learned helplessness, 28
Letters from participants, 31–34
Linguistic awareness, 85, 185
Logico-mathematical abilities, 205, 212. *See also* Mathematics disorders
Long-term needs, 4–5

Maps, difficulty with, 44
Mathematics ability, 205
Mathematics disorders, 17–20
  assessment of, 207
  computational skills and, 209–212
  daily living and, 214–215

intelligence and, 212–213
memory and, 213–214
nature of, 207
problem solving and, 208–209
sex differences in, 214
social maturity and, 44
Meaning problems, generalized, 277–278
Mechanical errors in writing, 259
Memory development, 93
Memory disorders
job performance and, 41
mathematics and, 207, 213–214
personal descriptions of, 150
writing as aid to, 200
Mental health, 261
Metalinguistic, 85
Middle ear impedance tests, 108
Money, problems with, 43–44, 215
Morphosyntactic rules, 26
Motivation, 16
Multisensory learning, 22
Multisensory processing problems, 149

National Advisory Committee on Handicapped Children, 1968, *297–298*
National Joint Committee for Learning Disabilities, *298*
Nonverbal cognitive processes, 17–20, 220
daily living and, 44
Nonverbal learning, 220. *See also* Nonverbal disorders
Nonverbal disorders, 3, 280
assessment of, 222–223
discussion of, 219–222
imagery and, 223–224
patterns in, 226–229
reading disabled, 229–230
perceptual analysis and, 223
rod task and, 76
social problems and, 42–43
symbolization and, 224–225
verbal learning and, 23
Note-taking, 37–38
in college, 253–254

Occupational history, 13. *See also* Vocational history
Open-set response in auditory processing, 112–113
Oral expressive disorders, 19–20, 148
Oral language disorders, 43. *See also* Auditory language disorders
complaints about, 38
rods task and, 74–76
verbal rules and, 26
Oral reading and decoding patterns
in context, 157–160
passage comprehension and, 164–165
reading comprehension and, 160–162
reading rate for, 165–166
silent reading and, 160
single words and, 154–157
summary of, 166
vocabulary and, 163–164
Oral Sentence Building task, 96–97
Oral syntax and morphology, 96–98
Oral and written language, 175–177
Organizational skills
for college, 254–255
daily living and, 44
problems with, 41
summary of, 281–282
Overload, 15

Passage comprehension, 164–165
Perception difficulties, social problems and, 42–43
Perceptual analysis, nonverbal disorders and, 223
Perceptual-motor disorders, social problems and, 42
Perceptual organization factor in intelligence tests, 57
Phoneme discrimination, 84–85
tests for, 22
Piaget, mathematical ability and, 205
Picture interpretation problems, 14
Picture Story Language Test (PSLT), 194–195, 196, 197–199
Planning disorders, 41
daily living and, 44
summary of, 281–282
Prerequisites for learning, 16
Priorities, problems establishing, 41
Problem solving, 208–209
assessment of. *See* Rods task
mathematics and, 208–209. *See also* Mathematics disorders
Productivity in written discourse, 194–195
Prosody, 91–92
PSLT, 194–195, 196, 197–199

Psychological process and learning disability, 3
Punctuation disorders, 257, 258–259
Pure tone sensitivity test
  conventional, 108, 109(*f*)
  experimental, 110–111

Quantitative disorders, 280

Reading comprehension, 15, 160–162
Reading disorders, 3, 37, 82
  assessment of, 151–153
  discussion of, 145–147
  handwriting and, 185–186
  independence and, 43
  job performance and, 41
  nonverbal disorders and, 229–230
  personal descriptions of, 147–151
  reading performance and, 153–154
  social problems and, 42
  summary of, 279–280
Reading performance, 153–154
Reading rate for oral reading, 165–166
Receptive language disorders, 20
  co-occurrence of, 10
Recognition of Melody Pattern, 92
Rehabilitation Act of 1973, 239–240, 242, 244, 268
Retrieval problems, social problems and, 42. *See also* Word retrieval,
*Review of Educational Research, February, 1969*, *297*
Rhythmic skills, social problems and, 42
Rods task
  conclusions and implications of, 77–78
  discussion of, 67–68
  mathematics and, 209
  procedural details for, 68–70
  qualitative aspects of performance in, 73–74
    nonverbal cases, 76
    oral language, 74–76
  strategy use in, 70–73
Rule systems, 24–27

Section 504 of Rehabilitation Act of 1973. *See* College programming, LD, Section 504 of Rehabilitation Act of 1973 and
Self-help group, social skills and, 261
Self-monitoring in diagnostic process, 14
Self-report, 31–34
Semantic relations
  assessment of, 133–140
  theories of, 132–133
Semi-autonomous systems, 22
Sensation level (SL) in speech testing, 108
Sentence perception in auditory processing, 121–126
Sex differences
  in mathematics disorders, 214
  in performance, 283–284
Silent reading, 160
Simultaneous and successive processing of information, 23–24
Single words and oral reading, 154–157
Social acceptance
  of LD student, 243, 260–261
Social/interpersonal skills for college student, 260–261
Social maturity, 43
Social perception, 14
Social problems
  in daily living, 43–44
  interpersonal, 41–43
Socio-economic levels of adults studied, 34
Special services, history of, 36–37
Speech perception, 83–84
Speech reception threshold (SRT), 108–110
Speech understanding in noise (SPIN), 121–126, 127
Speech understanding tests, conventional, 108–110
Spelling disorders, 257, 259, 279–280
  diagnostic and strategy use in, 192–193
  dictation and, 186–190, 191(*f*)
  job performance and, 40–41
  spontaneous, 191–192
Strategy usage, 10
  primary processing deficiencies and, 72–73
  rods task and, 67–68, 70–73. *See also* Rods task
Structured *v* spontaneous problem detection, 15
Subtypes of learning disabilities, 10, 166, 280
Syllable detection in auditory processing, 113
Syllable discrimination in auditory processing, 119–120
Syllable identification thresholds in auditory processing, 114–118
Symbolization, 16–20
  nonverbal disorders and, 224–225
Syntax, 258–259, 279
  morphology and, 96–98
  tests for, 111–112
  written discourse and, 197–199

Taped learning materials, 266–268, 269
Test of Academic Skills, 207
Tests for assessment, *313–316*
Test-taking strategies, 255–257
Text organization in written discourse, 195
Theories and procedures, 14–16
Therapeutic effect of diagnostic process, 13
Therapy, 37, 261
Time management skills, 15
  in college, 255
  complaints about, 38
Timing in oral communication, 99
Trust factor in group therapy, 234
T-unit analysis, 259
Turn-taking in conversation, 99

Verbal comprehension factor in intelligence tests, 56–57
Verbal and nonverbal learning, 22–23
Verbal-performance IQ discrepancies, 47, 48, 50–52, 61–64
  mathematics and, 213
  sex differences in, 283–284
Vineland Social Maturity Scale, 43
Visualization and related memory problems in handwriting, 184
Visual motor deficits, 14–15
Visual processing, problems related to, 148–149
Visual screening, 16
Visual spatial disorders, 280
  daily living and, 44
  mathematics and, 206–207, 212, 215
Visual-spatial-motor problems
  co-occurrence of, 10
  in handwriting, 179–183
Visual system, simultaneous and successive processing and, 23–24
Vocabulary, 37
  comprehension, 88–89
  oral reading and, 163–164
  social problems and, 41
  tests, 15
  written discourse and, 197
Vocational history of adults studied, 38–39
Vocational needs, future
  career awareness and, 286–287
  discussion of, 285–286, 287
  maintaining a job and, 287–288
  services for, 287
Vocational services, 39–40
Vocational studies, 28

Wechsler Adult Intelligence Scale (WAIS), 16, 47–48, 209. *See also* Intelligence tests, patterns in
  arithmetic subtest of, 207, 209
  auditory memory and, 94
  college admission and, 246, 249
  Digit Span subtest of, 213
  limitations of, 67
  mathematics and, 209, 212–213
  rods task and, 71–72
  semantic relations and, 133–140
  sex differences in, 283–284
Wechsler Adult Intelligence Scale-Revised (WAIS-R), 47–48. *See also* Intelligence tests, patterns in
Wide Range Achievement Test, 60, 63, 69. *See also* Intelligence tests, patterns in
  arithmetic subtest of, 207, 212
  auditory analysis and, 87
  oral reading and, 254–256, 257
  rods task and, 69, 71, 72
  sex differences in, 284
Woodcock-Johnson Psycho-educational Battery, mathematics and, 207, 209
Word problems, 208–209
Word retrieval, 94–95, 279
Writing disorders. *See also* Handwriting
  independence and, 43
  job performance and, 41
  summary of, 279
Writing, need for, 174–175
Written language, 17–20
Written language disorders
  assessment of, 177
  discussion of, 173–174, 199–200
  handwriting and. *See* Handwriting
  in non-LD college students, 262
  performance patterns and trends in, 177–179
  school and, 38
  summary of, 280
  written formulation and discourse in
    abstraction and story organization, 195
    discussion, 193–194
    productivity, 194–195
    syntax, 197–199
    text organization and audience, 195–196
    vocabulary, 197
Written language skills for college student, 257–260
Written and oral language, 175–177